THE CARTOON HISTORY OF THE
MODERN WORLD

PART II

ALSO BY LARRY GONICK

THE CARTOON HISTORY OF THE UNIVERSE, VOLUMES 1-7
THE CARTOON HISTORY OF THE UNIVERSE, VOLUMES 8-13
THE CARTOON HISTORY OF THE UNIVERSE, VOLUMES 14-19
THE CARTOON HISTORY OF THE MODERN WORLD, PART I
THE CARTOON HISTORY OF THE UNITED STATES
THE CARTOON GUIDE TO CHEMISTRY (WITH CRAIG CRIDDLE)
THE CARTOON GUIDE TO THE COMPUTER
THE CARTOON GUIDE TO THE ENVIRONMENT (WITH ALICE OUTWATER)
THE CARTOON GUIDE TO GENETICS (WITH MARK WHEELIS)
THE CARTOON GUIDE TO (NON)COMMUNICATION
THE CARTOON GUIDE TO PHYSICS (WITH ART HUFFMAN)
THE CARTOON GUIDE TO SEX (WITH CHRISTINE DEVAULT)
THE CARTOON GUIDE TO STATISTICS (WITH WOOLLCOTT SMITH)
KOKOPELLI AND COMPANY IN THE ATTACK OF THE SMART PIES

THE CARTOON HISTORY OF THE MODERN WORLD

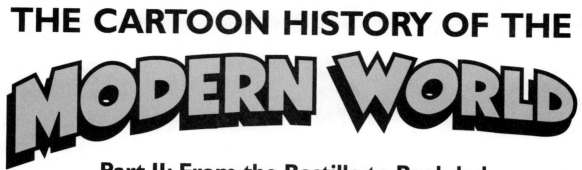

Part II: From the Bastille to Baghdad

LARRY GONICK

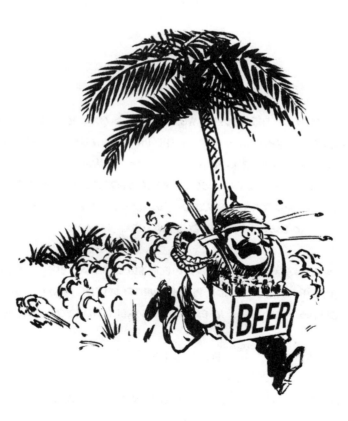

HARPER

NEW YORK • LONDON • TORONTO • SYDNEY

TO LISA, JUST LIKE THE FIRST ONE

HARPER

HARPERCOLLINS BOOKS MAY BE PURCHASED FOR EDUCATIONAL, BUSINESS, OR SALES PROMOTIONAL USE. FOR INFORMATION PLEASE WRITE: SPECIAL MARKETS DEPARTMENT, HARPERCOLLINS PUBLISHERS, 10 EAST 53RD STREET, NEW YORK, NY 10022.

FIRST EDITION

LIBRARY OF CONGRESS CATALOGING-IN-PUBLICATION DATA IS AVAILABLE ON REQUEST.

ISBN 978-0-06-076008-3

09 10 11 12 13 DT/RRD 10 9 8 7 6 5 4 3 2 1

CONTENTS

ACKNOWLEDGMENTS

I OWE THANKS TO MANY PEOPLE, AND SINCE, UNLIKE AN OSCAR ACCEPTANCE SPEECH, THIS CAN BE SKIPPED BY THE INDIFFERENT, HERE'S A QUASI-COMPLETE LIST, INCLUDING SOME NO LONGER LIVING: VICKY BIJUR, MY AGENT, WHO PULLED OFF THE MIRACLE THAT TURNED *THE CARTOON HISTORY OF THE MODERN WORLD* INTO TWO VOLUMES; ALL THE SUPPORTIVE HARPERCOLLINS EDITORS, MOST RECENTLY THE REDOUBTABLE AND CHEERFUL STEPHANIE MEYERS; DIANE BURROWES, ALWAYS READY TO SEND COMICS TO CURIOUS ACADEMICS; LESSING KAHN, WHO NEGOTIATED THE BUY-BACK OF A SOON-TO-BE-REMAINDERED HEAP OF AN EARLIER PAPERBACK VERSION OF *CARTOON HISTORY I* AND THEREBY TAUGHT ME SOME LESSONS ABOUT PUBLISHING; JACKIE ONASSIS AND NANCY EVANS, FOR GIVING ANOTHER SHOT TO *THE CARTOON HISTORY OF THE UNIVERSE*; EPPIE LEDERER ("ANN LANDERS"), FOR A PLUG THAT SENT ME ON AN EMOTIONAL AND PROFESSIONAL ROCKET RIDE; KARL KATZ, FOR SHOWING JACKIE; VIKRAM JAYANTI, FOR SHOWING KARL; ESTHER MITGANG, FOR EARLY SUPPORT IN NEW YORK; GILBERT SHELTON, FOR SETTING IT ALL IN MOTION; FRED TODD, FOR MAKING SURE GILBERT'S WISHES CAME OUT THE OTHER END OF A PRINTING PRESS; RIUS, FOR UNKNOWINGLY INSPIRING ME TO DO NONFICTION COMICS; STEVE ATLAS, FOR SHOWING ME RIUS' COMICS; JAMES ATLAS, FOR INTRODUCING ME TO STEVE; FRANCINE PROSE, FOR INTRODUCING ME TO JAMES; KIM STAPLEY, WHO GOT ME DRAWING AGAIN AFTER COLLEGE; MY DAD, FOR READING ME THE SUNDAY FUNNIES IN THE FIRST PLACE (GO, GORDO!); MY MOM, FOR FLOGGING THE EARLY *CARTOON HISTORY* COMICS; MOMO ZHOU, FOR HER TIRELESS, GOOD-HUMORED ASSISTANCE; MY STUDIOMATES PAT KOREN, LAURIE SMITH, LAURIE WIGHAM, ALISON WOOD, BILL VOLKMANN, JORDAN OLSHANSKY, AND DAN HUBIG, FOR EMOTIONAL SUPPORT, FEEDBACK ON DEMAND, AND MANY LUNCHES; MY WIFE LISA GOLDSCHMID AND DAUGHTERS SOPHIE AND ANNA, FOR TOO MANY THINGS TO NAME; AND A SPECIAL THANKS TO PETER BARNES AND THE MESA REFUGE, FOR PROVIDING TRANQUIL, PRODUCTIVE, AND UNINTERRUPTED HOURS ON THE VERDANT BLUFFS OF WEST MARIN. IF I'VE FORGOTTEN ANYONE, WRITE ME AND I'LL SEE IF WE CAN'T SLIP YOU INTO A REPRINT!

WHAT HAPPENS WHEN A COUNTRY TRIES TO RULE THE WORLD—AND FAILS? WHEN A RICH NATION EXHAUSTS ITS PEOPLE, ITS CREDIT, AND ITS CREDIBILITY?
IN THIS VOLUME, WE'LL SEE A COUNTRY LIKE THAT, WHERE THE CITIZENS ROSE UP, THREW OUT THE OLD ORDER, AND BROUGHT IN A NEW AGE OF UNIVERSAL—HEEHEEHEE—HAPPINESS!
THEIR REVOLUTION IMPROVED—SNICKER—EVERYTHING AND SPREAD ITS SHINING IDEALS TO—HEH—PEOPLE EVERYWHA-HA-HAHAHAHA... CHOKE... EXCUSE ME...
WHAHAHAHAHA
HAHAHA
HOHO HOHO
SOB
SOB
GROAN... HEEHEEHEE... WOW! THAT'S THE BEST THING ABOUT THIS JOB: YOU GET TO LAUGH AT YOUR OWN JOKES TILL YOU SOB!
WHAT? YOU DIDN'T GET IT? WELL, THEN, YOU OBVIOUSLY NEED TO READ ON, AS WE SET THE TIME MACHINE FOR THE YEAR 1789...

THE CARTOON HISTORY OF THE MODERN WORLD

Volume 6

GUNS, GOLD, AND GOOD INTENTIONS

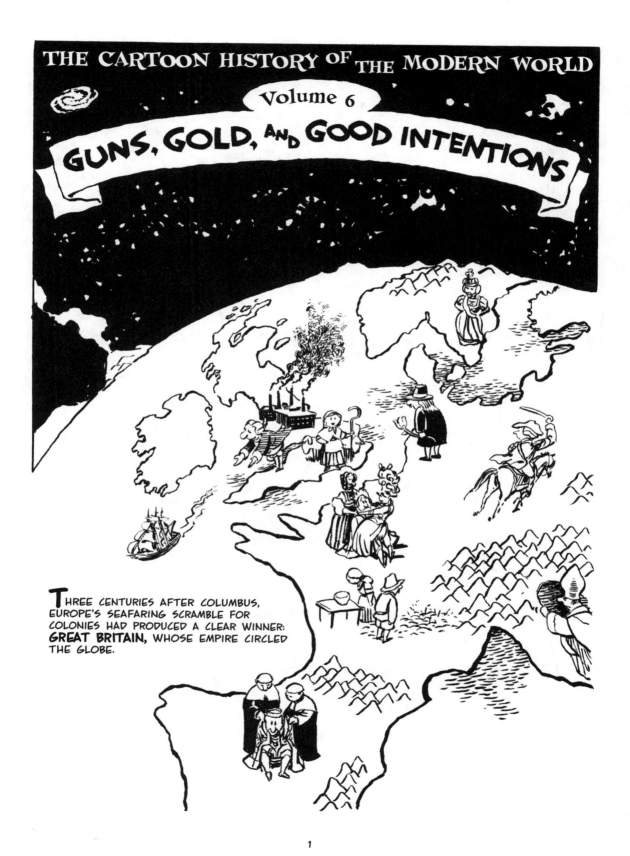

THREE CENTURIES AFTER COLUMBUS, EUROPE'S SEAFARING SCRAMBLE FOR COLONIES HAD PRODUCED A CLEAR WINNER: **GREAT BRITAIN,** WHOSE EMPIRE CIRCLED THE GLOBE.

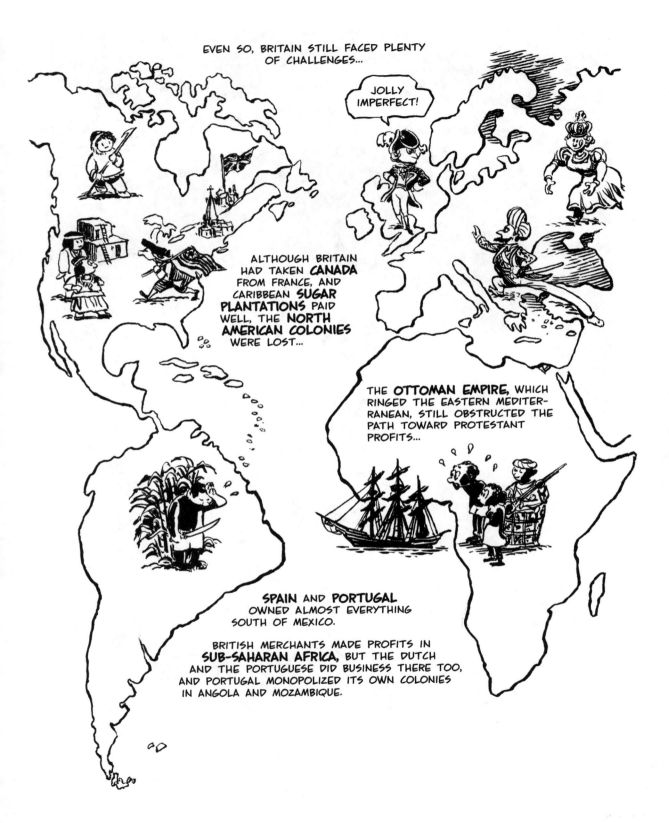

EVEN SO, BRITAIN STILL FACED PLENTY OF CHALLENGES...

JOLLY IMPERFECT!

ALTHOUGH BRITAIN HAD TAKEN **CANADA** FROM FRANCE, AND CARIBBEAN **SUGAR PLANTATIONS** PAID WELL, THE **NORTH AMERICAN COLONIES** WERE LOST...

THE **OTTOMAN EMPIRE,** WHICH RINGED THE EASTERN MEDITERRANEAN, STILL OBSTRUCTED THE PATH TOWARD PROTESTANT PROFITS...

SPAIN AND **PORTUGAL** OWNED ALMOST EVERYTHING SOUTH OF MEXICO.

BRITISH MERCHANTS MADE PROFITS IN **SUB-SAHARAN AFRICA,** BUT THE DUTCH AND THE PORTUGUESE DID BUSINESS THERE TOO, AND PORTUGAL MONOPOLIZED ITS OWN COLONIES IN ANGOLA AND MOZAMBIQUE.

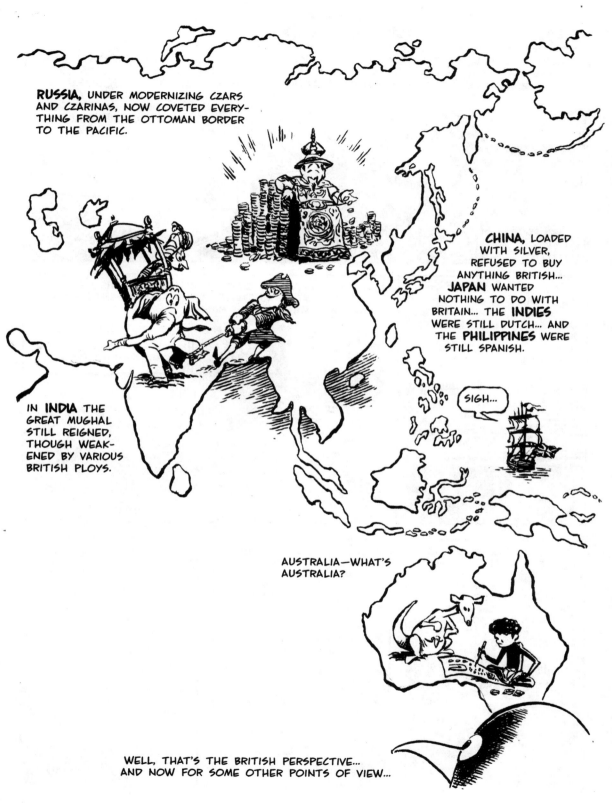

RUSSIA, UNDER MODERNIZING CZARS AND CZARINAS, NOW COVETED EVERYTHING FROM THE OTTOMAN BORDER TO THE PACIFIC.

CHINA, LOADED WITH SILVER, REFUSED TO BUY ANYTHING BRITISH... JAPAN WANTED NOTHING TO DO WITH BRITAIN... THE INDIES WERE STILL DUTCH... AND THE PHILIPPINES WERE STILL SPANISH.

IN INDIA THE GREAT MUGHAL STILL REIGNED, THOUGH WEAKENED BY VARIOUS BRITISH PLOYS.

SIGH...

AUSTRALIA—WHAT'S AUSTRALIA?

WELL, THAT'S THE BRITISH PERSPECTIVE... AND NOW FOR SOME OTHER POINTS OF VIEW...

LEGAL ALIENS

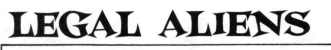

ONCE UPON A TIME, IN CHINA'S YOUTH, A RULING FAMILY'S FALL CAME AS A SHOCKING NOVELTY... BUT AFTER 2,000 YEARS, IT BEGAN TO SEEM **ROUTINE**.

THEY ALL LOOK ALIKE!

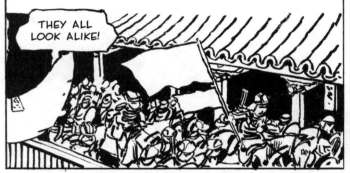

THE GOVERNMENT GROWS **CORRUPT**... TOO MANY **EUNUCHS*** HOLD OFFICE... A **WARLORD** REBELS... A ONCE-FAITHFUL **GENERAL** SUDDENLY TURNS **TRAITOR**... AND (OFTEN) **NORTHERN ALIENS** INVADE.

SAME OLD STORY...

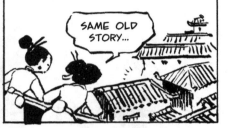

THE MING DYNASTY WENT THIS ROUTE IN THE 1600S... ITS EUNUCH PRIME MINISTER EVEN HAD AN **ALL-EUNUCH ARMY**, TOTALLY USELESS AGAINST THE INEVITABLE REBELLIOUS WARLORD.

SIGH... NOT AGAIN!

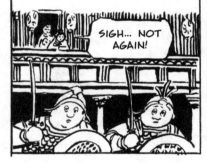

IN 1644, THE REBELS ENTERED BEIJING AND THE DYNASTY FELL—LITERALLY, AS THE EMPEROR AND HIS ENTOURAGE HANGED THEMSELVES EN MASSE.

HM, WELL, THAT'S KIND OF DIFFERENT...

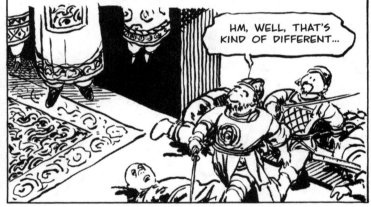

LEADERS WHO REWARD THEIR FOLLOWERS SOON FIND THEMSELVES ASKED TO REWARD THEIR FOLLOWERS' **FAMILIES** TOO: SONS, DAUGHTERS, GRANDKIDS, AN EVER-GROWING CROWD!

GAH!!

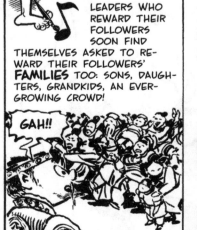

IN CHINA, AT LEAST, EMPERORS "SOLVED" THIS PROBLEM BY TURNING TO **EUNUCHS**, SURGICALLY CASTRATED ADVISERS **WITHOUT DESCENDANTS** TO CLAMOR FOR FAVORS.

SO PEACEFUL...

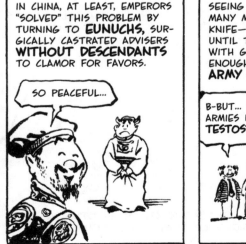

SEEING A CAREER PATH HERE, MANY MEN WENT UNDER THE KNIFE—TOO MANY, IN FACT, UNTIL THE COURT TEEMED WITH GELDED JOB APPLICANTS... ENOUGH TO MAKE A SMALL **ARMY** UNDER THE MING.

B-BUT... DON'T ARMIES RUN ON **TESTOSTERONE?**

SOLVE ONE PROBLEM, MAKE ANOTHER...

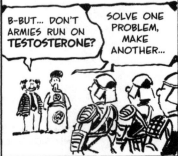

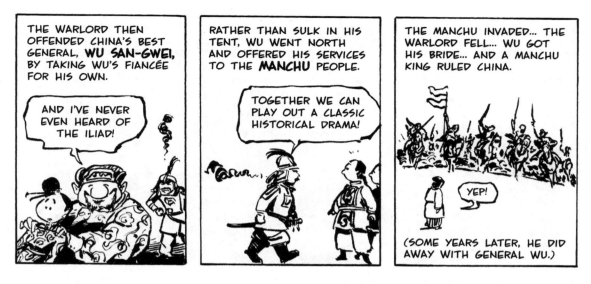

THE WARLORD THEN OFFENDED CHINA'S BEST GENERAL, **WU SAN-GWEI**, BY TAKING WU'S FIANCÉE FOR HIS OWN.

AND I'VE NEVER EVEN HEARD OF THE ILIAD!

RATHER THAN SULK IN HIS TENT, WU WENT NORTH AND OFFERED HIS SERVICES TO THE **MANCHU** PEOPLE.

TOGETHER WE CAN PLAY OUT A CLASSIC HISTORICAL DRAMA!

THE MANCHU INVADED... THE WARLORD FELL... WU GOT HIS BRIDE... AND A MANCHU KING RULED CHINA.

YEP!

(SOME YEARS LATER, HE DID AWAY WITH GENERAL WU.)

LIKE THE MONGOLS BEFORE THEM (*CHU III, P. 242*), THE MANCHU KEPT APART FROM THEIR CHINESE UNDERLINGS... BUT THEY DID REQUIRE ALL CHINESE MALES TO GET A **LOYALTY HAIRCUT**, MANCHU-STYLE, WITH FOREHEAD SHAVED AND A BRAID DOWN THE BACK.

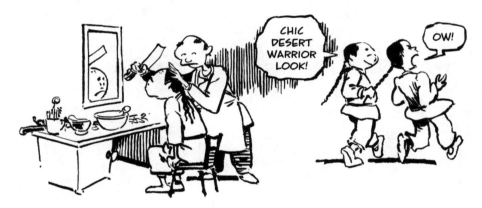

CHIC DESERT WARRIOR LOOK!

OW!

ON THE OTHER HAND, CHINA'S **LAW CODE, BUREAUCRACY,** AND **CIVIL SERVICE EXAMS** REMAINED ALL-CHINESE. CHINA RAN BEST, THE MANCHU BELIEVED, ON TRADITIONAL CHINESE LINES.

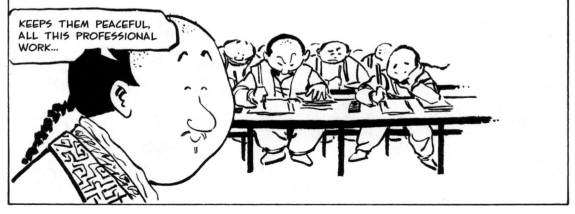

KEEPS THEM PEACEFUL, ALL THIS PROFESSIONAL WORK...

ALL THIS TIME, CHINA HAD BEEN IMPORTING MEXICAN AND PERUVIAN **SILVER** FROM THE PHILIPPINES, WHERE SPANISH MERCHANTS TRADED IT FOR CHINESE GOODS. THE CHINESE TOOK THE SILVER BARS, BUT BARRED THE BRASSY SPANIARDS.

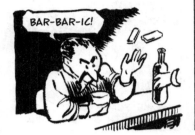

BAR-BAR-IC!

IN THE 1660S, THE MANCHU EMPEROR **KANGXI** PUT OUT THE NOVEL IDEA THAT THE OUTSIDE WORLD MIGHT HAVE SOMETHING TO OFFER! HE WELCOMED FOREIGNERS....

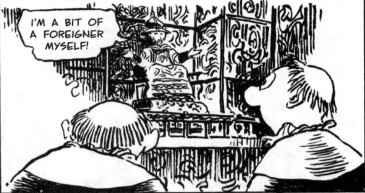

I'M A BIT OF A FOREIGNER MYSELF!

JESUIT PRIESTS HEADED KANGXI'S ASTRONOMY DEPARTMENT AND TAUGHT HIS ARMORERS HOW TO CAST HEAVY CANNON.

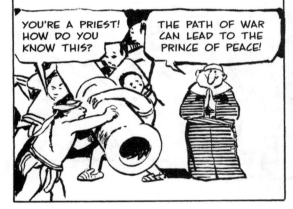

YOU'RE A PRIEST! HOW DO YOU KNOW THIS?

THE PATH OF WAR CAN LEAD TO THE PRINCE OF PEACE!

CHRISTIANITY HAD THE EMPEROR'S BLESSING... CHURCHES SPROUTED... OFFICIALS CONVERTED...

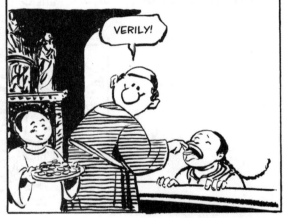

VERILY!

THE JESUITS, WHO MADE A POINT OF TRAVELING THE WORLD, EVEN SENT A MISSIONARY, FR. **DESIDERI**, TO **TIBET** IN THE EARLY 1700S.

WOW! TOP OF THE WORLD!

THE WORLD IS ROUND!

DESIDERI LEARNED TIBETAN, TRANSLATED BUDDHIST SUTRAS INTO LATIN, AND HAD MANY PHILOSOPHICAL DISPUTES WITH TIBETAN LAMAS, OFTEN TO HIS OWN DISADVANTAGE.

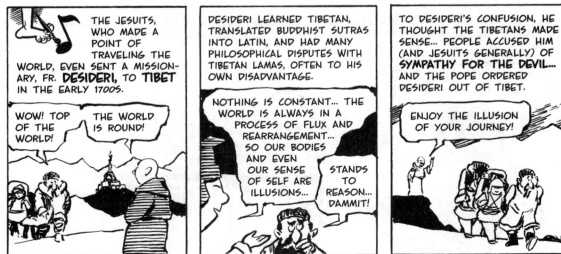

NOTHING IS CONSTANT... THE WORLD IS ALWAYS IN A PROCESS OF FLUX AND REARRANGEMENT... SO OUR BODIES AND EVEN OUR SENSE OF SELF ARE ILLUSIONS...

STANDS TO REASON... DAMMIT!

TO DESIDERI'S CONFUSION, HE THOUGHT THE TIBETANS MADE SENSE... PEOPLE ACCUSED HIM (AND JESUITS GENERALLY) OF **SYMPATHY FOR THE DEVIL**... AND THE POPE ORDERED DESIDERI OUT OF TIBET.

ENJOY THE ILLUSION OF YOUR JOURNEY!

THE NEXT EMPEROR, YONGZHENG, INHERITED SOME COMPLICATIONS: HE HAD THREE OLDER BROTHERS, RIVALS FOR THE ROYAL HAT.
SOME OF HIS ENEMIES MUST HAVE HAD CHRISTIAN BACKING... BECAUSE YONGZHENG SLAMMED THE RELIGION AS AN ALIEN CULT WITH A HIDDEN AGENDA.
NAMELY, IT'S AGAINST ME!
SO HE BANNED CHRISTIANITY AND EXPELLED EUROPEANS FROM CHINA.
YOU WANT PEACE? THEN GO AWAY!
STILL, FOR THE SILVER, HE LEFT OPEN A SINGLE CHINESE PORT, GUANGZHOU, WHERE EUROPEANS COULD TRADE.
AND PLEASE! DON'T TALK!
AND THE EMPIRE DID HAVE PEACE AND PROSPERITY... WHEN CROPS FAILED IN THE 1750S, THE GOVERNMENT WAS ABLE TO RUSH RICE TO THE NEEDY, AND NOBODY STARVED.
WELL, I'M SURE A CHRISTIAN NATION WOULD DO THE SAME THING!

TEMPURA TANTRUM

JAPAN ALSO CLAMPED DOWN ON CHRISTIANS AFTER AN INITIAL WARM EMBRACE.

LIKE HUGGING A SPINY URCHIN IT WAS...

IN THE MID-1500S, JAPAN WAS A **PIRATE ISLAND** DIVIDED AMONG NOBLE WARLORDS, ARMED BUDDHIST TEMPLES, FEROCIOUS HERMITS, ANGRY WOMEN WITH STICKS, ETC.

AT THIS POINT, THE PORTUGUESE ARRIVED WITH **FRIED FOOD** AND **FIREARMS.**
BOTH'LL KILL YOU, BUT THIS ONE'S FASTER...

ONE WARLORD, **ODA NOBUNAGA,** LEAPED AT THE CHANCE TO BUY GUNS—500 MATCHLOCKS IN 1549—WHILE THE OTHERS, I GUESS, WENT FOR THE FRITTERS.
SHOULDN'T **WE** DO SOMETHING TOO?
I DUNNO... THIS TEMPURA MAKES ME SO SLEEPY...

ONE THING LED TO ANOTHER... ODA TERRORIZED HIS RIVALS... ONE BY ONE THEY FELL... AND BY 1600, JAPAN WAS **UNIFIED** UNDER A LONE WARLORD, THE **SHOGUN.**
I TOTALLY BLAME THE TEMPURA...

ALL THIS TIME, PORTUGUESE PRIESTS AND MERCHANTS HAD BEEN DOING THEIR THING IN JAPAN.
PREACHING PEACE AND SELLING GUNS—WOW!
THEN THE DUTCH SHOWED UP AND GAVE THE JAPANESE AN EARFUL!
THESE PORTUGUESE WIN CONVERTS... TAKE CONTROL... THEN BURN YOU AT THE STAKE!
AND THEY OVER-CHARGE FOR EVERYTHING!
TO PROTECT THE JAPANESE WAY OF LIFE, THE SHOGUN EXPELLED THE PORTUGUESE, BANNED THE CHURCH, AND STOPPED ALL JAPANESE TRAVEL ABROAD.
WHO NEEDS 'EM?
ANY WOULD-BE WESTERN VISITOR HAD TO PROVE HIMSELF BY STEPPING ON A PORTRAIT OF THE VIRGIN MARY.
ONLY THE DUTCH PASSED THE TEST!
LET'S DO BUSINESS!
BUT EVEN THEY HAD TO STAY ON A SMALL ISLAND IN NAGASAKI HARBOR AND AVOID ALL CONTACT WITH ORDINARY JAPANESE.
EVEN EYE CONTACT...
FOR THE NEXT TWO CENTURIES, JAPAN KEPT UP THIS WALL AGAINST EUROPE.
DO YOU EVER WONDER WHAT'S BEHIND THERE?
A MENAGERIE OF MONSTERS, I IMAGINE...

THE COMPANY THAT KEEPS YOU

IN INDIA, THE MUGHAL STILL SAT SPLENDIDLY IN DELHI, BUT AS PROVINCES BROKE AWAY IN THE LATE 1600S, HIS SPLENDOR WENT SLIGHTLY SEEDY AROUND THE EDGES.

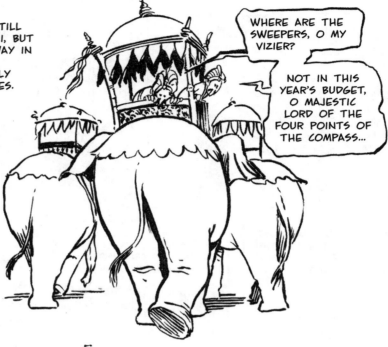

WHERE ARE THE SWEEPERS, O MY VIZIER?

NOT IN THIS YEAR'S BUDGET, O MAJESTIC LORD OF THE FOUR POINTS OF THE COMPASS...

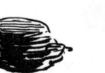

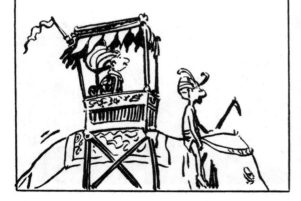

EVEN THE MUGHAL'S LOYAL NAWABS, OR GOVERNORS, BEGAN TO ACT LIKE LITTLE KINGS—FOR EXAMPLE, **SIRAJ UD-DAULAH,** NAWAB OF BENGAL, BIHAR, AND ORISSA.

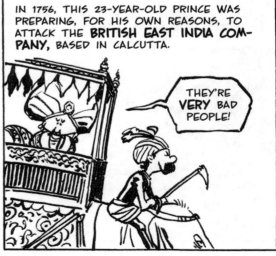

IN 1756, THIS 23-YEAR-OLD PRINCE WAS PREPARING, FOR HIS OWN REASONS, TO ATTACK THE **BRITISH EAST INDIA COMPANY,** BASED IN CALCUTTA.

THEY'RE **VERY** BAD PEOPLE!

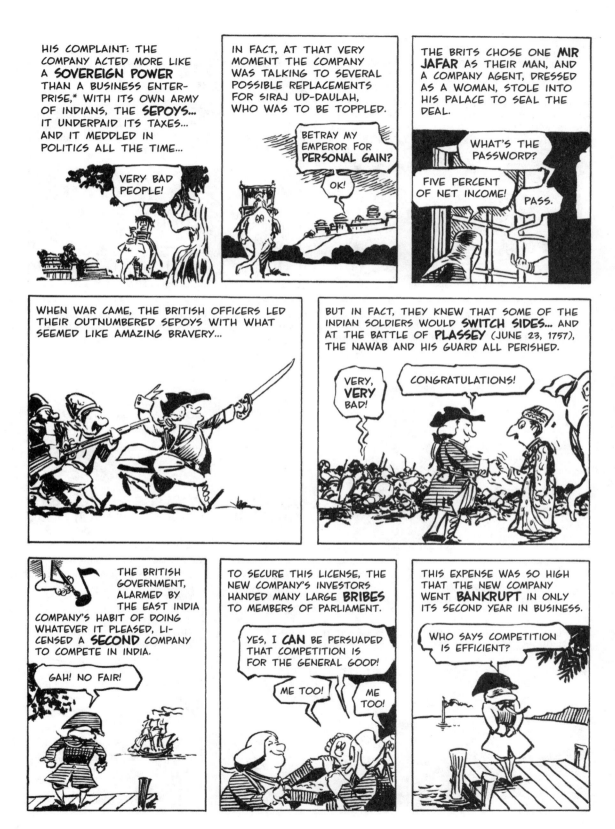

HIS COMPLAINT: THE COMPANY ACTED MORE LIKE A **SOVEREIGN POWER** THAN A BUSINESS ENTERPRISE,* WITH ITS OWN ARMY OF INDIANS, THE **SEPOYS**... IT UNDERPAID ITS TAXES... AND IT MEDDLED IN POLITICS ALL THE TIME...

VERY BAD PEOPLE!

IN FACT, AT THAT VERY MOMENT THE COMPANY WAS TALKING TO SEVERAL POSSIBLE REPLACEMENTS FOR SIRAJ UD-DAULAH, WHO WAS TO BE TOPPLED.

BETRAY MY EMPEROR FOR **PERSONAL GAIN?**

OK!

THE BRITS CHOSE ONE **MIR JAFAR** AS THEIR MAN, AND A COMPANY AGENT, DRESSED AS A WOMAN, STOLE INTO HIS PALACE TO SEAL THE DEAL.

WHAT'S THE PASSWORD?

FIVE PERCENT OF NET INCOME!

PASS.

WHEN WAR CAME, THE BRITISH OFFICERS LED THEIR OUTNUMBERED SEPOYS WITH WHAT SEEMED LIKE AMAZING BRAVERY...

BUT IN FACT, THEY KNEW THAT SOME OF THE INDIAN SOLDIERS WOULD **SWITCH SIDES**... AND AT THE BATTLE OF **PLASSEY** (JUNE 23, 1757), THE NAWAB AND HIS GUARD ALL PERISHED.

VERY, **VERY** BAD!

CONGRATULATIONS!

THE BRITISH GOVERNMENT, ALARMED BY THE EAST INDIA COMPANY'S HABIT OF DOING WHATEVER IT PLEASED, LICENSED A **SECOND** COMPANY TO COMPETE IN INDIA.

GAH! NO FAIR!

TO SECURE THIS LICENSE, THE NEW COMPANY'S INVESTORS HANDED MANY LARGE **BRIBES** TO MEMBERS OF PARLIAMENT.

YES, I **CAN** BE PERSUADED THAT COMPETITION IS FOR THE GENERAL GOOD!

ME TOO!

ME TOO!

THIS EXPENSE WAS SO HIGH THAT THE NEW COMPANY WENT **BANKRUPT** IN ONLY ITS SECOND YEAR IN BUSINESS.

WHO SAYS COMPETITION IS EFFICIENT?

11

NOW MIR JAFAR RAN BENGAL... OR DID HE? THE COMPANY DRAINED HIS TREASURY TO "COVER ITS EXPENSES."
YOU MAY KEEP THE ELEPHANT!
AND FEED HER WHAT?
WHEN HE COMPLAINED, THE BRITISH PUSHED HIM ASIDE ENTIRELY AND BEGAN COLLECTING TAXES DIRECTLY. THE COMPANY HAD BECOME A GOVERNMENT!
NICE TOUCH, THE HAT!
IN THE FACE OF SUCH LOOT, THE COMPANY MANAGERS HELPED THEMSELVES TO ASTONISHING SUMS... ROBERT CLIVE, CHAIRMAN OF THE EXECUTIVE COMMITTEE, MADE HIMSELF ONE OF BRITAIN'S RICHEST MEN OVERNIGHT.
THE COMPANY EXPANDED ITS SCOPE... IT HELPED THE MUGHAL MILITARY... JOINED THE MARATHAS TO PUT DOWN AN AMBITIOUS MAHARAJAH OF MYSORE, TIPU SULTAN... AND AT EVERY TURN, TOOK A CUT OF WHATEVER TREASURE TURNED UP...
WELL, WE ARE A BUSINESS!
THE EAST INDIAMEN PLANNED THEIR LOOTING WITH CARE, EVEN DRAWING UP CONTRACTS SPELLING OUT WHAT PERCENTAGE WOULD GO TO WHOM.
AND WE DID IT WITH A STRAIGHT FACE!
IN THE BUSINESS WITH MIR JAFAR, FOR INSTANCE, THEY MADE USE OF AN ARMENIAN MIDDLEMAN, KHOJAH WAJID, WHOSE CONTRACT GAVE HIM A PIECE OF THE TAKINGS FOR HIS SERVICES.
ALL PROPER AND BUSINESSLIKE IT IS!
THEN, BEHIND HIS BACK, THEY DREW UP A SECOND CONTRACT GIVING HIM NOTHING... WHICH IS WHAT HE GOT WHEN HE ASKED FOR HIS SHARE. AT THIS, IT IS SAID, KHOJAH WAJID WENT INSANE.
PROPER AND BUSINESSLIKE!
PROPER AND BUSINESSLIKE! WAH!!
TSK!

JAMES MILL, A HISTORIAN WHO LOOKED AT THE AC-COUNT BOOKS, CONCLUDED THAT THE COMPANY, AS A TRADING ENTERPRISE, NEVER TURNED A PROFIT: REVENUE FROM SALES ALWAYS FELL SHORT OF EXPENSES!
!
EXPENSES SUCH AS: THE PURCHASE OF PALACES, BARRACKS, BUNGALOWS, UNIFORMS, WEAPONS; THE UPKEEP OF ARMIES, SERVANTS, AND FORTS; PLUS THE HOGGISH PER-SONAL FORTUNES SKIMMED OFF BY EMPLOYEES.
TO STAY FLUSH, THE COMPANY HAD TO KEEP EXTORTING ONE-TIME "GIFTS" AND FINES FROM INDIAN TREASURIES.
I'M THIRSTY, MEN! GO OFF AND PILLAGE A NAWAB!
WHAT WAS SUPPOSED TO HAPPEN WHEN THIS DWINDLING POOL OF RICHES RAN DRY?
AND RUN DRY IT DID... INDIA FELL HELPLESSLY INTO POVERTY.
I WAS A NAWAB'S CHAMBERMAID ONCE...
I WAS A NAWAB...
THE COMPANY'S OWNERS IN BRITAIN COMPLAINED... BUT IT WAS HARD TO MAKE CHANGES FROM 10,000 MILES AWAY!
A LETTER TAKES SIX MONTHS TO ARRIVE...
AND NOBODY LISTENS ANYWAY...
BUT EVENTUALLY, THE MANAGERS IN INDIA FOUND NEW FIELDS TO HARVEST... FIELDS WE WILL REVISIT LATER...
LOVELY!

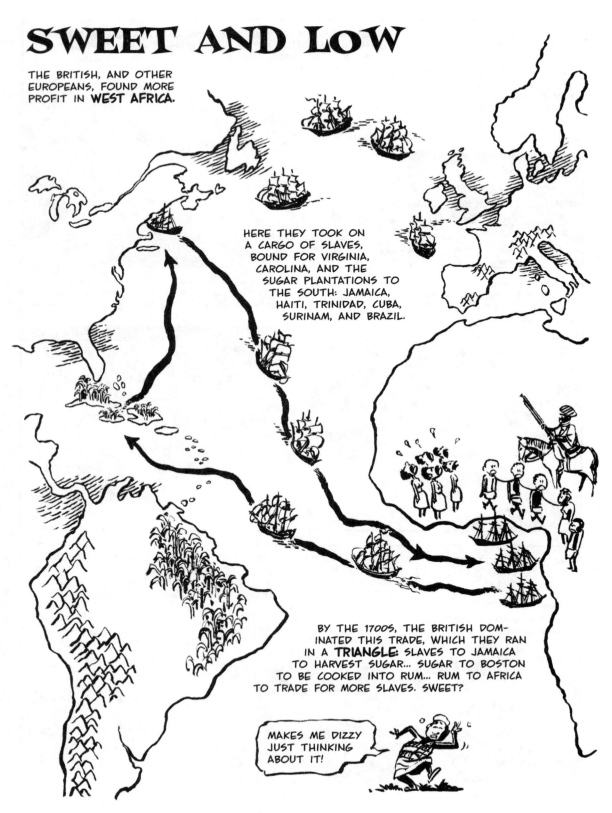

SWEET AND LOW

THE BRITISH, AND OTHER EUROPEANS, FOUND MORE PROFIT IN **WEST AFRICA**.

HERE THEY TOOK ON A CARGO OF SLAVES, BOUND FOR VIRGINIA, CAROLINA, AND THE SUGAR PLANTATIONS TO THE SOUTH: JAMAICA, HAITI, TRINIDAD, CUBA, SURINAM, AND BRAZIL.

BY THE 1700S, THE BRITISH DOMINATED THIS TRADE, WHICH THEY RAN IN A **TRIANGLE**: SLAVES TO JAMAICA TO HARVEST SUGAR... SUGAR TO BOSTON TO BE COOKED INTO RUM... RUM TO AFRICA TO TRADE FOR MORE SLAVES. SWEET?

MAKES ME DIZZY JUST THINKING ABOUT IT!

14

BESIDES SLAVES, THE EUROPEANS ALSO BOUGHT IVORY, GOLD DUST, AND CAFFEINE-LACED KOLA NUTS IN AFRICA, AND THE AFRICANS TOOK CLOTH, KNICK-KNACKS, COWRIE SHELLS, AND **MUSKETS.**

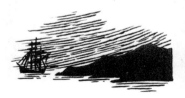

AS IN JAPAN, SOME CHIEFS BOUGHT ENOUGH GUNS TO EQUIP ARMIES AND CONQUER SIZABLE KINGDOMS, SUCH AS **DAHOMEY** AND **ASHANTI.**

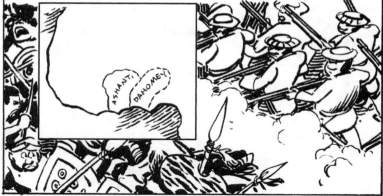

ASHANTI DAHOMEY

FIREARMS ALSO REACHED THE SLAVE RAIDERS WHO INFESTED THE BACK COUNTRY.

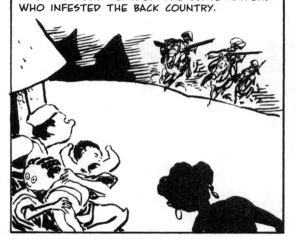

THEY CAPTURED MORE PEOPLE, IN FACT, THAN EUROPE COULD CARRY AWAY...

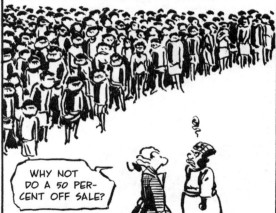

WHY NOT DO A 50 PER-CENT OFF SALE?

BUT NO MATTER! SLAVES COULD ALWAYS FIND AFRICAN BUYERS!

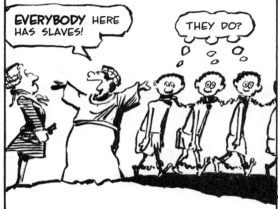

EVERYBODY HERE HAS SLAVES!

THEY DO?

AFRICAN DEALERS, IT'S SAID, TENDED TO SHIP THE FEISTIER SLAVES TO AMERICA, SINCE IN AFRICA, THEY'D BE TOO LIKELY TO BOLT FOR HOME.

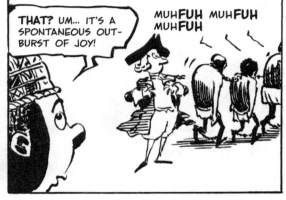

THAT? UM... IT'S A SPONTANEOUS OUT-BURST OF JOY!

MUH**FUH** MUH**FUH** MUH**FUH**

AS SLAVE CATCHERS RANGED FARTHER IN-
LAND, FARMERS FLED THEIR VILLAGES AND
TOOK TO THE HILLS OR THE FOREST.

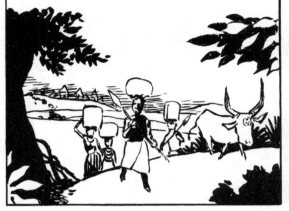

WHEN THEY FOUND OTHERS ON THE RUN
LIKE THEMSELVES, THEY MIGHT **JOIN** THEM—
OR **ENSLAVE** THEM, OR **BE** ENSLAVED,
DEPENDING.

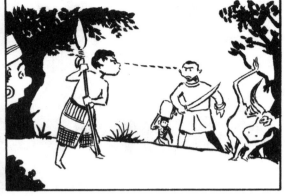

MOST PROTECTED THEMSELVES BY SWEARING
LOYALTY TO THE STRONGEST MAN IN THE
NEIGHBORHOOD. THEN YOU WERE SAFE...

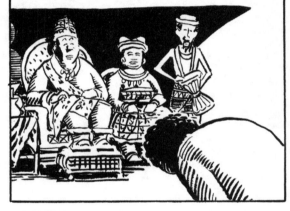

UNLESS, THAT IS, HE RAN SHORT OF CASH
AND DECIDED TO **SELL** YOU! RISKY BUSINESS,
LIVING IN A SLAVE DEPOT...

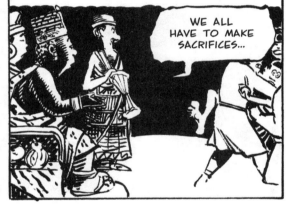

WE ALL
HAVE TO MAKE
SACRIFICES...

AFRICANS ALSO
PROTECTED
THEMSELVES BY
JOINING
SECRET SOCIETIES: CLUB
BUDDIES WERE SUPPOSED TO
HELP EACH OTHER STAY FREE.

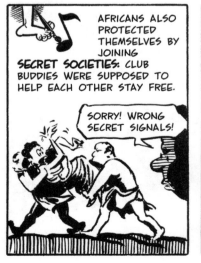

SORRY! WRONG
SECRET SIGNALS!

SLAVES BROUGHT THESE HUSH-
HUSH CLUBS TO AMERICA, LIKE
HAITI'S **VOODOO** SOCIETIES.

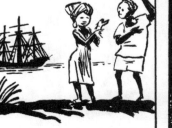

I WISH I COULD SAY MORE
ABOUT THIS FASCINATING SUB-
JECT, BUT WHAT DO I KNOW?
IT'S SECRET!

SH!

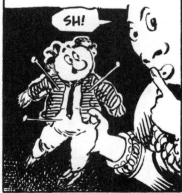

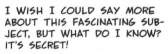

CAPTURED UP-COUNTRY, A SLAVE MIGHT SIT SHACKLED FOR MONTHS WHILE THE DEALER BUILT UP HIS INVENTORY... UNTIL ONE DAY COMES THE ORDER TO MARCH.
STARVING AND WEAK-KNEED, THE CAPTIVE WOULD HAVE TO STAND UP, SHOULDER A LOAD, AND MARCH FAR ON LITTLE FOOD.
HI, HOW ARE **YOU?**
DEPRESSED, BUT I HEAR IT'S AN INCURABLE BIOCHEMICAL IMBALANCE...
ON ARRIVAL, SLAVES PRESUMABLY GOT ENOUGH TO EAT TO MAKE THEM LOOK GOOD TO BUYERS.
FEEL ANY BETTER?
NO... IT'S ALL EMPTY CALORIES...
THEN, AFTER A LAST GOOD-BYE, THE EXPORTS WOULD PACK THEMSELVES BY THE HUNDREDS INTO WAITING SHIPS.
OHMIGOD... THIS IS JUST **AWFUL!**
MAN, DO YOU HAVE TO COMPLAIN ABOUT **EVERYTHING?**
IF ALL WENT WELL, THE CARGO SPENT SIX TO EIGHT WEEKS PACKED AND SHACKLED WITH THE REST IN THE DARK, STINKING HOLD, WITH A FEW SHORT BREAKS TOPSIDE FOR AIR.
YOU SNORE.
SHUT UP!
THINGS WENT WRONG OFTEN ENOUGH... ON AVERAGE, 25 TO 30 PERCENT WOULD DIE IN TRANSIT—**CREW** AS WELL AS **CARGO!**
WHEN MUM ADVISED ME TO GO TO SEA, I DON'T THINK SHE MEANT QUITE THIS CLOSE...

EVENTUALLY, THE SHIP ARRIVED IN AMERICA AND COUGHED UP ITS CARGO...
COUGH COUGH COUGH
...MOST OFTEN TO THE MAN-EATING SUGAR PLANTATIONS OF THE CARIBBEAN.
LOOKS BAD...
OH, BITCH, BITCH, BITCH...
THRIFTY OWNERS KNEW IT COST LESS TO WORK A SLAVE TO DEATH AND REPLACE HIM THAN TO WASTE TIME WITH PREGNANCY AND CHILD-REARING. THIS EXPLAINS WHY MOST SLAVES IMPORTED WERE MALE, AND WHY THEY USUALLY LIVED ONLY A FEW YEARS AFTER ARRIVING.
LOOK ON THE BRIGHT SIDE! WE'RE GIVING THE BRITS THE LEISURE TO DEVELOP LIBERAL PHILOSOPHY!
AND YET THOUSANDS SURVIVED, GAINED FREEDOM, AND SOMETIMES EVEN BOUGHT THEIR OWN SLAVE PLANTATIONS.
TO BE LIKE YOU IS MY DREAM...
OTHERS TOOK UP CRAFTS OR WENT TO SEA...
AND OF THESE, MANY LANDED IN NORTH AMERICA OR EUROPE.

DARKNESS AND ENLIGHTENMENT

MOST OF THE AFRICAN IMMIGRANTS TO EUROPE SETTLED DOCKSIDE, NEAR WORK. FROM HERE, THEY MAY NOT HAVE NOTICED THE COFFEEHOUSES FULL OF CAFFEINE-FUELED SCRIBBLERS AND TALKERS WORKING FURIOUSLY ON A **VAST INTELLECTUAL PROJECT.**

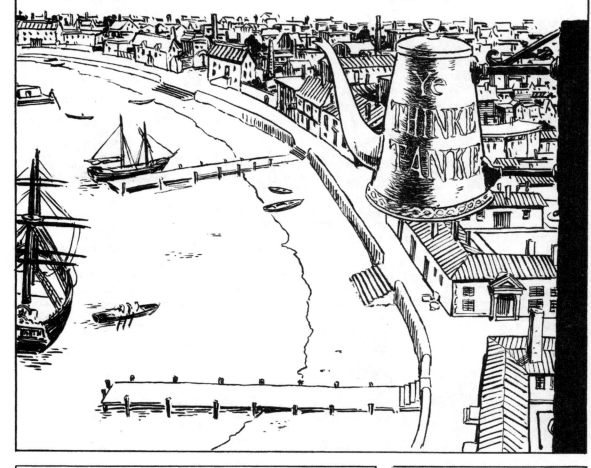

Ye THINKE TANKE

INSPIRED BY RECENT TRIUMPHS IN PHYSICS, CHEMISTRY, ELECTRICITY, AND ASTRONOMY, THESE PHILOSOPHERS HOPED TO PUT **SOCIETY** ON A RATIONAL, **"NATURAL"** FOUNDATION.

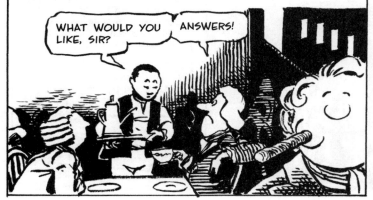

WHAT WOULD YOU LIKE, SIR?

ANSWERS!

SOME CALLED THIS MOVEMENT THE **ENLIGHTENMENT**... OTHERS CALLED IT **ATHEISM**... AND IN FACT SOME OF ITS PRACTITIONERS DID HAVE MIXED FEELINGS ABOUT RELIGION, TO SAY THE LEAST...

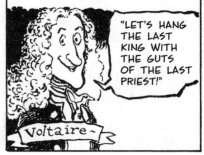

"LET'S HANG THE LAST KING WITH THE GUTS OF THE LAST PRIEST!"

Voltaire~

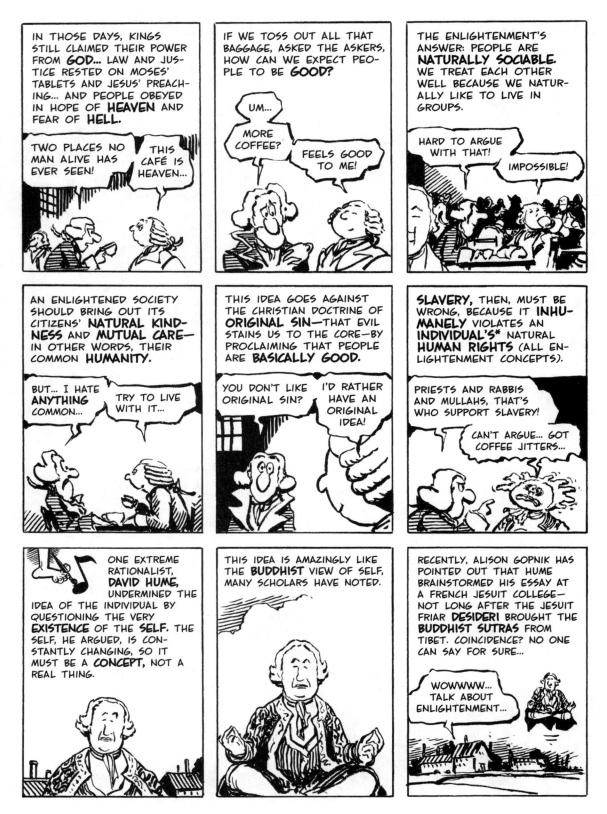

IN THOSE DAYS, KINGS STILL CLAIMED THEIR POWER FROM **GOD**... LAW AND JUSTICE RESTED ON MOSES' TABLETS AND JESUS' PREACHING... AND PEOPLE OBEYED IN HOPE OF **HEAVEN** AND FEAR OF **HELL**.

TWO PLACES NO MAN ALIVE HAS EVER SEEN!

THIS CAFÉ IS HEAVEN...

IF WE TOSS OUT ALL THAT BAGGAGE, ASKED THE ASKERS, HOW CAN WE EXPECT PEOPLE TO BE **GOOD**?

UM...

MORE COFFEE?

FEELS GOOD TO ME!

THE ENLIGHTENMENT'S ANSWER: PEOPLE ARE **NATURALLY SOCIABLE.** WE TREAT EACH OTHER WELL BECAUSE WE NATURALLY LIKE TO LIVE IN GROUPS.

HARD TO ARGUE WITH THAT!

IMPOSSIBLE!

AN ENLIGHTENED SOCIETY SHOULD BRING OUT ITS CITIZENS' **NATURAL KINDNESS** AND **MUTUAL CARE**—IN OTHER WORDS, THEIR COMMON **HUMANITY**.

BUT... I HATE **ANYTHING** COMMON...

TRY TO LIVE WITH IT...

THIS IDEA GOES AGAINST THE CHRISTIAN DOCTRINE OF **ORIGINAL SIN**—THAT EVIL STAINS US TO THE CORE—BY PROCLAIMING THAT PEOPLE ARE **BASICALLY GOOD**.

YOU DON'T LIKE ORIGINAL SIN?

I'D RATHER HAVE AN ORIGINAL IDEA!

SLAVERY, THEN, MUST BE WRONG, BECAUSE IT **INHUMANELY** VIOLATES AN **INDIVIDUAL'S*** NATURAL **HUMAN RIGHTS** (ALL ENLIGHTENMENT CONCEPTS).

PRIESTS AND RABBIS AND MULLAHS, THAT'S WHO SUPPORT SLAVERY!

CAN'T ARGUE... GOT COFFEE JITTERS...

ONE EXTREME RATIONALIST, **DAVID HUME,** UNDERMINED THE IDEA OF THE INDIVIDUAL BY QUESTIONING THE VERY **EXISTENCE** OF THE **SELF.** THE SELF, HE ARGUED, IS CONSTANTLY CHANGING, SO IT MUST BE A **CONCEPT,** NOT A REAL THING.

THIS IDEA IS AMAZINGLY LIKE THE **BUDDHIST** VIEW OF SELF, MANY SCHOLARS HAVE NOTED.

RECENTLY, ALISON GOPNIK HAS POINTED OUT THAT HUME BRAINSTORMED HIS ESSAY AT A FRENCH JESUIT COLLEGE—NOT LONG AFTER THE JESUIT FRIAR **DESIDERI** BROUGHT THE **BUDDHIST SUTRAS** FROM TIBET. COINCIDENCE? NO ONE CAN SAY FOR SURE...

WOWWWW... TALK ABOUT ENLIGHTENMENT...

ONE DAY IN 1765, AN AIMLESS YOUNG LON-DONER NAMED **GRANVILLE SHARP** DROPPED IN ON HIS BROTHER, A SURGEON, AT WORK.

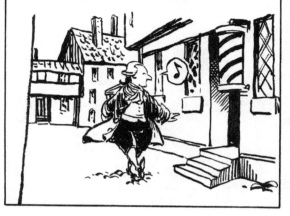

THERE A SHOCK GREETED SHARP: A SLAVE, **JONATHAN STRONG,** HIS FACE PISTOL-WHIPPED TO A PULP BY HIS MASTER.

STRONG EXPLAINED THAT THE MASTER, A JAMAICAN PLANTER VISITING LONDON, HAD BEATEN HIM IN A FURY, LEFT HIM FOR DEAD, AND SAILED HOME TO JAMAICA.

BLOODY VILLAINOUS!

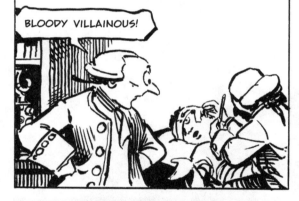

JONATHAN STRONG RECOVERED, AND TWO YEARS LATER, WHILE VISITING LONDON AGAIN, HIS FORMER MASTER HAPPENED TO SEE HIM.

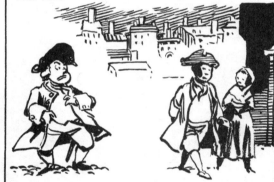

THE PLANTER HIRED SOME MUSCLE TO KIDNAP—OR RECLAIM—HIS HUMAN PROPERTY.

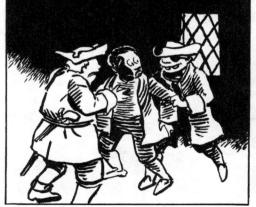

STRONG, WHO HAD LEARNED TO WRITE IN THE MEANTIME, SENT A NOTE TO THE SHARPS.

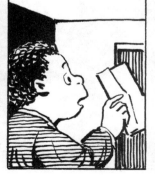

AND GRANVILLE SHARP SPRANG INTO ACTION!

NO, BY GOD!

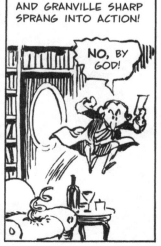

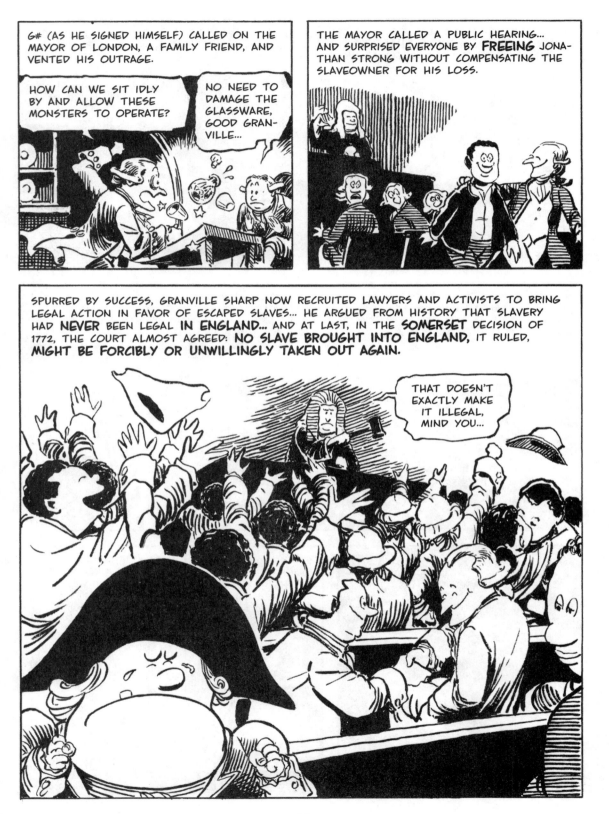

G# (AS HE SIGNED HIMSELF) CALLED ON THE MAYOR OF LONDON, A FAMILY FRIEND, AND VENTED HIS OUTRAGE.

HOW CAN WE SIT IDLY BY AND ALLOW THESE MONSTERS TO OPERATE?

NO NEED TO DAMAGE THE GLASSWARE, GOOD GRAN-VILLE...

THE MAYOR CALLED A PUBLIC HEARING... AND SURPRISED EVERYONE BY **FREEING** JONA-THAN STRONG WITHOUT COMPENSATING THE SLAVEOWNER FOR HIS LOSS.

SPURRED BY SUCCESS, GRANVILLE SHARP NOW RECRUITED LAWYERS AND ACTIVISTS TO BRING LEGAL ACTION IN FAVOR OF ESCAPED SLAVES... HE ARGUED FROM HISTORY THAT SLAVERY HAD **NEVER** BEEN LEGAL **IN ENGLAND**... AND AT LAST, IN THE **SOMERSET** DECISION OF 1772, THE COURT ALMOST AGREED: **NO SLAVE BROUGHT INTO ENGLAND,** IT RULED, **MIGHT BE FORCIBLY OR UNWILLINGLY TAKEN OUT AGAIN.**

THAT DOESN'T EXACTLY MAKE IT ILLEGAL, MIND YOU...

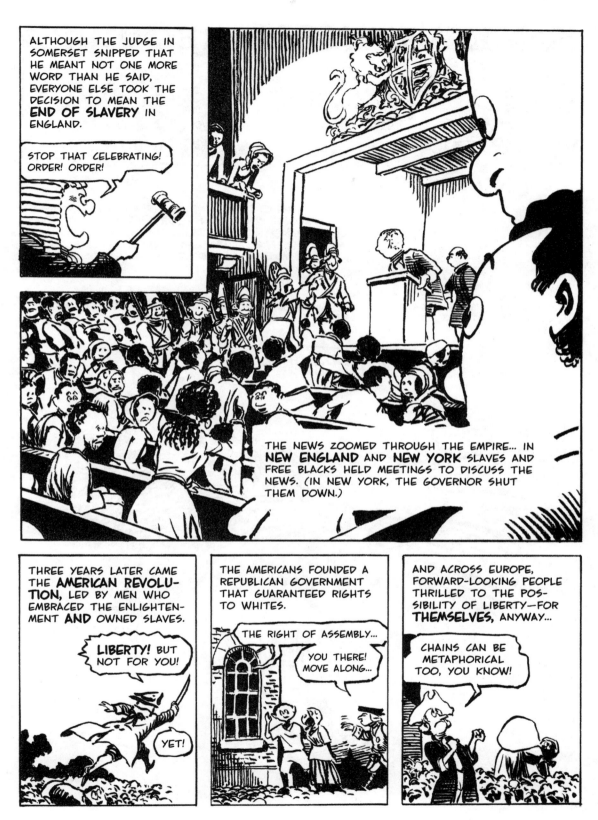

ALTHOUGH THE JUDGE IN SOMERSET SNIPPED THAT HE MEANT NOT ONE MORE WORD THAN HE SAID, EVERYONE ELSE TOOK THE DECISION TO MEAN THE **END OF SLAVERY** IN ENGLAND.

STOP THAT CELEBRATING! ORDER! ORDER!

THE NEWS ZOOMED THROUGH THE EMPIRE... IN **NEW ENGLAND** AND **NEW YORK** SLAVES AND FREE BLACKS HELD MEETINGS TO DISCUSS THE NEWS. (IN NEW YORK, THE GOVERNOR SHUT THEM DOWN.)

THREE YEARS LATER CAME THE **AMERICAN REVOLUTION,** LED BY MEN WHO EMBRACED THE ENLIGHTENMENT **AND** OWNED SLAVES.

LIBERTY! BUT NOT FOR YOU!

YET!

THE AMERICANS FOUNDED A REPUBLICAN GOVERNMENT THAT GUARANTEED RIGHTS TO WHITES.

THE RIGHT OF ASSEMBLY...

YOU THERE! MOVE ALONG...

AND ACROSS EUROPE, FORWARD-LOOKING PEOPLE THRILLED TO THE POSSIBILITY OF LIBERTY—FOR **THEMSELVES,** ANYWAY...

CHAINS CAN BE METAPHORICAL TOO, YOU KNOW!

SOME ASSEMBLY REQUIRED

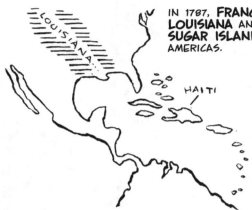

IN 1787, **FRANCE** STILL HELD **LOUISIANA** AND SOME PRECIOUS **SUGAR ISLANDS** IN THE AMERICAS.

OF THESE, **HAITI** WAS CALLED THE RICHEST—EVEN THOUGH MORE THAN **FOUR FIFTHS** OF ITS PEOPLE HAD **NOTHING AT ALL**... SLAVES IN THE CANE FIELDS FAR OUTNUMBERED WHITES, FREE BLACKS, AND MIXED-RACE PEOPLE PUT TOGETHER.

BY "RICH," THE FRENCH MEANT THAT HAITIAN **SUGAR SALES** BROUGHT A STEADY STREAM OF **MONEY** BACK TO THE MOTHER COUNTRY.

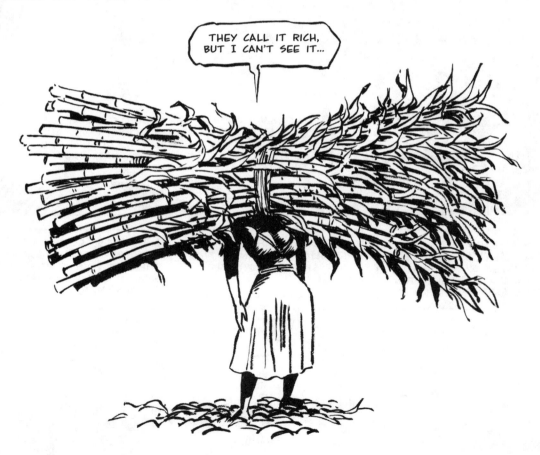

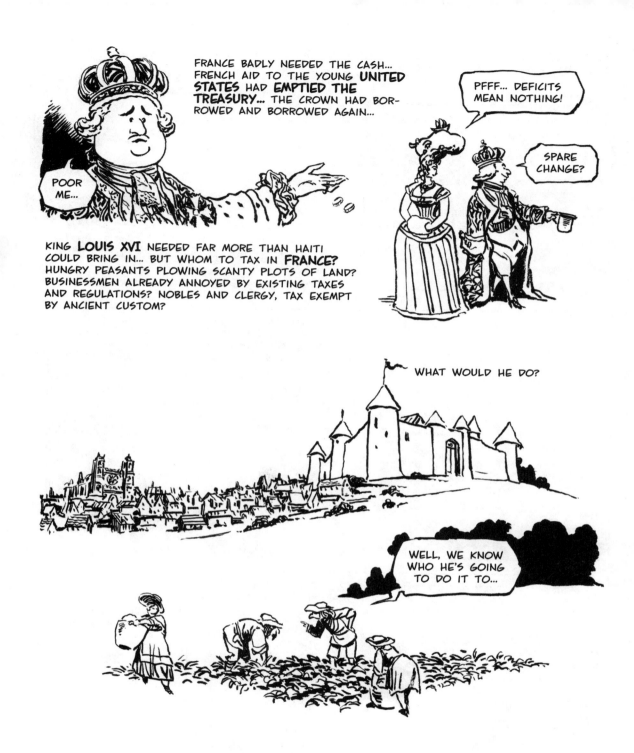

FRANCE BADLY NEEDED THE CASH... FRENCH AID TO THE YOUNG **UNITED STATES** HAD **EMPTIED THE TREASURY**... THE CROWN HAD BORROWED AND BORROWED AGAIN...

POOR ME...

PFFF... DEFICITS MEAN NOTHING!

SPARE CHANGE?

KING **LOUIS XVI** NEEDED FAR MORE THAN HAITI COULD BRING IN... BUT WHOM TO TAX IN **FRANCE?** HUNGRY PEASANTS PLOWING SCANTY PLOTS OF LAND? BUSINESSMEN ALREADY ANNOYED BY EXISTING TAXES AND REGULATIONS? NOBLES AND CLERGY, TAX EXEMPT BY ANCIENT CUSTOM?

WHAT WOULD HE DO?

WELL, WE KNOW WHO HE'S GOING TO DO IT TO...

TO ADDRESS THE PROBLEM, THE KING HIRED A SERIES OF FINANCE MINISTERS, BUT ALL THEIR BRILLIANT SCHEMES CAME TO NOTHING.

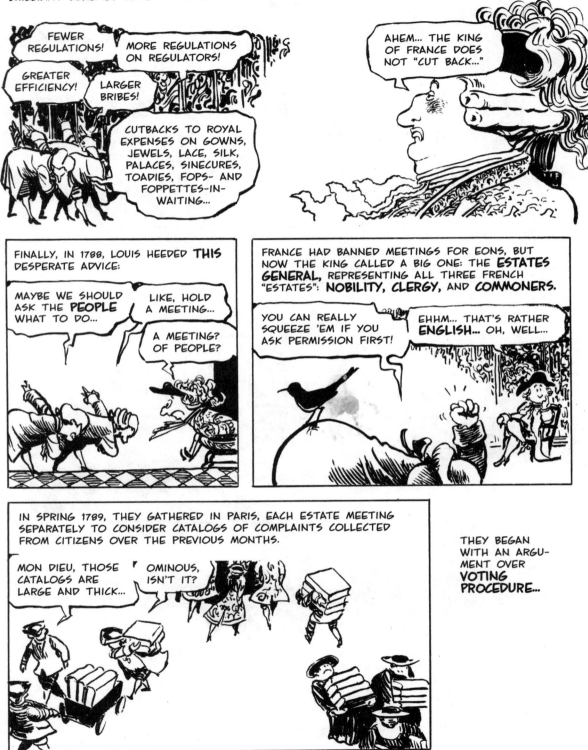

FEWER REGULATIONS!

MORE REGULATIONS ON REGULATORS!

GREATER EFFICIENCY!

LARGER BRIBES!

CUTBACKS TO ROYAL EXPENSES ON GOWNS, JEWELS, LACE, SILK, PALACES, SINECURES, TOADIES, FOPS- AND FOPPETTES-IN-WAITING...

AHEM... THE KING OF FRANCE DOES NOT "CUT BACK..."

FINALLY, IN 1788, LOUIS HEEDED **THIS** DESPERATE ADVICE:

MAYBE WE SHOULD ASK THE **PEOPLE** WHAT TO DO...

LIKE, HOLD A MEETING...

A MEETING? OF PEOPLE?

FRANCE HAD BANNED MEETINGS FOR EONS, BUT NOW THE KING CALLED A BIG ONE: THE **ESTATES GENERAL**, REPRESENTING ALL THREE FRENCH "ESTATES": **NOBILITY**, **CLERGY**, AND **COMMONERS**.

YOU CAN REALLY SQUEEZE 'EM IF YOU ASK PERMISSION FIRST!

EHHM... THAT'S RATHER **ENGLISH**... OH, WELL...

IN SPRING 1789, THEY GATHERED IN PARIS, EACH ESTATE MEETING SEPARATELY TO CONSIDER CATALOGS OF COMPLAINTS COLLECTED FROM CITIZENS OVER THE PREVIOUS MONTHS.

MON DIEU, THOSE CATALOGS ARE LARGE AND THICK...

OMINOUS, ISN'T IT?

THEY BEGAN WITH AN ARGU-MENT OVER **VOTING PROCEDURE...**

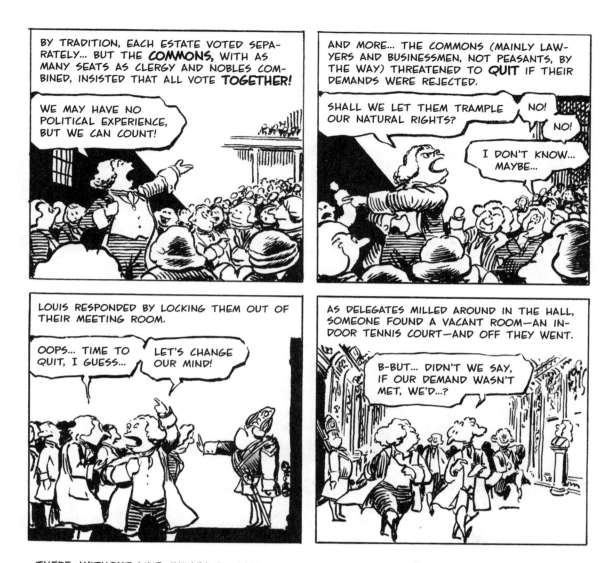

BY TRADITION, EACH ESTATE VOTED SEPARATELY... BUT THE **COMMONS**, WITH AS MANY SEATS AS CLERGY AND NOBLES COMBINED, INSISTED THAT ALL VOTE **TOGETHER!**

WE MAY HAVE NO POLITICAL EXPERIENCE, BUT WE CAN COUNT!

AND MORE... THE COMMONS (MAINLY LAWYERS AND BUSINESSMEN, NOT PEASANTS, BY THE WAY) THREATENED TO **QUIT** IF THEIR DEMANDS WERE REJECTED.

SHALL WE LET THEM TRAMPLE OUR NATURAL RIGHTS?

NO!

NO!

I DON'T KNOW... MAYBE...

LOUIS RESPONDED BY LOCKING THEM OUT OF THEIR MEETING ROOM.

OOPS... TIME TO QUIT, I GUESS...

LET'S CHANGE OUR MIND!

AS DELEGATES MILLED AROUND IN THE HALL, SOMEONE FOUND A VACANT ROOM—AN INDOOR TENNIS COURT—AND OFF THEY WENT.

B-BUT... DIDN'T WE SAY, IF OUR DEMAND WASN'T MET, WE'D...?

THERE, WITHOUT LINE JUDGES OR BALL BOYS, THEY TOOK THEIR FIRST OFFICIAL ACT: SWEARING TO STAY TOGETHER, NO MATTER WHAT, UNTIL THEIR WORK WAS DONE. THIS "TENNIS COURT OATH" TOOK MORE COURAGE THAN MANY YOU HEAR AT MATCHES TODAY...

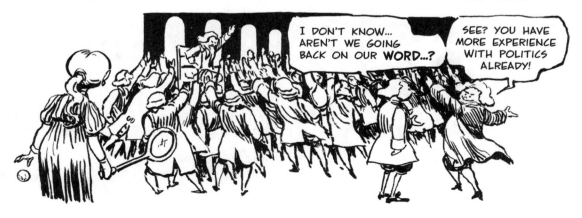

I DON'T KNOW... AREN'T WE GOING BACK ON OUR **WORD**...?

SEE? YOU HAVE MORE EXPERIENCE WITH POLITICS ALREADY!

AT THIS AFFRONT, LOUIS BACKED DOWN—PARTWAY: HE REOPENED THE COMMONERS' MEETING ROOM, BUT ALSO SENT 20,000 SOLDIERS TO PARIS TO KEEP ORDER.
AND SECURE THE TENNIS COURT!
BUT NO... LIBERAL PRIESTS AND NOBLES DEFIED THE KING TOO... THEY JOINED THE COMMONERS IN A GROUP HUG AND CALLED IT THE NATIONAL ASSEMBLY.
DON'T TOUCH ME THERE.
SWEPT AWAY BY BROTHERLY LOVE, THESE IDEALISTIC NOBLES NOW VOTED TO END THEIR OWN ANCIENT PRIVILEGES.
I'VE ALWAYS—SOB!!—WANTED TO PAY TAXES TOO!
MY BROTHER!
THE ASSEMBLY ARMED ITS OWN "NATIONAL GUARD," ORGANIZED AND LED BY COUNT DE LAFAYETTE, WHO HAD BEEN WITH WASHINGTON IN AMERICA.
PURELY FOR SELF-DEFENSE!
REALLY?
OH, DON'T BE SO REALITY-BASED, BROTHER!
LOUIS, LOATH TO FIGHT, MERELY FIRED HIS ADVISERS INSTEAD...
I'M STRONG! DECISIVE! IN CONTROL! BUT REASONABLE!
HECKUVA JOB, GUYS!
SO THE NATIONAL GUARD TOOK THE OFFENSIVE BY ATTACKING THE BASTILLE, A PARIS DUNGEON FOR POLITICAL PRISONERS.
ALL IN FAVOR OF DOING WHATEVER WE CAN GET AWAY WITH...

ON JULY 14, 1789, THE NATIONAL GUARD STORMED THE BASTILLE, A PARIS DUNGEON FOR POLITICAL PRISONERS.
AFTER FREEING ALL EIGHT(!) OF ITS INMATES, THEY RAZED THE BUILDING TO RUBBLE.
YES, WE'RE BUILDING SOMETHING GLORIOUS...
WITH THE BREAKDOWN IN GOVERNMENT, A NAMELESS FEAR SWEPT FRANCE... FEAR OF DISEASE, OF STARVATION, OF INVASION, OF THE NEIGHBORS FIVE MILES AWAY...
IN THE COUNTRYSIDE, ARMED MOBS FORMED TO DEFEND THEMSELVES—AGAINST NOTHING...
BUT, ARMED AND TOGETHER, THEY FOUND IT CONVENIENT TO ATTACK THE NOBLES' CHATEAUS, SYMBOLS OF FEUDALISM...
I MEAN, AS LONG AS WE'RE HERE...
AND HOME TO SOME VERY FINE WINE CELLARS.
FREE THE MOUTON ROTHSCHILD SIX!

BACK IN PARIS, THE ASSEMBLY WAS DIS- CUSSING THE BASIC PRINCIPLES OF THE NEW GOVERNMENT. TO BEGIN WITH, WHO WAS A **FRENCH CITIZEN?**

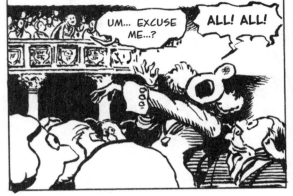

UM... EXCUSE ME...?

ALL! ALL!

FROM THE AUDIENCE, A HAITIAN NAMED **VIN- CENT OGÉ** PUT IN THAT FREE MEN OF COLOR, LIKE HIMSELF, WERE HAITI'S MOST LOYAL FRENCHMEN AND DESERVED EQUAL RIGHTS.

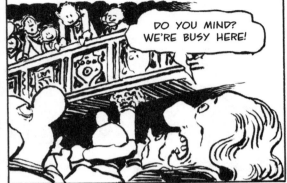

DO YOU MIND? WE'RE BUSY HERE!

AFTER EJECTING OGÉ, THE ASSEMBLY ISSUED A STIRRING PROCLAMATION THAT ALL MEN ARE BORN FREE AND EQUAL.

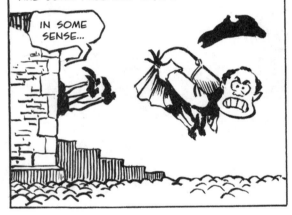

IN SOME SENSE...

THEN THEY RESTRICTED THE VOTE TO 15 PERCENT OF THE FRENCH POPULATION.

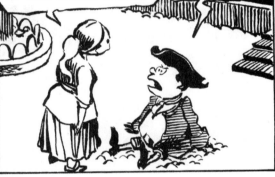

HOW ARE THE RIGHTS OF MAN COMING ALONG?

OH, MAN...

MEANWHILE, PARISIANS SHOWED WHAT THEY COULD DO WITHOUT A VOTE BY INVADING THE KING'S SUBURBAN PALACE AND KILLING DOZENS OF HIS GUARD.

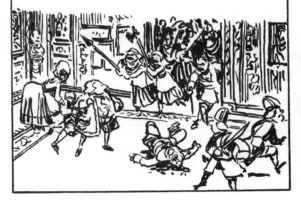

THE MOB "ESCORTED" THE ROYALS BACK TO THE CAPITAL, CLOSER TO THE VOICE—AND THE PIKES—OF THE PEOPLE, OR AT LEAST SOME OF THEM.

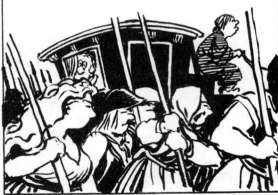

NONE OF THIS LIBERTY SOLVED THE GOVERNMENT'S ORIGINAL PROBLEM: THE **SHORTAGE OF MONEY.**

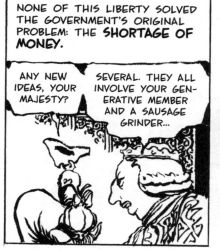

ANY NEW IDEAS, YOUR MAJESTY?

SEVERAL. THEY ALL INVOLVE YOUR GENERATIVE MEMBER AND A SAUSAGE GRINDER...

HOW TO RAISE FUNDS WHEN SO MANY DELEGATES WERE BUSINESSMEN WHO LOATHED TAXES? THEY CHOSE THIS PLAN: SEIZE **CHURCH PROPERTY** AND ISSUE MONEY AGAINST IT.

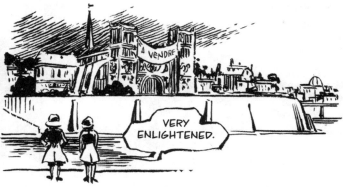

VERY ENLIGHTENED.

NEXT THE ASSEMBLY **ABOLISHED NOBILITY** COMPLETELY... DESPERATE, ANGRY NOBLES BEGAN TO FLEE FRANCE... AND SO, IN MID-1791, DID KING LOUIS AND QUEEN MARIE-ANTOINETTE.

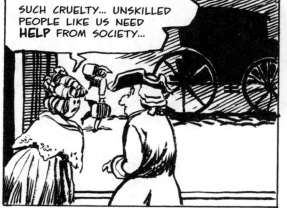

SUCH CRUELTY... UNSKILLED PEOPLE LIKE US NEED **HELP** FROM SOCIETY...

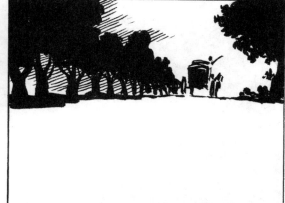

A WATCHFUL WAITRESS SPOTTED THE ROYALS AT A COUNTRY INN... THEY WERE DETAINED...

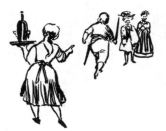

AND RETURNED TO PARIS UNDER GUARD.

WHAT'S THAT?

A CLOUD OF SUSPICION...

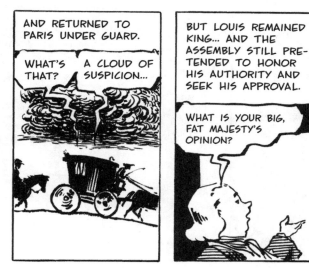

BUT LOUIS REMAINED KING... AND THE ASSEMBLY STILL PRETENDED TO HONOR HIS AUTHORITY AND SEEK HIS APPROVAL.

WHAT IS YOUR BIG, FAT MAJESTY'S OPINION?

AT THIS POINT, UPSETTING NEWS ARRIVED FROM **HAITI...**

VINCENT OGÉ, THE HAITIAN TURNED OUT OF THE ASSEMBLY DURING THE CITIZENSHIP DEBATE (SEE P. 30), RETURNED TO HAITI WITH LIBERATION ON HIS MIND.

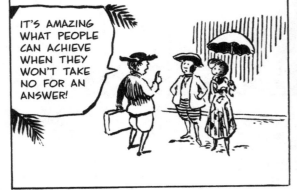

IT'S AMAZING WHAT PEOPLE CAN ACHIEVE WHEN THEY WON'T TAKE NO FOR AN ANSWER!

OGÉ ORGANIZED THE FREE PEOPLE OF COLOR TO DEMAND FULL CIVIL RIGHTS AND A PLACE IN THE ISLAND'S GOVERNMENT.

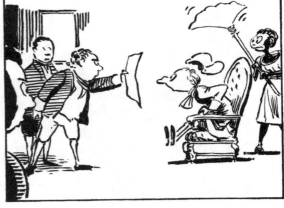

WHEN TALKING FAILED, HE AND HIS SUP-PORTERS LAUNCHED A **GUERRILLA WAR** AGAINST THE WHITE ESTABLISHMENT.

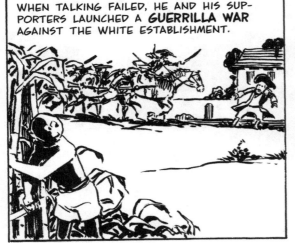

THE WHITES RAISED THEIR OWN MILITIA, AND FIGHTING WENT ON FOR SEVERAL MONTHS.

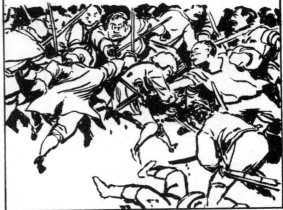

IN EARLY 1791, OGÉ FELL INTO HIS ENEMIES' HANDS.

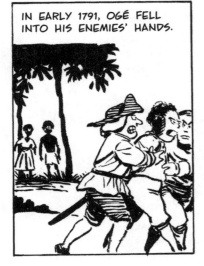

THEY EXECUTED HIM WITH THE NASTY TORTURES PEOPLE USE WHEN TRYING TO MAKE A POINT...

A SERIOUS ERROR! THIS RIFT AMONG THE FREE GAVE THE **SLAVES** AN OPPORTUNITY. IN A MID-AUGUST **VOODOO CEREMONY,** THEY PLANNED THEIR OWN REBELLION.

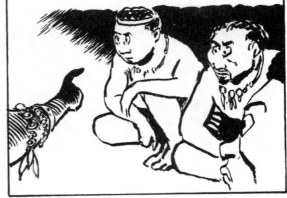

FOR SEVEN DAYS, THE WORD QUIETLY SPREAD...

ON AUGUST 21, SLAVES ACROSS HAITI ROSE AND BEGAN KILLING THEIR MASTERS, THEIR MASTERS' WIVES, THEIR MASTERS' CHILDREN, THEIR MASTERS' PUPPY DOGS...

SLAVE REBELLIONS ARE **UGLY!**

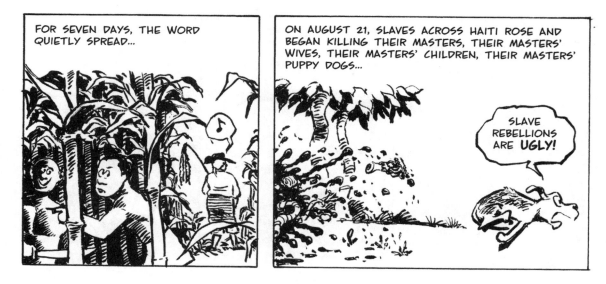

USING WHATEVER WEAPONS THEY COULD FIND, THE REBELS OVERRAN ARMORIES FOR GUNS, SWORDS, AND UNIFORMS. THEY FORMED MILITARY UNITS THAT TORCHED SUGAR PLANTATIONS, AND SOON THE WHOLE ISLAND SMELLED LIKE BARBECUE.

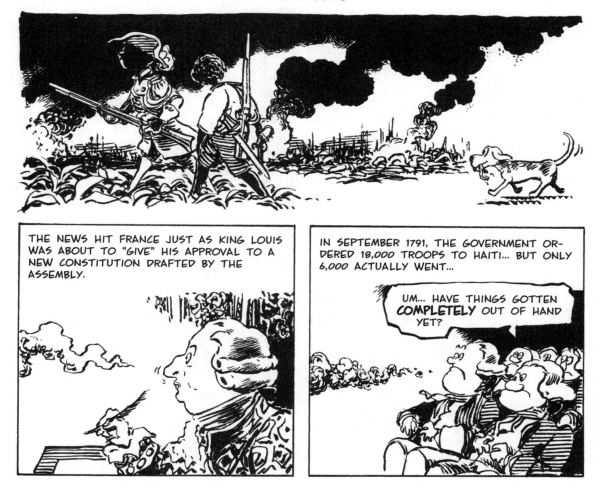

THE NEWS HIT FRANCE JUST AS KING LOUIS WAS ABOUT TO "GIVE" HIS APPROVAL TO A NEW CONSTITUTION DRAFTED BY THE ASSEMBLY.

IN SEPTEMBER 1791, THE GOVERNMENT ORDERED 18,000 TROOPS TO HAITI... BUT ONLY 6,000 ACTUALLY WENT...

UM... HAVE THINGS GOTTEN **COMPLETELY** OUT OF HAND YET?

A PERFECT TIME, THE ASSEMBLY DECIDED, TO **DISSOLVE** ITSELF!!
GOVERNMENT, IT'S A NICE PLACE TO VISIT...
BUT I WOULDN'T WANT
TO LIVE THERE!
HAITI, THE FINANCES, AND EVERYTHING ELSE WAS LEFT TO A NEW "LEGISLATIVE ASSEMBLY" TO BE ELECTED.
HEH... HAVE FUN!
SINCE, BY AGREEMENT, NO ONE FROM THE OLD ASSEMBLY COULD RUN AGAIN, THE INCOMING BODY HAD NO EXPERIENCE AT ALL!
WISE, WISE!
NO INSIDERS, PROFESSIONAL POLITICIANS, OR THAT LOT...
STILL FACED WITH STAGGERING MONEY PROBLEMS, THE NEW GOVERNMENT HAD A NEW IDEA: RAID THE **BANKS OF AMSTERDAM.**
BUT CALL IT "EXPORTING THE REVOLUTION"!
THIS WOULD INVOLVE CONQUERING HOLLAND, SO THE ARMY MARCHED OFF.
ATTACKED BY AUSTRIA JUST BEYOND THE FRONTIER, THE FRENCH FORCE COLLAPSED AND FELL BACK.
LAWMAKERS BLAMED ARISTOCRATS, TRAITORS, DISLOYAL OFFICERS, COUNTERREVOLUTIONARIES...
SNAKES IN THE GRASS...
BORING INSECTS...
WORMWOOD...
CANCER...
DRY ROT...
ANYONE BUT OURSELVES...

THE NATIONAL GUARD ARRESTED THOUSANDS OF SUSPECTS: BREAD-HOARDERS, ARISTOCRATS, UNPOPULAR PEOPLE, LOUDMOUTHS, AND FINALLY THE **ROYAL FAMILY.**

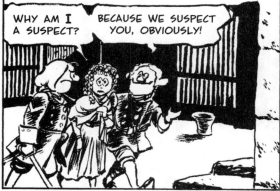

WHY AM **I** A SUSPECT?

BECAUSE WE SUSPECT YOU, OBVIOUSLY!

IMPATIENT WITH MERE ARRESTS, MILITANTS STORMED THE PRISONS AND SPENT FIVE DAYS MURDERING INMATES...

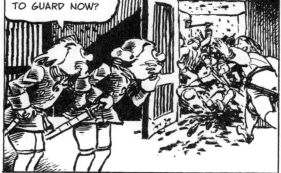

ULP... WHO ARE WE SUPPOSED TO GUARD NOW?

A FEW DAYS LATER, THE REVOLUTIONARIES CHASED AWAY THE ASSEMBLY AND REPLACED IT WITH A MORE RADICAL GOVERNMENT.*

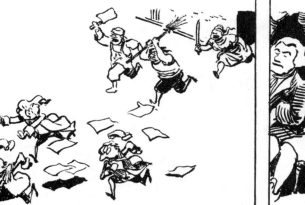

ON SEPTEMBER 21, 1792, THIS "CONVENTION" **OUTLAWED MONARCHY** AND DECLARED FRANCE A **REPUBLIC.**

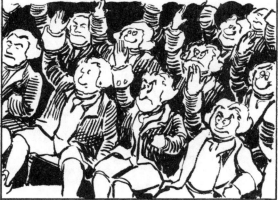

THE REVOLUTIONARY GOVERNMENT SAID IT WAS CARRYING OUT THE **"GENERAL WILL,"** THAT IS, AS REPRESENTATIVE OF THE NATION, THE CONVENTION MUST BE DOING WHAT FRANCE WANTED.

THIS IS VERY LOGICAL! DON'T YOU AGREE?

THE PROBLEM HERE (ASIDE FROM WHETHER A NATION CAN "WANT" SOMETHING OR THE REVOLUTIONARIES REPRESENTED THE NATION) IS THAT **OPPOSITION** NOW EQUALS **TREASON...** MAYBE NOT THE BEST WAY TO STIMULATE HONEST DEBATE...

WELL?

YES! I AGREE! SINCERELY! WHATEVER YOU SAY!

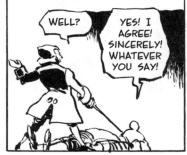

THE CONCEPT OF THE GENERAL WILL, ALONG WITH MANY OTHER ELOQUENTLY PHRASED FALSEHOODS, COMES FROM **JEAN-JACQUES ROUSSEAU,** A THINKER STILL TREATED WITH RESPECT, FOR SOME REASON...

HRRAF... ROUSSEAU INFLUENCED ROMANTICISM...

A PRECURSOR OF TOTALITARIANISM...

O.K.... I GET IT... BUT I DON'T HAVE TO **LIKE** HIM...

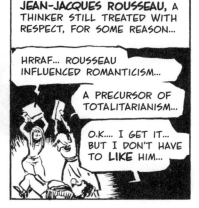

THE CONVENTION CALLED ON THE PARIS MOB TO DEFEND FRANCE BY **JOINING THE ARMY**... PARISIANS RESPONDED AND SURPRISED THEMSELVES BY PUSHING THE AUSTRIANS BACK.

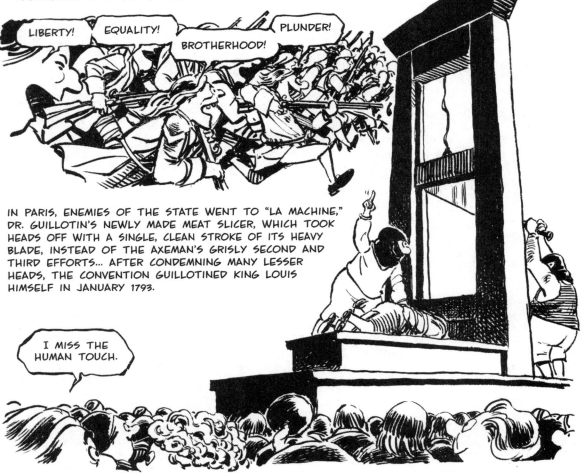

LIBERTY!

EQUALITY!

BROTHERHOOD!

PLUNDER!

IN PARIS, ENEMIES OF THE STATE WENT TO "LA MACHINE," DR. GUILLOTIN'S NEWLY MADE MEAT SLICER, WHICH TOOK HEADS OFF WITH A SINGLE, CLEAN STROKE OF ITS HEAVY BLADE, INSTEAD OF THE AXEMAN'S GRISLY SECOND AND THIRD EFFORTS... AFTER CONDEMNING MANY LESSER HEADS, THE CONVENTION GUILLOTINED KING LOUIS HIMSELF IN JANUARY 1793.

I MISS THE HUMAN TOUCH.

FRANCE DECLARED WAR AGAINST **BRITAIN** AND THEN AGAINST THE **CHURCH**... THE CONVENTION ORDERED PRIESTS TO BECOME **STATE EMPLOYEES** AND SWEAR LOYALTY TO THE REVOLUTION... AND AT THIS, THE COUNTRYSIDE REBELLED.

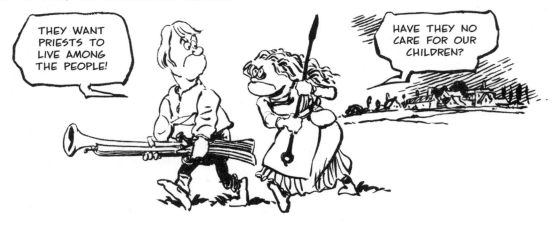

THEY WANT PRIESTS TO LIVE AMONG THE PEOPLE!

HAVE THEY NO CARE FOR OUR CHILDREN?

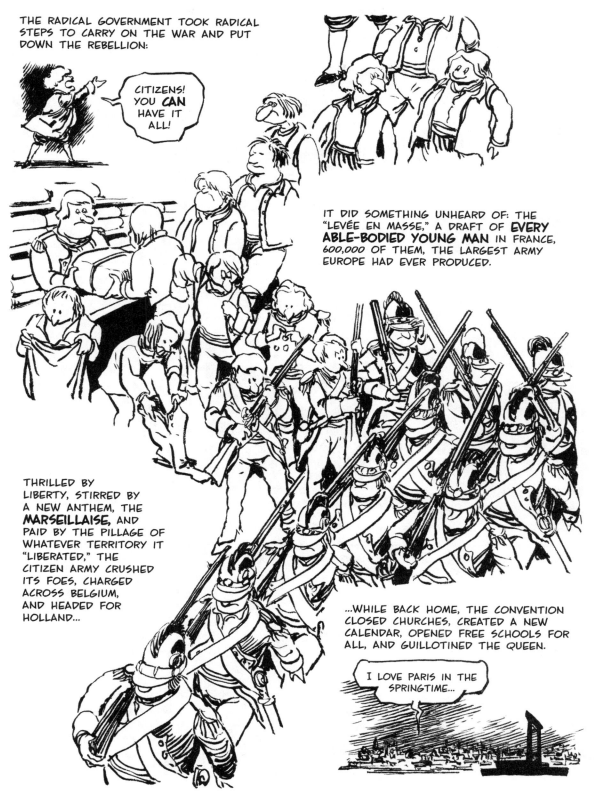

THE RADICAL GOVERNMENT TOOK RADICAL STEPS TO CARRY ON THE WAR AND PUT DOWN THE REBELLION:

CITIZENS! YOU **CAN** HAVE IT ALL!

IT DID SOMETHING UNHEARD OF: THE "LEVÉE EN MASSE," A DRAFT OF **EVERY ABLE-BODIED YOUNG MAN** IN FRANCE, 600,000 OF THEM, THE LARGEST ARMY EUROPE HAD EVER PRODUCED.

THRILLED BY LIBERTY, STIRRED BY A NEW ANTHEM, THE **MARSEILLAISE,** AND PAID BY THE PILLAGE OF WHATEVER TERRITORY IT "LIBERATED," THE CITIZEN ARMY CRUSHED ITS FOES, CHARGED ACROSS BELGIUM, AND HEADED FOR HOLLAND...

...WHILE BACK HOME, THE CONVENTION CLOSED CHURCHES, CREATED A NEW CALENDAR, OPENED FREE SCHOOLS FOR ALL, AND GUILLOTINED THE QUEEN.

I LOVE PARIS IN THE SPRINGTIME...

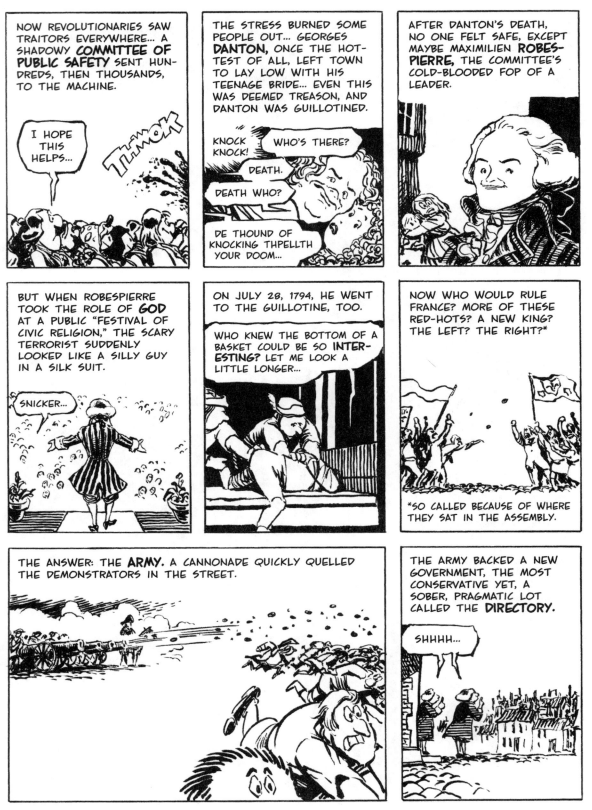

NOW REVOLUTIONARIES SAW TRAITORS EVERYWHERE... A SHADOWY **COMMITTEE OF PUBLIC SAFETY** SENT HUNDREDS, THEN THOUSANDS, TO THE MACHINE.

I HOPE THIS HELPS...

TH-WOK

THE STRESS BURNED SOME PEOPLE OUT... GEORGES **DANTON**, ONCE THE HOTTEST OF ALL, LEFT TOWN TO LAY LOW WITH HIS TEENAGE BRIDE... EVEN THIS WAS DEEMED TREASON, AND DANTON WAS GUILLOTINED.

KNOCK KNOCK!

WHO'S THERE?

DEATH.

DEATH WHO?

DE THOUND OF KNOCKING THPELLTH YOUR DOOM...

AFTER DANTON'S DEATH, NO ONE FELT SAFE, EXCEPT MAYBE MAXIMILIEN **ROBESPIERRE**, THE COMMITTEE'S COLD-BLOODED FOP OF A LEADER.

BUT WHEN ROBESPIERRE TOOK THE ROLE OF **GOD** AT A PUBLIC "FESTIVAL OF CIVIC RELIGION," THE SCARY TERRORIST SUDDENLY LOOKED LIKE A SILLY GUY IN A SILK SUIT.

SNICKER...

ON JULY 28, 1794, HE WENT TO THE GUILLOTINE, TOO.

WHO KNEW THE BOTTOM OF A BASKET COULD BE SO **INTERESTING?** LET ME LOOK A LITTLE LONGER...

NOW WHO WOULD RULE FRANCE? MORE OF THESE RED-HOTS? A NEW KING? THE LEFT? THE RIGHT?*

*SO CALLED BECAUSE OF WHERE THEY SAT IN THE ASSEMBLY.

THE ANSWER: THE **ARMY**. A CANNONADE QUICKLY QUELLED THE DEMONSTRATORS IN THE STREET.

THE ARMY BACKED A NEW GOVERNMENT, THE MOST CONSERVATIVE YET, A SOBER, PRAGMATIC LOT CALLED THE **DIRECTORY**.

SHHHH...

BY 1795, THE CITIZEN ARMY WAS THE TERROR OF EUROPE. TOPPED UP YEARLY WITH NEW 18-YEAR-OLDS, LED BY OFFICERS PROMOTED ON MERIT, AND FULL OF SUCCESS, THE FRENCH TOOK THE NETHERLANDS AND A GOOD PIECE OF ITALY.

IN THE ITALIAN CAMPAIGN, ONE ARTILLERY OFFICER IMPRESSED EVERYONE, ESPECIALLY HIMSELF: **NAPOLEON BONAPARTE.**

I'M AMAZING!

BONAPARTE'S QUICK GRASP OF BATTLEFIELDS, THOROUGH PREPARATION, AMAZING ENERGY, RAPID MOVEMENT, SELF-ASSURANCE, AND COOLNESS UNDER FIRE COMBINED TO MAKE HIM A WINNER IN WAR AND THE GOVERNMENT'S DARLING, ESPECIALLY BECAUSE HE SENT REGULAR WAGON-LOADS OF CASH BACK TO PARIS.

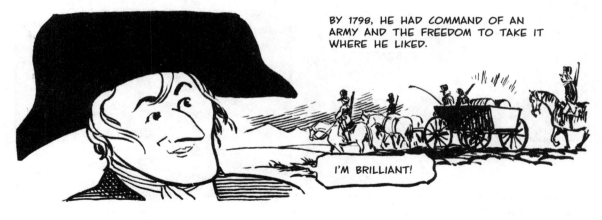

BY 1798, HE HAD COMMAND OF AN ARMY AND THE FREEDOM TO TAKE IT WHERE HE LIKED.

I'M BRILLIANT!

AT THE MOMENT, HE LIKED **EGYPT**... SO, WITH AN ARMY, A NAVY, AND DOZENS OF SCIENTISTS, SURVEYORS, AND SCHOLARS, NAPOLEON LAUNCHED AN INVASION...

I'M SEASICK!

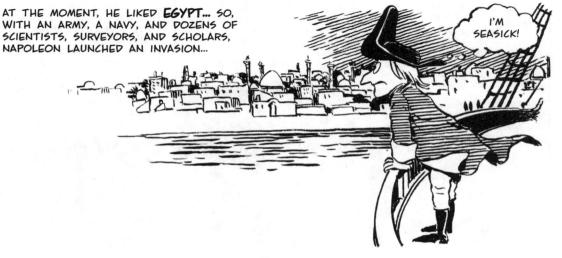

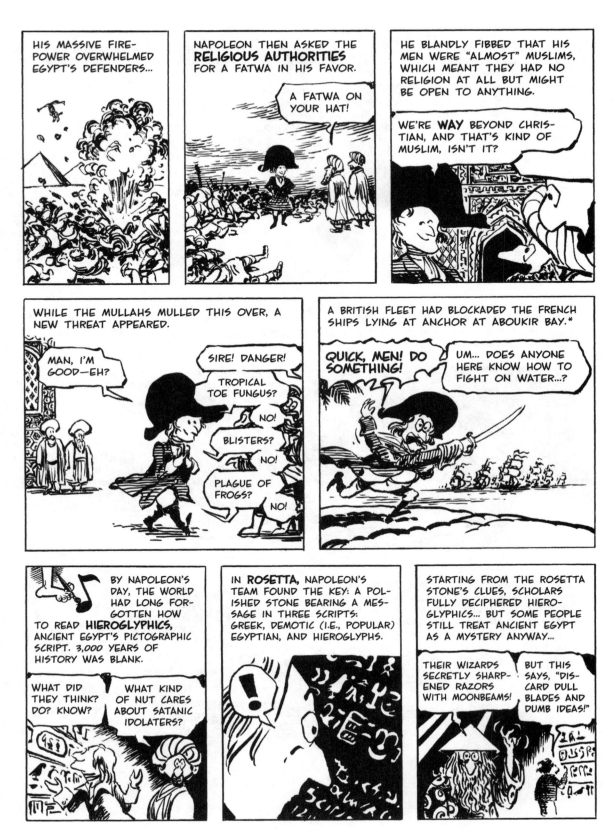

HIS MASSIVE FIRE-POWER OVERWHELMED EGYPT'S DEFENDERS...

NAPOLEON THEN ASKED THE **RELIGIOUS AUTHORITIES** FOR A FATWA IN HIS FAVOR.

A FATWA ON YOUR HAT!

HE BLANDLY FIBBED THAT HIS MEN WERE "ALMOST" MUSLIMS, WHICH MEANT THEY HAD NO RELIGION AT ALL BUT MIGHT BE OPEN TO ANYTHING.

WE'RE **WAY** BEYOND CHRISTIAN, AND THAT'S KIND OF MUSLIM, ISN'T IT?

WHILE THE MULLAHS MULLED THIS OVER, A NEW THREAT APPEARED.

MAN, I'M GOOD—EH?

SIRE! DANGER!

TROPICAL TOE FUNGUS?

NO!

BLISTERS?

NO!

PLAGUE OF FROGS?

NO!

A BRITISH FLEET HAD BLOCKADED THE FRENCH SHIPS LYING AT ANCHOR AT ABOUKIR BAY.*

QUICK, MEN! DO SOMETHING!

UM... DOES ANYONE HERE KNOW HOW TO FIGHT ON WATER...?

BY NAPOLEON'S DAY, THE WORLD HAD LONG FORGOTTEN HOW TO READ **HIEROGLYPHICS**, ANCIENT EGYPT'S PICTOGRAPHIC SCRIPT. 3,000 YEARS OF HISTORY WAS BLANK.

WHAT DID THEY THINK? DO? KNOW?

WHAT KIND OF NUT CARES ABOUT SATANIC IDOLATERS?

IN **ROSETTA**, NAPOLEON'S TEAM FOUND THE KEY: A POLISHED STONE BEARING A MESSAGE IN THREE SCRIPTS: GREEK, DEMOTIC (I.E., POPULAR) EGYPTIAN, AND HIEROGLYPHS.

STARTING FROM THE ROSETTA STONE'S CLUES, SCHOLARS FULLY DECIPHERED HIEROGLYPHICS... BUT SOME PEOPLE STILL TREAT ANCIENT EGYPT AS A MYSTERY ANYWAY...

THEIR WIZARDS SECRETLY SHARPENED RAZORS WITH MOONBEAMS!

BUT THIS SAYS, "DISCARD DULL BLADES AND DUMB IDEAS!"

BY SEA, IT TURNED OUT, NAPOLEON
HAD NOTHING LIKE HIS AMAZING
ABILITY ON LAND. THE FRENCH LINE
OF SHIPS HAD A GAP, INTO WHICH
THE BRITISH NAVY PLUNGED.

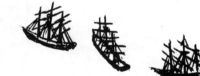

THE BRITISH ADMIRAL **HORATIO NELSON,** ON
THE OTHER HAND, WAS A BRILLIANT IF ECCENTRIC
COMMANDER. HIS CAPTAINS RAN THEIR SHIPS AS
THEY PLEASED, AND AT ABOUKIR BAY SEVERAL
CREWMEN'S WIVES WERE ABOARD, INCLUDING ONE
WHO WAS NINE MONTHS PREGNANT.

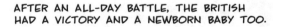

WAAAH!

AFTER AN ALL-DAY BATTLE, THE BRITISH
HAD A VICTORY AND A NEWBORN BABY TOO.

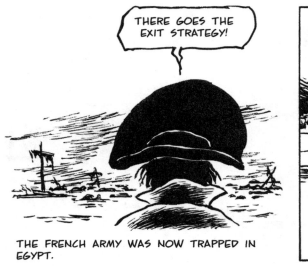

THERE GOES THE EXIT STRATEGY!

THE FRENCH ARMY WAS NOW TRAPPED IN EGYPT.

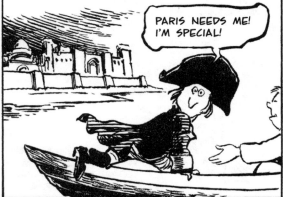

NAPOLEON DEFTLY SLIPPED AWAY AND ABANDONED HIS MEN TO THEIR FATE (LEPROSY, CONVERSION, PIRACY, SLAVERY).

PARIS NEEDS ME! I'M SPECIAL!

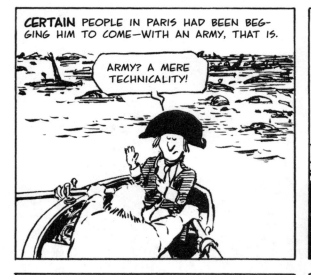

CERTAIN PEOPLE IN PARIS HAD BEEN BEGGING HIM TO COME—WITH AN ARMY, THAT IS.

ARMY? A MERE TECHNICALITY!

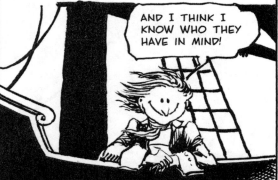

CERTAIN PEOPLE SNEERED AT THE CURRENT GOVERNMENT'S WEAKNESS AND BICKERING. **CERTAIN PEOPLE** WANTED A STRONG, DYNAMIC, CHARISMATIC LEADER.

AND I THINK I KNOW WHO THEY HAVE IN MIND!

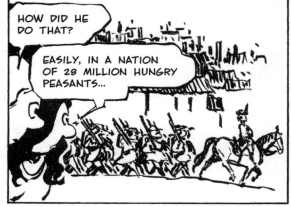

NAPOLEON, WHO SUPPORTED THIS GOAL WITH ALL HIS HEART, SOMEHOW RAISED A NEW ARMY AND TOOK IT TO PARIS.

HOW DID HE DO THAT?

EASILY, IN A NATION OF 28 MILLION HUNGRY PEASANTS...

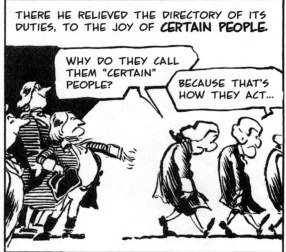

THERE HE RELIEVED THE DIRECTORY OF ITS DUTIES, TO THE JOY OF **CERTAIN PEOPLE.**

WHY DO THEY CALL THEM "CERTAIN" PEOPLE?

BECAUSE THAT'S HOW THEY ACT...

IN OTHER WORDS, THE "ENLIGHTENED" REVOLUTION HAD PRODUCED A DICTATOR!

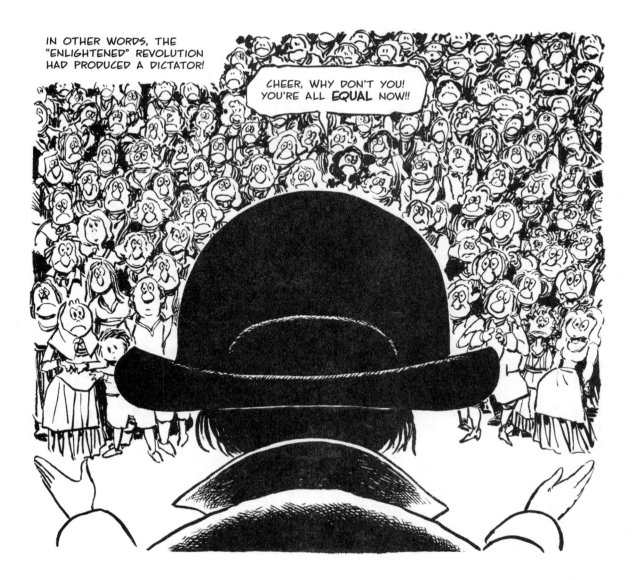

CHEER, WHY DON'T YOU! YOU'RE ALL **EQUAL** NOW!!

AND AN ENERGETIC DICTATOR HE WAS! NAPOLEON TORE INTO EVERYTHING: THE LAW CODE, THE SYSTEM OF WEIGHTS AND MEASURES, MATHEMATICS, SCIENCE, TECHNOLOGY, ART, FINANCES...

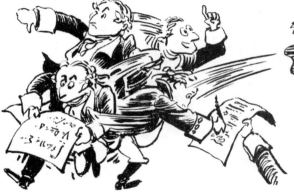

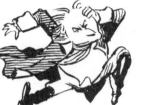

AH, MERDE! FINANCES AGAIN?

YES, THE FINANCES... TO FIX THE FINANCES, HE HAD TO TAX SUGAR... TO TAX SUGAR HE HAD TO **HAVE** SUGAR... AND TO HAVE SUGAR, HE HAD TO HAVE **HAITI**...

ONE TOO MANY

MUCH HAD HAPPENED IN HAITI SINCE 1791...

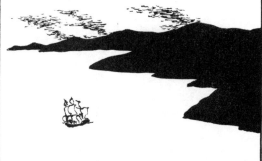

THE SLAVE REVOLT HAD CREATED A THREE-WAY WAR AMONG WHITES, BLACKS, AND MIXED-RACE *GENS DU COULEUR.*

EARLY ON, THE FRENCH GOVERNMENT REALIZED THAT VINCENT OGÉ HAD SPOKEN THE TRUTH: **WHITES** MOSTLY CRAVED INDEPENDENCE... **SLAVES** CARED NOTHING FOR FRANCE, WHILE THE *GENS DU COULEUR* SAW FRANCE AS A PROTECTOR AGAINST THE OTHER TWO GROUPS...

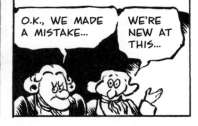

O.K., WE MADE A MISTAKE...

WE'RE NEW AT THIS...

IN MID-1792, AFTER CHANGING ITS MIND TWICE, THE ASSEMBLY GRANTED CITIZENSHIP TO THE *GENS DU COULEUR* AND SENT AN ENVOY, **LEGER SONTHONAX,** TO HAITI.

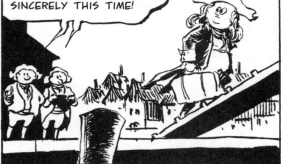

TELL THEM WE MEAN IT SINCERELY THIS TIME!

SONTHONAX, A GIFTED DIPLOMAT, SOON WON OVER THE NEW CITIZENS TO FRANCE'S SIDE.

LIBERTY, EQUALITY, AND GUNS FOR YOU ALL!

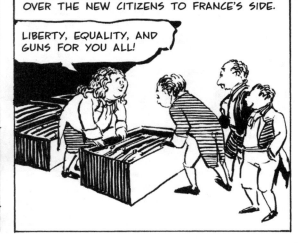

ALLIED WITH THE FRENCH, THEY PUT DOWN THE WHITE REBELS AND CORNERED THE SLAVE ARMY.

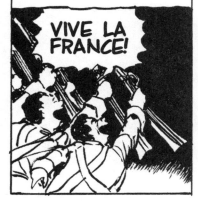

VIVE LA FRANCE!

BUT WHEN FRANCE KILLED KING LOUIS, AND ITS WARS BROUGHT A BRITISH INVASION OF HAITI, THE *GENS DU COULEUR* SOURED ON THE FRENCH REVOLUTIONARIES.

YOU PEOPLE ARE INSANE!

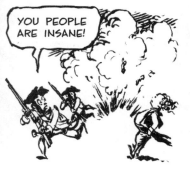

THEY DESERTED SONTHONAX... THE SLAVE REBELS BROKE OUT AND ESCAPED TO THE MOUNTAINS... AND THE COMMISSIONER PONDERED HIS OPTIONS.

EQUALITY... HM...

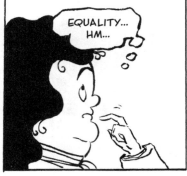

ON AUGUST 29, 1793, SONTHONAX ANNOUNCED THE END OF SLAVERY IN HAITI.
YOU'RE FREE! TO HELP US!
WHEN THE SLAVE REBELS GOT THE WORD, MOST WERE WARY.
NOBODY ELSE TRUSTS HIM—WHY SHOULD WE?
BUT ONE, TOUSSAINT L'OUVERTURE, BROUGHT HIS FOLLOWERS OVER TO SONTHONAX IN 1794.
THANK YOU THANK YOU THANK YOU!
MADE BRIGADIER GENERAL, L'OUVERTURE TURNED OUT TO BE HAITI'S MOST ABLE COMMANDER.
BY 1798, THE BRITS HAD PULLED OUT, AND THE FIGHT BETWEEN L'OUVERTURE'S BLACKS AND THE GENS DU COULEUR GREW FIERCE AND ATROCIOUS.
OH, DEAR...
SONTHONAX HAD LOST CONTROL... THE BLACKS COULD NOW OUTMUSCLE THE FRENCH IF THEY CHOSE... SO THE COMMISSIONER BOWED TO THE FACTS AND WENT HOME.
I'VE LOST EVERYTHING... EXCEPT WEIGHT...
BY 1801, L'OUVERTURE HAD CONQUERED THE ISLAND, MADE A NEW CONSTITUTION, AND NAMED HIMSELF GOVERNOR FOR LIFE.
SORRY. WHAT?

BY THIS TIME, NAPOLEON HAD SEIZED POWER... AND IT IRKED HIM THOROUGHLY TO SEE SOMEONE MAKE HIMSELF DICTATOR OF HAITI WITHOUT FIRST CONSULTING THE DICTATOR OF FRANCE.
I UNDERSTAND THE TYPE ALL TOO WELL...
L'OUVERTURE ACTED INDEPENDENTLY IN OTHER WAYS TOO: HAITI SOLD SUGAR TO BRITAIN AND THE U.S., NOT LIKE A PROPER FRENCH COLONY AT ALL!
I FEEL SO... SO... VIOLATED, DON'T YOU, JOSIE, MY PET?
ONLY BY YOU.
JOSEPHINE BEAUHARNAIS, NAPOLEON'S WIFE, WHO HAD LOVERS BEFORE, DURING, AND AFTER THEIR MARRIAGE.
NAPOLEON, THE ENLIGHTENED RULER WHO MADE ALL FRENCH CITIZENS EQUAL BEFORE THE LAW, DECIDED TO RE-ENSLAVE HAITI.
ENOUGH ENLIGHTEN-MENT IS ENOUGH!
12,000 CITIZENS HIT HAITI'S SHORES AND THE BLACK ARMY BATTLED BACK...
THE FRENCH GENERAL, LE-CLERC, SWORE THAT HE WANTED NOTHING BUT HAITI'S LOYALTY... NO ONE, HE SAID, EVER WANTED TO BRING BACK SLAVERY... AND AT LAST, L'OUVERTURE SURRENDERED...
NEVER NEVER NEVER NEVER EVER!
THE FORMER SLAVE GENERAL RETIRED TO HIS COUNTRY ESTATE...
AND THERE THE FRENCH SURPRISED HIM AND SENT HIM BACK TO FRANCE.

AS USUAL, NAPOLEON HAD A **GRAND PLAN**: RE-ENSLAVE THE FRENCH ISLANDS... FEED THEM WITH GRAIN FROM FRENCH **LOUISIANA**... AND EVENTUALLY DRIVE THE BRITISH OUT OF THE CARIBBEAN.

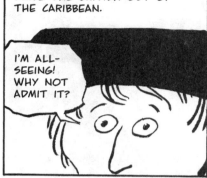

I'M ALL-SEEING! WHY NOT ADMIT IT?

BUT L'OUVERTURE'S ARREST HAD ALARMED THE EX-SLAVES, AND WHEN THE FRENCH TRIED TO **DISARM** THEM, FIERCE FIGHTING FLARED AGAIN.

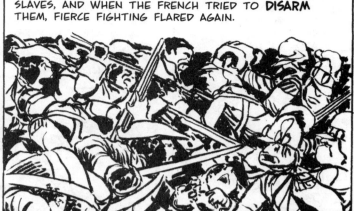

BY EARLY 1803, NAPOLEON CHANGED HIS GRAND PLAN. MORE THRILLING PROSPECTS LAY CLOSER TO HOME. HE DECIDED TO **INVADE BRITAIN** AND **CUT HAITI LOOSE.**

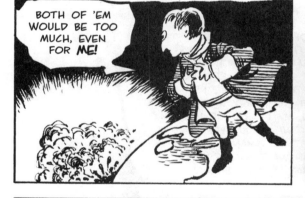

BOTH OF 'EM WOULD BE TOO MUCH, EVEN FOR **ME!**

FOR THE SECOND TIME, HE ABANDONED AN ARMY WITHOUT SUPPLIES, MEDICINE, OR MEANS OF ESCAPE.

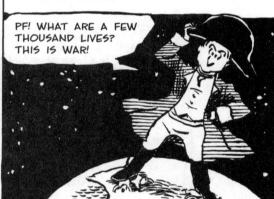

PF! WHAT ARE A FEW THOUSAND LIVES? THIS IS WAR!

WITHOUT HAITI, NAPOLEON NO LONGER NEEDED LOUISIANA, SO HE **SOLD** IT—FRANCE'S LAST, VAST NORTH AMERICAN HOLDINGS—FOR 15 MILLION DOLLARS (CHEAP!) TO THE **UNITED STATES,** WHICH DOUBLED IN SIZE OVERNIGHT.

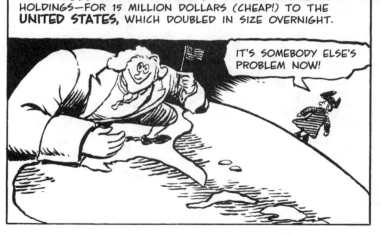

IT'S SOMEBODY ELSE'S PROBLEM NOW!

SIX MONTHS LATER, THE DICTATOR FINALLY RESCUED HIS ARMY IN HAITI, OR WHAT WAS LEFT OF IT.

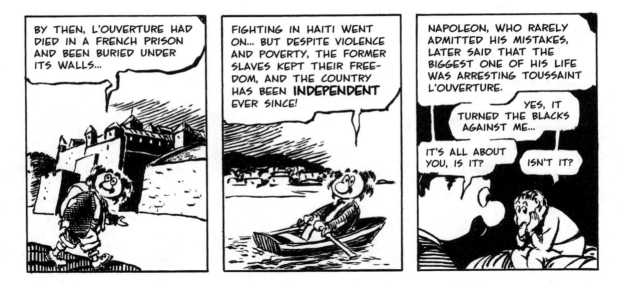

BY THEN, L'OUVERTURE HAD DIED IN A FRENCH PRISON AND BEEN BURIED UNDER ITS WALLS...

FIGHTING IN HAITI WENT ON... BUT DESPITE VIOLENCE AND POVERTY, THE FORMER SLAVES KEPT THEIR FREE-DOM, AND THE COUNTRY HAS BEEN **INDEPENDENT** EVER SINCE!

NAPOLEON, WHO RARELY ADMITTED HIS MISTAKES, LATER SAID THAT THE BIGGEST ONE OF HIS LIFE WAS ARRESTING TOUSSAINT L'OUVERTURE.

YES, IT TURNED THE BLACKS AGAINST ME...

IT'S ALL ABOUT YOU, IS IT?

ISN'T IT?

BUT AS USUAL, THE DICTATOR WAS TOO FULL OF PLANS FOR THE **FUTURE** TO LINGER ON ANY REGRETS!

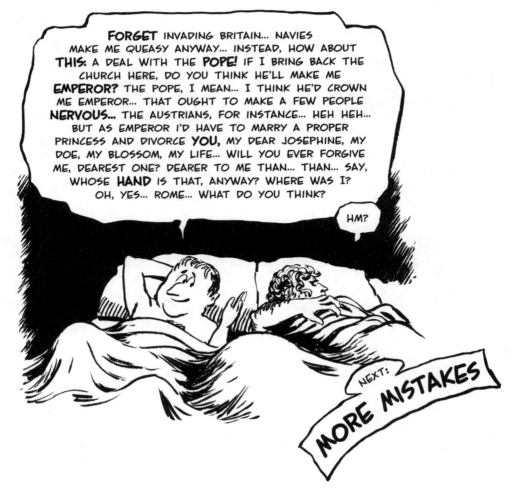

FORGET INVADING BRITAIN... NAVIES MAKE ME QUEASY ANYWAY... INSTEAD, HOW ABOUT **THIS:** A DEAL WITH THE **POPE!** IF I BRING BACK THE CHURCH HERE, DO YOU THINK HE'LL MAKE ME **EMPEROR?** THE POPE, I MEAN... I THINK HE'D CROWN ME EMPEROR... THAT OUGHT TO MAKE A FEW PEOPLE **NERVOUS...** THE AUSTRIANS, FOR INSTANCE... HEH HEH... BUT AS EMPEROR I'D HAVE TO MARRY A PROPER PRINCESS AND DIVORCE **YOU,** MY DEAR JOSEPHINE, MY DOE, MY BLOSSOM, MY LIFE... WILL YOU EVER FORGIVE ME, DEAREST ONE? DEARER TO ME THAN... THAN... SAY, WHOSE **HAND** IS THAT, ANYWAY? WHERE WAS I? OH, YES... ROME... WHAT DO YOU THINK?

HM?

NEXT: **MORE MISTAKES**

GOSH, I LOVE FREEDOM! AND I'LL BET YOU DO TOO!
ISN'T IT GREAT TO BE ABLE TO SAY WHAT WE THINK? READ WHAT WE WANT? GO WHERE WE PLEASE? POLLUTE THE PLANET UNTIL WE CHOKE?
WELL, MAYBE NOT THAT LAST BIT...
TO BE HONEST, WHAT I ACTUALLY MEAN IS, IT'S GREAT FOR ME TO BE ABLE TO DO ALL THAT STUFF... AND I IMAGINE YOU LIKE IT FOR YOU!
BUT HOW MUCH DO YOU REALLY CARE ABOUT ME? IF SOME THUGS TRIED TO SELL ME, WOULD THAT BOTHER YOU? IN FACT, WHAT IF SOMEBODY OFFERED YOU 500 BUCKS FOR ME?
IN THIS VOLUME, WE'LL SPEND SOME TIME AT A MOMENT WHEN AN ENTIRE NATION DECIDED TO CARE... TO STOP THE ENSLAVEMENT OF FOREIGNERS... AND GIVE UP THE DOUGH THAT WENT WITH IT!
VERY UNUSUAL!
SO, AS WE HEAD FOR THE YEAR 1782, KEEP THIS IN MIND: I CARE ABOUT YOU—AND, UM, IF ANYONE OFFERS TO BUY ME, I'LL PAY YOU DOUBLE TO LEAVE ME ALONE!

THE CARTOON HISTORY OF THE MODERN WORLD

Volume 7

FREE TRADE

HEAVE!

IN THE GROSS AND GRISLY HISTORY OF SLAVERY, FEW EVENTS MADE WAVES LIKE THE VOYAGE OF THE SLAVE SHIP **ZONG**, OUT OF LIVERPOOL... IN LATE 1782, WITH SEVERAL HUNDRED SLAVES ABOARD, THE **ZONG** WENT OFF COURSE AND RAN SHORT OF WATER... SOME OF THE CAPTIVES FELL ILL... THE DISEASE SPREAD... DOZENS OF SLAVES AND DECKHANDS DIED... AND AS THE CREW BEGAN PITCHING BODIES OVERBOARD, THE CAPTAIN, **LUKE COLLINGWOOD,** WORRIED ABOUT THE **LOSSES** TO HIS **BOSSES!**

IF THE CARGO DIED, HE KNEW, THE OWNERS WOULD LOSE ALL... BUT IF IT HAD TO BE SCUTTLED TO SAVE THE SHIP, THEN THE OWNERS' INSURANCE WOULD PAY.
A NO-BRAINER, REALLY!
SO CAPTAIN COLLINGWOOD ORDERED ALL THE LIVING SLAVES THROWN OVERBOARD.
IT'S THE ONLY HUMANE OPTION FOR MY EMPLOYERS...
IT TOOK THREE DAYS TO HEAVE EVERYONE INTO THE SEA.
DAMME, YOU LOT ARE SELFISH!
WAIL
SHRIEK
THE ZONG SAILED TO PORT AND MADE ITS CLAIM: 133 SLAVES AT 30 POUNDS PER HEAD.
THE INSURANCE COMPANY REFUSED TO PAY, ON THE GROUNDS THAT THE ACTION HAD NOT BEEN STRICTLY NECESSARY.
BESIDES, WE DON'T REIMBURSE MURDER...
OUT-RAGEOUS!
THE SHIPS' OWNERS SUED THE INSURERS... A JURY HEARD THE DETAILS...
A PERFECT RIGHT TO DISPOSE BLAH BLAH BLAH... CAPTAIN'S SOLE DISCRETION BLAH BLAH BLAH... SLEAZY INSURANCE COMPANY BLAH BLAH BLAH...
AND DECIDED WITHIN MINUTES—AGAINST THE INSURANCE COMPANY!
JUSTICE, AND LUNCH, ARE SERVED!

HOW COULD THE JURY COM-
PENSATE KILLERS? BECAUSE,
FROM THE LAW'S POINT OF
VIEW, SLAVES WERE **PEOPLE**
AND **PROPERTY** AT THE
SAME TIME...

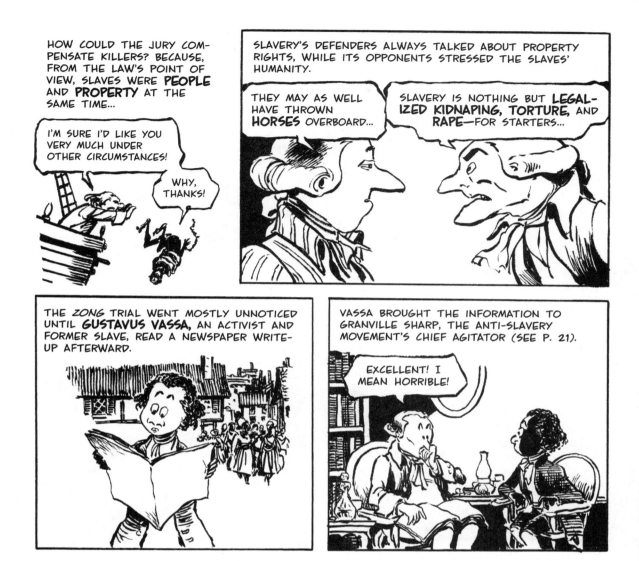

I'M SURE I'D LIKE YOU VERY MUCH UNDER OTHER CIRCUMSTANCES!

WHY, THANKS!

SLAVERY'S DEFENDERS ALWAYS TALKED ABOUT PROPERTY RIGHTS, WHILE ITS OPPONENTS STRESSED THE SLAVES' HUMANITY.

THEY MAY AS WELL HAVE THROWN **HORSES** OVERBOARD...

SLAVERY IS NOTHING BUT **LEGAL-IZED KIDNAPING, TORTURE,** AND **RAPE**—FOR STARTERS...

THE **ZONG** TRIAL WENT MOSTLY UNNOTICED UNTIL **GUSTAVUS VASSA,** AN ACTIVIST AND FORMER SLAVE, READ A NEWSPAPER WRITE-UP AFTERWARD.

VASSA BROUGHT THE INFORMATION TO GRANVILLE SHARP, THE ANTI-SLAVERY MOVEMENT'S CHIEF AGITATOR (SEE P. 21).

EXCELLENT! I MEAN HORRIBLE!

SHARP ORGANIZED HIS USUAL TEAM OF LAWYERS AND PUBLICISTS, AND SOON THEIR PAMPHLETS, LETTERS, AND LEGAL BRIEFS STARTED A NEW WAVE OF ANTISLAVERY ACTIVISM...

A PAPER TSUNAMI!

AND NOW ENGLAND LISTENED... IT WAS LATE 1783... BRITAIN HAD JUST LOST ITS 13 AMERICAN COLONIES, WHERE "LIBERTY" COULD MEAN THE FREEDOM TO BUY AND SELL HUMAN BEINGS... AN ATTITUDE THAT MADE SOME PEOPLE SICK...

SICK ENOUGH TO **ACT**, IN SOME CASES...

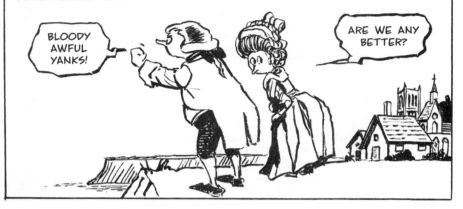

BLOODY AWFUL YANKS!

ARE WE ANY BETTER?

THOMAS CLARKSON, A CAMBRIDGE STUDENT WHO WROTE A PRIZE-WINNING ESSAY AGAINST SLAVERY IN 1784, DEVOTED HIS LIFE TO ABOLITION.

IT'S NOT JUST WORDS ON PAPER!

WILLIAM WILBERFORCE, A YOUNG M.P., CAME TO THE CAUSE (ALSO IN 1784) AFTER MEETING THE REFORMED SLAVE CAPTAIN WHO WROTE "AMAZING GRACE."

THAT SAME YEAR, **JAMES RAMSAY,** A DOCTOR TURNED MINISTER, PUBLISHED A TRACT ABOUT CARIBBEAN HORRORS HE HAD SEEN.

RAMSAY IN TURN DREW HIS SALARY FROM AN ANTI-SLAVERY NOBLEMAN, SIR **CHARLES MIDDLETON.** MIDDLETON AND HIS WIFE **MARGARET** BEGAN HOSTING MEETINGS OF ACTIVISTS, AS THEY PLANNED THE NEXT STAGE OF THE ABOLITION CAMPAIGN.

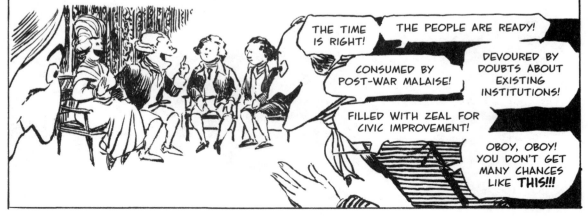

THE TIME IS RIGHT!

THE PEOPLE ARE READY!

CONSUMED BY POST-WAR MALAISE!

DEVOURED BY DOUBTS ABOUT EXISTING INSTITUTIONS!

FILLED WITH ZEAL FOR CIVIC IMPROVEMENT!

OBOY, OBOY! YOU DON'T GET MANY CHANCES LIKE **THIS!!!**

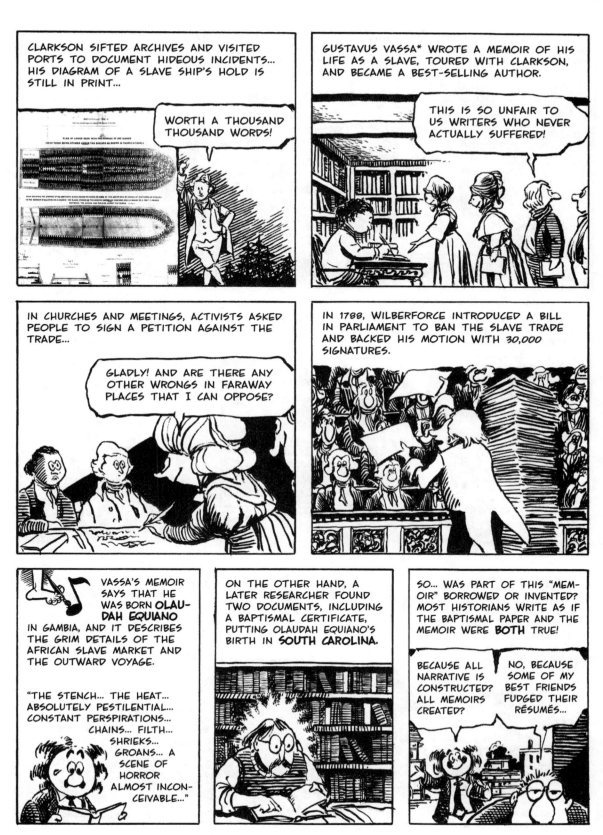

CLARKSON SIFTED ARCHIVES AND VISITED PORTS TO DOCUMENT HIDEOUS INCIDENTS... HIS DIAGRAM OF A SLAVE SHIP'S HOLD IS STILL IN PRINT...

WORTH A THOUSAND THOUSAND WORDS!

GUSTAVUS VASSA* WROTE A MEMOIR OF HIS LIFE AS A SLAVE, TOURED WITH CLARKSON, AND BECAME A BEST-SELLING AUTHOR.

THIS IS SO UNFAIR TO US WRITERS WHO NEVER ACTUALLY SUFFERED!

IN CHURCHES AND MEETINGS, ACTIVISTS ASKED PEOPLE TO SIGN A PETITION AGAINST THE TRADE...

GLADLY! AND ARE THERE ANY OTHER WRONGS IN FARAWAY PLACES THAT I CAN OPPOSE?

IN 1788, WILBERFORCE INTRODUCED A BILL IN PARLIAMENT TO BAN THE SLAVE TRADE AND BACKED HIS MOTION WITH 30,000 SIGNATURES.

VASSA'S MEMOIR SAYS THAT HE WAS BORN **OLAU-DAH EQUIANO** IN GAMBIA, AND IT DESCRIBES THE GRIM DETAILS OF THE AFRICAN SLAVE MARKET AND THE OUTWARD VOYAGE.

"THE STENCH... THE HEAT... ABSOLUTELY PESTILENTIAL... CONSTANT PERSPIRATIONS... CHAINS... FILTH... SHRIEKS... GROANS... A SCENE OF HORROR ALMOST INCON-CEIVABLE..."

ON THE OTHER HAND, A LATER RESEARCHER FOUND TWO DOCUMENTS, INCLUDING A BAPTISMAL CERTIFICATE, PUTTING OLAUDAH EQUIANO'S BIRTH IN **SOUTH CAROLINA.**

SO... WAS PART OF THIS "MEM-OIR" BORROWED OR INVENTED? MOST HISTORIANS WRITE AS IF THE BAPTISMAL PAPER AND THE MEMOIR WERE **BOTH** TRUE!

BECAUSE ALL NARRATIVE IS CONSTRUCTED? ALL MEMOIRS CREATED?

NO, BECAUSE SOME OF MY BEST FRIENDS FUDGED THEIR RÉSUMÉS...

BUT THE HOUSE OF COMMONS VOTED WILBERFORCE DOWN.

NAY
NAY   NAY
NAY

AND KEPT VOTING HIM DOWN EVERY TIME HE RAISED THE ISSUE AGAIN.

NAY   NAY   NAY
NAY   NAY   NAY
NAY   NAY   NA
NAY   NAY   NAY
NAY   NAY   NAY

HOW COULD THEY?

DON'T YOU PEOPLE HAVE A HEART?

OF GOLD, WILBY, SOLID GOLD!

YOU KNOW HOW THEY COULD... SLAVES WERE PROPERTY... PROPERTY WAS WEALTH... AND LOVE OF WEALTH GOVERNS REASON AS OFTEN AS NOT!

SLAVERY IS AN INSTITUTION SANCTIONED BY CUSTOM, LAW, AND RELIGION...

IF WE DON'T DO IT, SOMEONE ELSE WILL...

SENTIMENT (NO MATTER HOW FINE) IS NO GUIDE TO SOUND POLICY!

YOU VILLAINS ARE CHOKING THE PAGE WITH TYPE...

IN BRITAIN, A SEAFARING LAND, THOUSANDS OF WORKERS LIVED OFF THE TRADE... IN SOME PORTS, SLAVING WAS A RESPECTABLE BUSINESS... A FORMER MAYOR OF LIVERPOOL WAS PART OWNER OF THE *ZONG!*

END THE TRADE AND BRITAIN GOES BUST!

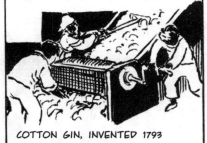

BESIDES, THANKS TO NEW **TECHNOLOGY,** THE COLONIES ACTUALLY NEEDED **MORE** SLAVES ALL THE TIME. STEAM-DRIVEN REFINERIES COULD PRODUCE MORE SUGAR... A MECHANICAL SEED-PULLER COULD PROCESS MORE COTTON...

COTTON GIN, INVENTED 1793

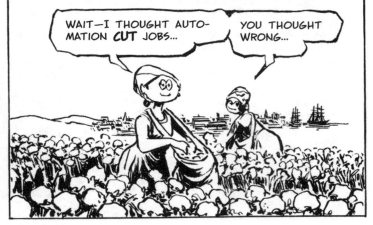

RESULT: MORE ACRES PLANTED... MORE HANDS NEEDED... MORE SHIPFULS OF SLAVES AFLOAT THAN EVER BEFORE!

WAIT—I THOUGHT AUTOMATION **CUT** JOBS...

YOU THOUGHT WRONG...

THERE WAS ALSO THE LITTLE MATTER OF THE **FRENCH REVOLUTION**...

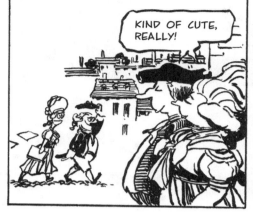

BEFORE 1789, SLAVERY'S DEFENDERS VIEWED ABOLITIONISTS AS A SORT OF KOOKY ANNOYANCE.

KIND OF CUTE, REALLY!

BUT ONCE FRENCH BLOOD STARTED GUSHING, REFORMERS BEGAN TO LOOK A LITTLE MORE DANGEROUS!

GASP!

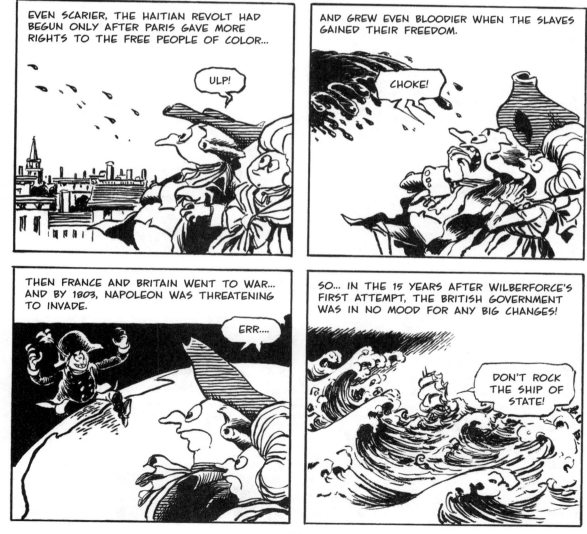

EVEN SCARIER, THE HAITIAN REVOLT HAD BEGUN ONLY AFTER PARIS GAVE MORE RIGHTS TO THE FREE PEOPLE OF COLOR...

ULP!

AND GREW EVEN BLOODIER WHEN THE SLAVES GAINED THEIR FREEDOM.

CHOKE!

THEN FRANCE AND BRITAIN WENT TO WAR... AND BY 1803, NAPOLEON WAS THREATENING TO INVADE.

ERR....

SO... IN THE 15 YEARS AFTER WILBERFORCE'S FIRST ATTEMPT, THE BRITISH GOVERNMENT WAS IN NO MOOD FOR ANY BIG CHANGES!

DON'T ROCK THE SHIP OF STATE!

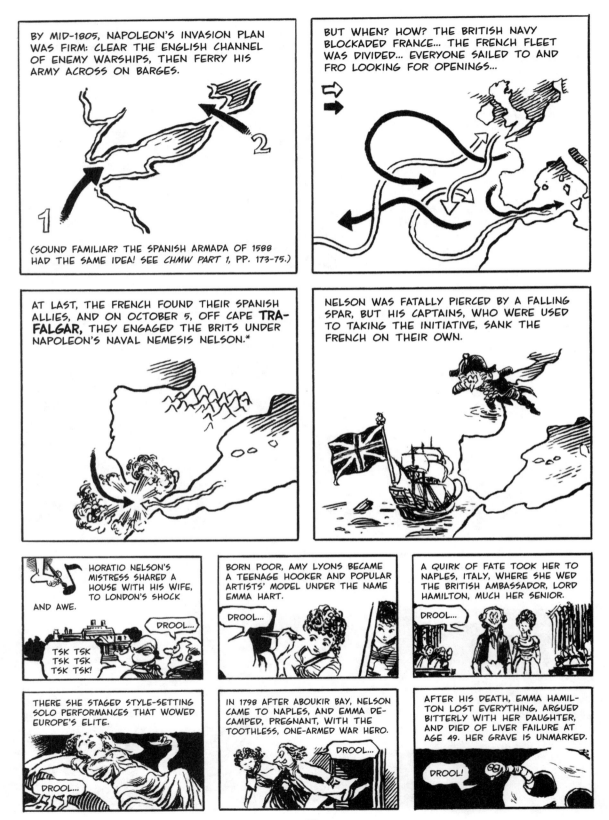

BY MID-1805, NAPOLEON'S INVASION PLAN WAS FIRM: CLEAR THE ENGLISH CHANNEL OF ENEMY WARSHIPS, THEN FERRY HIS ARMY ACROSS ON BARGES.

1

2

(SOUND FAMILIAR? THE SPANISH ARMADA OF 1588 HAD THE SAME IDEA! SEE *CHMW PART 1*, PP. 173-75.)

BUT WHEN? HOW? THE BRITISH NAVY BLOCKADED FRANCE... THE FRENCH FLEET WAS DIVIDED... EVERYONE SAILED TO AND FRO LOOKING FOR OPENINGS...

AT LAST, THE FRENCH FOUND THEIR SPANISH ALLIES, AND ON OCTOBER 5, OFF CAPE **TRA-FALGAR,** THEY ENGAGED THE BRITS UNDER NAPOLEON'S NAVAL NEMESIS NELSON.*

NELSON WAS FATALLY PIERCED BY A FALLING SPAR, BUT HIS CAPTAINS, WHO WERE USED TO TAKING THE INITIATIVE, SANK THE FRENCH ON THEIR OWN.

HORATIO NELSON'S MISTRESS SHARED A HOUSE WITH HIS WIFE, TO LONDON'S SHOCK AND AWE.

TSK TSK TSK TSK TSK TSK!

DROOL....

BORN POOR, AMY LYONS BECAME A TEENAGE HOOKER AND POPULAR ARTISTS' MODEL UNDER THE NAME EMMA HART.

DROOL...

A QUIRK OF FATE TOOK HER TO NAPLES, ITALY, WHERE SHE WED THE BRITISH AMBASSADOR, LORD HAMILTON, MUCH HER SENIOR.

DROOL...

THERE SHE STAGED STYLE-SETTING SOLO PERFORMANCES THAT WOWED EUROPE'S ELITE.

DROOL...

IN 1798 AFTER ABOUKIR BAY, NELSON CAME TO NAPLES, AND EMMA DE-CAMPED, PREGNANT, WITH THE TOOTHLESS, ONE-ARMED WAR HERO.

DROOL...

AFTER HIS DEATH, EMMA HAMIL-TON LOST EVERYTHING, ARGUED BITTERLY WITH HER DAUGHTER, AND DIED OF LIVER FAILURE AT AGE 49. HER GRAVE IS UNMARKED.

DROOL!

AFTER TRAFALGAR, THE BRITISH NAVY HAD NO RIVAL ANYWHERE, AND NAPOLEON'S THREATENED INVASION EVAPORATED...
OUR NAVY KICKS BUTT!
THIS GAVE WILBERFORCE AND HIS ALLIES AN IDEA...
WHAT IF BRITAIN BANNED **ALL NATIONS** FROM SHIPPING SLAVES?
WE CAN IMPROVE THE WORLD **AND** KICK BUTT!
BY ENFORCING A BAN, BRITAIN WOULD SHOW THE WORLD IT COULD BOARD ANY SHIP UNDER ANY FLAG FOR ANY REASON. BRITANNIA WOULD RULE THE WAVES!
AND WAIVE THE RULES, IF YOU'LL PARDON MY SAYING SO...
SO... FOR THE 37TH $&#% TIME, I HEREBY MOVE...
NEARLY 20 YEARS AFTER HIS FIRST TRY, WILBERFORCE AGAIN MOVED TO BAN THE SLAVE TRADE—AS AN **ANTI-PIRACY BILL.** SO MOVED, SO PASSED!
NOTE: THE LAW BANNED SHIPPING ONLY, NOT SLAVERY ITSELF. JAMAICA AND THE REST KEPT THEIR SLAVES.
BUT MAYBE NOW YOU'LL TREAT 'EM BETTER, AS THEY'RE HARDER TO REPLACE!
A TAKING! A TAKING! OF MY PROPERTY RIGHTS!
AT FIRST, BRITAIN DID LITTLE TO ENFORCE THE BAN—JUST FOUR OR FIVE SLOW, OLD SHIPS WATCHED THE ENTIRE AFRICAN COAST.
HALT AND BE BOARDED! PLEEASE?
BUT OVER THE COURSE OF THE CENTURY, BRITAIN FREED TENS OF THOUSANDS ON THE OPEN SEA...
NOT BAD!

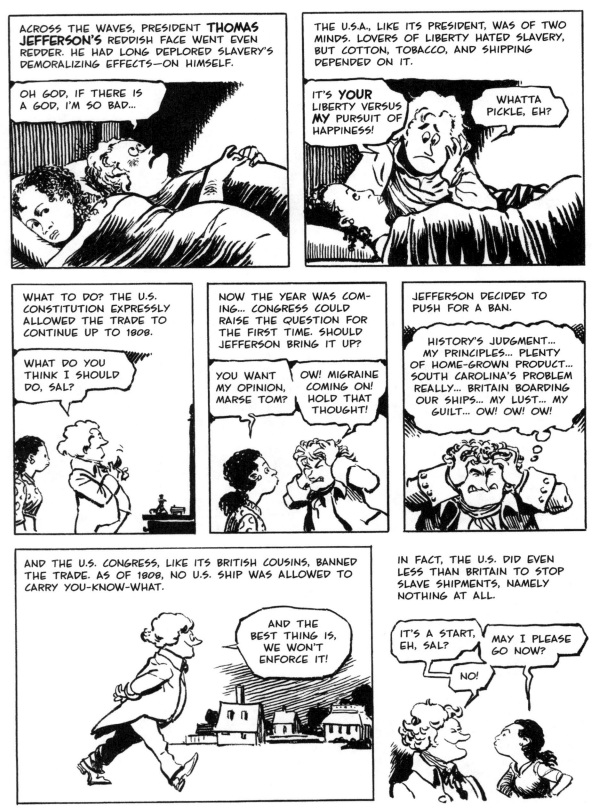

ACROSS THE WAVES, PRESIDENT **THOMAS JEFFERSON'S** REDDISH FACE WENT EVEN REDDER. HE HAD LONG DEPLORED SLAVERY'S DEMORALIZING EFFECTS—ON HIMSELF.

OH GOD, IF THERE IS A GOD, I'M SO BAD...

THE U.S.A., LIKE ITS PRESIDENT, WAS OF TWO MINDS. LOVERS OF LIBERTY HATED SLAVERY, BUT COTTON, TOBACCO, AND SHIPPING DEPENDED ON IT.

IT'S **YOUR** LIBERTY VERSUS **MY** PURSUIT OF HAPPINESS!

WHATTA PICKLE, EH?

WHAT TO DO? THE U.S. CONSTITUTION EXPRESSLY ALLOWED THE TRADE TO CONTINUE UP TO 1808.

WHAT DO YOU THINK I SHOULD DO, SAL?

NOW THE YEAR WAS COMING... CONGRESS COULD RAISE THE QUESTION FOR THE FIRST TIME. SHOULD JEFFERSON BRING IT UP?

YOU WANT MY OPINION, MARSE TOM?

OW! MIGRAINE COMING ON! HOLD THAT THOUGHT!

JEFFERSON DECIDED TO PUSH FOR A BAN.

HISTORY'S JUDGMENT... MY PRINCIPLES... PLENTY OF HOME-GROWN PRODUCT... SOUTH CAROLINA'S PROBLEM REALLY... BRITAIN BOARDING OUR SHIPS... MY LUST... MY GUILT... OW! OW! OW!

AND THE U.S. CONGRESS, LIKE ITS BRITISH COUSINS, BANNED THE TRADE. AS OF 1808, NO U.S. SHIP WAS ALLOWED TO CARRY YOU-KNOW-WHAT.

AND THE BEST THING IS, WE WON'T ENFORCE IT!

IN FACT, THE U.S. DID EVEN LESS THAN BRITAIN TO STOP SLAVE SHIPMENTS, NAMELY NOTHING AT ALL.

IT'S A START, EH, SAL?

NO!

MAY I PLEASE GO NOW?

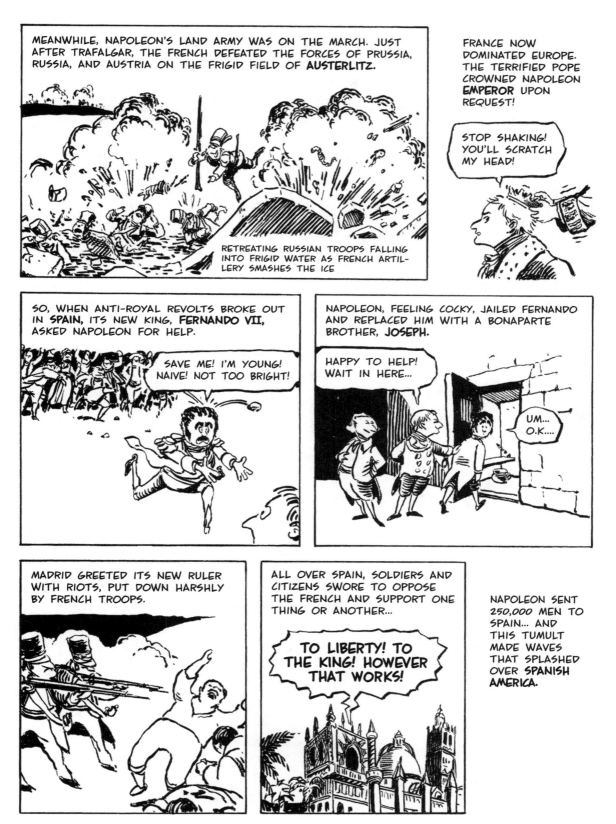

MEANWHILE, NAPOLEON'S LAND ARMY WAS ON THE MARCH. JUST AFTER TRAFALGAR, THE FRENCH DEFEATED THE FORCES OF PRUSSIA, RUSSIA, AND AUSTRIA ON THE FRIGID FIELD OF **AUSTERLITZ**.

RETREATING RUSSIAN TROOPS FALLING INTO FRIGID WATER AS FRENCH ARTILLERY SMASHES THE ICE

FRANCE NOW DOMINATED EUROPE. THE TERRIFIED POPE CROWNED NAPOLEON **EMPEROR** UPON REQUEST!

STOP SHAKING! YOU'LL SCRATCH MY HEAD!

SO, WHEN ANTI-ROYAL REVOLTS BROKE OUT IN **SPAIN**, ITS NEW KING, **FERNANDO VII**, ASKED NAPOLEON FOR HELP.

SAVE ME! I'M YOUNG! NAIVE! NOT TOO BRIGHT!

NAPOLEON, FEELING COCKY, JAILED FERNANDO AND REPLACED HIM WITH A BONAPARTE BROTHER, **JOSEPH**.

HAPPY TO HELP! WAIT IN HERE...

UM... O.K....

MADRID GREETED ITS NEW RULER WITH RIOTS, PUT DOWN HARSHLY BY FRENCH TROOPS.

ALL OVER SPAIN, SOLDIERS AND CITIZENS SWORE TO OPPOSE THE FRENCH AND SUPPORT ONE THING OR ANOTHER...

TO LIBERTY! TO THE KING! HOWEVER THAT WORKS!

NAPOLEON SENT 250,000 MEN TO SPAIN... AND THIS TUMULT MADE WAVES THAT SPLASHED OVER **SPANISH AMERICA**.

MIRANDA DECISION

SPANISH AMERICA REACTED CHAOTICALLY TO NAPOLEON'S INVASION OF SPAIN (NOT UNUSUAL FOR SPANISH AMERICA).

TO ARMS!

YOU INSULT LEGS!

SOME ADMIRED NAPOLEON'S DASH AND MODERNITY... SOME STUCK BY THEIR KING... SOME SAW A CHANCE FOR INDEPENDENCE AND DEMOCRACY... SOME WANTED INDEPENDENCE WITH A DICTATOR... YOU NAME IT, SOMEONE WANTED IT...

I JUST WANT TO STAND HERE...

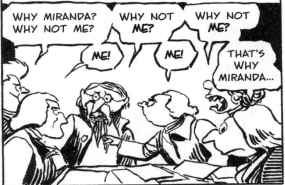

IN 1810, A COMMITTEE, OR JUNTA, MET IN **CARACAS**, VENEZUELA, DECLARED INDEPENDENCE, AND INVITED **FRANCISCO DE MIRANDA** TO COME HOME AND LEAD THEM.

WHY MIRANDA? WHY NOT ME?

WHY NOT ME?

WHY NOT ME?

ME!

ME!

THAT'S WHY MIRANDA...

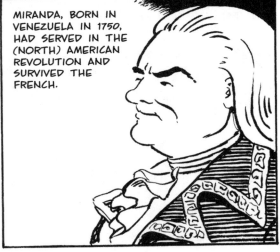

MIRANDA, BORN IN VENEZUELA IN 1750, HAD SERVED IN THE (NORTH) AMERICAN REVOLUTION AND SURVIVED THE FRENCH.

NOW IN LONDON, HE HAD FOUNDED A POLITICAL CLUB, THE **LODGE OF RATIONAL KNIGHTS** (!), TO ADVANCE HIS PLAN: A UNIFIED, INDEPENDENT SOUTH AMERICA RULED BY A LEGISLATURE AND AN EMPEROR FOR LIFE CALLED THE **INCA.** GO FIGURE!

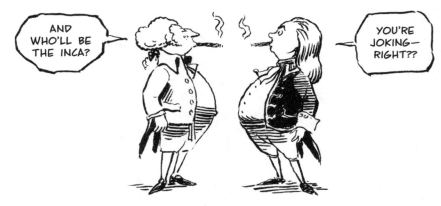

AND WHO'LL BE THE INCA?

YOU'RE JOKING— RIGHT??

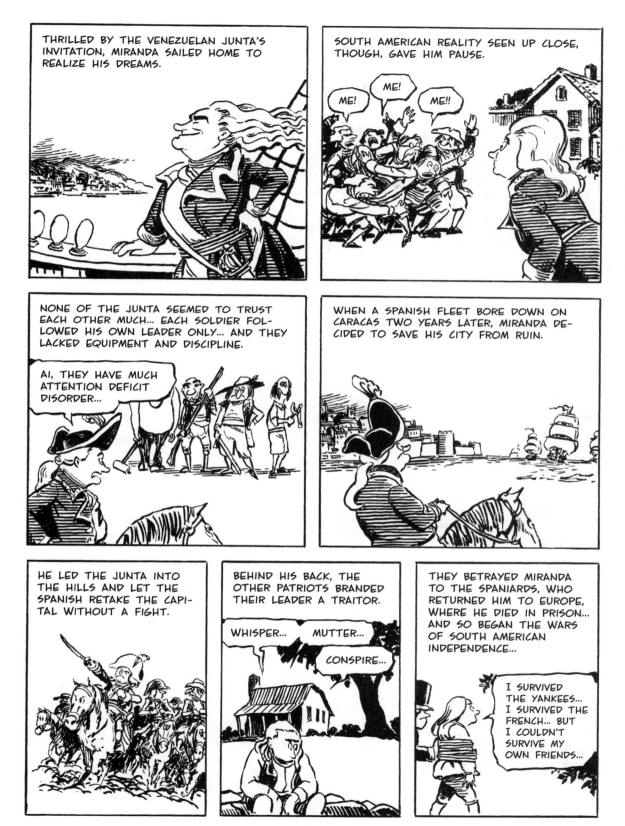

THRILLED BY THE VENEZUELAN JUNTA'S INVITATION, MIRANDA SAILED HOME TO REALIZE HIS DREAMS.

SOUTH AMERICAN REALITY SEEN UP CLOSE, THOUGH, GAVE HIM PAUSE.

ME!
ME!
ME!!

NONE OF THE JUNTA SEEMED TO TRUST EACH OTHER MUCH... EACH SOLDIER FOLLOWED HIS OWN LEADER ONLY... AND THEY LACKED EQUIPMENT AND DISCIPLINE.

AI, THEY HAVE MUCH ATTENTION DEFICIT DISORDER...

WHEN A SPANISH FLEET BORE DOWN ON CARACAS TWO YEARS LATER, MIRANDA DECIDED TO SAVE HIS CITY FROM RUIN.

HE LED THE JUNTA INTO THE HILLS AND LET THE SPANISH RETAKE THE CAPITAL WITHOUT A FIGHT.

BEHIND HIS BACK, THE OTHER PATRIOTS BRANDED THEIR LEADER A TRAITOR.

WHISPER...   MUTTER...
CONSPIRE...

THEY BETRAYED MIRANDA TO THE SPANIARDS, WHO RETURNED HIM TO EUROPE, WHERE HE DIED IN PRISON... AND SO BEGAN THE WARS OF SOUTH AMERICAN INDEPENDENCE...

I SURVIVED THE YANKEES... I SURVIVED THE FRENCH... BUT I COULDN'T SURVIVE MY OWN FRIENDS...

1812 INTERMEZZO

THE ROYAL NAVY, WHILE POLICING THE SEAS, ESPECIALLY LIKED BOARDING SHIPS FROM THE U.S.A.: THEY SPOKE ENGLISH!

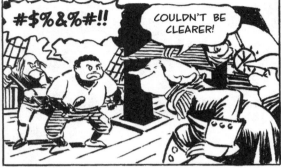

#$%&%#!!

COULDN'T BE CLEARER!

IN THE PROCESS, THE BRITS OFTEN DRAFTED AMERICAN CREWMEN INTO BRITISH SERVICE TO REPLACE THEIR OWN EVER-PLENTIFUL LOSSES.

SORRY... RUM, SODOMY, AND THE LASH TAKE A TOLL, BUT THEY WORK FOR US...

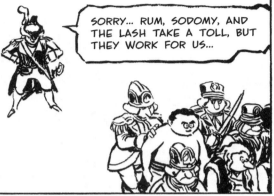

THIS PROVOKED THE YOUNG U.S.A. TO DECLARE WAR IN 1812...* BRITAIN INVADED, TORCHED WASHINGTON, D.C. (THEN BRAND-NEW), AND CALLED IT A WIN.

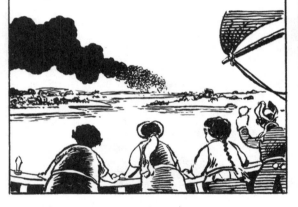

EXCEPT THAT THE "LOSERS" MANAGED TO ACQUIRE **INDIANA, ILLINOIS,** AND **MICHIGAN,** AND TO DRIVE THE BRITISH OUT OF **NEW ORLEANS** AS WELL.

GAH! EVEN WHEN THEY LOSE, THEY WIN!

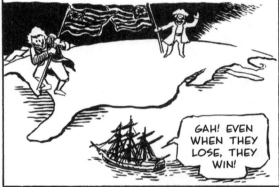

THE WAR OF 1812 WAS ALSO PUSHED BY AMERICANS WHO WANTED THE BRITS OUT OF CANADA AND ANYWHERE ELSE THAT CHECKED AMERICA'S WESTWARD EXPANSION.

IT'S MY GOD-GIVEN RIGHT AS AN AMERICAN TO GET LAND AND SELL IT FOR TEN TIMES WHAT I PAID FOR IT!

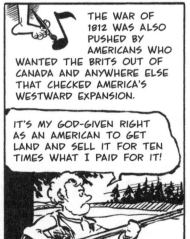

THE IROQUOIS CONFEDERACY AND OTHER NATIVE PEOPLES ON THE FRONTIER MAINLY BACKED BRITAIN AND HELPED FOIL AN AMERICAN INVASION OF CANADA.

DON'T THEY SEE? IT'S NOT THE LAND THAT'S SACRED, IT'S THE PROFIT FROM LAND!

A TRAGIC CULTURAL MISUNDERSTANDING...

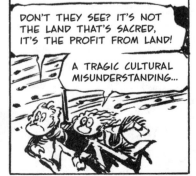

ONE PRO-BRITISH WAR CHIEF, **JOHN NORTON** (HALF CHEROKEE, HALF SCOTTISH, MOHAWK BY ADOPTION, AND ANCESTOR OF SOFTWARE GURU PETER NORTON), WROTE A VERY GOOD BOOK ABOUT THE WAR'S WESTERN FRONT.

I'M TRYING TO **UNERASE** OUR HISTORY!

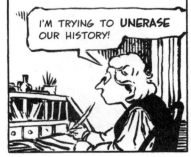

WAR AND PEACE

BACK IN EUROPE, NAPOLEON HAD A NEW PROBLEM: THE CZAR OF **RUSSIA** REFUSED TO MAKE PEACE... SO NAPOLEON ACTED.

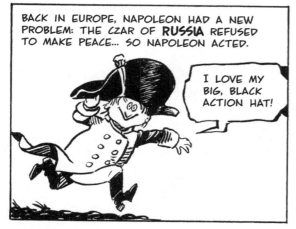

I LOVE MY BIG, BLACK ACTION HAT!

HIS PLAN: QUICK-MARCH INTO RUSSIA (EVEN WITHOUT THE 250,000 MEN IN SPAIN, NAPOLEON HAD 350,000 ON HAND), WASTE A FEW CITIES, AND GET OUT.

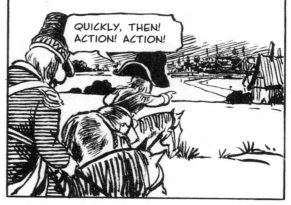

QUICKLY, THEN! ACTION! ACTION!

THE FRENCH BEGAN THE CAMPAIGN WITH A COSTLY WIN AT **BORODINO,** THE BLOODIEST SINGLE DAY OF FIGHTING IN EUROPEAN HISTORY, SAY HISTORIANS.

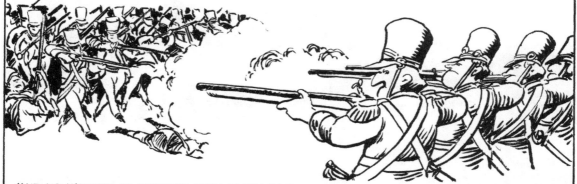

(AND NO WONDER: IT COMBINED HUGE ARMIES WITH THE "MODERN" TACTIC OF MARCHING IN ROWS DIRECTLY INTO HEAVY ENEMY FIRE.)

ALTHOUGH NAPOLEON HELD THE FIELD, THE RUSSIANS REFUSED TO SURRENDER. INSTEAD, THEY RETREATED...

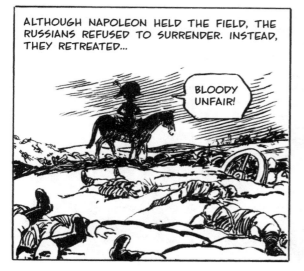

BLOODY UNFAIR!

AND THE FRENCH PURSUED...

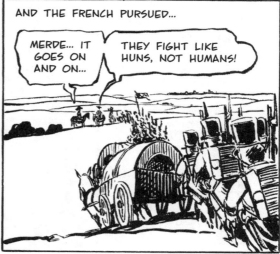

MERDE... IT GOES ON AND ON...

THEY FIGHT LIKE HUNS, NOT HUMANS!

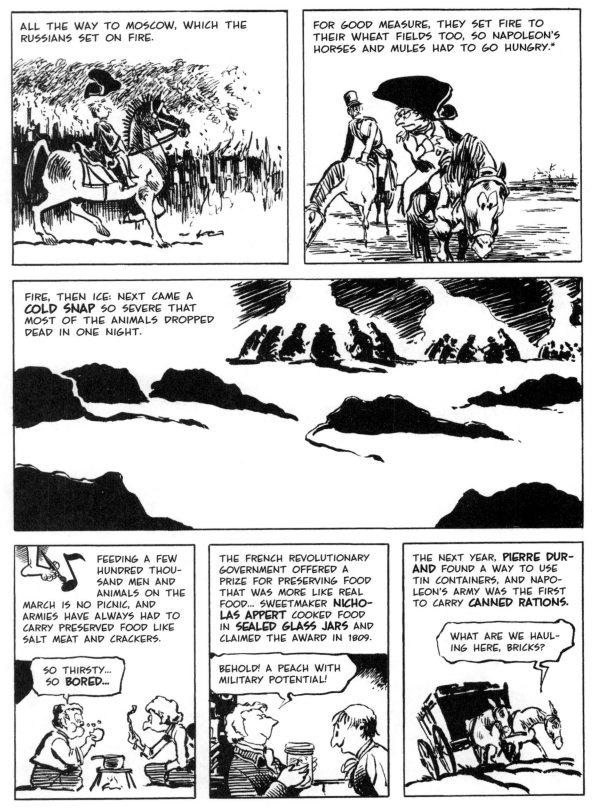

ALL THE WAY TO MOSCOW, WHICH THE RUSSIANS SET ON FIRE.

FOR GOOD MEASURE, THEY SET FIRE TO THEIR WHEAT FIELDS TOO, SO NAPOLEON'S HORSES AND MULES HAD TO GO HUNGRY.*

FIRE, THEN ICE: NEXT CAME A **COLD SNAP** SO SEVERE THAT MOST OF THE ANIMALS DROPPED DEAD IN ONE NIGHT.

FEEDING A FEW HUNDRED THOUSAND MEN AND ANIMALS ON THE MARCH IS NO PICNIC, AND ARMIES HAVE ALWAYS HAD TO CARRY PRESERVED FOOD LIKE SALT MEAT AND CRACKERS.

SO THIRSTY... SO **BORED**...

THE FRENCH REVOLUTIONARY GOVERNMENT OFFERED A PRIZE FOR PRESERVING FOOD THAT WAS MORE LIKE REAL FOOD... SWEETMAKER **NICHOLAS APPERT** COOKED FOOD IN **SEALED GLASS JARS** AND CLAIMED THE AWARD IN 1809.

BEHOLD! A PEACH WITH MILITARY POTENTIAL!

THE NEXT YEAR, **PIERRE DURAND** FOUND A WAY TO USE TIN CONTAINERS, AND NAPOLEON'S ARMY WAS THE FIRST TO CARRY **CANNED RATIONS.**

WHAT ARE WE HAULING HERE, BRICKS?

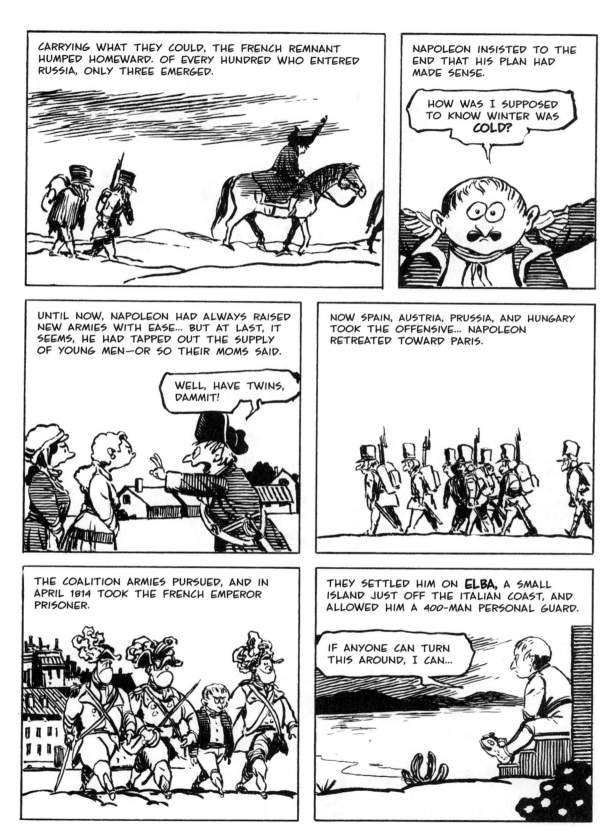

CARRYING WHAT THEY COULD, THE FRENCH REMNANT HUMPED HOMEWARD. OF EVERY HUNDRED WHO ENTERED RUSSIA, ONLY THREE EMERGED.

NAPOLEON INSISTED TO THE END THAT HIS PLAN HAD MADE SENSE.

HOW WAS I SUPPOSED TO KNOW WINTER WAS **COLD?**

UNTIL NOW, NAPOLEON HAD ALWAYS RAISED NEW ARMIES WITH EASE... BUT AT LAST, IT SEEMS, HE HAD TAPPED OUT THE SUPPLY OF YOUNG MEN—OR SO THEIR MOMS SAID.

WELL, HAVE TWINS, DAMMIT!

NOW SPAIN, AUSTRIA, PRUSSIA, AND HUNGARY TOOK THE OFFENSIVE... NAPOLEON RETREATED TOWARD PARIS.

THE COALITION ARMIES PURSUED, AND IN APRIL 1814 TOOK THE FRENCH EMPEROR PRISONER.

THEY SETTLED HIM ON **ELBA**, A SMALL ISLAND JUST OFF THE ITALIAN COAST, AND ALLOWED HIM A 400-MAN PERSONAL GUARD.

IF ANYONE CAN TURN THIS AROUND, I CAN...

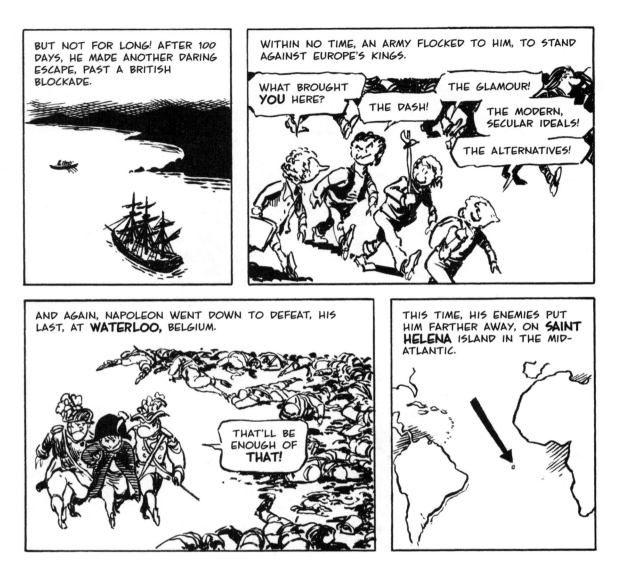

THERE HE WROTE HIS MEMOIRS AND PONDERED HIS LEGACY UNTIL HIS DEATH IN 1821.

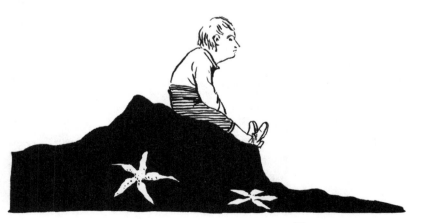

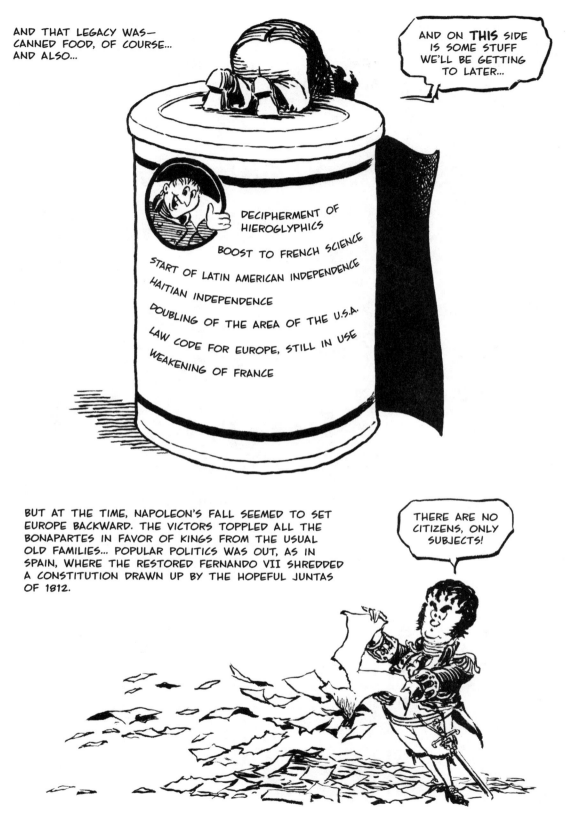

AND THAT LEGACY WAS—CANNED FOOD, OF COURSE... AND ALSO...

AND ON **THIS** SIDE IS SOME STUFF WE'LL BE GETTING TO LATER...

DECIPHERMENT OF HIEROGLYPHICS

BOOST TO FRENCH SCIENCE

START OF LATIN AMERICAN INDEPENDENCE

HAITIAN INDEPENDENCE

DOUBLING OF THE AREA OF THE U.S.A.

LAW CODE FOR EUROPE, STILL IN USE

WEAKENING OF FRANCE

BUT AT THE TIME, NAPOLEON'S FALL SEEMED TO SET EUROPE BACKWARD. THE VICTORS TOPPLED ALL THE BONAPARTES IN FAVOR OF KINGS FROM THE USUAL OLD FAMILIES... POPULAR POLITICS WAS OUT, AS IN SPAIN, WHERE THE RESTORED FERNANDO VII SHREDDED A CONSTITUTION DRAWN UP BY THE HOPEFUL JUNTAS OF 1812.

THERE ARE NO CITIZENS, ONLY SUBJECTS!

FERNANDO MAY HAVE HELD SPAIN AGAIN, BUT HE NEVER REGAINED **SOUTH AMERICA.** ALREADY A REBEL ARMY HAD RE-TAKEN CARACAS, VENEZUELA.

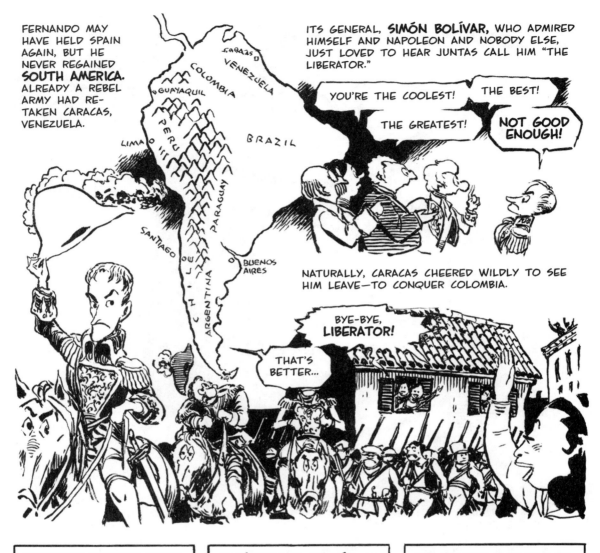

ITS GENERAL, **SIMÓN BOLÍVAR,** WHO ADMIRED HIMSELF AND NAPOLEON AND NOBODY ELSE, JUST LOVED TO HEAR JUNTAS CALL HIM "THE LIBERATOR."

YOU'RE THE COOLEST!

THE BEST!

THE GREATEST!

NOT GOOD ENOUGH!

NATURALLY, CARACAS CHEERED WILDLY TO SEE HIM LEAVE—TO CONQUER COLOMBIA.

BYE-BYE, **LIBERATOR!**

THAT'S BETTER...

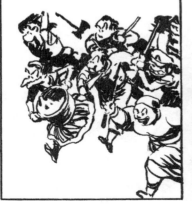

MEANWHILE, FARTHER SOUTH, REVOLT FLARED AMONG THE DOCKWORKERS OF **BUENOS AIRES.**

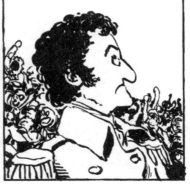

JOSÉ DE SAN MARTÍN, A "RATIONAL KNIGHT" (AND DEFINITELY MORE RATIONAL THAN BOLÍVAR), LED THE ARGENTINE REBEL ARMY.

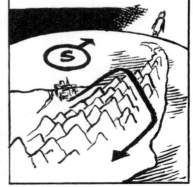

SAN MARTÍN'S PLAN WAS TO MARCH OVER THE ANDES, FIND ALLIES IN CHILE, AND ATTACK **LIMA,** PERU, STILL SPANISH AMERICA'S HUB.

SO... TWO AMAZING MOUNTAIN CAMPAIGNS, BOLÍVAR IN THE NORTH AND SAN MARTÍN IN THE SOUTH. (THEY AMAZED EUROPEANS, ANYWAY. THE INCAS USED TO DO THIS KIND OF THING ALL THE TIME!)

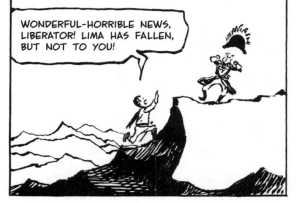

SAN MARTÍN, WHO HAD PLANNED CAREFULLY, REACHED CHILE QUICKLY AND WAS ALREADY MARCHING ON PERU WHILE BOLÍVAR, WHO HAD NOT, WAS STILL STUCK IN COLOMBIA.

WONDERFUL-HORRIBLE NEWS, LIBERATOR! LIMA HAS FALLEN, BUT NOT TO YOU!

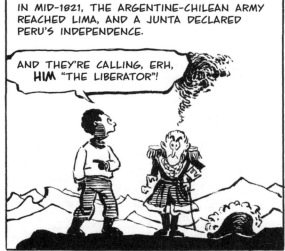

IN MID-1821, THE ARGENTINE-CHILEAN ARMY REACHED LIMA, AND A JUNTA DECLARED PERU'S INDEPENDENCE.

AND THEY'RE CALLING, ERH, **HIM** "THE LIBERATOR"!

BOLÍVAR, WHOSE KNACK FOR MAKING ENEMIES SLOWED HIM UP, APPROACHED LIMA A YEAR LATER.

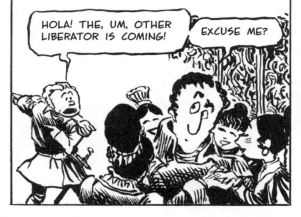

HOLA! THE, UM, OTHER LIBERATOR IS COMING!

EXCUSE ME?

SAN MARTÍN SAILED NORTH AND MET BOLÍVAR AT **GUAYAQUIL**, ECUADOR.

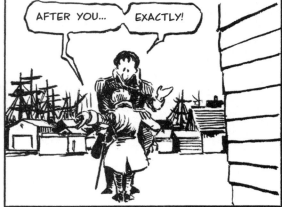

AFTER YOU...

EXACTLY!

THE TWO ENTERED A PRIVATE ROOM.

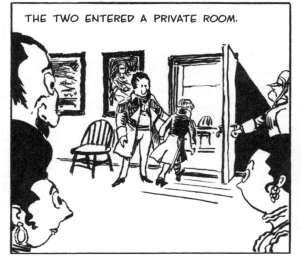

THEY HAD A LOT TO TALK ABOUT—THEY SPENT ALL DAY IN THERE—BUT NO ONE KNOWS WHAT WAS SAID...

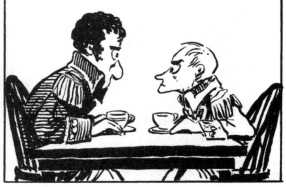

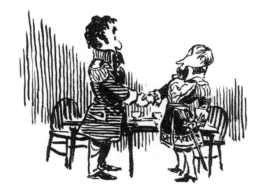

AND AFTER THE MEETING, JOSÉ DE SAN MARTÍN RETIRED FROM POLITICS FOREVER!

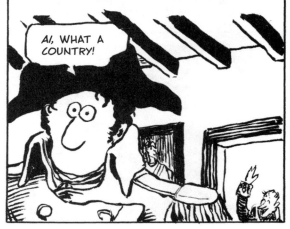

AI, WHAT A COUNTRY!

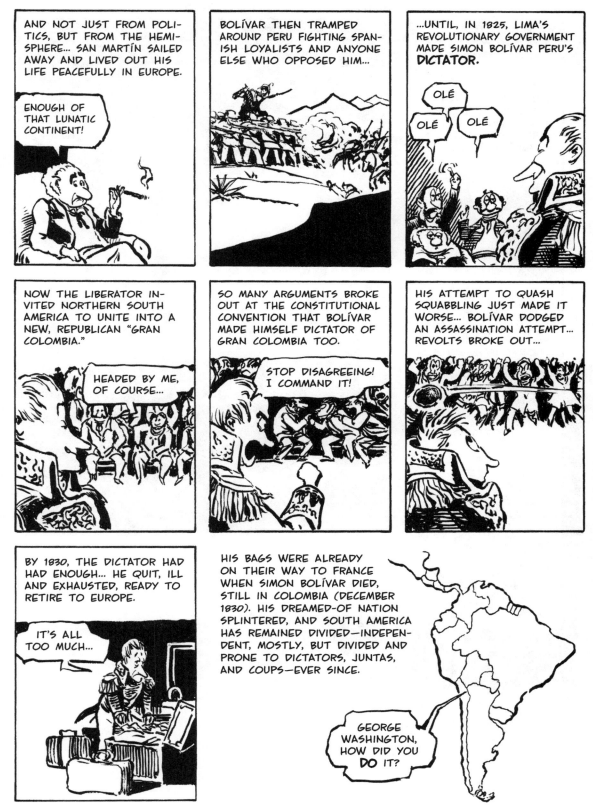

AND NOT JUST FROM POLITICS, BUT FROM THE HEMISPHERE... SAN MARTÍN SAILED AWAY AND LIVED OUT HIS LIFE PEACEFULLY IN EUROPE.

ENOUGH OF THAT LUNATIC CONTINENT!

BOLÍVAR THEN TRAMPED AROUND PERU FIGHTING SPANISH LOYALISTS AND ANYONE ELSE WHO OPPOSED HIM...

...UNTIL, IN 1825, LIMA'S REVOLUTIONARY GOVERNMENT MADE SIMON BOLÍVAR PERU'S **DICTATOR.**

OLÉ
OLÉ OLÉ

NOW THE LIBERATOR INVITED NORTHERN SOUTH AMERICA TO UNITE INTO A NEW, REPUBLICAN "GRAN COLOMBIA."

HEADED BY ME, OF COURSE...

SO MANY ARGUMENTS BROKE OUT AT THE CONSTITUTIONAL CONVENTION THAT BOLÍVAR MADE HIMSELF DICTATOR OF GRAN COLOMBIA TOO.

STOP DISAGREEING! I COMMAND IT!

HIS ATTEMPT TO QUASH SQUABBLING JUST MADE IT WORSE... BOLÍVAR DODGED AN ASSASSINATION ATTEMPT... REVOLTS BROKE OUT...

BY 1830, THE DICTATOR HAD HAD ENOUGH... HE QUIT, ILL AND EXHAUSTED, READY TO RETIRE TO EUROPE.

IT'S ALL TOO MUCH...

HIS BAGS WERE ALREADY ON THEIR WAY TO FRANCE WHEN SIMON BOLÍVAR DIED, STILL IN COLOMBIA (DECEMBER 1830). HIS DREAMED-OF NATION SPLINTERED, AND SOUTH AMERICA HAS REMAINED DIVIDED—INDEPENDENT, MOSTLY, BUT DIVIDED AND PRONE TO DICTATORS, JUNTAS, AND COUPS—EVER SINCE.

GEORGE WASHINGTON, HOW DID YOU **DO** IT?

PROGRESS

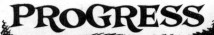

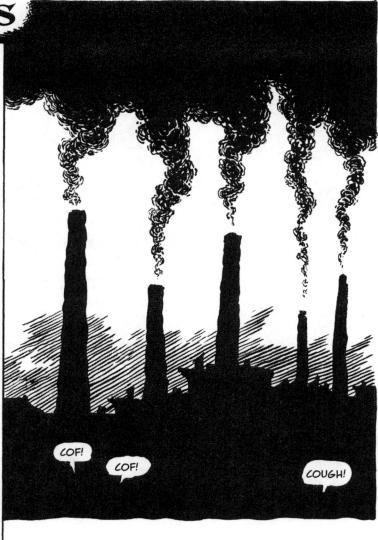

IN POST-NAPOLEONIC EUROPE, PLAYGROUND OF KINGS, ONE COUNTRY KEPT ITS MIXED GOVERN-MENT, FULL OF TALK AND COMPROMISE: **GREAT BRITAIN.**

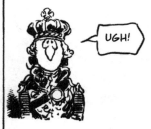

UGH!

STRANGELY, EUROPE'S ROYALS **ENVIED** BRITAIN, NOT FOR ITS MESSY POLITICS (OR INSIPID FOOD), BUT FOR ITS AWESOME **MACHINERY:** STEAM-POWERED FACTORIES, SHIPS, AND RAILWAY LOCOMOTIVES.

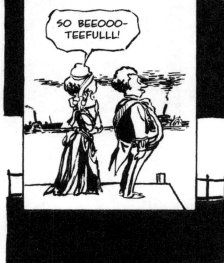

SO BEEOOO-TEEFULLL!

COF!

COF!

COUGH!

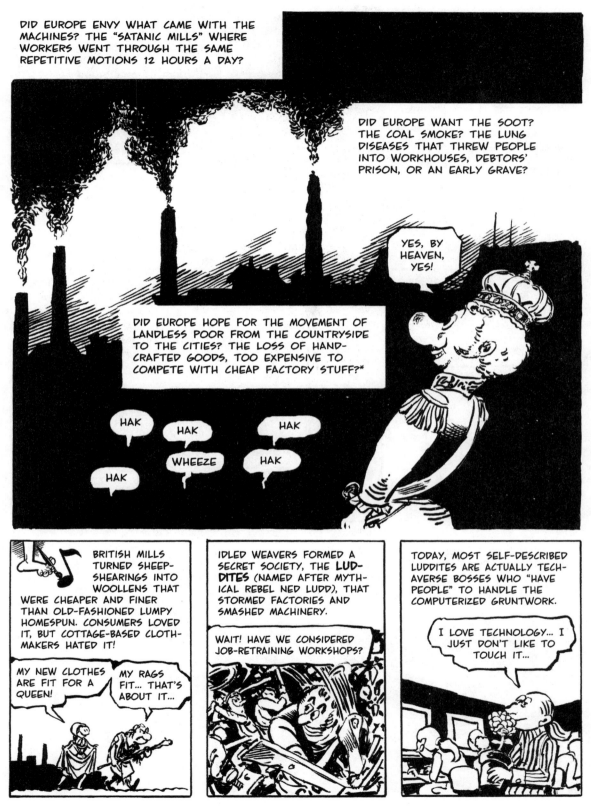

DID EUROPE ENVY WHAT CAME WITH THE MACHINES? THE "SATANIC MILLS" WHERE WORKERS WENT THROUGH THE SAME REPETITIVE MOTIONS 12 HOURS A DAY?

DID EUROPE WANT THE SOOT? THE COAL SMOKE? THE LUNG DISEASES THAT THREW PEOPLE INTO WORKHOUSES, DEBTORS' PRISON, OR AN EARLY GRAVE?

YES, BY HEAVEN, YES!

DID EUROPE HOPE FOR THE MOVEMENT OF LANDLESS POOR FROM THE COUNTRYSIDE TO THE CITIES? THE LOSS OF HAND-CRAFTED GOODS, TOO EXPENSIVE TO COMPETE WITH CHEAP FACTORY STUFF?*

HAK

HAK

HAK

HAK

WHEEZE

HAK

HAK

BRITISH MILLS TURNED SHEEP-SHEARINGS INTO WOOLLENS THAT WERE CHEAPER AND FINER THAN OLD-FASHIONED LUMPY HOMESPUN. CONSUMERS LOVED IT, BUT COTTAGE-BASED CLOTH-MAKERS HATED IT!

MY NEW CLOTHES ARE FIT FOR A QUEEN!

MY RAGS FIT... THAT'S ABOUT IT...

IDLED WEAVERS FORMED A SECRET SOCIETY, THE **LUD-DITES** (NAMED AFTER MYTH-ICAL REBEL NED LUDD), THAT STORMED FACTORIES AND SMASHED MACHINERY.

WAIT! HAVE WE CONSIDERED JOB-RETRAINING WORKSHOPS?

TODAY, MOST SELF-DESCRIBED LUDDITES ARE ACTUALLY TECH-AVERSE BOSSES WHO "HAVE PEOPLE" TO HANDLE THE COMPUTERIZED GRUNTWORK.

I LOVE TECHNOLOGY... I JUST DON'T LIKE TO TOUCH IT...

WHAT THOSE ROYALS HAD A HARD TIME SEEING WAS HOW BRITISH FREEDOMS PROMOTED INDUSTRIAL SUCCESS... BUT THE BRITS DID SEE IT, AND DURING THE 1820S AND '30S, THE BRITISH GOVERNMENT EXPANDED FREEDOM IN VARIOUS WAYS...

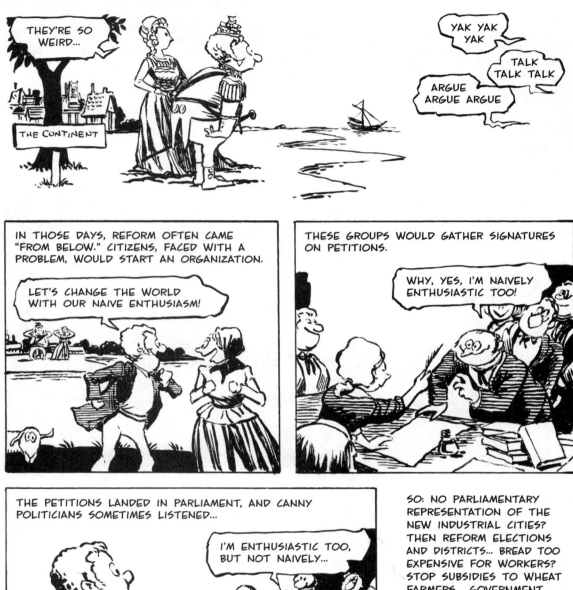

THEY'RE SO WEIRD...

THE CONTINENT

YAK YAK YAK

TALK TALK TALK

ARGUE ARGUE ARGUE

IN THOSE DAYS, REFORM OFTEN CAME "FROM BELOW." CITIZENS, FACED WITH A PROBLEM, WOULD START AN ORGANIZATION.

LET'S CHANGE THE WORLD WITH OUR NAIVE ENTHUSIASM!

THESE GROUPS WOULD GATHER SIGNATURES ON PETITIONS.

WHY, YES, I'M NAIVELY ENTHUSIASTIC TOO!

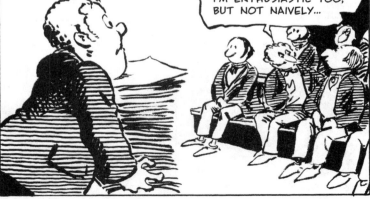

THE PETITIONS LANDED IN PARLIAMENT, AND CANNY POLITICIANS SOMETIMES LISTENED...

I'M ENTHUSIASTIC TOO, BUT NOT NAIVELY...

SO: NO PARLIAMENTARY REPRESENTATION OF THE NEW INDUSTRIAL CITIES? THEN REFORM ELECTIONS AND DISTRICTS... BREAD TOO EXPENSIVE FOR WORKERS? STOP SUBSIDIES TO WHEAT FARMERS... GOVERNMENT DEAF TO COMMERCIAL NEEDS? LET THE MIDDLE CLASS VOTE!

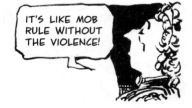

IT'S LIKE MOB RULE WITHOUT THE VIOLENCE!

IN THE 1830S, GOVERNMENT CAPPED THESE REFORMS WITH TWO THAT WOULD HAVE SEEMED UNTHINKABLE A FEW YEARS EARLIER.
GOSH, WHAT'S GOTTEN INTO US?
COAL SMOKE?
IN 1831, IT GRANTED **FULL CIVIL RIGHTS** TO ROMAN CATHOLICS, A MISTRUSTED MINORITY THAT HAD SUFFERED DISCRIMINATION SINCE THE REIGN OF QUEEN ELIZABETH I.
MAYBE NOW THE **IRISH** WILL LIKE US!
NOW **THAT** REALLY **IS** UNTHINKABLE...
COUGH
COUGH
IN 1833, PARLIAMENT **ABOLISHED SLAVERY** THROUGHOUT THE BRITISH EMPIRE.
UNTIL THEN, ONLY THE TRAFFIC IN HUMANS WAS BANNED... NOW, EVERY SLAVE IN THE EMPIRE WAS FREED.
DID WE REALLY JUST **DO** THAT?
COUGH!
DESPITE THESE REFORMS, **POOR BRITONS** STILL HAD NO SAY IN GOVERNMENT. ONLY PROPERTY OWNERS COULD VOTE OR HOLD OFFICE.
YOU WOULDN'T WANT THE NATION'S WEALTH MANAGED BY PEOPLE WITH NO EXPERIENCE WITH IT, WOULD YOU? DON'T ANSWER! I'M NOT LISTENING!
IN 1838, **3 MILLION PEOPLE** SIGNED A PETITION IN FAVOR OF ENDING ALL PROPERTY QUALIFICATIONS FOR VOTING.
PARLIAMENT TURNED IT DOWN FLAT.
B-B-BUT... THREE MILLION!
YES, TOO MANY OF YOU—THAT'S THE PROBLEM PRECISELY!

STILL, THE ABOLITION OF SLAVERY WAS AMAZING! EVERY SLAVEOWNER IN THE BRITISH EMPIRE LOST HIS HUMAN PROPERTY OVERNIGHT.

THIS IS SOME KIND OF JOKE, RIGHT?

I'M AFRAID NOT!

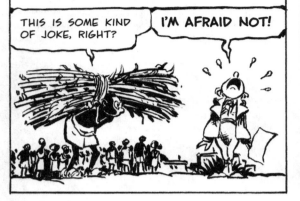

TRUE, THE GOVERNMENT HAD SET ASIDE 20 MILLION POUNDS STERLING* TO PAY OWNERS FOR THEIR LOSS, BUT EVEN SO...

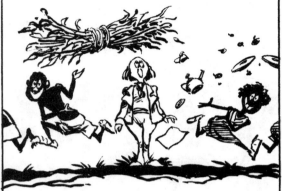

JAMAICA AND THE OTHER SUGAR COLONIES SAW THEIR PROFITS PLUNGE...

WHAT IN THE EVER-LOVIN' **WORLD** JUST **HAPPENED?**

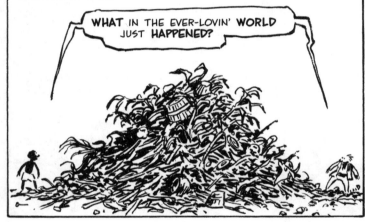

AND YET BRITISH BUSINESS PROSPERED—WELL ENOUGH TO PROVIDE PARLIAMENT WITH 20 MILLION EXTRA POUNDS STERLING! THIS WAGE-PAYING BUSINESS MODEL CERTAINLY MADE MONEY... BUT HOW? FROM WHERE...?

NOT FROM HERE ANY LONGER...

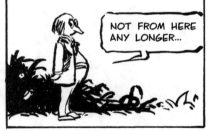

TO RECEIVE PAY-MENT FOR FREED SLAVES, AN OWNER HAD TO COLLECT THROUGH AN AGENT IN LONDON, AND IF YOU HAD NO AGENT IN LONDON, TOO BAD...

THIS IS BIASED AGAINST THE SMALL, INDEPENDENT OWNER OF HUMANS!

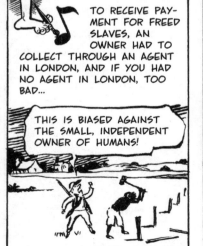

FOR EXAMPLE, **SOUTH AFRICA'S** DUTCH FARMERS, OR **BOERS,** HAD NO LONDON AGENTS... THEIR DISGUST FOR BRITAIN'S NEW LAW WAS LIMITLESS...

UGH! ECH!

PFAUGH!!

AND IT SOUNDS EVEN WORSE IN THE ORIGINAL DUTCH...

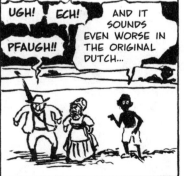

SO IN 1834, THOUSANDS OF THEM PACKED THEIR WAGONS AND TOOK A "GREAT TREK" TO GET THEMSELVES AND THEIR SLAVES AS FAR AWAY FROM THE BRITISH AS THEY COULD.

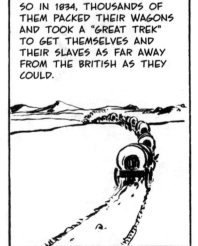

VISIONARIES

IN THE VERY EARLY 1800s, BRITAIN HAD A DREAM... A FREE-TRADE FANTASY OF SELLING ITS FACTORY GOODS EVERYWHERE AT A PROFIT THAT WOULD BUILD MORE FACTORIES, MAKE MORE GOODS, AND BRING MORE PROFIT... A DREAM OF "FOREIGN MARKETS"... A DREAM OF **CHINA,** A COUNTRY WITH 150 MILLION CUSTOMERS.

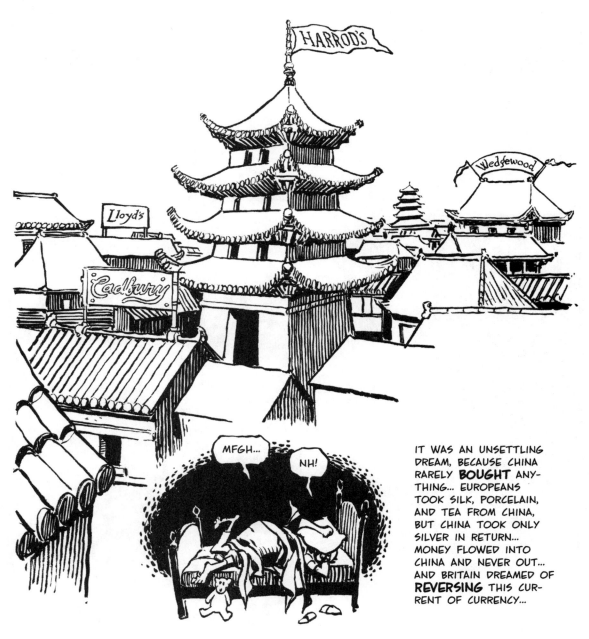

MFGH...

NH!

IT WAS AN UNSETTLING DREAM, BECAUSE CHINA RARELY **BOUGHT** ANYTHING... EUROPEANS TOOK SILK, PORCELAIN, AND TEA FROM CHINA, BUT CHINA TOOK ONLY SILVER IN RETURN... MONEY FLOWED INTO CHINA AND NEVER OUT... AND BRITAIN DREAMED OF **REVERSING** THIS CURRENT OF CURRENCY...

AROUND THIS TIME, THE CANNY GENTS OF THE **BRITISH EAST INDIA COMPANY** FIGURED OUT HOW TO TURN IT AROUND—AND THAT SHOULD ALARM YOU RIGHT THERE.

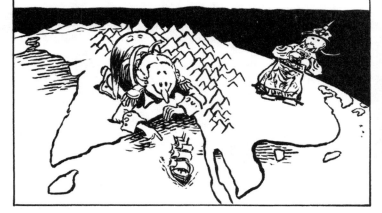

FIRST, THE COMPANY PLANTED TEA IN **INDIA**, WHERE COSTS COULD BE SQUEEZED.

WE'LL PAY YOU IN WOOL SWEATERS.

NOW THE HOME COUNTRY COULD TAKE CHEAP INDIAN TEA INSTEAD OF BUYING FROM CHINA.

DEVIOUS OCCIDENTALS...

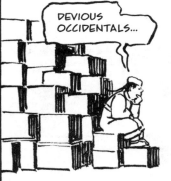

THEN THE COMPANY FOUND A PRODUCT THE CHINESE WOULD BUY...

NO WAY... NEVER HAPPEN... NOTHING FOREIGN IS ANY GOOD—

AHEM!

NAMELY OPIUM.

JUST **TRY** IT...

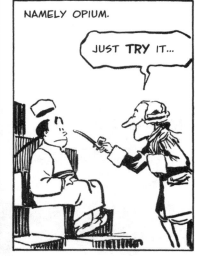

THE COMPANY PLANTED POPPY FIELDS IN INDIA... THEY YIELDED A RANGE OF GRADES, FROM CRUMMY, GUMMY BOMBAY GOOP, TO MELLOW MORPHIA FROM MADRAS...

IT'S **GOOD** FOR YOU!

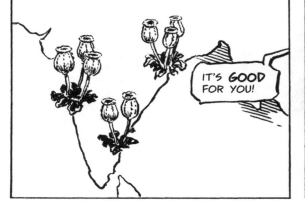

IN THE LATE 1700S, THE COMPANY SHIPPED A FEW SAMPLES OF OPIUM TO GUANGZHOU, AND THE CHINESE TOOK A TASTE.

SEE? ISN'T IT **DREAMY?**

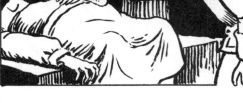

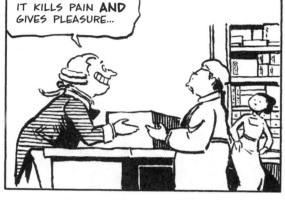

AT FIRST, THE CHINESE BOUGHT SMALL LOTS FOR MEDICINAL USE... BUT THIS WAS A VERY SPECIAL MEDICINE...

IT KILLS PAIN **AND** GIVES PLEASURE...

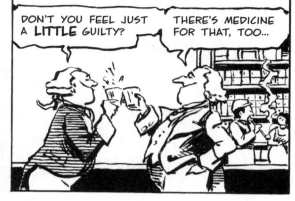

AND AS YOU KNOW FROM "ISSUES AND CHOICES" (OR WHATEVER IT'S CALLED AT YOUR SCHOOL), OPIUM HOOKS PEOPLE EVEN WORSE THAN, SAY, TEA.

DON'T YOU FEEL JUST A **LITTLE** GUILTY?

THERE'S MEDICINE FOR THAT, TOO...

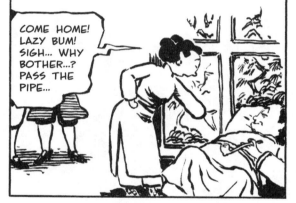

WHO KNOWS WHY A COUNTRY TURNS TO DRUGS? NAMELESS CRAVINGS, VAGUE MALAISE, A REALITY TOO PAINFUL OR BORING TO FACE SOBERLY?

COME HOME! LAZY BUM! SIGH... WHY BOTHER...? PASS THE PIPE...

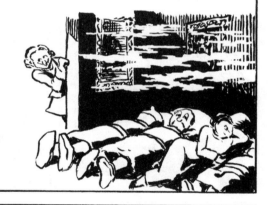

BY THE 1830S, MILLIONS OF CHINESE— MANDARINS, MERCHANTS, HOUSEWIVES, HOOKERS, YOU NAME IT—WERE WASTING THEIR TIME AND MONEY GETTING WASTED.

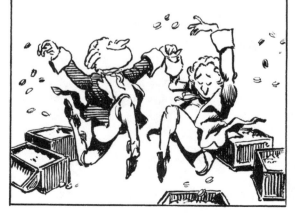

AND THE CASH, MINUS A CUT FOR THE DISTRIBUTOR AND RETAILER, ENDED UP IN BRITISH BANK ACCOUNTS.

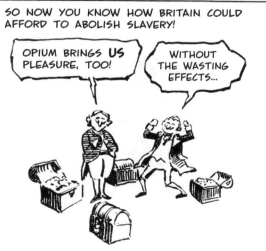

SO NOW YOU KNOW HOW BRITAIN COULD AFFORD TO ABOLISH SLAVERY!

OPIUM BRINGS **US** PLEASURE, TOO!

WITHOUT THE WASTING EFFECTS...

BRITISH LAW GAVE THE EAST INDIA COMPANY SOLE CONTROL OF "O," AND CHINA ALLOWED IMPORTS ONLY THROUGH ONE PORT, GUANGZHOU... BUT TEMPTED BY PROFIT, FREE-LANCE SMUGGLERS FOUND WAYS TO DODGE THE LAW AND MOVE PRODUCT ELSEWHERE.

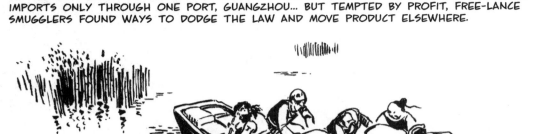

OPIUM PRODUCES VISIONS, AND NOT JUST IN USERS. BRITISH SHIPPERS SAW DAZZLING VISTAS OF WEALTH!

AND I NEVER COME DOWN...

THESE SMUGGLERS, LED BY ONE **WILLIAM JARDINE,** CONFESSED THEIR CRAVINGS TO FRIENDS IN GOVERNMENT.

CAN YOU FEEL IT TOO?

YES, NOW THAT YOU MENTION IT...

SOON THE HOUSE OF COMMONS RANG WITH PRAISE FOR FREE TRADE AND ABUSE OF MONOPOLY.

THE COMPANY IS SO INEFFICIENT!

HEAR HEAR!

IT CAN'T SELL THE STUFF FAST ENOUGH!

IN 1838, PARLIAMENT OPENED THE OPIUM TRADE TO ALL. FREE TRADE HAD PREVAILED!

ON PRINCIPLE, OF COURSE!

IT WAS A VOTE THAT LAUNCHED A THOUSAND SHIPS.

THE CHINESE GOVERNMENT WAS APPALLED, AT LEAST THAT PART OF THE GOVERNMENT NOT SUCKING ON PIPES.
AWFUL!
HORRIBLE!
WHATEVER...
NOT ONLY HAD BRITAIN UNLEASHED A PACK OF PUSHERS, BUT IT ALSO SENT A COMMISSIONER TO DISCUSS WAYS OF WIDENING THE TRADE EVEN FURTHER.
HELLO?
MONEY WAS DRAINING AWAY... ADDICTION WAS SPREADING... AND NOW SOME **FOREIGN COUNTRY** WANTED TO NEGOTIATE WITH CHINA AS AN **EQUAL!**
YOO-HOO?
IT'S ALL SO WRONG...
SO THE CHINESE OFFICIALS IGNORED THE BRITISH COMMISSIONER UNTIL HE WENT AWAY.
HIS MAJESTY'S GOVERNMENT INSISTS!
TSK! IF ONLY HE'D LAIN ON HIS FACE AND SAID PLEASE...
FOR THE NEXT FOUR YEARS, THE CHINESE GOVERNMENT ARGUED ABOUT HOW TO DEAL WITH THE OPIUM PROBLEM.
LEGALIZE AND TAX IT!
WIPE IT OUT!
PASS SOME TO ME!
TO ME!
TO ME!
AT LAST, IN 1838, THE EMPEROR RULED: HE ORDERED THE **DEATH PENALTY** FOR CHINESE OPIUM DEALERS AND SENT AN HONEST OFFICIAL, **LIN ZEXU,** TO DEAL WITH THE FOREIGNERS IN GUANGZHOU.

COMMISSIONER LIN HAD ALWAYS TAKEN A HARD LINE ON OPIUM, AND NOW HE HAD A CHANCE TO APPLY HIS IDEAS.*

I HATE IT WHEN THAT HAPPENS...

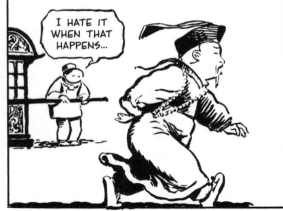

HE MADE THE EUROPEANS AN OFFER: TRADE THE NARCOTICS FOR TEA, OR LOSE THEM. THE FOREIGNERS, THINKING LIN WAS BLUFFING, SIMPLY SCOFFED.

HM! NO EXPERIENCE WITH HONEST MEN, I GUESS...

SCOFF

SCOFF

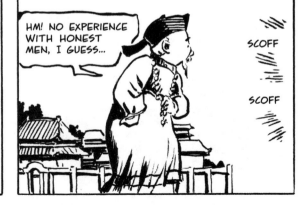

IMAGINE THEIR SURPRISE WHEN THE DEADLINE CAME, AND LIN'S MEN SEALED THE WAREHOUSES.

I'M GOING TO BE SICK...

AND THEY BLOODY WELL JUST LOCKED UP THE ANTI-NAUSEA MEDICATION...

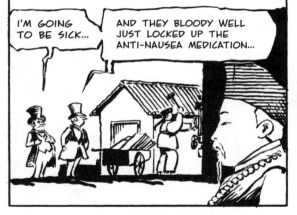

THEN THE CHINESE CARTED OFF THE OPIUM—OVER A **MILLION KILOS**—AND DESTROYED IT.

SAD, REALLY, HOW LITTLE REGARD THE BENIGHTED HEATHEN HAS FOR PROPERTY RIGHTS...

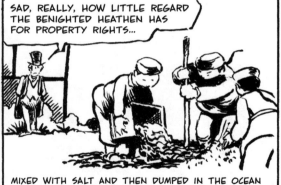

MIXED WITH SALT AND THEN DUMPED IN THE OCEAN

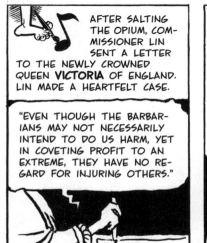 AFTER SALTING THE OPIUM, COMMISSIONER LIN SENT A LETTER TO THE NEWLY CROWNED QUEEN **VICTORIA** OF ENGLAND. LIN MADE A HEARTFELT CASE.

"EVEN THOUGH THE BARBARIANS MAY NOT NECESSARILY INTEND TO DO US HARM, YET IN COVETING PROFIT TO AN EXTREME, THEY HAVE NO REGARD FOR INJURING OTHERS."

"WHERE IS YOUR CONSCIENCE?... THE SMOKING OF OPIUM IS VERY STRICTLY **FORBIDDEN** BY **YOUR** COUNTRY... BECAUSE THE HARM CAUSED BY OPIUM IS CLEARLY UNDERSTOOD. SINCE IT IS NOT PERMITTED TO DO HARM TO YOUR OWN COUNTRY, THEN EVEN LESS SHOULD YOU LET IT BE PASSED ON TO THE HARM OF **OTHER** COUNTRIES."

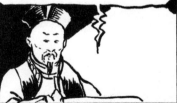

THIS LETTER WAS PUBLISHED IN THE LONDON *TIMES*, THOUGH APPARENTLY NEVER SHOWN TO THE YOUNG QUEEN.

THIS SILLY THING? JUST MORE HEATHEN RANTING!

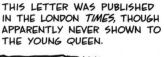

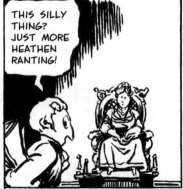

IN THE IMMORTAL WORDS OF BUGS BUNNY, THIS MEANT **WAR.**

HOW DARE THEY INTERFERE WITH A NEW WORLD ORDER BASED ON TRANSPARENCY AND THE RULE OF LAW?

BRITISH GUNBOATS STEAMED UP THE RIVER TO DEFEND, AS THEY PUT IT, BRITAIN'S RIGHT TO HAVE "NORMAL" RELATIONS WITH CHINA.

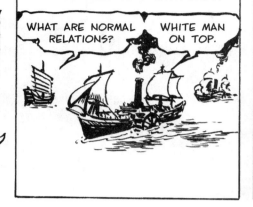

WHAT ARE NORMAL RELATIONS?

WHITE MAN ON TOP.

THE MANCHU/CHINESE ARMY HAD NO DEFENSE AGAINST MODERN WEAPONS.

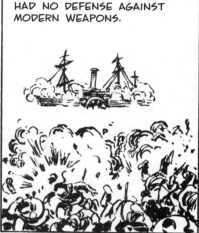

IN 1843, CHINA SURRENDERED AND OPENED MORE THAN **FOUR DOZEN** PORTS TO EUROPEANS. ONE, **HONG KONG,** WENT TO BRITAIN ALONE... IN THESE ZONES CHINA "ALLOWED" EUROPEANS TO GOVERN THEMSELVES BY EUROPEAN LAWS... CHRISTIAN MISSIONARIES RETURNED TO CHINA... AND TRADE FLOURISHED, INCLUDING THE OPIUM TRADE.

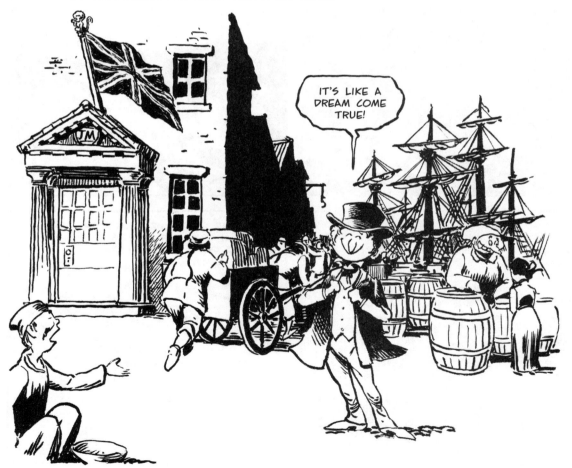

IT'S LIKE A DREAM COME TRUE!

HOW COULD UPSTARTS FROM NOWHERE HAVE BEATEN MIGHTY CHINA? SOME CHINESE BLAMED THEIR MANCHU RULERS... SOME BLAMED OPIUM... SOME **TOOK** OPIUM... AND SOME GREW OBSESSED WITH THE WEST.

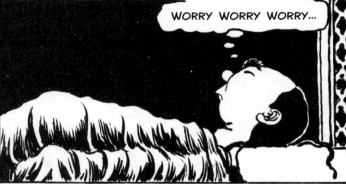

WORRY WORRY WORRY...

HONG XIQUAN, FOR INSTANCE, HAD PUZZLING DREAMS IN WHICH A BLOND-BEARDED FIGURE CALLED HIM "SON."

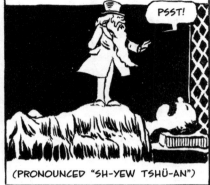

PSST!

(PRONOUNCED "SH-YEW TSHÜ-AN")

HONG, WHOSE SCRAMBLED SENSE OF THE CLASSICS HAD CAUSED HIM TO FAIL THE CIVIL SERVICE EXAM REPEATEDLY, TURNED TO **CHRISTIANITY**—AND ALL BECAME CLEAR!

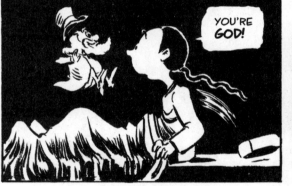

YOU'RE **GOD!**

NOW HE SCRAMBLED THE BIBLE TOO, PUTTING HIMSELF AT THE CENTER, AND HIS PREACHING ATTRACTED A FOLLOWING.

JESUS IS MY OLDER BROTHER!

YES! YES! I LOVE BELIEVING THINGS WHEN THERE'S NO EVIDENCE ONE WAY OR THE OTHER...

BY 1851, HE LED AN ANTI-MANCHU, OPIUM-FREE "HEAVENLY KINGDOM" WITH ITS OWN ARMY AND CIVIL SERVICE EXAMS BASED ON THE BIBLE(!).

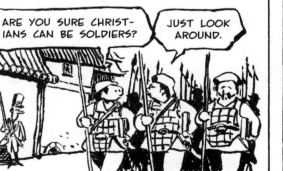

ARE YOU SURE CHRISTIANS CAN BE SOLDIERS?

JUST LOOK AROUND.

WHEN THE GOVERNMENT DECIDED THINGS HAD GONE TOO FAR, HONG'S "TAIPINGS" SHOCKED EVERYONE BY DEFEATING THE CHINESE ARMY.

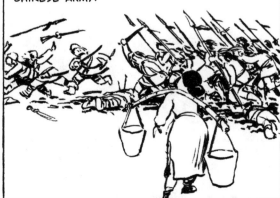

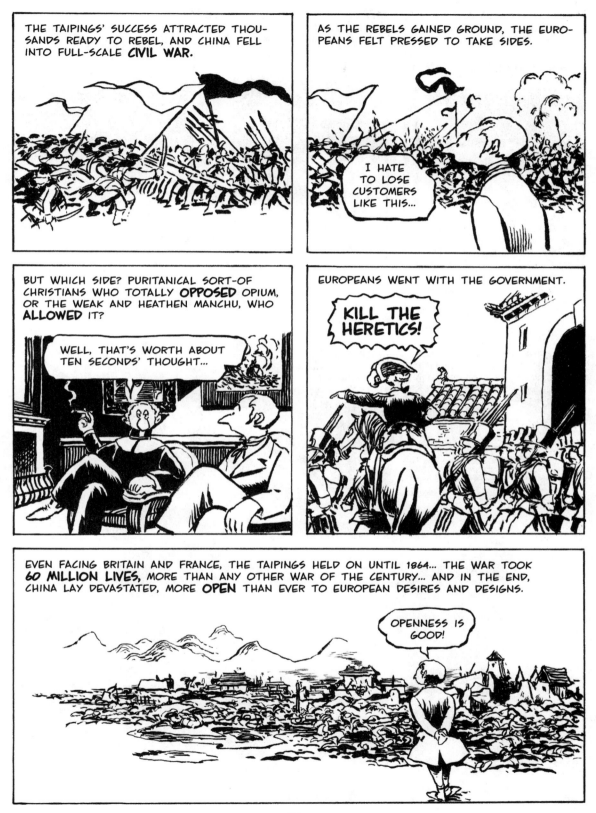

THE TAIPINGS' SUCCESS ATTRACTED THOUSANDS READY TO REBEL, AND CHINA FELL INTO FULL-SCALE **CIVIL WAR.**

AS THE REBELS GAINED GROUND, THE EUROPEANS FELT PRESSED TO TAKE SIDES.

I HATE TO LOSE CUSTOMERS LIKE THIS...

BUT WHICH SIDE? PURITANICAL SORT-OF CHRISTIANS WHO TOTALLY **OPPOSED** OPIUM, OR THE WEAK AND HEATHEN MANCHU, WHO **ALLOWED** IT?

WELL, THAT'S WORTH ABOUT TEN SECONDS' THOUGHT...

EUROPEANS WENT WITH THE GOVERNMENT.

KILL THE HERETICS!

EVEN FACING BRITAIN AND FRANCE, THE TAIPINGS HELD ON UNTIL 1864... THE WAR TOOK **60 MILLION LIVES,** MORE THAN ANY OTHER WAR OF THE CENTURY... AND IN THE END, CHINA LAY DEVASTATED, MORE **OPEN** THAN EVER TO EUROPEAN DESIRES AND DESIGNS.

OPENNESS IS GOOD!

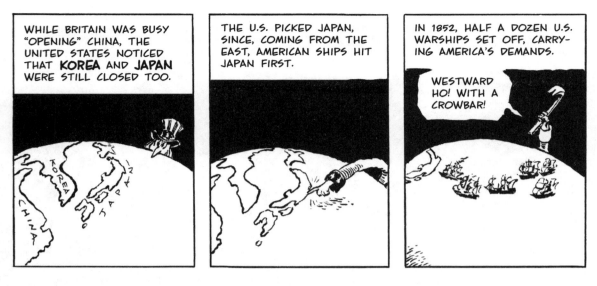

WHILE BRITAIN WAS BUSY "OPENING" CHINA, THE UNITED STATES NOTICED THAT **KOREA** AND **JAPAN** WERE STILL CLOSED TOO.

THE U.S. PICKED JAPAN, SINCE, COMING FROM THE EAST, AMERICAN SHIPS HIT JAPAN FIRST.

IN 1852, HALF A DOZEN U.S. WARSHIPS SET OFF, CARRYING AMERICA'S DEMANDS.

WESTWARD HO! WITH A CROWBAR!

ON JULY 8, 1853, THESE BLACK-HULLED MONSTERS CHUGGED INTO TOKYO BAY.

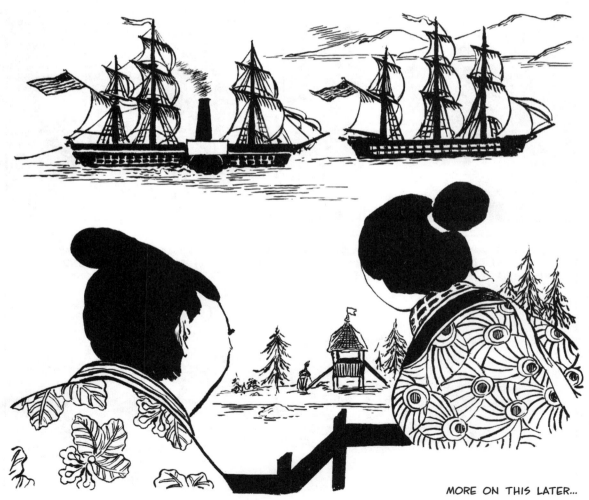

MORE ON THIS LATER...

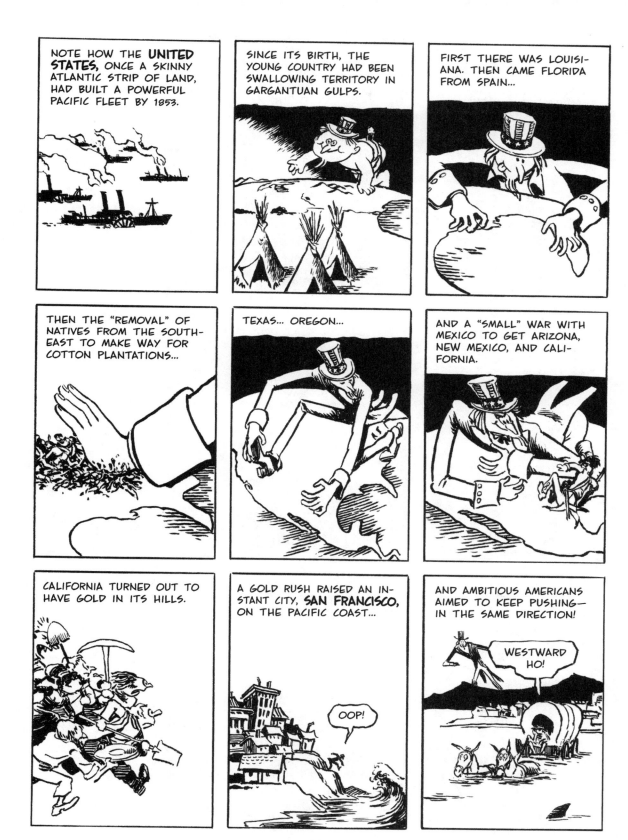

NOTE HOW THE **UNITED STATES**, ONCE A SKINNY ATLANTIC STRIP OF LAND, HAD BUILT A POWERFUL PACIFIC FLEET BY 1853.

SINCE ITS BIRTH, THE YOUNG COUNTRY HAD BEEN SWALLOWING TERRITORY IN GARGANTUAN GULPS.

FIRST THERE WAS LOUISI-ANA. THEN CAME FLORIDA FROM SPAIN...

THEN THE "REMOVAL" OF NATIVES FROM THE SOUTH-EAST TO MAKE WAY FOR COTTON PLANTATIONS...

TEXAS... OREGON...

AND A "SMALL" WAR WITH MEXICO TO GET ARIZONA, NEW MEXICO, AND CALI-FORNIA.

CALIFORNIA TURNED OUT TO HAVE GOLD IN ITS HILLS.

A GOLD RUSH RAISED AN IN-STANT CITY, **SAN FRANCISCO**, ON THE PACIFIC COAST...

OOP!

AND AMBITIOUS AMERICANS AIMED TO KEEP PUSHING— IN THE SAME DIRECTION!

WESTWARD HO!

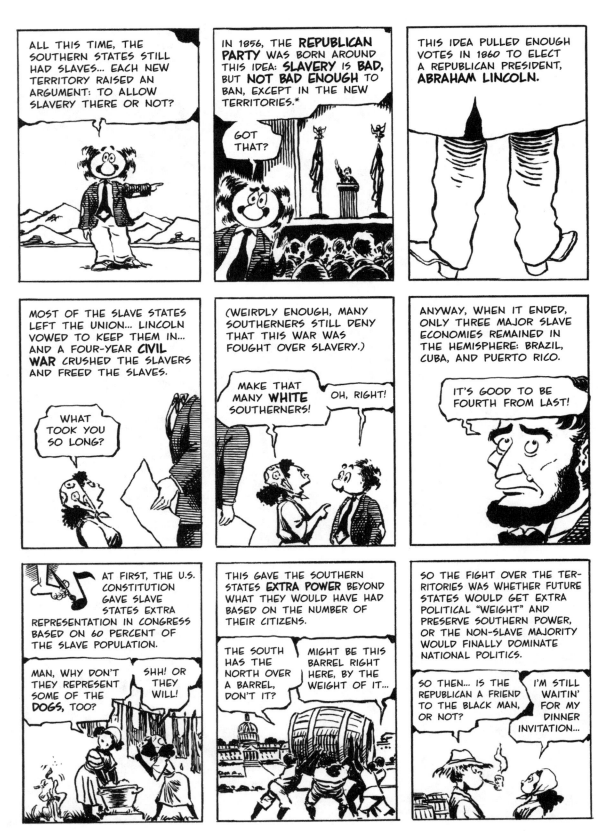

ALL THIS TIME, THE SOUTHERN STATES STILL HAD SLAVES... EACH NEW TERRITORY RAISED AN ARGUMENT: TO ALLOW SLAVERY THERE OR NOT?

IN 1856, THE **REPUBLICAN PARTY** WAS BORN AROUND THIS IDEA: **SLAVERY** IS **BAD**, BUT **NOT BAD ENOUGH** TO BAN, EXCEPT IN THE NEW TERRITORIES.*

GOT THAT?

THIS IDEA PULLED ENOUGH VOTES IN 1860 TO ELECT A REPUBLICAN PRESIDENT, **ABRAHAM LINCOLN.**

MOST OF THE SLAVE STATES LEFT THE UNION... LINCOLN VOWED TO KEEP THEM IN... AND A FOUR-YEAR **CIVIL WAR** CRUSHED THE SLAVERS AND FREED THE SLAVES.

WHAT TOOK YOU SO LONG?

(WEIRDLY ENOUGH, MANY SOUTHERNERS STILL DENY THAT THIS WAR WAS FOUGHT OVER SLAVERY.)

MAKE THAT MANY **WHITE** SOUTHERNERS!

OH, RIGHT!

ANYWAY, WHEN IT ENDED, ONLY THREE MAJOR SLAVE ECONOMIES REMAINED IN THE HEMISPHERE: BRAZIL, CUBA, AND PUERTO RICO.

IT'S GOOD TO BE FOURTH FROM LAST!

AT FIRST, THE U.S. CONSTITUTION GAVE SLAVE STATES EXTRA REPRESENTATION IN CONGRESS BASED ON 60 PERCENT OF THE SLAVE POPULATION.

MAN, WHY DON'T THEY REPRESENT SOME OF THE **DOGS**, TOO?

SHH! OR THEY WILL!

THIS GAVE THE SOUTHERN STATES **EXTRA POWER** BEYOND WHAT THEY WOULD HAVE HAD BASED ON THE NUMBER OF THEIR CITIZENS.

THE SOUTH HAS THE NORTH OVER A BARREL, DON'T IT?

MIGHT BE THIS BARREL RIGHT HERE, BY THE WEIGHT OF IT...

SO THE FIGHT OVER THE TER- RITORIES WAS WHETHER FUTURE STATES WOULD GET EXTRA POLITICAL "WEIGHT" AND PRESERVE SOUTHERN POWER, OR THE NON-SLAVE MAJORITY WOULD FINALLY DOMINATE NATIONAL POLITICS.

SO THEN... IS THE REPUBLICAN A FRIEND TO THE BLACK MAN, OR NOT?

I'M STILL WAITIN' FOR MY DINNER INVITATION...

AFRICA AFTER

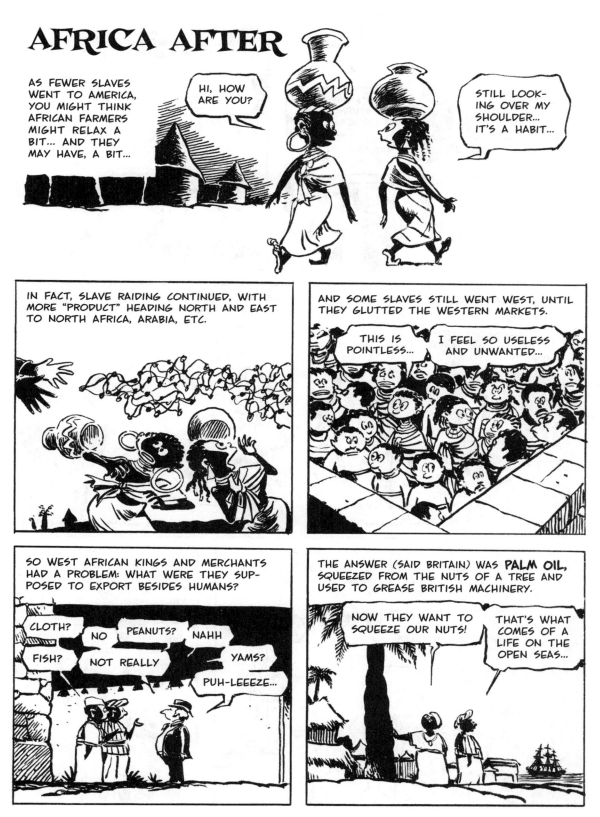

AS FEWER SLAVES WENT TO AMERICA, YOU MIGHT THINK AFRICAN FARMERS MIGHT RELAX A BIT... AND THEY MAY HAVE, A BIT...

HI, HOW ARE YOU?

STILL LOOKING OVER MY SHOULDER... IT'S A HABIT...

IN FACT, SLAVE RAIDING CONTINUED, WITH MORE "PRODUCT" HEADING NORTH AND EAST TO NORTH AFRICA, ARABIA, ETC.

AND SOME SLAVES STILL WENT WEST, UNTIL THEY GLUTTED THE WESTERN MARKETS.

THIS IS POINTLESS...

I FEEL SO USELESS AND UNWANTED...

SO WEST AFRICAN KINGS AND MERCHANTS HAD A PROBLEM: WHAT WERE THEY SUPPOSED TO EXPORT BESIDES HUMANS?

CLOTH? NO PEANUTS? NAHH
FISH? NOT REALLY YAMS?
PUH-LEEEZE...

THE ANSWER (SAID BRITAIN) WAS **PALM OIL**, SQUEEZED FROM THE NUTS OF A TREE AND USED TO GREASE BRITISH MACHINERY.

NOW THEY WANT TO SQUEEZE OUR NUTS!

THAT'S WHAT COMES OF A LIFE ON THE OPEN SEAS...

SO WEST AFRICA HAD TO RETOOL: PLANT PALM GROVES, BUY NUT PRESSES, MAKE NEW JARS AND DEPOTS. (SLAVE PRISONS MAKE LOUSY WAREHOUSES.)
TOO $#*& HARD TO MOVE STUFF IN AND OUT OF HERE!
THAT WAS ON PURPOSE, MY BROTHER...
AND AFTER ALL THAT, YOU HAVE AN OIL JAR, WHICH, UNLIKE A SELF-PROPELLED SLAVE, WILL NOT CARRY ITSELF TO MARKET.
IT... JUST... SITS THERE...
TO MOVE A JAR, YOU HAD TO PUT LEGS UNDER IT.
SO WASTEFUL...
AND WHEN YOU SOLD THE JAR, THE LEGS WERE STILL STANDING THERE!
SIGH...
TRUE, YOU COULD HIRE THE LEGS TO CARRY IMPORTS UP-COUNTRY, BUT THEN YOU HAD TO FEED THE MOUTH AND CLOTHE THE BODY ON TOP OF THE LEGS...
THIS IS **SO** MUCH BETTER THAN THREE MONTHS BELOW-DECKS GETTING PUKED ON!
GROAN...
IN OTHER WORDS, AFRICAN MERCHANTS SPENT MORE AND EARNED LESS THAN THEY USED TO.
WE DO FINE, THOUGH!
NUTS AREN'T THE ONLY THING BEING SQUEEZED HERE...

WITH PROFITS FALLING, CHIEFTAINS MOVED TO SECURE THEIR WEALTH AND STATUS.*

WHEN MARGINS FALL, HONEY, YOU HAVE TO INCREASE YOUR **VOLUME!**

YOU THINK VOLUME'S MY PROBLEM?

THEY INVESTED IN ARMIES OF SLAVES, WHICH THEY SENT TO TAKE LAND FROM THEIR NEIGHBORS.

VOLUME! VOLUME!

THESE WARS, AS WARS WILL, DISRUPTED BUSINESS... AND THE BRITISH, WHO DEPENDED ON A STEADY SUPPLY OF PALM OIL, GROUSED LOUDLY.

STOP!

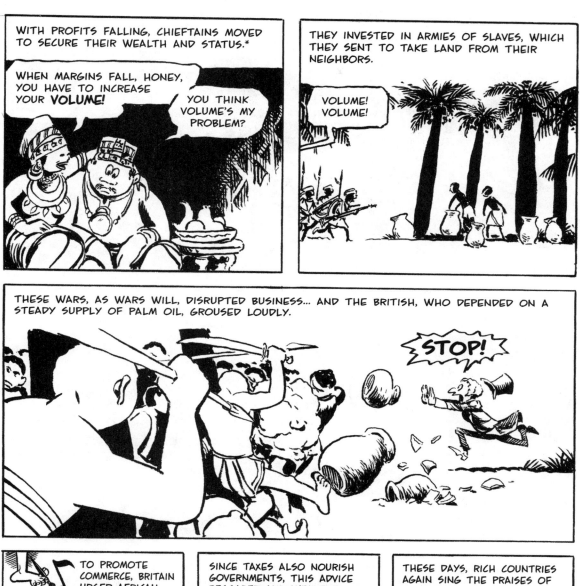

TO PROMOTE COMMERCE, BRITAIN URGED AFRICAN LEADERS NOT TO TAX IMPORTS OR EXPORTS. TAXES, THEY SAID, STIFLE **FREE TRADE.**

OUR ECONOMISTS HAVE WORKED IT ALL OUT MATHEMATICALLY... THE VOLUME OF TRADE WILL INCREASE... EMPLOYMENT WILL RISE... **EVERYONE** BENEFITS, EH? EH? EH?

NO ROOM... TO REPLY...

SINCE TAXES ALSO NOURISH GOVERNMENTS, THIS ADVICE BEGGARED AND WEAKENED THE AFRICAN LEADERS WHO FOLLOWED IT.

OH, BY THE WAY, **I'M** "EVERYONE"!

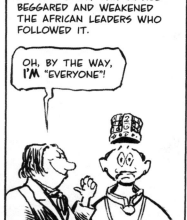

THESE DAYS, RICH COUNTRIES AGAIN SING THE PRAISES OF FREE TRADE.

HALLELUJAH! IT'S A BLEEDIN' MIRACLE!

LIKE STIGMATA?

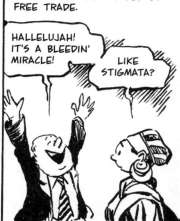

BRITISH MACHINERY NEEDED THAT PALM OIL LUBRICATION...
SQUEE SQUEE SQUEE
WITHOUT IT, BAD THINGS HAPPENED!
CRUNK
(THIS WAS B.P., BEFORE PETROLEUM.)
AS EARLY AS 1821, THE BRITISH INTERVENED IN THE ASHANTI KINGDOM TO KEEP PEACE.
THE SQUEAKING HAS TO STOP!
BY 1830, BRITAIN HAD DECIDED TO TAKE OVER THE TERRITORY, RULE IT DIRECTLY, AND RENAME IT THE GOLD COAST.
NO BEATING AROUND THE BUSH FROM THIS LOT, IS THERE??
FIGHTING STOPPED... PALM OIL FLOWED... AND BRITAIN LIKED WHAT IT SAW.
AN EMPIRE SHOULD RUN LIKE A WELL-OILED MACHINE!
TIP ME SOME MORE LUBRICATION, OLD CHAP...
THE GOVERNMENT WENT FOR MORE OF THIS DIRECT ADMINISTRATION, A CHANGE FROM THE COMPANY-RUN COLONIES OF THE PAST.
CORPORATE RULE IZJUST WRONG... 'NLESS THE COLONY ENDS WITH "Q"...
IN 1857, PARLIAMENT EVEN DUMPED THE EAST INDIA COMPANY AND TOOK CHARGE OF THE BIGGEST COLONY OF ALL...
HEY! BACK TO AFRICA!
SORRY!

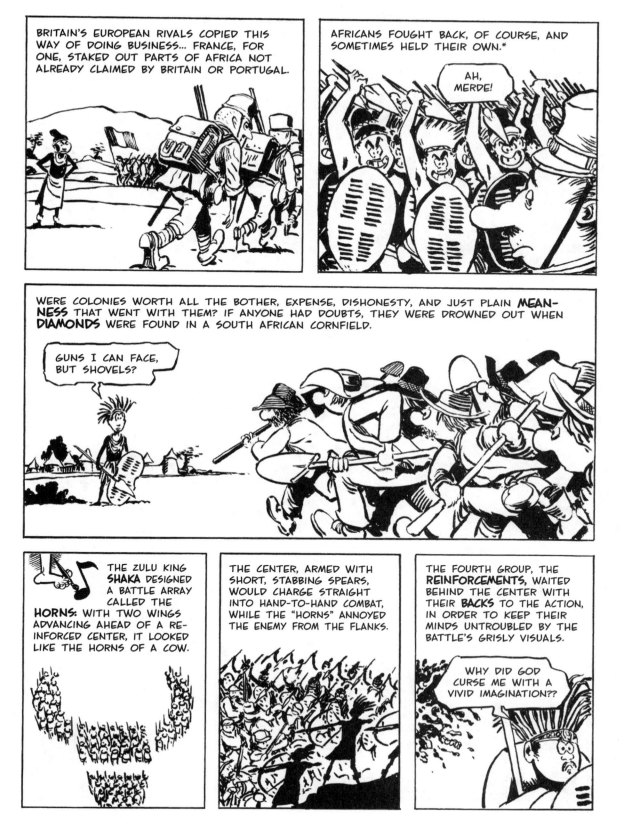

BRITAIN'S EUROPEAN RIVALS COPIED THIS WAY OF DOING BUSINESS... FRANCE, FOR ONE, STAKED OUT PARTS OF AFRICA NOT ALREADY CLAIMED BY BRITAIN OR PORTUGAL.

AFRICANS FOUGHT BACK, OF COURSE, AND SOMETIMES HELD THEIR OWN.*

AH, MERDE!

WERE COLONIES WORTH ALL THE BOTHER, EXPENSE, DISHONESTY, AND JUST PLAIN **MEANNESS** THAT WENT WITH THEM? IF ANYONE HAD DOUBTS, THEY WERE DROWNED OUT WHEN **DIAMONDS** WERE FOUND IN A SOUTH AFRICAN CORNFIELD.

GUNS I CAN FACE, BUT SHOVELS?

THE ZULU KING **SHAKA** DESIGNED A BATTLE ARRAY CALLED THE **HORNS:** WITH TWO WINGS ADVANCING AHEAD OF A REINFORCED CENTER, IT LOOKED LIKE THE HORNS OF A COW.

THE CENTER, ARMED WITH SHORT, STABBING SPEARS, WOULD CHARGE STRAIGHT INTO HAND-TO-HAND COMBAT, WHILE THE "HORNS" ANNOYED THE ENEMY FROM THE FLANKS.

THE FOURTH GROUP, THE **REINFORCEMENTS,** WAITED BEHIND THE CENTER WITH THEIR **BACKS** TO THE ACTION, IN ORDER TO KEEP THEIR MINDS UNTROUBLED BY THE BATTLE'S GRISLY VISUALS.

WHY DID GOD CURSE ME WITH A VIVID IMAGINATION??

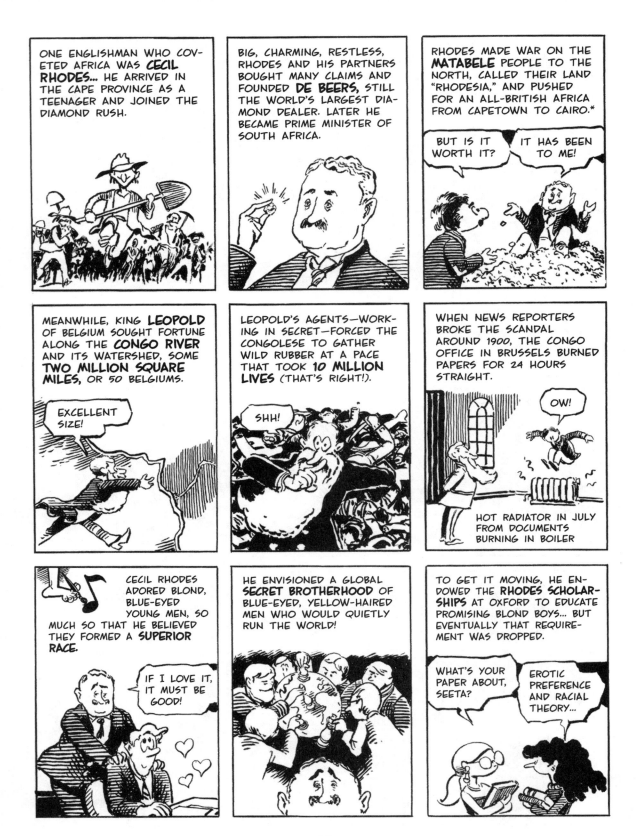

ONE ENGLISHMAN WHO COVETED AFRICA WAS **CECIL RHODES**... HE ARRIVED IN THE CAPE PROVINCE AS A TEENAGER AND JOINED THE DIAMOND RUSH.

BIG, CHARMING, RESTLESS, RHODES AND HIS PARTNERS BOUGHT MANY CLAIMS AND FOUNDED **DE BEERS**, STILL THE WORLD'S LARGEST DIAMOND DEALER. LATER HE BECAME PRIME MINISTER OF SOUTH AFRICA.

RHODES MADE WAR ON THE **MATABELE** PEOPLE TO THE NORTH, CALLED THEIR LAND "RHODESIA," AND PUSHED FOR AN ALL-BRITISH AFRICA FROM CAPETOWN TO CAIRO.*

BUT IS IT WORTH IT?

IT HAS BEEN TO ME!

MEANWHILE, KING **LEOPOLD** OF BELGIUM SOUGHT FORTUNE ALONG THE **CONGO RIVER** AND ITS WATERSHED, SOME **TWO MILLION SQUARE MILES,** OR 50 BELGIUMS.

EXCELLENT SIZE!

LEOPOLD'S AGENTS—WORKING IN SECRET—FORCED THE CONGOLESE TO GATHER WILD RUBBER AT A PACE THAT TOOK **10 MILLION LIVES** (THAT'S RIGHT!).

SHH!

WHEN NEWS REPORTERS BROKE THE SCANDAL AROUND 1900, THE CONGO OFFICE IN BRUSSELS BURNED PAPERS FOR 24 HOURS STRAIGHT.

OW!

HOT RADIATOR IN JULY FROM DOCUMENTS BURNING IN BOILER

CECIL RHODES ADORED BLOND, BLUE-EYED YOUNG MEN, SO MUCH SO THAT HE BELIEVED THEY FORMED A **SUPERIOR RACE.**

IF I LOVE IT, IT MUST BE GOOD!

HE ENVISIONED A GLOBAL **SECRET BROTHERHOOD** OF BLUE-EYED, YELLOW-HAIRED MEN WHO WOULD QUIETLY RUN THE WORLD!

TO GET IT MOVING, HE ENDOWED THE **RHODES SCHOLARSHIPS** AT OXFORD TO EDUCATE PROMISING BLOND BOYS... BUT EVENTUALLY THAT REQUIREMENT WAS DROPPED.

WHAT'S YOUR PAPER ABOUT, SEETA?

EROTIC PREFERENCE AND RACIAL THEORY...

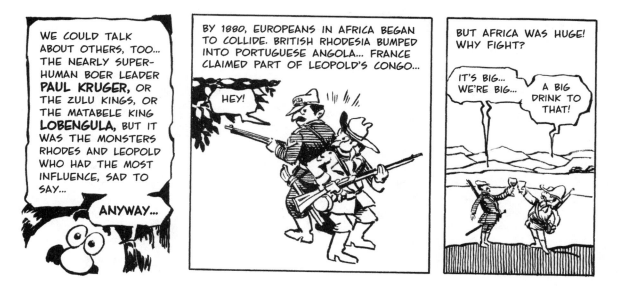

WE COULD TALK ABOUT OTHERS, TOO... THE NEARLY SUPER-HUMAN BOER LEADER **PAUL KRUGER,** OR THE ZULU KINGS, OR THE MATABELE KING **LOBENGULA,** BUT IT WAS THE MONSTERS RHODES AND LEOPOLD WHO HAD THE MOST INFLUENCE, SAD TO SAY...

ANYWAY...

BY 1880, EUROPEANS IN AFRICA BEGAN TO COLLIDE. BRITISH RHODESIA BUMPED INTO PORTUGUESE ANGOLA... FRANCE CLAIMED PART OF LEOPOLD'S CONGO...

HEY!

BUT AFRICA WAS HUGE! WHY FIGHT?

IT'S BIG... WE'RE BIG...

A BIG DRINK TO THAT!

IN 1884, A STELLAR CROWD OF EUROPEAN OFFICIALS, PRINCES, ONE KING (LEOPOLD, NATURALLY), AND ALL THEIR TOTALLY NON-AFRICAN ENTOURAGES MET IN **BERLIN,** GERMANY, TO SETTLE THE "AFRICA QUESTION," WHICH WAS, IN THREE WORDS, WHO GOT WHAT.

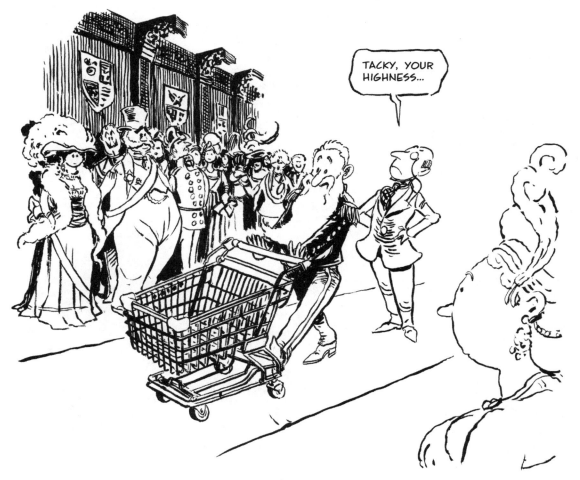

TACKY, YOUR HIGHNESS...

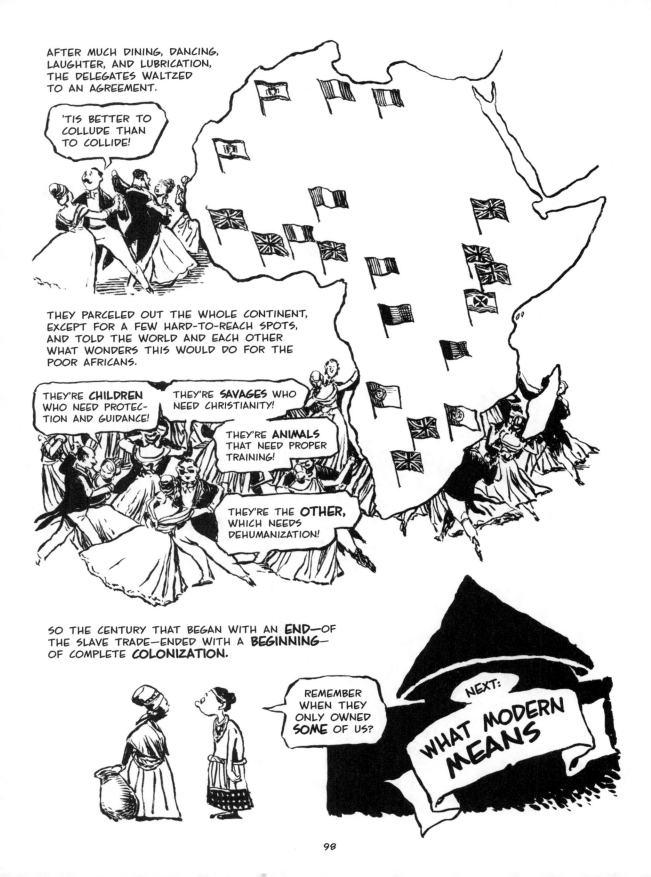

AFTER MUCH DINING, DANCING, LAUGHTER, AND LUBRICATION, THE DELEGATES WALTZED TO AN AGREEMENT.

'TIS BETTER TO COLLUDE THAN TO COLLIDE!

THEY PARCELED OUT THE WHOLE CONTINENT, EXCEPT FOR A FEW HARD-TO-REACH SPOTS, AND TOLD THE WORLD AND EACH OTHER WHAT WONDERS THIS WOULD DO FOR THE POOR AFRICANS.

THEY'RE **CHILDREN** WHO NEED PROTECTION AND GUIDANCE!

THEY'RE **SAVAGES** WHO NEED CHRISTIANITY!

THEY'RE **ANIMALS** THAT NEED PROPER TRAINING!

THEY'RE THE **OTHER**, WHICH NEEDS DEHUMANIZATION!

SO THE CENTURY THAT BEGAN WITH AN **END**—OF THE SLAVE TRADE—ENDED WITH A **BEGINNING**— OF COMPLETE **COLONIZATION**.

REMEMBER WHEN THEY ONLY OWNED **SOME** OF US?

NEXT: WHAT MODERN MEANS

YOU KNOW HOW WHEN YOU REPEAT A WORD OVER AND OVER, IT SEEMS TO LOSE ITS **MEANING** AND SOUND **ABSURD?**
MODERN ISMS
IT'S HAPPENING TO ME WITH "MODERN"... MODERN WORLD, MODERN ART, MODERN SCIENCE, MODERN WARFARE, MODERN MEDICINE, MODERN CAT FOOD...
MODERN MODERN MODRRN MODERN MODERN MODERN MODERN MODRRN MODERN MODERN MODERN MODERN MODERN MODERN MODERN MODERN MODERN... YUP!
MEANING-LESS!
BUT WAIT! DID "MODERN" EVER REALLY MEAN **ANYTHING** TO BEGIN WITH? OR IS IT NOTHING BUT A SYNONYM FOR "NEW"?
WELL, THAT'S EASY... YES, MODERNITY **DOES** HAVE A MEANING! IN THIS VOLUME, WE'LL SEE A NATION GO IN SEARCH OF THAT MEANING—AND **FIND** IT!
MEANING THAT THE MEANING HAS... ER... MEANING... FOR... UM... MEANING... MEANING MEANING MEANING MEANING MEANIN© MEANING MEANING MEANING MEANING MEANING...
OOPS!
JAPAN ETC

THE CARTOON HISTORY OF THE MODERN WORLD

Volume 8

WHAT MODERN MEANS

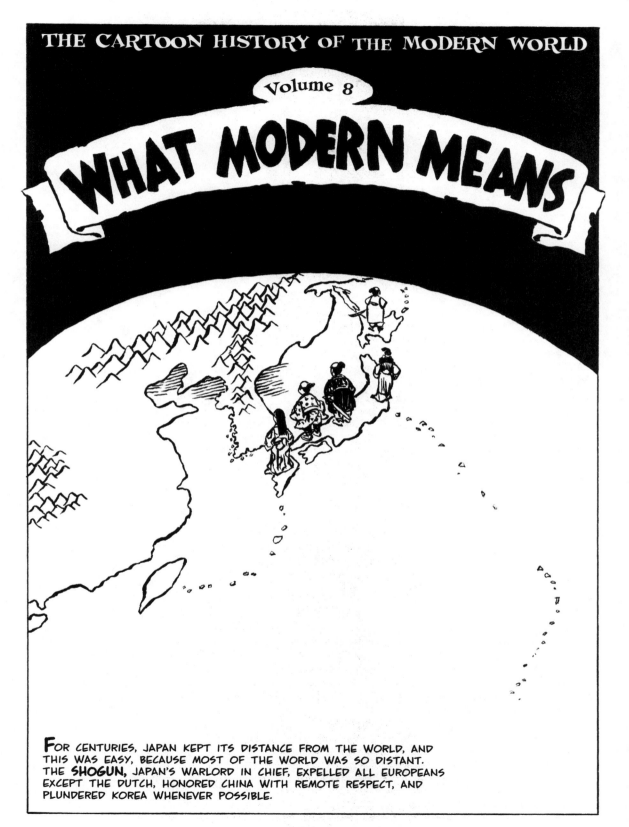

FOR CENTURIES, JAPAN KEPT ITS DISTANCE FROM THE WORLD, AND THIS WAS EASY, BECAUSE MOST OF THE WORLD WAS SO DISTANT. THE **SHOGUN,** JAPAN'S WARLORD IN CHIEF, EXPELLED ALL EUROPEANS EXCEPT THE DUTCH, HONORED CHINA WITH REMOTE RESPECT, AND PLUNDERED KOREA WHENEVER POSSIBLE.

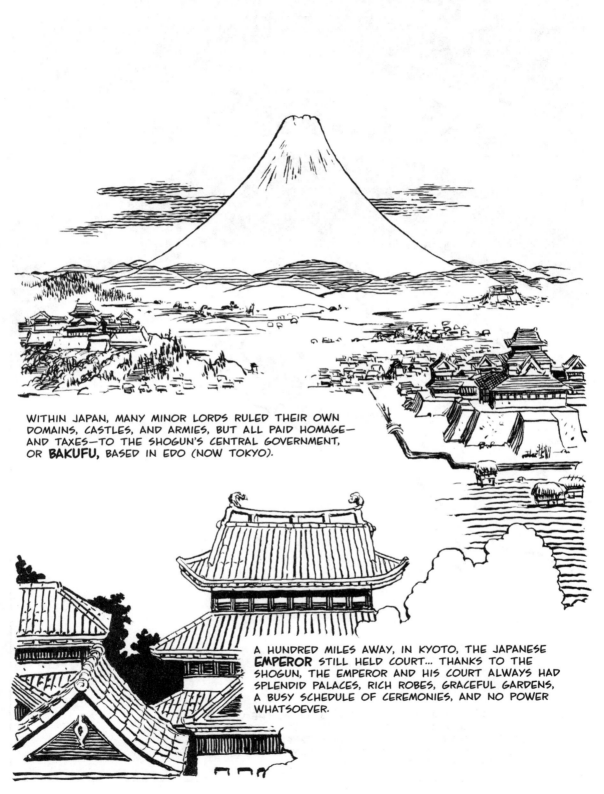

WITHIN JAPAN, MANY MINOR LORDS RULED THEIR OWN DOMAINS, CASTLES, AND ARMIES, BUT ALL PAID HOMAGE— AND TAXES—TO THE SHOGUN'S CENTRAL GOVERNMENT, OR **BAKUFU,** BASED IN EDO (NOW TOKYO).

A HUNDRED MILES AWAY, IN KYOTO, THE JAPANESE **EMPEROR** STILL HELD COURT... THANKS TO THE SHOGUN, THE EMPEROR AND HIS COURT ALWAYS HAD SPLENDID PALACES, RICH ROBES, GRACEFUL GARDENS, A BUSY SCHEDULE OF CEREMONIES, AND NO POWER WHATSOEVER.

FOR 200 YEARS, THIS SYSTEM PROSPERED... IN THIS LONG PEACE, BABIES GREW UP TO MAKE EVEN MORE BABIES, AND BY THE LATE 1700S, THESE MADE QUITE A CROWD... HUNGRY FARMERS RAISED REVOLTS SEVERAL TIMES BUT WITHOUT MUCH SUCCESS*... SO WHEN EUROPEANS AGAIN ARRIVED IN SOME NUMBERS, THE JAPANESE WERE ALREADY A BIT GRUMPY...

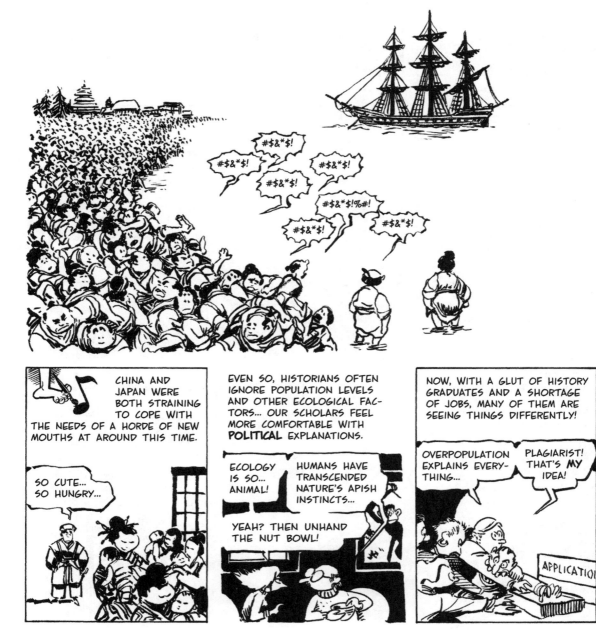

CHINA AND JAPAN WERE BOTH STRAINING TO COPE WITH THE NEEDS OF A HORDE OF NEW MOUTHS AT AROUND THIS TIME.

SO CUTE... SO HUNGRY...

EVEN SO, HISTORIANS OFTEN IGNORE POPULATION LEVELS AND OTHER ECOLOGICAL FAC- TORS... OUR SCHOLARS FEEL MORE COMFORTABLE WITH **POLITICAL** EXPLANATIONS.

ECOLOGY IS SO... ANIMAL!

HUMANS HAVE TRANSCENDED NATURE'S APISH INSTINCTS...

YEAH? THEN UNHAND THE NUT BOWL!

NOW, WITH A GLUT OF HISTORY GRADUATES AND A SHORTAGE OF JOBS, MANY OF THEM ARE SEEING THINGS DIFFERENTLY!

OVERPOPULATION EXPLAINS EVERY- THING...

PLAGIARIST! THAT'S **MY** IDEA!

APPLICATION

AFTER 1800, ALIEN SHIPS SKIRTED JAPANESE SHORES MORE FREQUENTLY.
DON'T LOOK! THEY'RE DEVILS!
IN 1808, SOME HUNGRY BRITS IMPATIENTLY RAIDED NAGASAKI FOR SUPPLIES.
YOU SEE? DEVILS!
AS STEAMSHIPS CAME ON LINE, THE FOREIGNERS REQUIRED FUEL, TOO.
WE'RE HUMAN! WITH NEEDS! JUST LIKE YOU!
COASTAL GOVERNORS BEGGED THE BAKUFU (THE CENTRAL GOVERNMENT) FOR GUIDANCE.
THEY SAY THEY HAVE NEEDS! CAN THIS BE TRUE?
DEVILS HAVE NEEDS TOO.
IN 1811, THE BAKUFU FORMED A COMMITTEE TO STUDY THE WEST—BY READING BOOKS IN CHINESE AND DUTCH(!).
EVEN THOUGH THE STATE TRIED TO KEEP THE WORK **SECRET,** SOME INFORMATION DID LEAK OUT.
SO STRANGE... [redacted] BELIEVE THAT [redacted] AND [redacted] BUT [redacted] SAYS [redacted], DON'T YOU [redacted]?
[redacted]
SOME OF THE STUDENTS SHOWED AN ALARMING TENDENCY TO **ADMIRE** WHAT THEY READ: THE STRANGE IDEA OF **FREEDOM,** FOR EXAMPLE (IN DUTCH).
VREJHEID
VREJHEID
VREJHEID
BUT TALKING ABOUT IT ALWAYS LANDED THEM IN JAIL.
SO... WHAT **IS** VREJHEID?
NOT THIS...

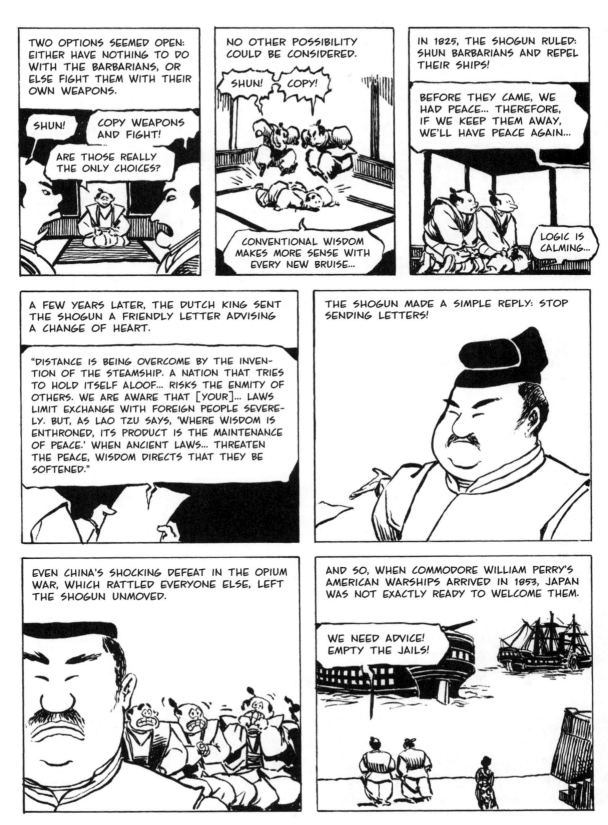

TWO OPTIONS SEEMED OPEN: EITHER HAVE NOTHING TO DO WITH THE BARBARIANS, OR ELSE FIGHT THEM WITH THEIR OWN WEAPONS.

SHUN!

COPY WEAPONS AND FIGHT!

ARE THOSE REALLY THE ONLY CHOICES?

NO OTHER POSSIBILITY COULD BE CONSIDERED.

SHUN! COPY!

CONVENTIONAL WISDOM MAKES MORE SENSE WITH EVERY NEW BRUISE...

IN 1825, THE SHOGUN RULED: SHUN BARBARIANS AND REPEL THEIR SHIPS!

BEFORE THEY CAME, WE HAD PEACE... THEREFORE, IF WE KEEP THEM AWAY, WE'LL HAVE PEACE AGAIN...

LOGIC IS CALMING...

A FEW YEARS LATER, THE DUTCH KING SENT THE SHOGUN A FRIENDLY LETTER ADVISING A CHANGE OF HEART.

"DISTANCE IS BEING OVERCOME BY THE INVENTION OF THE STEAMSHIP. A NATION THAT TRIES TO HOLD ITSELF ALOOF... RISKS THE ENMITY OF OTHERS. WE ARE AWARE THAT [YOUR]... LAWS LIMIT EXCHANGE WITH FOREIGN PEOPLE SEVERELY. BUT, AS LAO TZU SAYS, 'WHERE WISDOM IS ENTHRONED, ITS PRODUCT IS THE MAINTENANCE OF PEACE.' WHEN ANCIENT LAWS... THREATEN THE PEACE, WISDOM DIRECTS THAT THEY BE SOFTENED."

THE SHOGUN MADE A SIMPLE REPLY: STOP SENDING LETTERS!

EVEN CHINA'S SHOCKING DEFEAT IN THE OPIUM WAR, WHICH RATTLED EVERYONE ELSE, LEFT THE SHOGUN UNMOVED.

AND SO, WHEN COMMODORE WILLIAM PERRY'S AMERICAN WARSHIPS ARRIVED IN 1853, JAPAN WAS NOT EXACTLY READY TO WELCOME THEM.

WE NEED ADVICE! EMPTY THE JAILS!

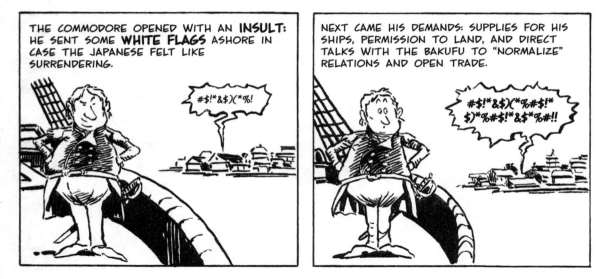

THE COMMODORE OPENED WITH AN **INSULT:** HE SENT SOME **WHITE FLAGS** ASHORE IN CASE THE JAPANESE FELT LIKE SURRENDERING.

#$!*&$)(*%!

NEXT CAME HIS DEMANDS: SUPPLIES FOR HIS SHIPS, PERMISSION TO LAND, AND DIRECT TALKS WITH THE BAKUFU TO "NORMALIZE" RELATIONS AND OPEN TRADE.

#$!*&$)(*%#$!* $)*%#$!*&$*%#!!

BAKUFU OFFICIALS, FROZEN WITH DOUBT, ASKED FOR ADVICE FROM GOVERNORS, WESTERN-STUDY MAJORS FRESH OUT OF JAIL, SCHOOLTEACHERS, ANYONE WITH AN OPINION.

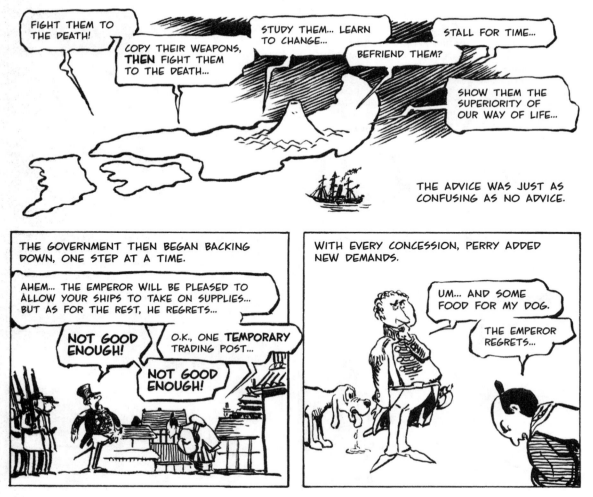

FIGHT THEM TO THE DEATH!

COPY THEIR WEAPONS, **THEN** FIGHT THEM TO THE DEATH...

STUDY THEM... LEARN TO CHANGE...

BEFRIEND THEM?

STALL FOR TIME...

SHOW THEM THE SUPERIORITY OF OUR WAY OF LIFE...

THE ADVICE WAS JUST AS CONFUSING AS NO ADVICE.

THE GOVERNMENT THEN BEGAN BACKING DOWN, ONE STEP AT A TIME.

AHEM... THE EMPEROR WILL BE PLEASED TO ALLOW YOUR SHIPS TO TAKE ON SUPPLIES... BUT AS FOR THE REST, HE REGRETS...

NOT GOOD ENOUGH!

O.K., ONE **TEMPORARY** TRADING POST...

NOT GOOD ENOUGH!

WITH EVERY CONCESSION, PERRY ADDED NEW DEMANDS.

UM... AND SOME FOOD FOR MY DOG.

THE EMPEROR REGRETS...

SO, IN THE END, JAPAN OPENED AS CHINA HAD OPENED: WESTERNERS WOULD TRADE IN CERTAIN PORTS LIGHTLY TAXED, GOVERN THEMSELVES BY THEIR OWN LAWS, AND (OF COURSE) PREACH CHRISTIANITY.

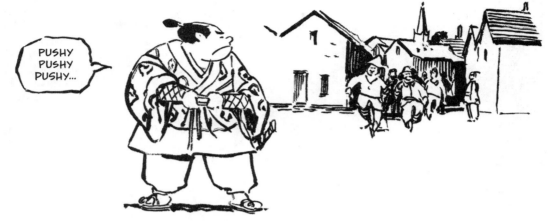

PUSHY PUSHY PUSHY...

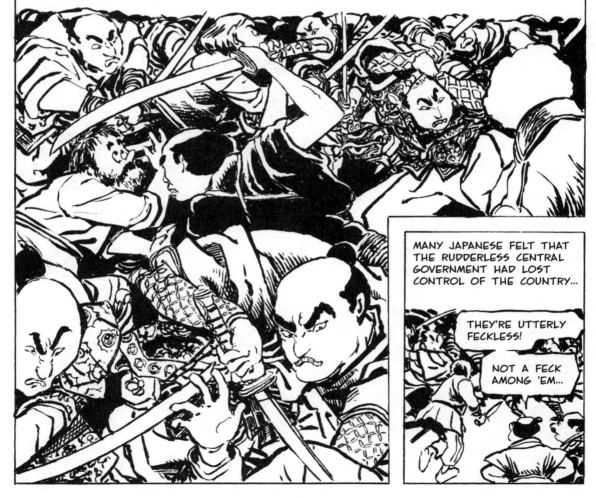

JAPANESE TEMPERS FLARED AT THIS BULLYING... ESPECIALLY AFTER REGULAR SHIPLOADS OF FOREIGNERS BEGAN TO ARRIVE. ONE DOCKSIDE MELÉE KILLED 15 FRENCH SAILORS.

MANY JAPANESE FELT THAT THE RUDDERLESS CENTRAL GOVERNMENT HAD LOST CONTROL OF THE COUNTRY...

THEY'RE UTTERLY FECKLESS!

NOT A FECK AMONG 'EM...

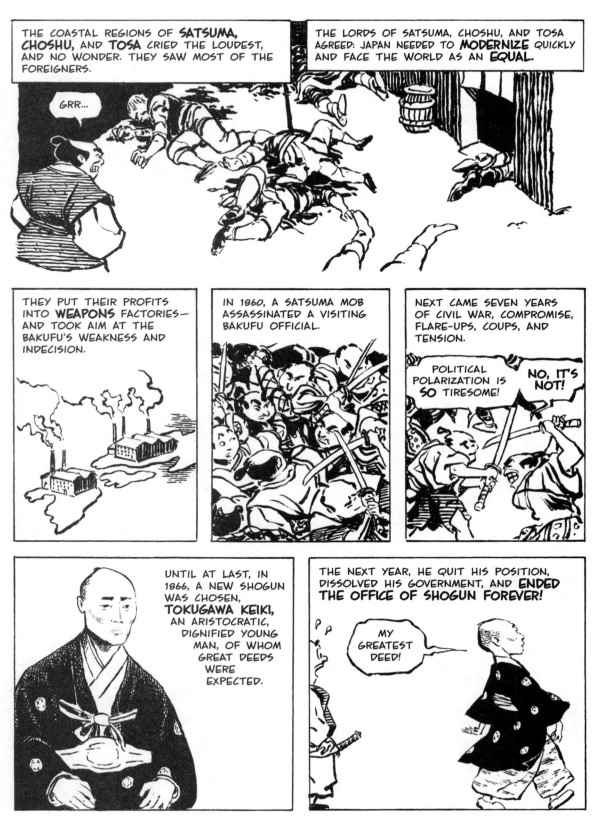

THE COASTAL REGIONS OF **SATSUMA,** **CHOSHU,** AND **TOSA** CRIED THE LOUDEST, AND NO WONDER. THEY SAW MOST OF THE FOREIGNERS.

GRR...

THE LORDS OF SATSUMA, CHOSHU, AND TOSA AGREED: JAPAN NEEDED TO **MODERNIZE** QUICKLY AND FACE THE WORLD AS AN **EQUAL.**

THEY PUT THEIR PROFITS INTO **WEAPONS** FACTORIES— AND TOOK AIM AT THE BAKUFU'S WEAKNESS AND INDECISION.

IN 1860, A SATSUMA MOB ASSASSINATED A VISITING BAKUFU OFFICIAL.

NEXT CAME SEVEN YEARS OF CIVIL WAR, COMPROMISE, FLARE-UPS, COUPS, AND TENSION.

POLITICAL POLARIZATION IS **SO** TIRESOME!

NO, IT'S NOT!

UNTIL AT LAST, IN 1866, A NEW SHOGUN WAS CHOSEN, **TOKUGAWA KEIKI,** AN ARISTOCRATIC, DIGNIFIED YOUNG MAN, OF WHOM GREAT DEEDS WERE EXPECTED.

THE NEXT YEAR, HE QUIT HIS POSITION, DISSOLVED HIS GOVERNMENT, AND **ENDED THE OFFICE OF SHOGUN FOREVER!**

MY GREATEST DEED!

WITHOUT A SHOGUN, ONLY THE **EMPEROR** COULD RULE JAPAN, AND TO SHOW OFF THE CHANGE, THE ENTIRE IMPERIAL COURT MOVED FROM KYOTO TO **TOKYO,** THE SHOGUN'S FORMER HEADQUARTERS. THE PROCESSION, CREEPING FORWARD LIKE AN INCHWORM IN SILKS, LASTED NINE MONTHS.

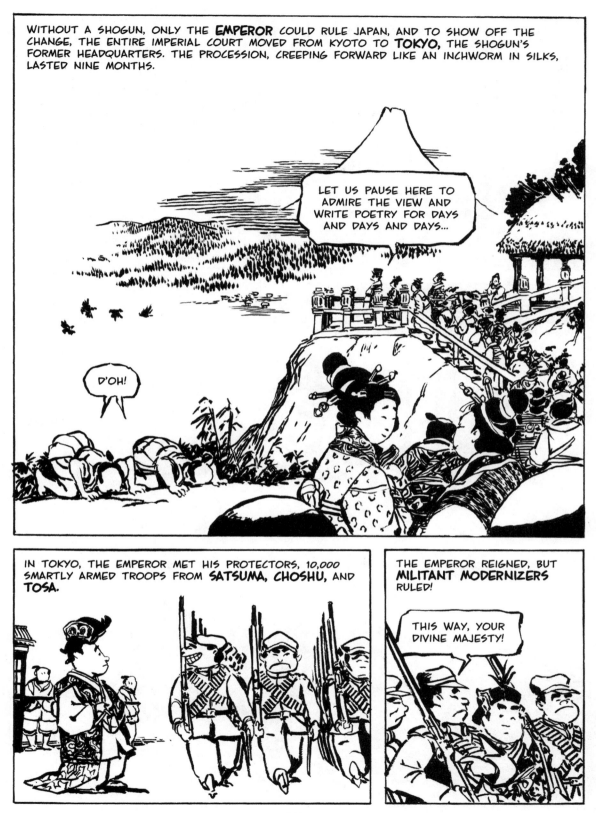

LET US PAUSE HERE TO ADMIRE THE VIEW AND WRITE POETRY FOR DAYS AND DAYS AND DAYS...

D'OH!

IN TOKYO, THE EMPEROR MET HIS PROTECTORS, 10,000 SMARTLY ARMED TROOPS FROM **SATSUMA, CHOSHU,** AND **TOSA.**

THE EMPEROR REIGNED, BUT **MILITANT MODERNIZERS** RULED!

THIS WAY, YOUR DIVINE MAJESTY!

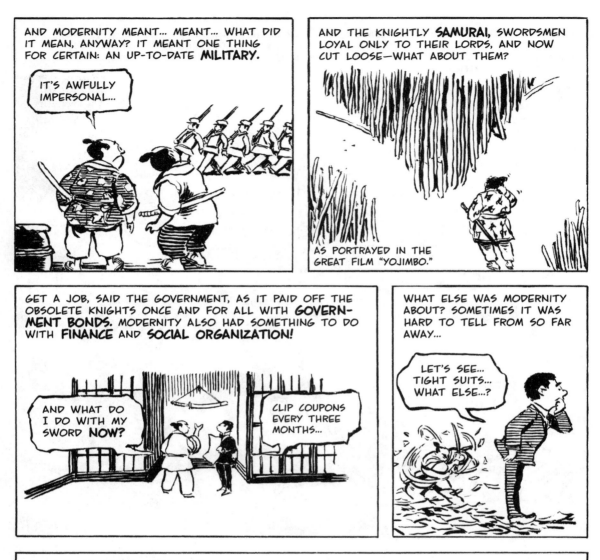

AND MODERNITY MEANT... MEANT... WHAT DID IT MEAN, ANYWAY? IT MEANT ONE THING FOR CERTAIN: AN UP-TO-DATE **MILITARY.**

IT'S AWFULLY IMPERSONAL...

AND THE KNIGHTLY **SAMURAI,** SWORDSMEN LOYAL ONLY TO THEIR LORDS, AND NOW CUT LOOSE—WHAT ABOUT THEM?

AS PORTRAYED IN THE GREAT FILM "YOJIMBO."

GET A JOB, SAID THE GOVERNMENT, AS IT PAID OFF THE OBSOLETE KNIGHTS ONCE AND FOR ALL WITH **GOVERNMENT BONDS.** MODERNITY ALSO HAD SOMETHING TO DO WITH **FINANCE** AND **SOCIAL ORGANIZATION!**

AND WHAT DO I DO WITH MY SWORD **NOW?**

CLIP COUPONS EVERY THREE MONTHS...

WHAT ELSE WAS MODERNITY ABOUT? SOMETIMES IT WAS HARD TO TELL FROM SO FAR AWAY...

LET'S SEE... TIGHT SUITS... WHAT ELSE...?

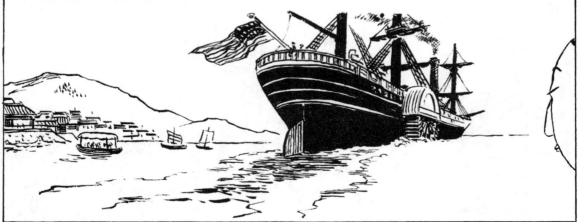

SO THE NEW GOVERNMENT SENT ITS TOP 50 OFFICIALS, PLUS 50 AIDES, AROUND THE WORLD TO SEE HOW IT WORKED!

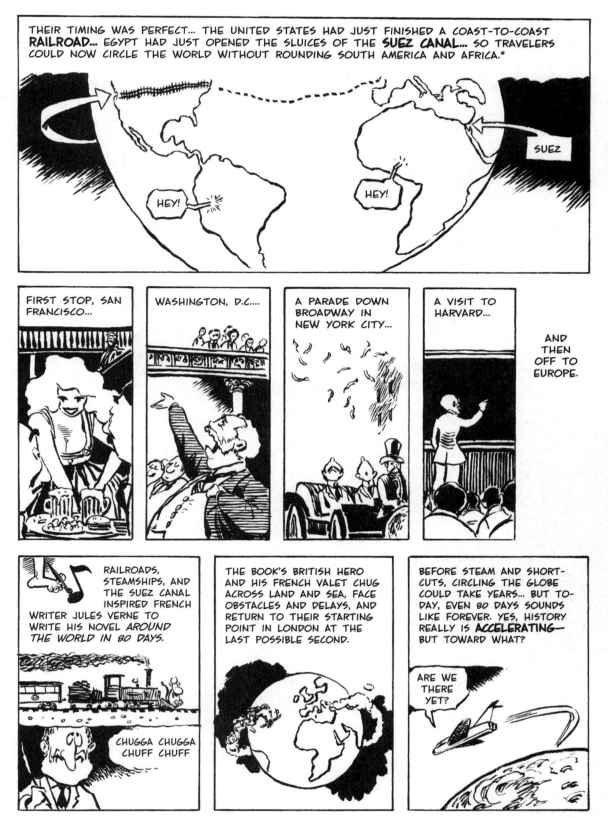

THEIR TIMING WAS PERFECT... THE UNITED STATES HAD JUST FINISHED A COAST-TO-COAST **RAILROAD**... EGYPT HAD JUST OPENED THE SLUICES OF THE **SUEZ CANAL**... SO TRAVELERS COULD NOW CIRCLE THE WORLD WITHOUT ROUNDING SOUTH AMERICA AND AFRICA.*

SUEZ

HEY!

HEY!

FIRST STOP, SAN FRANCISCO...

WASHINGTON, D.C....

A PARADE DOWN BROADWAY IN NEW YORK CITY...

A VISIT TO HARVARD...

AND THEN OFF TO EUROPE.

RAILROADS, STEAMSHIPS, AND THE SUEZ CANAL INSPIRED FRENCH WRITER JULES VERNE TO WRITE HIS NOVEL *AROUND THE WORLD IN 80 DAYS*.

CHUGGA CHUGGA CHUFF CHUFF

THE BOOK'S BRITISH HERO AND HIS FRENCH VALET CHUG ACROSS LAND AND SEA, FACE OBSTACLES AND DELAYS, AND RETURN TO THEIR STARTING POINT IN LONDON AT THE LAST POSSIBLE SECOND.

BEFORE STEAM AND SHORT-CUTS, CIRCLING THE GLOBE COULD TAKE YEARS... BUT TO-DAY, EVEN 80 DAYS SOUNDS LIKE FOREVER. YES, HISTORY REALLY IS **ACCELERATING**— BUT TOWARD WHAT?

ARE WE THERE YET?

BEFORE FINDING OUT WHAT THE JAPANESE SAW,
LET'S BACK UP THE TIME MACHINE 60 YEARS.

POWER SHIFT

AFTER NAPOLEON'S FALL IN 1815, EUROPE'S GREAT POWERS SOUGHT A WAY TO PREVENT FURTHER WAR. THEY REDREW THE MAP SO THAT STRENGTH AMONG THEM WAS **BALANCED**... NO KINGDOM WOULD BE TEMPTED TO BULLY ANOTHER... AND IF PROBLEMS SHOULD ARISE, AS THEY MUST, THE POWERS SWORE TO WORK **COOPERATIVELY** FOR PEACEFUL SOLUTIONS.

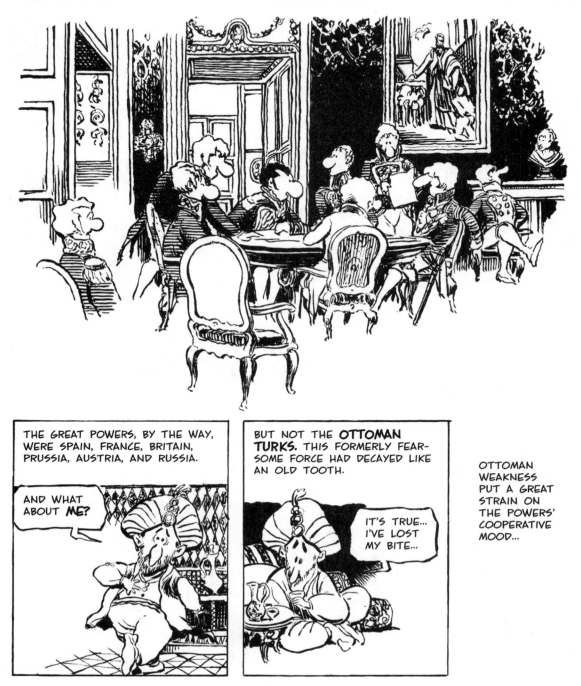

THE GREAT POWERS, BY THE WAY, WERE SPAIN, FRANCE, BRITAIN, PRUSSIA, AUSTRIA, AND RUSSIA.

AND WHAT ABOUT **ME?**

BUT NOT THE **OTTOMAN TURKS.** THIS FORMERLY FEARSOME FORCE HAD DECAYED LIKE AN OLD TOOTH.

IT'S TRUE... I'VE LOST MY BITE...

OTTOMAN WEAKNESS PUT A GREAT STRAIN ON THE POWERS' COOPERATIVE MOOD...

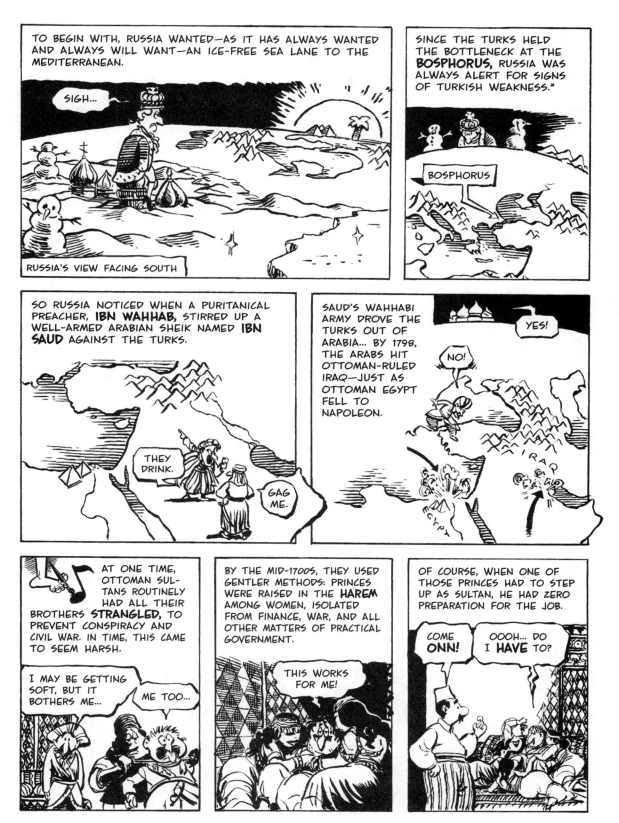

TO BEGIN WITH, RUSSIA WANTED—AS IT HAS ALWAYS WANTED AND ALWAYS WILL WANT—AN ICE-FREE SEA LANE TO THE MEDITERRANEAN.

SIGH...

RUSSIA'S VIEW FACING SOUTH

SINCE THE TURKS HELD THE BOTTLENECK AT THE **BOSPHORUS**, RUSSIA WAS ALWAYS ALERT FOR SIGNS OF TURKISH WEAKNESS.*

BOSPHORUS

SO RUSSIA NOTICED WHEN A PURITANICAL PREACHER, **IBN WAHHAB**, STIRRED UP A WELL-ARMED ARABIAN SHEIK NAMED **IBN SAUD** AGAINST THE TURKS.

THEY DRINK.

GAG ME.

SAUD'S WAHHABI ARMY DROVE THE TURKS OUT OF ARABIA... BY 1798, THE ARABS HIT OTTOMAN-RULED IRAQ—JUST AS OTTOMAN EGYPT FELL TO NAPOLEON.

YES!

NO!

IRAQ

EGYPT

AT ONE TIME, OTTOMAN SULTANS ROUTINELY HAD ALL THEIR BROTHERS **STRANGLED**, TO PREVENT CONSPIRACY AND CIVIL WAR. IN TIME, THIS CAME TO SEEM HARSH.

I MAY BE GETTING SOFT, BUT IT BOTHERS ME...

ME TOO...

BY THE MID-1700S, THEY USED GENTLER METHODS: PRINCES WERE RAISED IN THE **HAREM** AMONG WOMEN, ISOLATED FROM FINANCE, WAR, AND ALL OTHER MATTERS OF PRACTICAL GOVERNMENT.

THIS WORKS FOR ME!

OF COURSE, WHEN ONE OF THOSE PRINCES HAD TO STEP UP AS SULTAN, HE HAD ZERO PREPARATION FOR THE JOB.

COME **ONN!**

OOOH... DO I **HAVE** TO?

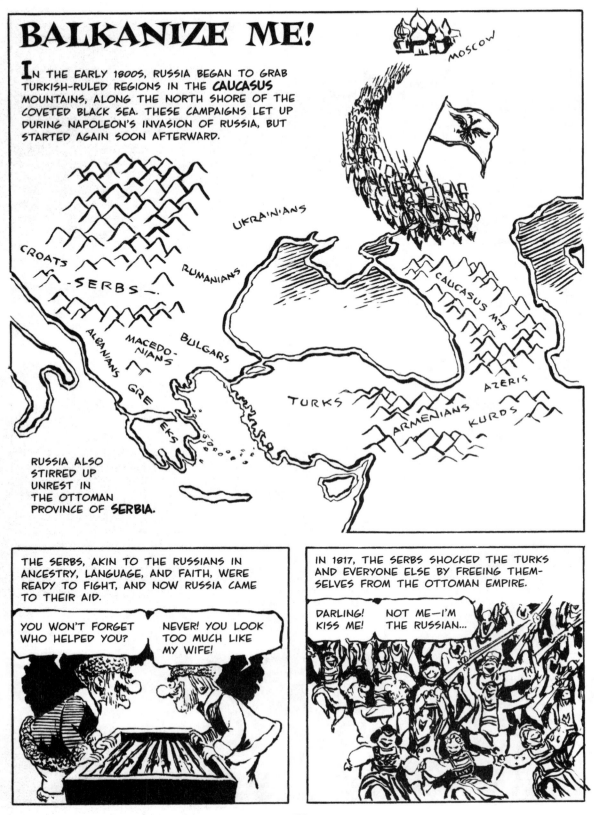

BALKANIZE ME!

IN THE EARLY 1800S, RUSSIA BEGAN TO GRAB TURKISH-RULED REGIONS IN THE **CAUCASUS** MOUNTAINS, ALONG THE NORTH SHORE OF THE COVETED BLACK SEA. THESE CAMPAIGNS LET UP DURING NAPOLEON'S INVASION OF RUSSIA, BUT STARTED AGAIN SOON AFTERWARD.

RUSSIA ALSO STIRRED UP UNREST IN THE OTTOMAN PROVINCE OF **SERBIA.**

THE SERBS, AKIN TO THE RUSSIANS IN ANCESTRY, LANGUAGE, AND FAITH, WERE READY TO FIGHT, AND NOW RUSSIA CAME TO THEIR AID.

> YOU WON'T FORGET WHO HELPED YOU?

> NEVER! YOU LOOK TOO MUCH LIKE MY WIFE!

IN 1817, THE SERBS SHOCKED THE TURKS AND EVERYONE ELSE BY FREEING THEM-SELVES FROM THE OTTOMAN EMPIRE.

> DARLING! KISS ME!

> NOT ME—I'M THE RUSSIAN...

FOUR YEARS LATER, RUSSIAN-SUPPORTED GREEK REBELS BEGAN THEIR OWN REVOLT AGAINST THE TURKS.
IT SET BRITAIN FRETTING TO SEE RUSSIA MUCKING ABOUT ON MEDITERRANEAN SHORES.
RUSSIA BY SEA? BUGGER!
SPEAKING OF WHICH, WE MUST EVER REMEMBER OUR CULTURAL DEBT TO THE ANCIENT GREEKS...
BUT COOPERATION HAD BEEN PROMISED! THE BRITS MUST STAY PALS WITH THE CZAR...
YES, WE'LL BE EVERYBODY'S FRIEND...
HOW WICKEDLY DEVIOUS...
SO BRITAIN "COOPERATED" BY SENDING MASSIVE AID TO THE GREEK REBELS.*
WE ADORE GREECE! YOUR ANCIENT LANGUAGE, YOUR PHILOSOPHY, YOUR MATHEMATICS, YOUR DORMITORY CUSTOMS!
I HAVEN'T FULLY RECOVERED TO THIS DAY...
TWENTY YEARS EARLIER, IN 1801, THE BRITISH AMBASSADOR TO THE OTTOMANS, LORD ELGIN, BEGAN CHOPPING STATUES OFF THE PARTHENON, THE GLORIOUS ATHENIAN TEMPLE, AND SENDING THEM BACK TO ENGLAND.
HEY, I HAVE VAGUELY WRITTEN PERMISSION!
MOVING THIS LARGER-THAN-LIFESIZE LOAD COST ELGIN A FORTUNE... SO HE SOLD THE LOT TO THE BRITISH MUSEUM, WHERE THE STATUES STILL SIT, IRKING THE GREEKS THEN AND NOW.
HOW CAN YOU SELL SOMETHING YOU DON'T OWN?
THE MUSEUM PAID ELGIN FAR LESS THAN HE'D SPENT, AND OUR ART VANDAL TRIED TO RECOUP THE LOSS BY SUING HIS WIFE'S LOVER FOR THE DIFFERENCE.
SORRY TO BOTHER YOU... IT'S FOR THE GREATER GLORY OF ENGLAND...

THE GREEK WAR TURNED LONG AND COMPLEX, WITH MOUNTAIN FIGHTING, NAVAL BATTLES, AND BRITISH ADVISERS, WHO SHOULDERED THE RUSSIANS ASIDE.

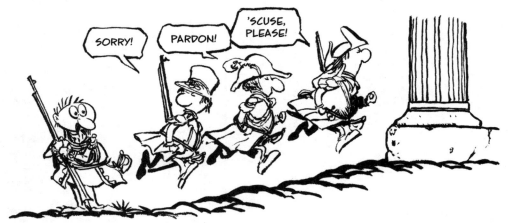

IN THE END, IT PETERED OUT INTO ENDLESS TALKING, WITH GREECE AND THE WESTERNERS ON ONE SIDE OF THE TABLE, THE SULTAN ON THE OTHER, AND RUSSIA STUCK IN THE BACKGROUND.

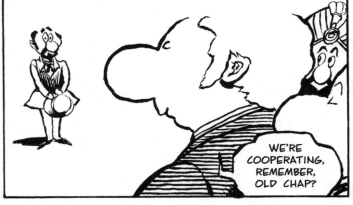

THE POWERS AGREED THEY WOULD RATHER **HOLD THE OTTOMAN EMPIRE TOGETHER** THAN SEE IT TORN APART BY WILD DOGS THAT MIGHT FIGHT EACH OTHER FOR THE SCRAPS.

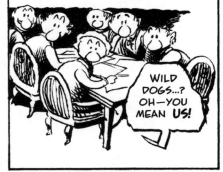

SO, EVEN THOUGH THEY ALL WANTED SOME PIECE OF THE OTTOMAN EMPIRE, THE POWERS VOWED TO PROTECT IT FOR THE SAKE OF PEACE AND "BALANCE."

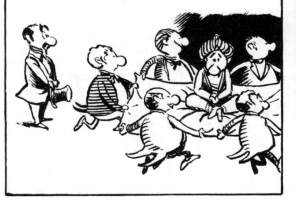

IN RETURN FOR THIS PROTECTION, THE SULTAN GAVE UP GREECE IN 1833.

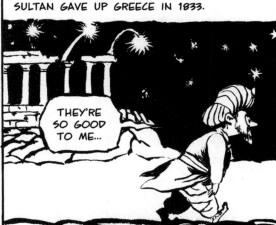

116

TO PUT IT ANOTHER WAY, THE SULTAN WAS LETTING THE POWERS DISMEMBER HIS EMPIRE ONE SLICE AT A TIME—COOPERATIVELY!

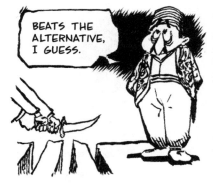

BEATS THE ALTERNATIVE, I GUESS.

JUST TO DRIVE HOME THE POINT, FRANCE SEIZED OTTOMAN ALGERIA IN 1830.

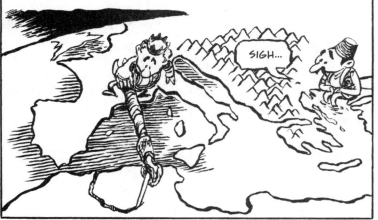

SIGH...

NOW ALL THE EMPIRE'S MINORITIES—CROATS, ALBANIANS, BULGARS, MACEDONIANS, ARMENIANS—DARED TO DREAM OF FREEDOM.

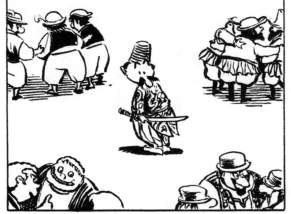

ACTIVISTS BEGAN TO HOLD MEETINGS, WRITE PAMPHLETS, STAGE DEMONSTRATIONS, REVIVE LANGUAGES, OPEN SCHOOLS, DESIGN FLAGS, BLOW UP POLICE STATIONS...

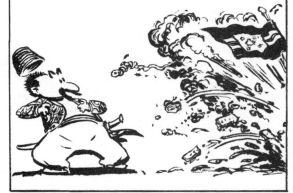

NOT EVERY EUROPEAN POWER WAS THRILLED: HABSBURG **AUSTRIA,** RIGHT NEXT DOOR, ALSO RULED AN ETHNIC GOULASH OF HUNGARIANS, GERMANS, POLES, JEWS, CZECHS, ITALIANS, ETC. WHAT IF THEY CAUGHT THE SAME CRAVING?

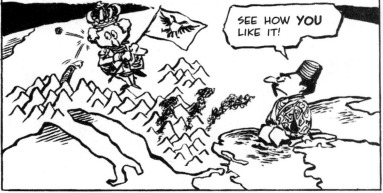

SEE HOW **YOU** LIKE IT!

WHAT IF, FOR EXAMPLE, THE **GERMANS** ALL GOT TOGETHER?

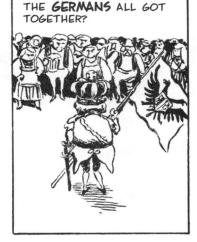

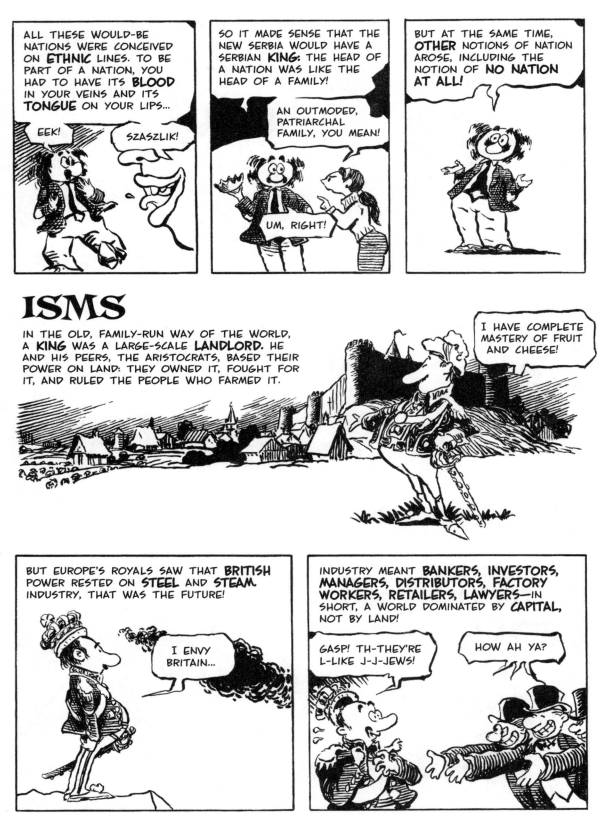

ALL THESE WOULD-BE NATIONS WERE CONCEIVED ON **ETHNIC** LINES. TO BE PART OF A NATION, YOU HAD TO HAVE ITS **BLOOD** IN YOUR VEINS AND ITS **TONGUE** ON YOUR LIPS...

EEK!

SZASZLIK!

SO IT MADE SENSE THAT THE NEW SERBIA WOULD HAVE A SERBIAN **KING:** THE HEAD OF A NATION WAS LIKE THE HEAD OF A FAMILY!

AN OUTMODED, PATRIARCHAL FAMILY, YOU MEAN!

UM, RIGHT!

BUT AT THE SAME TIME, **OTHER** NOTIONS OF NATION AROSE, INCLUDING THE NOTION OF **NO NATION AT ALL!**

ISMS

IN THE OLD, FAMILY-RUN WAY OF THE WORLD, A **KING** WAS A LARGE-SCALE **LANDLORD.** HE AND HIS PEERS, THE ARISTOCRATS, BASED THEIR POWER ON LAND: THEY OWNED IT, FOUGHT FOR IT, AND RULED THE PEOPLE WHO FARMED IT.

I HAVE COMPLETE MASTERY OF FRUIT AND CHEESE!

BUT EUROPE'S ROYALS SAW THAT **BRITISH** POWER RESTED ON **STEEL** AND **STEAM.** INDUSTRY, THAT WAS THE FUTURE!

I ENVY BRITAIN...

INDUSTRY MEANT **BANKERS, INVESTORS, MANAGERS, DISTRIBUTORS, FACTORY WORKERS, RETAILERS, LAWYERS**—IN SHORT, A WORLD DOMINATED BY **CAPITAL,** NOT BY LAND!

GASP! TH-THEY'RE L-LIKE J-J-JEWS!

HOW AH YA?

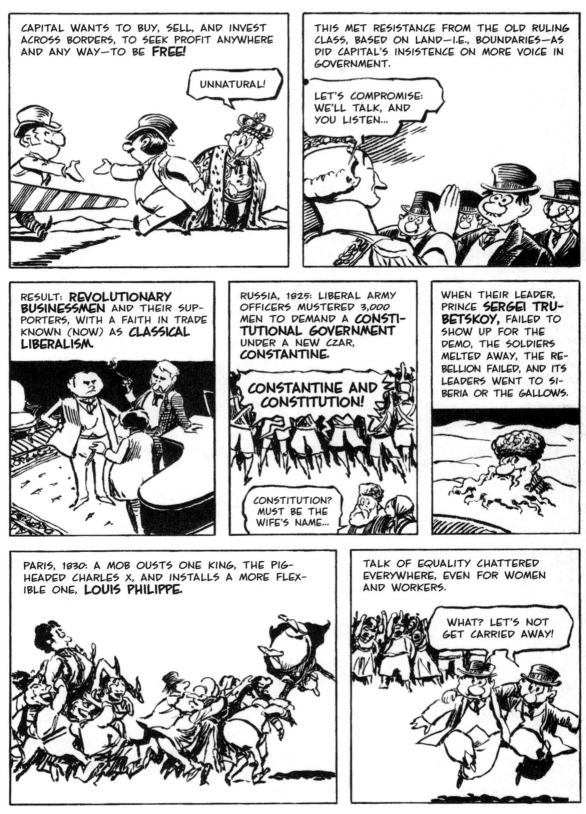

CAPITAL WANTS TO BUY, SELL, AND INVEST ACROSS BORDERS, TO SEEK PROFIT ANYWHERE AND ANY WAY—TO BE **FREE!**

UNNATURAL!

THIS MET RESISTANCE FROM THE OLD RULING CLASS, BASED ON LAND—I.E., BOUNDARIES—AS DID CAPITAL'S INSISTENCE ON MORE VOICE IN GOVERNMENT.

LET'S COMPROMISE: WE'LL TALK, AND YOU LISTEN...

RESULT: **REVOLUTIONARY BUSINESSMEN** AND THEIR SUPPORTERS, WITH A FAITH IN TRADE KNOWN (NOW) AS **CLASSICAL LIBERALISM.**

RUSSIA, 1825: LIBERAL ARMY OFFICERS MUSTERED 3,000 MEN TO DEMAND A **CONSTITUTIONAL GOVERNMENT** UNDER A NEW CZAR, **CONSTANTINE.**

CONSTANTINE AND CONSTITUTION!

CONSTITUTION? MUST BE THE WIFE'S NAME...

WHEN THEIR LEADER, PRINCE **SERGEI TRUBETSKOY,** FAILED TO SHOW UP FOR THE DEMO, THE SOLDIERS MELTED AWAY, THE REBELLION FAILED, AND ITS LEADERS WENT TO SIBERIA OR THE GALLOWS.

PARIS, 1830: A MOB OUSTS ONE KING, THE PIG-HEADED CHARLES X, AND INSTALLS A MORE FLEXIBLE ONE, **LOUIS PHILIPPE.**

TALK OF EQUALITY CHATTERED EVERYWHERE, EVEN FOR WOMEN AND WORKERS.

WHAT? LET'S NOT GET CARRIED AWAY!

UTOPIA NOW! OR LATER'S O.K., TOO...

FREE-MARKET BACKERS OFTEN SAID, AND STILL SAY, THAT **CAPITALISM** BENEFITS **EVERYONE:** HEALTHY BUSINESSES CREATE JOBS, PROMOTE PROSPERITY, AND MAKE THE WORLD A BETTER PLACE, DON'T THEY?

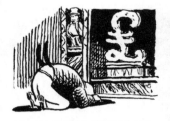

AS INDUSTRY THREW UP MORE SOOT AND MORE SLUMS,* ITS PARTISANS CRIED OUT—FOR EVEN **MORE CAPITALISM!**

GOD, I LOVE THE STENCH OF PROGRESS!

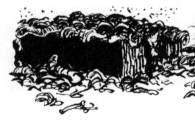

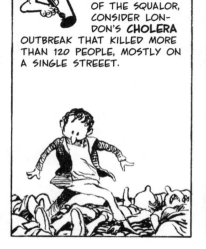

TO GET A SENSE OF THE SQUALOR, CONSIDER LONDON'S **CHOLERA** OUTBREAK THAT KILLED MORE THAN 120 PEOPLE, MOSTLY ON A SINGLE STREEET.

DR. **JOHN SNOW** TRIED TO SLEUTH OUT THE SOURCE BY INTERVIEWING SURVIVORS AND RELATIVES... AND CAME TO SUSPECT A SINGLE **PUBLIC PUMP** FROM WHICH EVERY VICTIM HAD DRUNK.

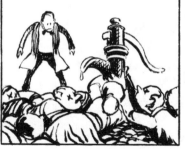

IN NEARBY BUILDINGS, IT TURNED OUT, TENANTS WERE DUMPING THEIR **SEWAGE** INTO **PITS** IN THEIR YARDS, AND THE LIQUID SEEPED INTO THE GROUNDWATER.

THERE'S NO IN-DOOR PLUMBING, AND THE WHOLE CITY REEKS!

REEKING'S AB-NORMAL?

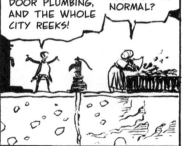

OTHERS BEGGED TO DIFFER, MOST NOTABLY THOSE CRITICS KNOWN AS

SOCIALISTS.

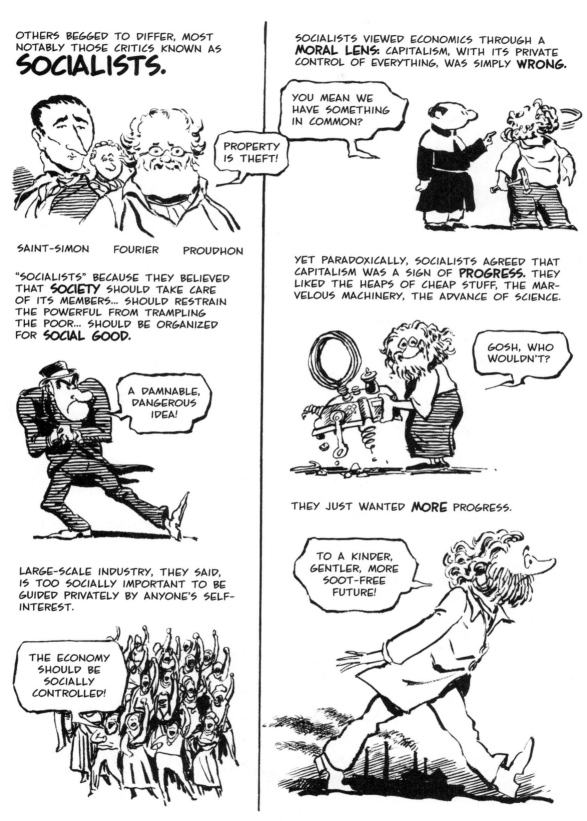

SAINT-SIMON   FOURIER   PROUDHON

PROPERTY IS THEFT!

"SOCIALISTS" BECAUSE THEY BELIEVED THAT **SOCIETY** SHOULD TAKE CARE OF ITS MEMBERS... SHOULD RESTRAIN THE POWERFUL FROM TRAMPLING THE POOR... SHOULD BE ORGANIZED FOR **SOCIAL GOOD.**

A DAMNABLE, DANGEROUS IDEA!

LARGE-SCALE INDUSTRY, THEY SAID, IS TOO SOCIALLY IMPORTANT TO BE GUIDED PRIVATELY BY ANYONE'S SELF-INTEREST.

THE ECONOMY SHOULD BE SOCIALLY CONTROLLED!

SOCIALISTS VIEWED ECONOMICS THROUGH A **MORAL LENS:** CAPITALISM, WITH ITS PRIVATE CONTROL OF EVERYTHING, WAS SIMPLY **WRONG.**

YOU MEAN WE HAVE SOMETHING IN COMMON?

YET PARADOXICALLY, SOCIALISTS AGREED THAT CAPITALISM WAS A SIGN OF **PROGRESS.** THEY LIKED THE HEAPS OF CHEAP STUFF, THE MARVELOUS MACHINERY, THE ADVANCE OF SCIENCE.

GOSH, WHO WOULDN'T?

THEY JUST WANTED **MORE** PROGRESS.

TO A KINDER, GENTLER, MORE SOOT-FREE FUTURE!

BUT HOW TO ACHIEVE IT? WHAT WOULD IT LOOK LIKE? NO ONE SEEMED TO AGREE!*

EVERY BUSINESS SHOULD BE OWNED BY ITS **WORKERS!**
THE **STATE** SHOULD OWN ALL BUSINESSES, AND WORKERS SHOULD RUN THE STATE!
THE STATE ITSELF IS OUTMODED!
OWNERS SHOULD KEEP SOME BUSINESSES, BUT WORKERS SHOULD HAVE A SHARE OF THE MANAGEMENT!
ALL **PRIVATE PROPERTY** SHOULD BE **ABOLISHED!**
ABSOLUTELY NOT! ONLY **MOST** PRIVATE PROPERTY SHOULD BE ABOLISHED!
I OWN THAT IDEA, BY THE WAY...
WORKERS SHOULD BE FREE TO JOIN **UNIONS** AND TO **STRIKE** TO ACHIEVE THEIR DEMANDS!
BUT ONCE THE WORKERS RULE, STRIKES WILL BE ABSURD! HOW CAN WORKERS STRIKE AGAINST **THEMSELVES?**
STUPID! **SOME** PRIVATE PROPERTY SHOULD BE ABOLISHED!
WORKERS SHOULD GET THE **VOTE** AND CHANGE SOCIETY **DEMOCRATICALLY!**
WE SHOULD WORK FOR REFORMS **GRADUALLY!**
ANYONE WHO DISAGREES WITH ME IS AN IDIOT!
DEMOCRACY IS JUST A TOOL OF CAPITAL!
GRADUALISM PERPETUATES OPPRESSION! REVOLUTION **NOW!**
AM NOT!
I HATE MEETINGS...
ARE TOO!
NO YOU DON'T!
EVERYTHING SHOULD BE **SCRAPPED** AND REPLACED WITH A BUNCH OF DIPPY LITTLE COLLECTIVES...

COMBINE ALL THE FLAVORS OF SOCIALISM WITH THE OTHER ISMS IN PLAY, AND ONLY A MATHEMATICIAN COULD LIST ALL THE PERMUTATIONS... THESE INCLUDED: MONARCHIST ETHNIC NATIONALISTS, SOCIALIST ETHNIC NATIONALISTS, SPIRITUALIST SOCIALIST FEMINISTS, ATHEIST CAPITALIST FEMINISTS, DEMOCRATIC SOCIALISTS, DEMOCRATIC LIBERAL NATIONALISTS, SOCIALIST LABOR UNIONISTS, NON-SOCIALIST LABOR UNIONISTS, INTERNATIONALIST CAPITALISTS, NIHILISTS, UTILITARIANS, ANARCHISTS...

AND THEN THERE'S **ME!**

SINCE SOCIALISTS AND OTHER REFORMERS WANTED TO MAKE A NEW SOCIETY LIKE NONE EVER SEEN, MANY OF THEM MADE PLANS FOR **MODEL COMMUNITIES** BASED ON **COOPERATION.**
COMPETITION IS **SO** 18TH CENTURY!

CHARLES FOURIER, FOR INSTANCE, SAID THAT PEOPLE FELL INTO EXACTLY 810 **PERSONALITY TYPES.** IDEALLY, THEN, 1620 PEOPLE—TWO OF EACH TYPE—WOULD LIVE TOGETHER IN A BIG DORM.
MATING WILL BE DONE BASED ON A CARD CATALOG...

MANY EXPERIMENTAL COMMUNES SPRANG UP IN THE EARLY 1800S, BUT FOR SOME REASON, FEW LASTED LONG.
LOOK AT OUR CARDS! WE **HAVE** TO DO IT!
BUT I DON'T **FEEL** LIKE IT...
UNPRINCIPLED CAPITALIST! I QUIT!

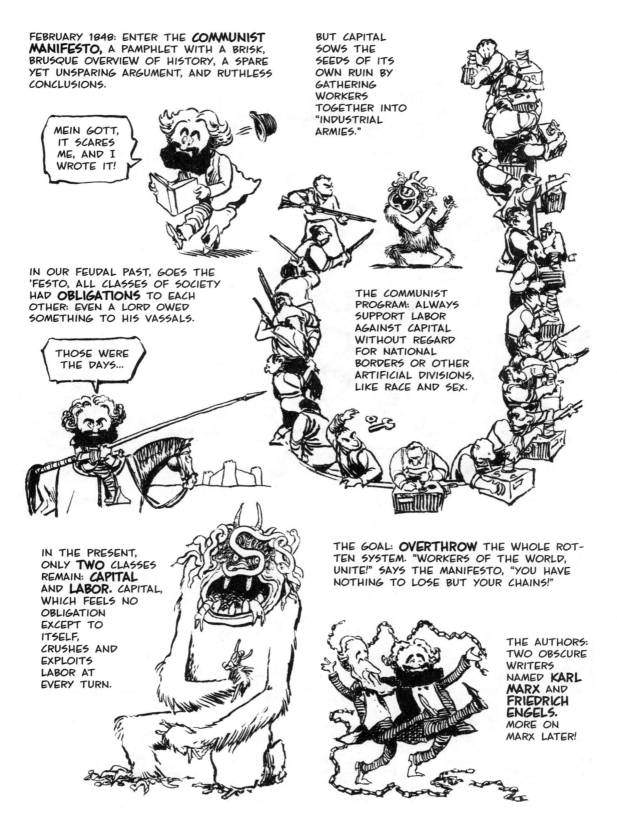

FEBRUARY 1848: ENTER THE **COMMUNIST MANIFESTO,** A PAMPHLET WITH A BRISK, BRUSQUE OVERVIEW OF HISTORY, A SPARE YET UNSPARING ARGUMENT, AND RUTHLESS CONCLUSIONS.

MEIN GOTT, IT SCARES ME, AND I WROTE IT!

IN OUR FEUDAL PAST, GOES THE 'FESTO, ALL CLASSES OF SOCIETY HAD **OBLIGATIONS** TO EACH OTHER: EVEN A LORD OWED SOMETHING TO HIS VASSALS.

THOSE WERE THE DAYS...

BUT CAPITAL SOWS THE SEEDS OF ITS OWN RUIN BY GATHERING WORKERS TOGETHER INTO "INDUSTRIAL ARMIES."

THE COMMUNIST PROGRAM: ALWAYS SUPPORT LABOR AGAINST CAPITAL WITHOUT REGARD FOR NATIONAL BORDERS OR OTHER ARTIFICIAL DIVISIONS, LIKE RACE AND SEX.

IN THE PRESENT, ONLY **TWO** CLASSES REMAIN: **CAPITAL** AND **LABOR.** CAPITAL, WHICH FEELS NO OBLIGATION EXCEPT TO ITSELF, CRUSHES AND EXPLOITS LABOR AT EVERY TURN.

THE GOAL: **OVERTHROW** THE WHOLE ROTTEN SYSTEM. "WORKERS OF THE WORLD, UNITE!" SAYS THE MANIFESTO, "YOU HAVE NOTHING TO LOSE BUT YOUR CHAINS!"

THE AUTHORS: TWO OBSCURE WRITERS NAMED **KARL MARX** AND **FRIEDRICH ENGELS.** MORE ON MARX LATER!

WITHIN DAYS, AS IF ON CUE, REVOLUTIONS ERUPTED ACROSS EUROPE.*

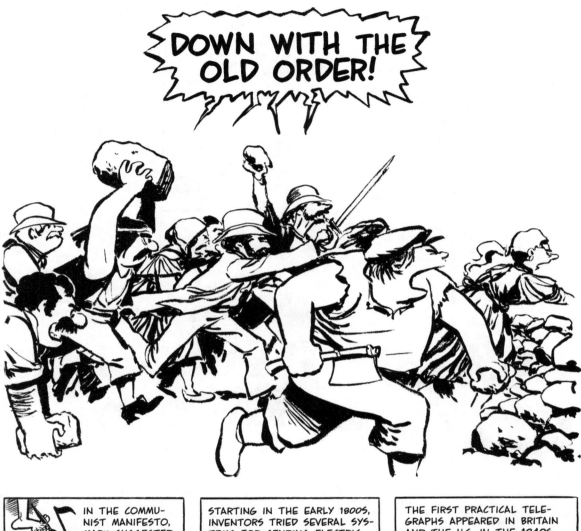

DOWN WITH THE OLD ORDER!

IN THE COMMUNIST MANIFESTO, MARX SUGGESTED THAT THE NEW **ELECTRIC TELEGRAPH** COULD AID REVOLUTIONARIES BY LETTING THEM COORDINATE THEIR ACTIONS.

NOW IF ONLY THERE WERE A MACHINE TO MAKE EVERYONE AGREE WITH ME...

STARTING IN THE EARLY 1800s, INVENTORS TRIED SEVERAL SYSTEMS FOR SENDING ELECTRIC SIGNALS DOWN WIRES.

I RUN 26 WIRES, ONE FOR EACH LETTER, INTO A TUB OF WATER... WHEN BUBBLES APPEAR ON THE **FIRST** WIRE, IT'S AN A, ETC., ETC....

VOT ABOUT UMLAUTS?

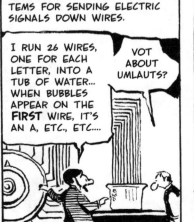

THE FIRST PRACTICAL TELEGRAPHS APPEARED IN BRITAIN AND THE U.S. IN THE 1840s, BUT CONTINENTAL EUROPE STILL HAD ALMOST NOTHING TO USE IN 1848.

SIGH... THE REVOLUTION WILL NOT BE TELEGRAPHED...

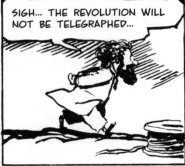

NOT THAT THESE WERE COMMUNIST REVOLUTIONS... NOT AT ALL... EVERY UPRISING HAD ITS OWN LOCAL GOALS: HUNGARIANS, POLES, BOHEMIANS, AND ITALIANS AIMED FOR FREEDOM FROM AUSTRIA... GERMANS WANTED A UNITED GERMANY... THE FRENCH DEMANDED BREAD... NEARLY EVERYONE CALLED FOR **CONSTITUTIONS** AND **ELECTIONS**... BUT COMMUNISM? NOT SO MUCH...

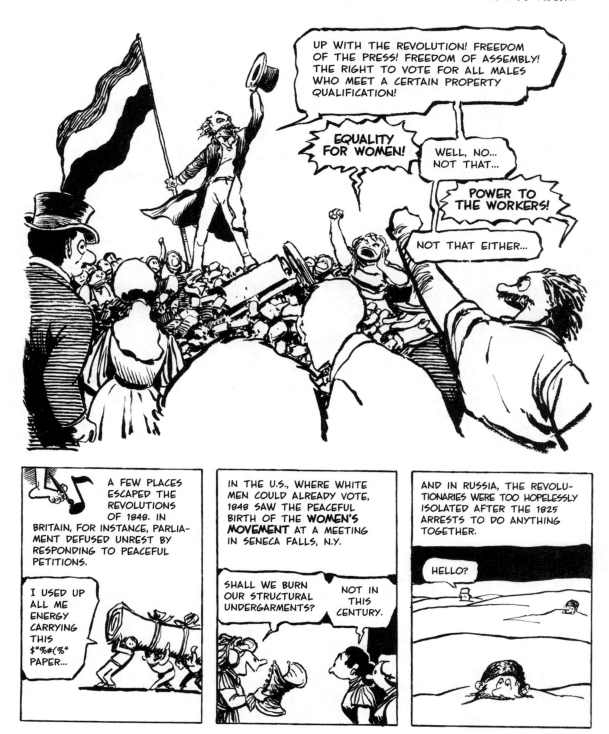

UP WITH THE REVOLUTION! FREEDOM OF THE PRESS! FREEDOM OF ASSEMBLY! THE RIGHT TO VOTE FOR ALL MALES WHO MEET A CERTAIN PROPERTY QUALIFICATION!

EQUALITY FOR WOMEN!

WELL, NO... NOT THAT...

POWER TO THE WORKERS!

NOT THAT EITHER...

A FEW PLACES ESCAPED THE REVOLUTIONS OF 1848. IN BRITAIN, FOR INSTANCE, PARLIAMENT DEFUSED UNREST BY RESPONDING TO PEACEFUL PETITIONS.

I USED UP ALL ME ENERGY CARRYING THIS $*%#(%* PAPER...

IN THE U.S., WHERE WHITE MEN COULD ALREADY VOTE, 1848 SAW THE PEACEFUL BIRTH OF THE **WOMEN'S MOVEMENT** AT A MEETING IN SENECA FALLS, N.Y.

SHALL WE BURN OUR STRUCTURAL UNDERGARMENTS?

NOT IN THIS CENTURY.

AND IN RUSSIA, THE REVOLUTIONARIES WERE TOO HOPELESSLY ISOLATED AFTER THE 1825 ARRESTS TO DO ANYTHING TOGETHER.

HELLO?

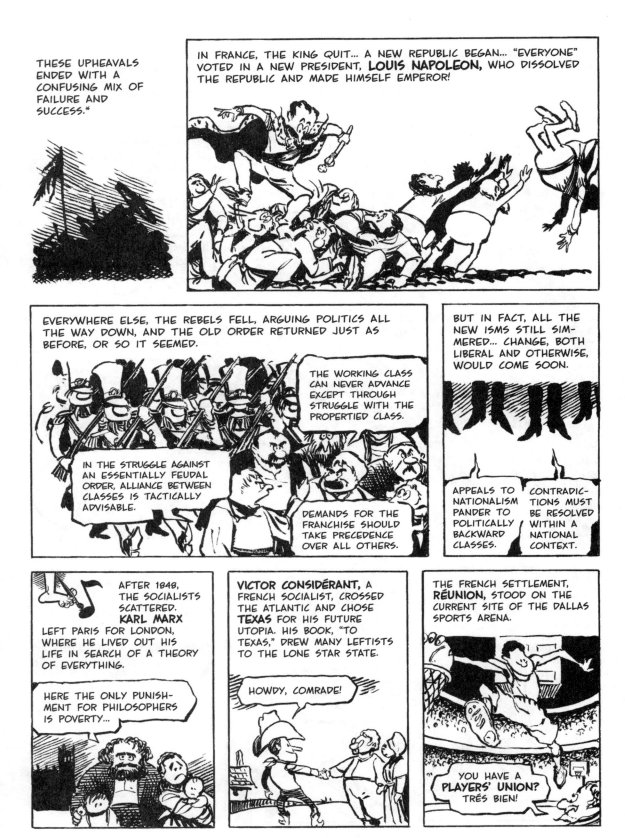

THESE UPHEAVALS ENDED WITH A CONFUSING MIX OF FAILURE AND SUCCESS.*

IN FRANCE, THE KING QUIT... A NEW REPUBLIC BEGAN... "EVERYONE" VOTED IN A NEW PRESIDENT, **LOUIS NAPOLEON,** WHO DISSOLVED THE REPUBLIC AND MADE HIMSELF EMPEROR!

EVERYWHERE ELSE, THE REBELS FELL, ARGUING POLITICS ALL THE WAY DOWN, AND THE OLD ORDER RETURNED JUST AS BEFORE, OR SO IT SEEMED.

THE WORKING CLASS CAN NEVER ADVANCE EXCEPT THROUGH STRUGGLE WITH THE PROPERTIED CLASS.

IN THE STRUGGLE AGAINST AN ESSENTIALLY FEUDAL ORDER, ALLIANCE BETWEEN CLASSES IS TACTICALLY ADVISABLE.

DEMANDS FOR THE FRANCHISE SHOULD TAKE PRECEDENCE OVER ALL OTHERS.

BUT IN FACT, ALL THE NEW ISMS STILL SIMMERED... CHANGE, BOTH LIBERAL AND OTHERWISE, WOULD COME SOON.

APPEALS TO NATIONALISM PANDER TO POLITICALLY BACKWARD CLASSES.

CONTRADICTIONS MUST BE RESOLVED WITHIN A NATIONAL CONTEXT.

AFTER 1848, THE SOCIALISTS SCATTERED. **KARL MARX** LEFT PARIS FOR LONDON, WHERE HE LIVED OUT HIS LIFE IN SEARCH OF A THEORY OF EVERYTHING.

HERE THE ONLY PUNISHMENT FOR PHILOSOPHERS IS POVERTY...

VICTOR CONSIDÉRANT, A FRENCH SOCIALIST, CROSSED THE ATLANTIC AND CHOSE **TEXAS** FOR HIS FUTURE UTOPIA. HIS BOOK, "TO TEXAS," DREW MANY LEFTISTS TO THE LONE STAR STATE.

HOWDY, COMRADE!

THE FRENCH SETTLEMENT, **RÉUNION,** STOOD ON THE CURRENT SITE OF THE DALLAS SPORTS ARENA.

YOU HAVE A **PLAYERS' UNION?** TRÉS BIEN!

RUSSIA, SPARED THE TUMULT OF 1848, TOOK ADVANTAGE BY PRESSING ITS OWN INTERESTS ONCE AGAIN.

B-BUT... WHAT ABOUT CO-OPERATION?

GOOD! FINE! SO COOPERATE WITH ME!

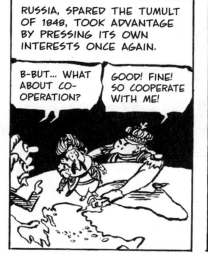

RUSSIA DEMANDED FROM THE TURKISH SULTAN THE RIGHT TO "PROTECT" ORTHODOX CHRISTIANS IN THE OTTOMAN NEAR EAST.

TRANSLATION: YOU WANT TO PUT **SOLDIERS** THERE?

WHENEVER WE LIKE, YOUR PATHETIC, MOTH-EATEN HIGHNESS...

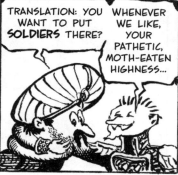

FRANCE'S FEISTY NEW EMPEROR CRIED FOUL... DITTO BRITAIN... AND THE RUSSIANS MARCHED SOUTH, WHICH ALARMED AUSTRIA AND MOBILIZED THE TURKS.

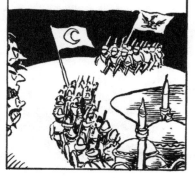

TO HONOR THE SPIRIT OF 1815, THE POWERS AGREED TO TALK, BUT THEIR TALK BROUGHT NO AGREEMENT.

WHY DON'T YOU GO BACK WHERE YOU CAME FROM?

HAVE YOU **SEEN** WHERE I COME FROM?

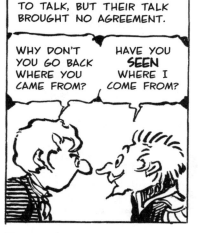

RUSSIANS AND TURKS OPENED FIRE... BRITAIN AND FRANCE DECLARED WAR, WHICH THEY CARRIED TO THE **CRIMEAN PENINSULA,*** ON RUSSIA'S SOUTHERN FLANK.

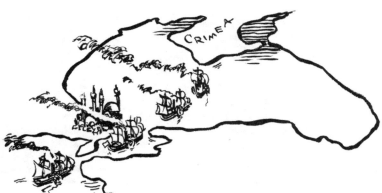

ALONG WITH OLD-FASHIONED CAVALRY TACTICS, THE CRIMEAN WAR ALSO USED MODERN EQUIPMENT LIKE RAILROADS, TELEGRAPHS, AND **STATISTICS.**

STATISTICS?

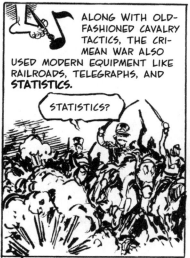

FLORENCE NIGHTINGALE, A BRITISH HOSPITAL NURSE, CAREFULLY TALLIED THE CAUSES OF DEATH—AND DISCOVERED THAT MOST OF THEM CAME FROM **INFECTION** AND **DISEASE,** NOT FROM WOUNDS.

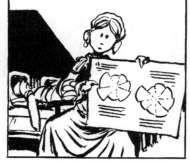

HER NUMBERS PERSUADED THE BRITS THAT A BIT OF SANITATION MIGHT SAVE LIVES, AND GET SOLDIERS BACK INTO BATTLE FASTER AS WELL.

SOAP, OUR SECRET WEAPON!

SHHH! ENEMY EARS ARE EVERYWHERE!

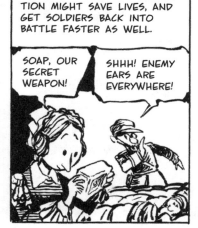

THREE YEARS OF CRIMEAN CARNAGE SEEMED TO END IN A DRAW, AND EVERYONE WENT HOME.

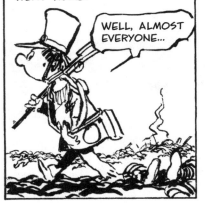

WELL, ALMOST EVERYONE...

ON THE OTHER HAND, RUSSIA HAS NEVER SINCE TRIED TO PUSH PAST TURKEY, SO BRITAIN AND FRANCE MUST HAVE WON... AND IN FACT, FRANCE BECAME THE "PROTECTOR" OF SYRIA AND LEBANON.

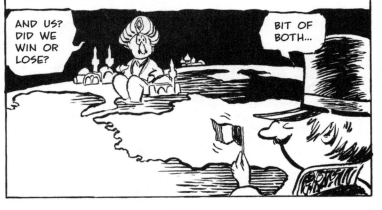

AND US? DID WE WIN OR LOSE?

BIT OF BOTH...

CLEARLY, THE POWERS WERE READY TO FIGHT EACH OTHER AGAIN! SOON FRANCE WAS BACK AT IT, SUPPORTING ITALIAN NATIONALISTS* AGAINST AUSTRIAN RULE.

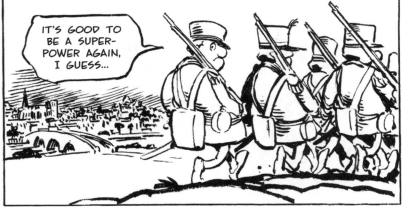

IT'S GOOD TO BE A SUPER-POWER AGAIN, I GUESS...

AND THEN THERE WAS GERMANY...

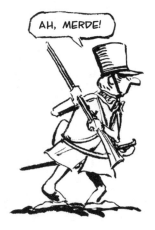

AH, MERDE!

ITALY HAD BEEN DIVIDED FOR AGES, WITH ITS VARIOUS PARTS DOMINATED BY FRANCE, SPAIN, OR AUSTRIA, AND A STRIP ACROSS THE MIDDLE RULED BY THE POPE.

IN THE 1830S, A MOVEMENT FOR UNION AROSE... IN 1848 SERIOUS REVOLTS BROKE OUT.

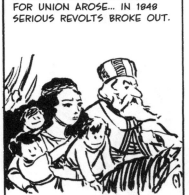

GENERAL GIUSEPPI GARIBALDI AND HIS WIFE, THE PASSIONATE AND TRAGIC BRAZILIAN ANITA RIBEIRO.

FRANCE, WHILE HAPPILY HELPING THE ITALIANS FIGHT AUSTRIA, STILL LIKED ITALY DIVIDED (I.E., WEAKER THAN FRANCE)... SO THE FRENCH ALSO STATIONED TROOPS IN ROME TO GUARD THE **POPE** AND HIS LANDS.

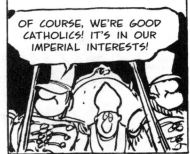

OF COURSE, WE'RE GOOD CATHOLICS! IT'S IN OUR IMPERIAL INTERESTS!

BIRTH OF A NATION

THE 40 GERMAN STATES, SO LONG DIVIDED, SLOWLY MOVED TOWARD UNION... AS EARLY AS 1842, THEY AGREED THAT GOODS COULD MOVE AMONG THE STATES UNTAXED, AND IN THIS "TOLL-FREE ZONE," BUSINESS BOOMED.

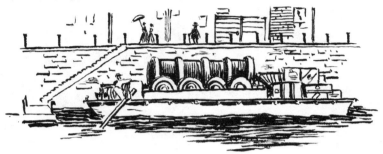

BUSINESS LEADERS WANTED **POLITICAL** UNION, TOO, SO THEY COULD OPERATE UNDER A SINGLE SET OF LAWS.

IT'S ONLY RATIONAL, DON'T YOU SEE? ALL THOSE **THOUSANDS** OF SILLY TRADITIONS YOU HAVE... SUCH AN OBSOLETE **NUISANCE**...

SILLY?

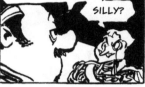

THE NOBILITY BALKED AT SUBMITTING ITSELF TO A CENTRAL GOVERNMENT, ESPECIALLY A LONG-WINDED LIBERAL ONE.

EHMMM... YOU **DO** BELIEVE IN RATIONALITY, DON'T YOU?

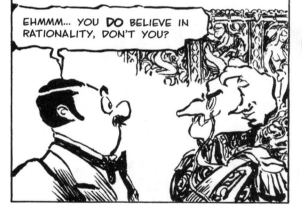

SOMETIME AFTER 1848, ONE PRUSSIAN NOBLEMAN, **OTTO VON BISMARCK,** CHANGED HIS MIND.

LET GERMANY **UNITE,** THOUGHT BISMARCK, AND LET HIS OWN STATE, **PRUSSIA,** WITH ITS ARISTOCRATIC, MILITARY CULTURE, DOMINATE THE UNION!

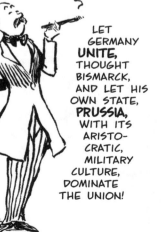

IN 1862, BISMARCK BECAME PRUSSIA'S CHANCELLOR, OR PRIME MINISTER, AND MADE THIS PROMISE TO LIBERALS:

"YOU'RE GOING TO GET EVERYTHING YOU WANT—NOT BY DEBATE AND RESOLUTIONS, BUT BY **IRON** AND **BLOOD!**"

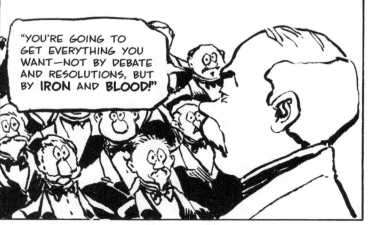

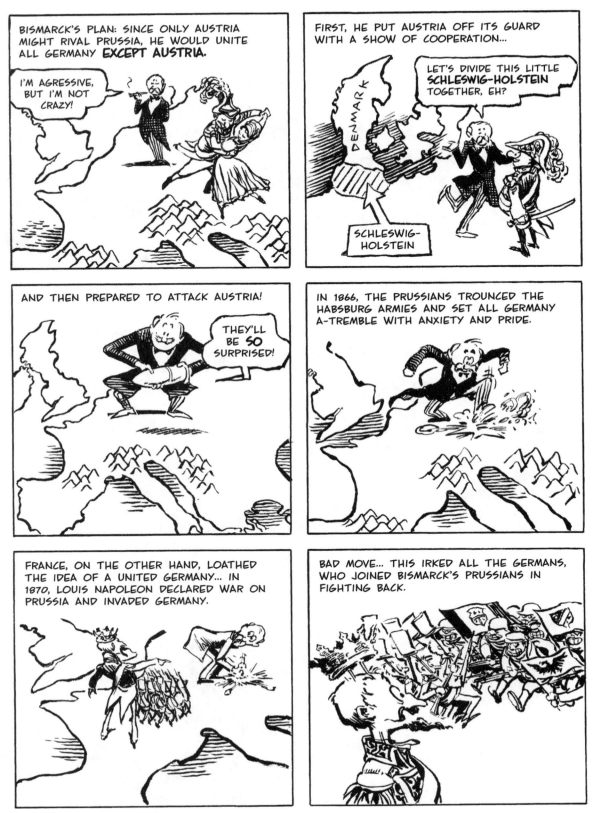

BISMARCK'S PLAN: SINCE ONLY AUSTRIA MIGHT RIVAL PRUSSIA, HE WOULD UNITE ALL GERMANY **EXCEPT AUSTRIA.**

I'M AGRESSIVE, BUT I'M NOT CRAZY!

FIRST, HE PUT AUSTRIA OFF ITS GUARD WITH A SHOW OF COOPERATION...

LET'S DIVIDE THIS LITTLE **SCHLESWIG-HOLSTEIN** TOGETHER, EH?

DENMARK

SCHLESWIG-HOLSTEIN

AND THEN PREPARED TO ATTACK AUSTRIA!

THEY'LL BE **SO** SURPRISED!

IN 1866, THE PRUSSIANS TROUNCED THE HABSBURG ARMIES AND SET ALL GERMANY A-TREMBLE WITH ANXIETY AND PRIDE.

FRANCE, ON THE OTHER HAND, LOATHED THE IDEA OF A UNITED GERMANY... IN 1870, LOUIS NAPOLEON DECLARED WAR ON PRUSSIA AND INVADED GERMANY.

BAD MOVE... THIS IRKED ALL THE GERMANS, WHO JOINED BISMARCK'S PRUSSIANS IN FIGHTING BACK.

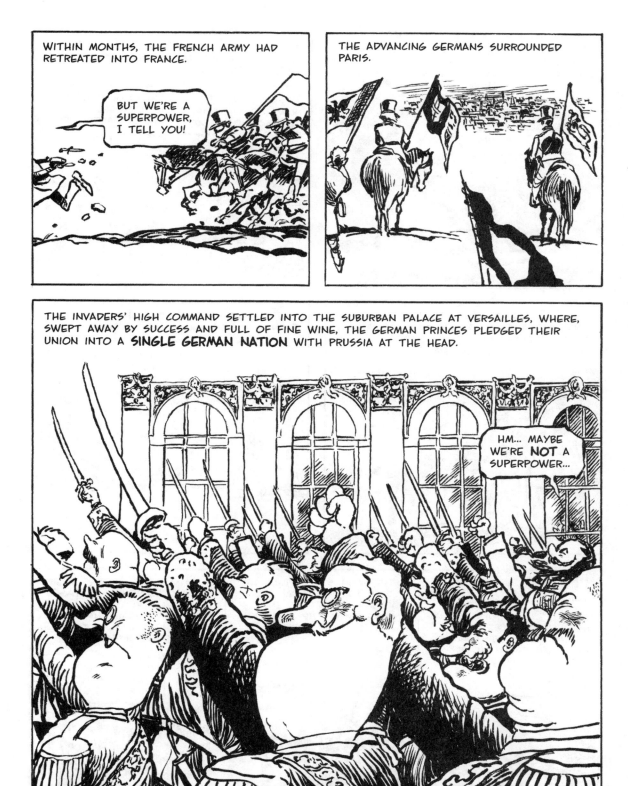

WITHIN MONTHS, THE FRENCH ARMY HAD RETREATED INTO FRANCE.

BUT WE'RE A SUPERPOWER, I TELL YOU!

THE ADVANCING GERMANS SURROUNDED PARIS.

THE INVADERS' HIGH COMMAND SETTLED INTO THE SUBURBAN PALACE AT VERSAILLES, WHERE, SWEPT AWAY BY SUCCESS AND FULL OF FINE WINE, THE GERMAN PRINCES PLEDGED THEIR UNION INTO A **SINGLE GERMAN NATION** WITH PRUSSIA AT THE HEAD.

HM... MAYBE WE'RE **NOT** A SUPERPOWER...

PARIS RESPONDED WITH YET ANOTHER REVOLUTION. UP WENT THE BARRICADES, OUT WENT THE EMPEROR... IN CAME A COMMUNE... AND THEN ANOTHER REPUBLIC.*
IT'S GOOD TO BE BACK IN THE STREETS AGAIN!
BISMARCK LET THE FRENCH DO AS THEY LIKED... HE HAD WHAT HE WANTED: **GERMAN UNION.**
WE'RE A **COMMUNE** NOW, BRO! WHAT ARE **YOU** GON' DO ABOUT IT? EH? EH?
THE SAME THING AS IF YOU WERE A COLONY OF EARTHWORMS.
THE CHANCELLOR WAS SATISFIED TO SET FOOT IN PARIS FOR A FEW MINUTES—AND TO STRIP FRANCE OF TWO BORDER PROVINCES, **ALSACE** AND **LORRAINE.**
YOU REALLY SHOULD FIX THIS PAVEMENT...
THE GERMANS WENT HOME AND LEFT THE FRENCH WONDERING WHAT TO DO NEXT.
?
?
PAINTING HAZY LIGHT... THAT SOUNDS GOOD...
BEFORE THE FRANCO-PRUSSIAN WAR, FRENCH TROOPS IN ROME GUARDED THE POPE (P. 128)... BUT AS THINGS WENT BADLY IN FRANCE, THEY HAD TO HURRY HOME TO HELP OUT.
GOTTA GO!
SORRY!
CIAO!
THE PAPAL STATES THEN LAY OPEN TO THE ITALIAN REBELS, WHO WERE ABLE TO ENTER ROME EASILY AND COMPLETE ITALY'S UNIFICATION.
FINALLY, THE ITALIANS HIRED A PHOTOGRAPHER, **RESTAGED** THE WALK-IN AS A GALLOPING CAVALRY CHARGE, AND SPREAD THE PHOTO AROUND TO INSPIRE THE MASSES.
O.K.! NOW LET'S GET A SNAP OF THE POPE WITH A BIG GRIN!

AT THIS POINT, JUST AFTER THE FRANCO-PRUSSIAN WAR, THE TRAVELING JAPANESE GOVERNMENT CAME TO EUROPE... THEY SAW A NEW GERMANY, A NEW ITALY, EVEN A NEW FRANCE ALL GRAPPLING WITH NEW CONSTITUTIONS... AND ALSO RAILROADS, POSTAL SERVICES, FACTORIES, TELEGRAPHS, NEWSPAPERS... AND THEY **MISSED** SOME THINGS TOO...

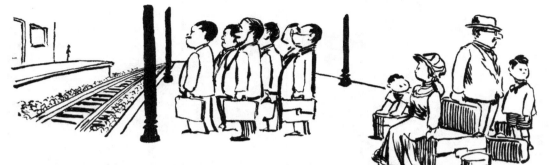

ONE MORE NATION

FOR EXAMPLE, ALMOST NO ONE WOULD HAVE NOTICED THE FAMILY **DREYFUS** OF **ALSACE**, ONE OF THE BORDER PROVINCES ANNEXED BY GERMANY.

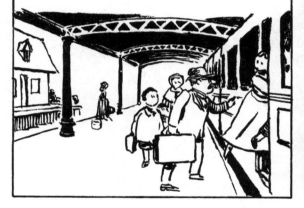

WHEN ALSACE BECAME GERMAN, THIS FRENCH-SPEAKING FAMILY MOVED TO PARIS.

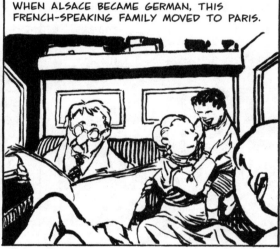

ONE OF THE DREYFUS BOYS, **ALFRED**, GREW UP TO JOIN THE FRENCH ARMY AS AN **INTELLIGENCE OFFICER.**

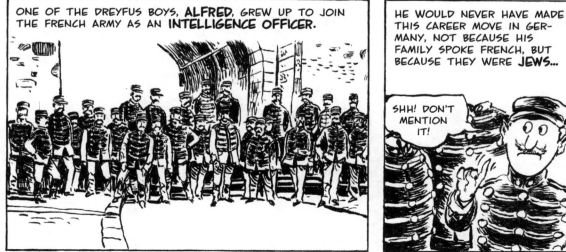

HE WOULD NEVER HAVE MADE THIS CAREER MOVE IN GERMANY, NOT BECAUSE HIS FAMILY SPOKE FRENCH, BUT BECAUSE THEY WERE **JEWS**...

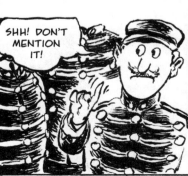

SHH! DON'T MENTION IT!

DURING THE LATE MIDDLE AGES, JEWS HAD FLED MOST EUROPEAN STATES AND TAKEN REFUGE IN **POLAND.**

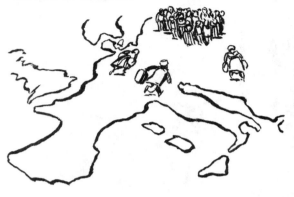

POLISH JEWS LIVED IN MUCH THE SAME WAY AS THEIR POLISH NEIGHBORS, A TRADITIONAL, NARROW, RELIGIOUS LIFE, AND PROUD OF IT.

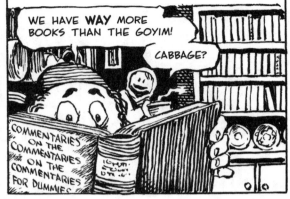

WE HAVE **WAY** MORE BOOKS THAN THE GOYIM!

CABBAGE?

COMMENTARIES ON THE COMMENTARIES ON THE COMMENTARIES FOR DUMMIES

THOSE WHO DID STAY IN THE WEST WERE CONFINED TO GHETTOS AND TREATED AS PERPETUAL OUTSIDERS.

THEY LIKE US SOBER, DOCILE, AND FEW!

THEY LIKE US?

IN THE LATE 1700S, POLAND FELL TO PRUSSIA, RUSSIA, AND AUSTRIA... THEY SPLIT THE KINGDOM AMONG THEMSELVES AND SO ACQUIRED ALL THE POLISH JEWS.

CATHERINE I "THE GREAT"

FREDERICK II "THE GREAT"

MARIA TERESA "NOT SO GREAT"

OY GEVALT!

RUSSIA SHOVED ITS JEWS **BEYOND THE PALE,** I.E., A CERTAIN LINE ON THE MAP, AND GENERALLY OPPRESSED THEM.

SUCH SOFT, FEMININE HANDS...

AUSTRIA, ALTERNATING BETWEEN **ENLIGHTENED** AND **CATHOLIC** RULERS, GAVE JEWS RIGHTS, TOOK THEM AWAY, GAVE, TOOK...

ONLY THE OLDEST SON CAN MARRY!

OUT!

PERMITS PLEASE!

YOU SHOULD HAVE SEEN IT **BEFORE** WE HAD RIGHTS...

PRUSSIA, ON THE OTHER HAND, PROVED MORE PLEASANT, AT LEAST FOR NOW...

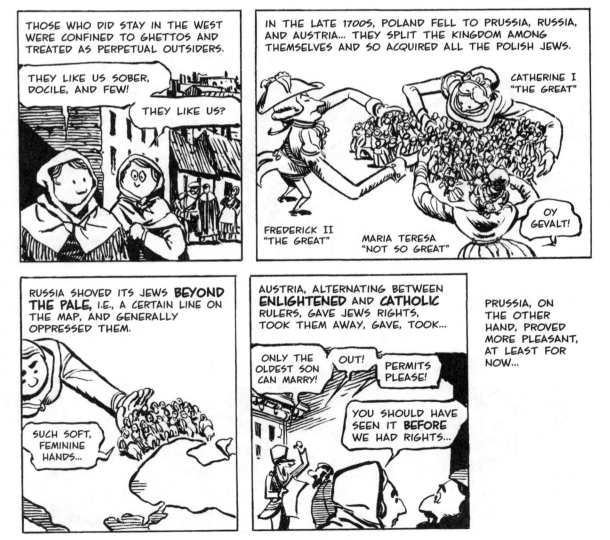

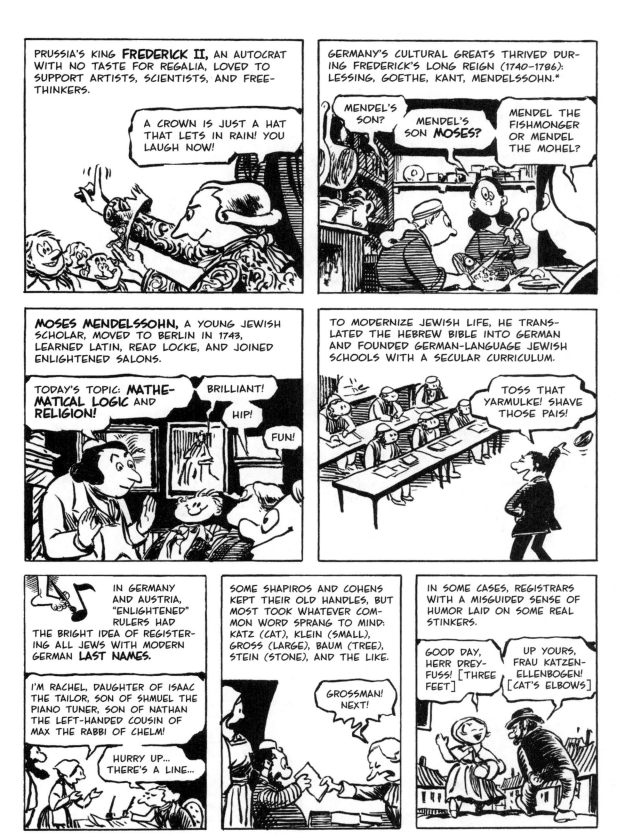

PRUSSIA'S KING **FREDERICK II,** AN AUTOCRAT WITH NO TASTE FOR REGALIA, LOVED TO SUPPORT ARTISTS, SCIENTISTS, AND FREE-THINKERS.

A CROWN IS JUST A HAT THAT LETS IN RAIN! YOU LAUGH NOW!

GERMANY'S CULTURAL GREATS THRIVED DURING FREDERICK'S LONG REIGN (1740–1786): LESSING, GOETHE, KANT, MENDELSSOHN.*

MENDEL'S SON?

MENDEL'S SON **MOSES**?

MENDEL THE FISHMONGER OR MENDEL THE MOHEL?

MOSES MENDELSSOHN, A YOUNG JEWISH SCHOLAR, MOVED TO BERLIN IN 1743, LEARNED LATIN, READ LOCKE, AND JOINED ENLIGHTENED SALONS.

TODAY'S TOPIC: **MATHEMATICAL LOGIC** AND **RELIGION!**

BRILLIANT!

HIP!

FUN!

TO MODERNIZE JEWISH LIFE, HE TRANSLATED THE HEBREW BIBLE INTO GERMAN AND FOUNDED GERMAN-LANGUAGE JEWISH SCHOOLS WITH A SECULAR CURRICULUM.

TOSS THAT YARMULKE! SHAVE THOSE PAIS!

IN GERMANY AND AUSTRIA, "ENLIGHTENED" RULERS HAD THE BRIGHT IDEA OF REGISTERING ALL JEWS WITH MODERN GERMAN **LAST NAMES.**

I'M RACHEL, DAUGHTER OF ISAAC THE TAILOR, SON OF SHMUEL THE PIANO TUNER, SON OF NATHAN THE LEFT-HANDED COUSIN OF MAX THE RABBI OF CHELM!

HURRY UP... THERE'S A LINE...

SOME SHAPIROS AND COHENS KEPT THEIR OLD HANDLES, BUT MOST TOOK WHATEVER COMMON WORD SPRANG TO MIND: KATZ (CAT), KLEIN (SMALL), GROSS (LARGE), BAUM (TREE), STEIN (STONE), AND THE LIKE.

GROSSMAN! NEXT!

IN SOME CASES, REGISTRARS WITH A MISGUIDED SENSE OF HUMOR LAID ON SOME REAL STINKERS.

GOOD DAY, HERR DREY-FUSS! [THREE FEET]

UP YOURS, FRAU KATZEN-ELLENBOGEN! [CAT'S ELBOWS]

MENDELSSOHN'S MODERNIZING MOVEMENT, THE HASKALAH, PUSHED THOUSANDS OF JEWS OUT OF "OUTMODED" CUSTOMS AND INTO THE SECULAR MAINSTREAM.
OY, I HATE TO SEE THEM GO NAKED LIKE THAT!
ABOUT HALF OF THESE MODERNIZERS CONVERTED TO CHRISTIANITY, INCLUDING SEVERAL OF MENDELSSOHN'S OWN KIDS.
MOISHE! WHAT DID YOU START??!!
I-I'M NOT SURE...
A PROTESTANT GRANDSON, FELIX MENDELSSOHN, BECAME GERMANY'S FOREMOST MUSICIAN, WHO REVIVED THE FORGOTTEN CLASSICS OF BACH.
BUT FELIX'S MUSICAL TASTE WAS TOO CONSERVATIVE FOR AT LEAST ONE AVANT-GARDE COMPOSER, RICHARD WAGNER.
RICKY, RICKY, RICKY! RESTRAIN YOUR HISTRIONICS! WE CREATE MUSIC, NOT VIOLENCE!
A LOT YOU KNOW...
IN 1850, WAGNER BLASTED MENDELSSOHN IN AN ESSAY CALLED "JEWISHNESS IN MUSIC."
WAGNER CALLED FOR A NEW, PURELY "GERMAN" MUSIC, WHICH NO JEW COULD EVER WRITE, HE SAID, BECAUSE GERMANNESS AND JEWISHNESS WERE IN THE BLOOD.
MY BLOOD IS BETTER THAN YOUR BLOOD!
OKAYYY...

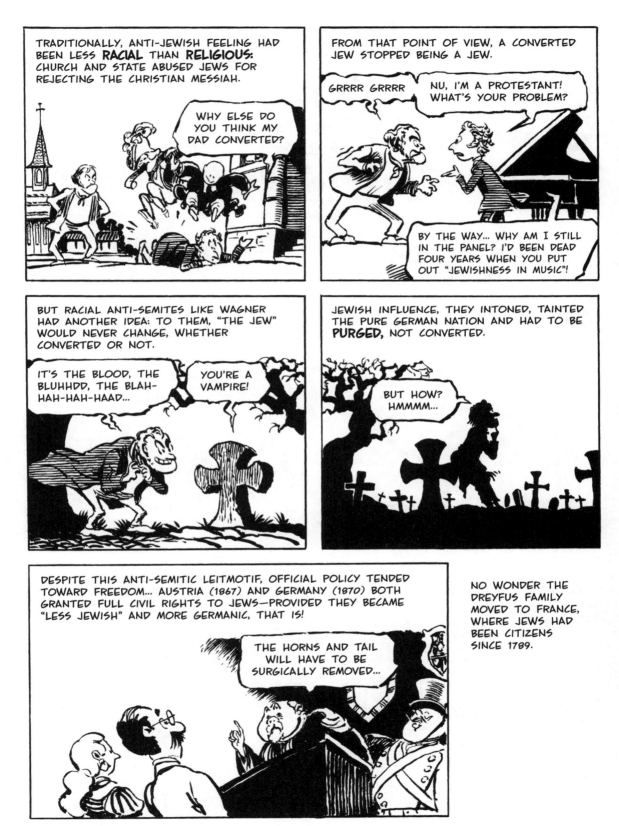

TRADITIONALLY, ANTI-JEWISH FEELING HAD BEEN LESS **RACIAL** THAN **RELIGIOUS:** CHURCH AND STATE ABUSED JEWS FOR REJECTING THE CHRISTIAN MESSIAH.

WHY ELSE DO YOU THINK MY DAD CONVERTED?

FROM THAT POINT OF VIEW, A CONVERTED JEW STOPPED BEING A JEW.

GRRRR GRRRR

NU, I'M A PROTESTANT! WHAT'S YOUR PROBLEM?

BY THE WAY... WHY AM I STILL IN THE PANEL? I'D BEEN DEAD FOUR YEARS WHEN YOU PUT OUT "JEWISHNESS IN MUSIC"!

BUT RACIAL ANTI-SEMITES LIKE WAGNER HAD ANOTHER IDEA: TO THEM, "THE JEW" WOULD NEVER CHANGE, WHETHER CONVERTED OR NOT.

IT'S THE BLOOD, THE BLUHHDD, THE BLAH-HAH-HAH-HAAD...

YOU'RE A VAMPIRE!

JEWISH INFLUENCE, THEY INTONED, TAINTED THE PURE GERMAN NATION AND HAD TO BE **PURGED,** NOT CONVERTED.

BUT HOW? HMMMM...

DESPITE THIS ANTI-SEMITIC LEITMOTIF, OFFICIAL POLICY TENDED TOWARD FREEDOM... AUSTRIA (1867) AND GERMANY (1870) BOTH GRANTED FULL CIVIL RIGHTS TO JEWS—PROVIDED THEY BECAME "LESS JEWISH" AND MORE GERMANIC, THAT IS!

THE HORNS AND TAIL WILL HAVE TO BE SURGICALLY REMOVED...

NO WONDER THE DREYFUS FAMILY MOVED TO FRANCE, WHERE JEWS HAD BEEN CITIZENS SINCE 1789.

FRANCE'S IDEA OF NATIONHOOD WAS BASED ON LANG-UAGE, CULTURE, WINE, AND CHEESE, NOT ETHNICITY.

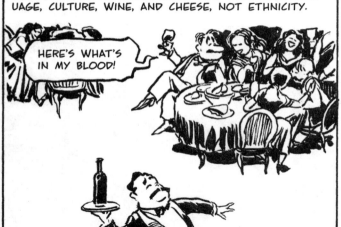

HERE'S WHAT'S IN MY BLOOD!

CAPTAIN DREYFUS MUST HAVE APPRECIATED FRANCE EVEN MORE WHEN LOOKING AT GERMANY IN THE 1880S AND '90S.

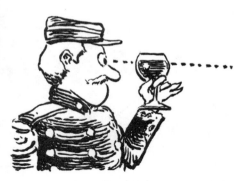

AFTER 1870'S EMANCIPATION, GERMAN JEWS HAD SURGED OUT OF THE STIFLING GHETTOS LIKE ATHLETES ON OXYGEN BOOSTERS.

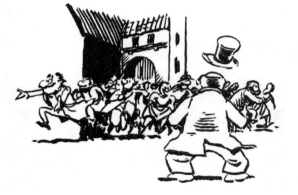

ONLY TWO PERCENT OF THE POPULATION, JEWS SUDDENLY MADE UP AT LEAST TEN PER-CENT OF SCIENCE STUDENTS AND FULLY **ONE THIRD** OF THE SHOPKEEPERS IN GERMANY.

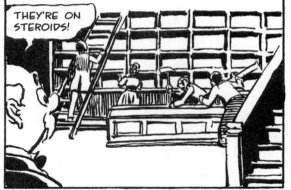

THEY'RE ON STEROIDS!

SOME GERMANS REACTED BY "GOING WAGNERIAN."

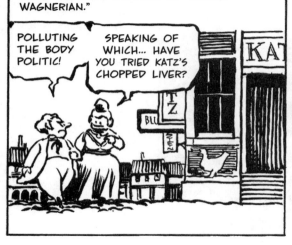

POLLUTING THE BODY POLITIC!

SPEAKING OF WHICH... HAVE YOU TRIED KATZ'S CHOPPED LIVER?

STARTING IN 1877, SEVERAL SMALL POLITI-CAL PARTIES AROSE WITH THE MAIN GOAL OF "ELIMINATING" JEWS FROM GERMANY.

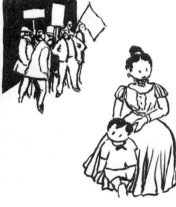

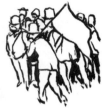

BUT THAT WAS GERMANY... FRANCE WAS—WELL, FRANCE WAS THE COUNTRY WHERE ALFRED DREYFUS WAS **ARRESTED** IN 1894 ON CHARGES OF **SPYING** FOR **GERMANY!**

SECRET DIAGRAMS OF FRENCH WEAPONRY HAD BEEN FOUND IN A GERMAN ATTACHÉ'S WASTEBASKET... SOMEONE SAID THE HANDWRITING LOOKED LIKE DREYFUS'S.

DON'T WORRY, SIS... IT'S ALL A SILLY MISUNDERSTANDING!

WHO DOESN'T UNDERSTAND WHAT, AL?

WITH NO FURTHER EVIDENCE (HE WAS INNOCENT, AFTER ALL), DREYFUS WAS PUT ON TRIAL...

AND WOULD YOU SAY THE J— I MEAN, THE CAPTAIN—EVER ACTED STRANGELY?

WELL, HE **COULD** BE RATHER **STANDOFFISH...**

GASP!!

... CONVICTED, AND SENTENCED TO **10 YEARS** ON **DEVIL'S ISLAND**, A HARSH PENAL ROCK OFF SOUTH AMERICA.

WHAT WAS YOUR CRIME?

HIGH EXPECTATIONS...

139

ONE JEWISH NEWSMAN WHO COVERED THE TRIAL CONCLUDED THAT NO JEW COULD GET A FAIR TRIAL IN CHRISTIAN EUROPE...

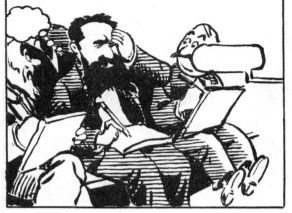

THE REPORTER, **THEODOR HERZL**, SAW ONLY ONE WAY OUT: AN INDEPENDENT **JEWISH STATE**—SO ADD **ZIONISM** TO THE LIST OF ETHNIC NATIONALISMS.

HEY, EVERYONE ELSE HAS ONE!

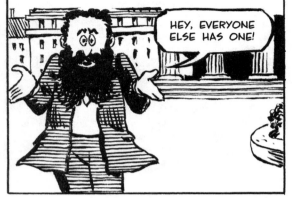

HERZL DEVOTED HIMSELF TO WRITING, TRAVELING, SPEAKING, AND RAISING FUNDS FOR THE CAUSE.

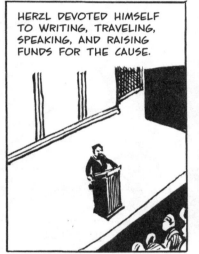

WHERE TO PUT THE NEW ISRAEL? **UGANDA** LOOKED GOOD, FOR A WHILE...

THESE BENIGHTED SAVAGES KNOW NOTHING OF ANTI-SEMITISM...

TAKE MY LAND; I CAN LEARN!

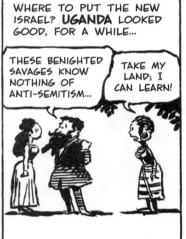

HERZL ASKED THE SULTAN ABOUT USING **PALESTINE**, THEN OTTOMAN-RULED... THE SULTAN SAID:

I'D RATHER BE IMPALED ON AN IRON BAR!

BUT YOU'RE NOT SAYING "NO"?

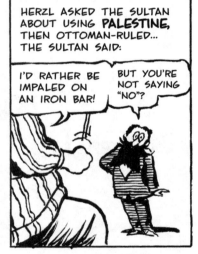

MEANWHILE, IN FRANCE, THE DREYFUS CASE RAISED A RUCKUS... HIS DEFENDERS AND ENEMIES BATTLED IN THE PRESS AND THE STREET... ONE SIDE CALLED FOR JUSTICE... THE OTHER DEFENDED THE ARMY'S "HONOR"...

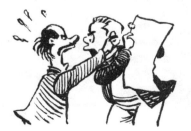

IN 1898, A MAJOR **ESTER-HAZY** ADMITTED WRITING THE ORIGINAL INCRIMINATING PAPER.

I HAD DRINKING AND GAMBLING ADDICTIONS TO SUPPORT... I'M A VICTIM TOO...

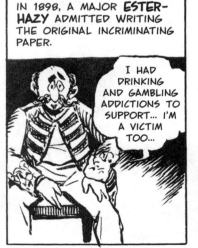

DREYFUS WAS PARDONED, HIS RANK RESTORED... AND SINCE THEN FRANCE HAS HAD 4.25 JEWISH PRESIDENTS... BUT THE ZIONIST MOVEMENT CONTINUED!

PATIENCE!

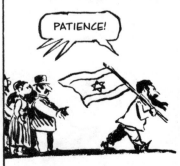

INSTANT MODERNITY

THE TRAVELING JAPANESE GOVERNMENT RETURNED FROM ITS 20-MONTH, ROUND-THE-WORLD JUNKET IN 1873 AND PONDERED ITS LESSONS.

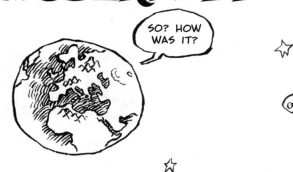

SO? HOW WAS IT?

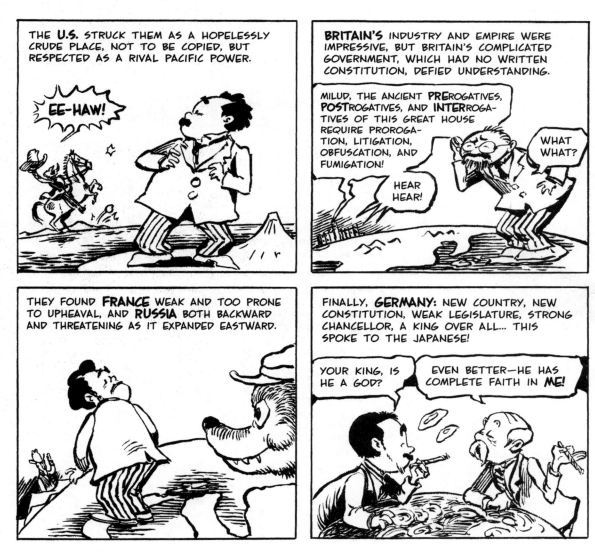

THE **U.S.** STRUCK THEM AS A HOPELESSLY CRUDE PLACE, NOT TO BE COPIED, BUT RESPECTED AS A RIVAL PACIFIC POWER.

EE-HAW!

BRITAIN'S INDUSTRY AND EMPIRE WERE IMPRESSIVE, BUT BRITAIN'S COMPLICATED GOVERNMENT, WHICH HAD NO WRITTEN CONSTITUTION, DEFIED UNDERSTANDING.

MILUD, THE ANCIENT **PRE**ROGATIVES, **POST**ROGATIVES, AND **INTER**ROGATIVES OF THIS GREAT HOUSE REQUIRE PROROGATION, LITIGATION, OBFUSCATION, AND FUMIGATION!

HEAR HEAR!

WHAT WHAT?

THEY FOUND **FRANCE** WEAK AND TOO PRONE TO UPHEAVAL, AND **RUSSIA** BOTH BACKWARD AND THREATENING AS IT EXPANDED EASTWARD.

FINALLY, **GERMANY:** NEW COUNTRY, NEW CONSTITUTION, WEAK LEGISLATURE, STRONG CHANCELLOR, A KING OVER ALL... THIS SPOKE TO THE JAPANESE!

YOUR KING, IS HE A GOD?

EVEN BETTER—HE HAS COMPLETE FAITH IN **ME!**

EDUCATION

SCHOOLS AND PLENTY OF THEM, WITH A CURRICULUM STRONG IN SCIENCE, TECHNOLOGY, AND ENGINEERING, AS WELL AS LITERATURE AND PHILOSOPHY.

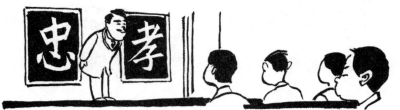

TO SUM UP, THEY CAME HOME WITH THE UNDERSTANDING THAT MODERNITY HAD SEVERAL KEY INGREDIENTS:

INDUSTRY

A MODERN COUNTRY SHOULD PRODUCE AS MUCH OF ITS OWN HIGH-VALUE PRODUCT AS POSSIBLE: STEEL, MACHINERY, TOOLS, BEARINGS, RAIL CARS, ENGINES, SHIPS.

IN TIMES OF CRISIS, DON'T DEPEND ON OTHERS!

COMPLEX TRADE ARRANGEMENTS

THE WEST TALKED UP FREE TRADE, BUT ONLY WITH WEAKER COUNTRIES. MODERN COUNTRIES HAD ALL SORTS OF TAXES, QUOTAS, AND REGULATIONS TO PROTECT THEIR OWN INDUSTRIES FROM FOREIGN COMPETITION.

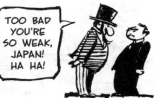

TOO BAD YOU'RE SO WEAK, JAPAN! HA HA!

CONSTITUTIONAL GOVERNMENT

INDUSTRY NEEDED CLEAR, CONSISTENT CODES OF LAW ISSUED BY IMPARTIAL GOVERNMENTS THAT INCLUDED SOME MEASURE OF POPULAR PARTICIPATION.

OTHERWISE, HOW CAN THE LAW RESPOND QUICKLY TO NEW NEEDS?

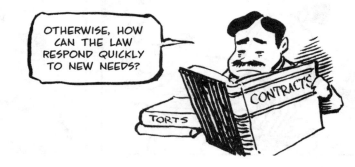

SO...

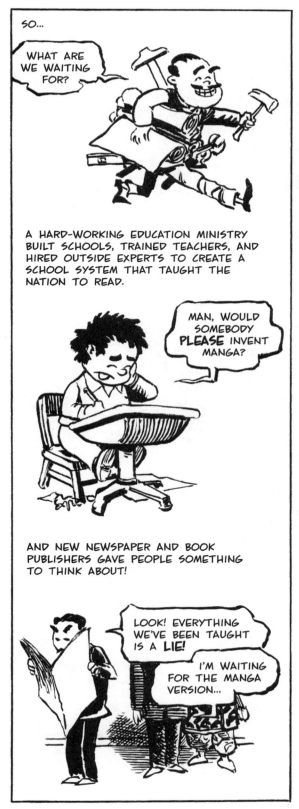

WHAT ARE WE WAITING FOR?

A HARD-WORKING EDUCATION MINISTRY BUILT SCHOOLS, TRAINED TEACHERS, AND HIRED OUTSIDE EXPERTS TO CREATE A SCHOOL SYSTEM THAT TAUGHT THE NATION TO READ.

MAN, WOULD SOMEBODY **PLEASE** INVENT MANGA?

AND NEW NEWSPAPER AND BOOK PUBLISHERS GAVE PEOPLE SOMETHING TO THINK ABOUT!

LOOK! EVERYTHING WE'VE BEEN TAUGHT IS A **LIE!**

I'M WAITING FOR THE MANGA VERSION...

TRADE AGREEMENTS WERE HARDER... JAPAN WANTED TO SLOW WESTERN IMPORTS AND GIVE HOME-GROWN INDUSTRIES A COMPETITIVE ADVANTAGE.

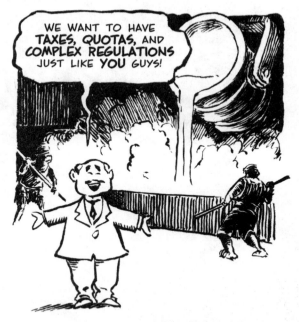

WE WANT TO HAVE **TAXES, QUOTAS,** AND **COMPLEX REGULATIONS** JUST LIKE **YOU** GUYS!

UNFORTUNATELY, THE WEST HAD ALREADY FORCED JAPAN TO TAKE WESTERN GOODS TAX-FREE (OR NEARLY SO), AND JAPAN WAS TOO WEAK TO DEMAND ANY CHANGES.

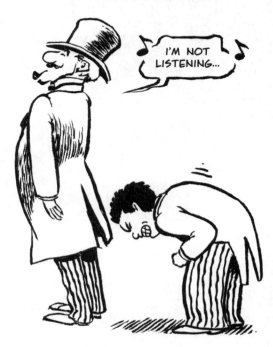

♪ I'M NOT LISTENING... ♪

SO JAPANESE BUSINESSES HELD DOWN COSTS BY PAYING LOW WAGES THAT IMPOVERISHED MILLIONS OF WORKERS.

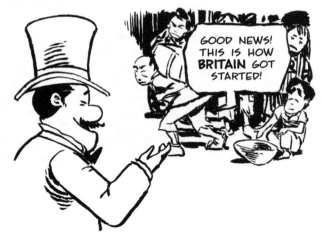

GOOD NEWS! THIS IS HOW **BRITAIN** GOT STARTED!

MEANWHILE, AT THE TOP, GOVERNMENT KEPT THE OLD FEUDAL LORDS HAPPY BY INVITING THEM INTO THE NEW INDUSTRIAL MANAGEMENT.

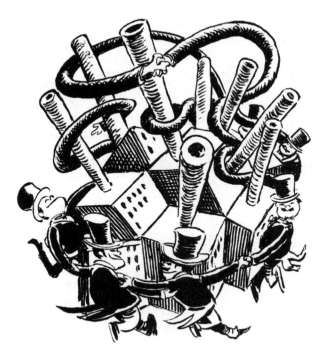

RESULT: A FEW BIG COMPANIES RUN BY A FEW RICH AND WELL-CONNECTED MEN. SOME OF THESE COMPANIES—MITSUBISHI, NIPPON ELECTRIC (NEC), MATSUSHITA, MATSUI—HAVE SURVIVED TO THIS DAY.

ALL THIS WAS DONE WITHOUT A CONSTITUTION.

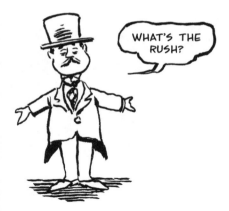

WHAT'S THE RUSH?

IN 1884, GOVERNMENT STARTED PLANNING ONE AND HIRED **HERMANN ROESLER,** A GERMAN LEGAL SCHOLAR, TO CONSULT.

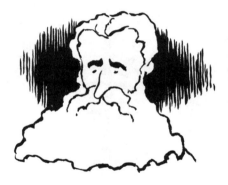

ROESLER WARNED THEM OFF BRITISH- AND AMERICAN-STYLE **CHECKS** AND **BALANCES.** WHEN PARTS OF THE GOVERNMENT OPPOSE EACH OTHER, HE SAID, "SOCIAL UNITY" SUFFERS... AND THE JAPANESE AGREED!

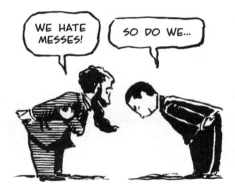

WE HATE MESSES!

SO DO WE...

TO BEGIN WITH, THE CON-
STITUTION SAID THAT THE
GOVERNMENT EXISTED,
NOT BY THE WILL OF
THE PEOPLE, BUT
BY THE DIVINE
GRACE OF THE
EMPEROR, A
LIVING GOD.
ROESLER
OBJECTED, BUT
WHAT COULD
HE DO?

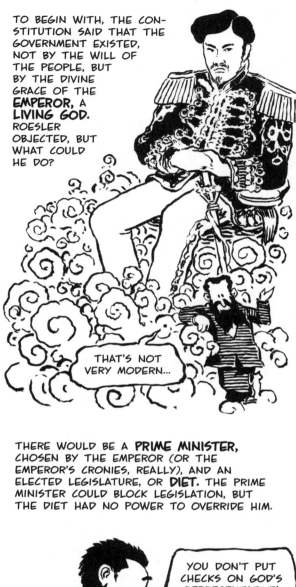

THAT'S NOT
VERY MODERN...

THERE WOULD BE A **PRIME MINISTER,**
CHOSEN BY THE EMPEROR (OR THE
EMPEROR'S CRONIES, REALLY), AND AN
ELECTED LEGISLATURE, OR **DIET.** THE PRIME
MINISTER COULD BLOCK LEGISLATION, BUT
THE DIET HAD NO POWER TO OVERRIDE HIM.

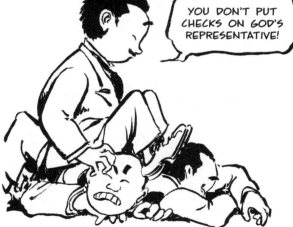

YOU DON'T PUT
CHECKS ON GOD'S
REPRESENTATIVE!

THE CONSTITUTION TOOK EFFECT IN
1890, AND THE FIRST ELECTIONS RAN
SMOOTHLY...

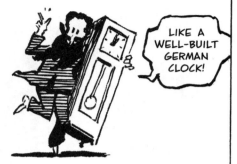

LIKE A
WELL-BUILT
GERMAN
CLOCK!

AND, LO, THE DIET TURNED OUT TO
HAVE MORE POWER THAN YOU MIGHT
HAVE EXPECTED, BECAUSE THE DIET
CONTROLLED ALL **TAXING AND
SPENDING...** SOON, PRIME MINISTERS
AND DIETS WERE BUTTING HEADS
EVERY YEAR OR TWO.

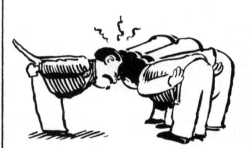

SO, EVERY YEAR OR TWO, THE PRIME
MINISTER WOULD RESIGN, AND THE
EMPEROR WOULD SEND DOWN A
NEW ONE.

SUCH A HEADACHE,
THIS DEMOCRACY!

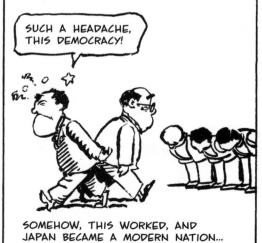

SOMEHOW, THIS WORKED, AND
JAPAN BECAME A MODERN NATION...

IN 1894 CAME A BREAK: BRITAIN AGREED TO END THE UNEQUAL TREATIES THAT HAD HELD JAPAN DOWN.

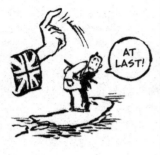

AT LAST!

THE JAPANESE GOVERNMENT TOOK THIS AS A LICENSE TO DECLARE **WAR** ON **CHINA.**

HUH?

WE'RE BIG BOYS NOW!

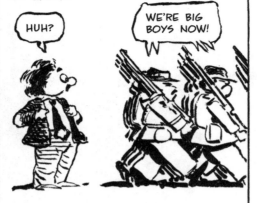

THE ISSUE: **KOREA,** WHERE CHINA AND JAPAN HAD BEEN VYING FOR INFLUENCE... CHINA BACKED KOREA'S TRADITION-MINDED KING... JAPAN FAVORED KOREAN MODERNIZERS, IN HOPES OF EXPANDING JAPANESE BUSINESS THERE... OVER THE YEARS, THERE HAD BEEN PLOTS, MURDERS, "INCIDENTS"...

IN LATE 1894, JAPAN ATTACKED CHINA AND IN SHORT ORDER THRASHED THE MAINLAND GIANT BY LAND AND SEA.

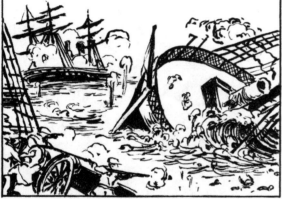

WITHIN A YEAR, CHINA ABANDONED KOREA, CEDED TAIWAN TO JAPAN, AND PROMISED TO PAY JAPAN A SIZABLE SUM.

GREAT! NOW WE CAN BRING DEMOCRACY TO KOREA AND GET LUCRATIVE CONTRACTS!

A NOBLE GOAL...

BUT WHEN JAPAN TRIED TO WORK ITS WILL ON KOREA, THE KOREANS FOUND MANY WAYS TO RESIST.

YOU **ONLY** NEED TO CREATE A NEW TAX STRUCTURE, LAW CODE, SCHOOL SYSTEM, BUREAUCRACY...

YES! EXACTLY! IN A MINUTE...

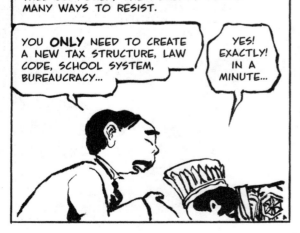

ONE WAY WAS TO LOOK TO **RUSSIA** FOR SUPPORT.

WE **INSIST** ON HELPING...

OH, THANK YOU!

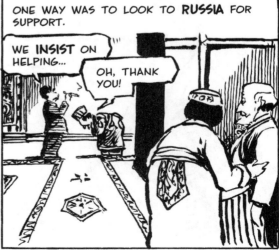

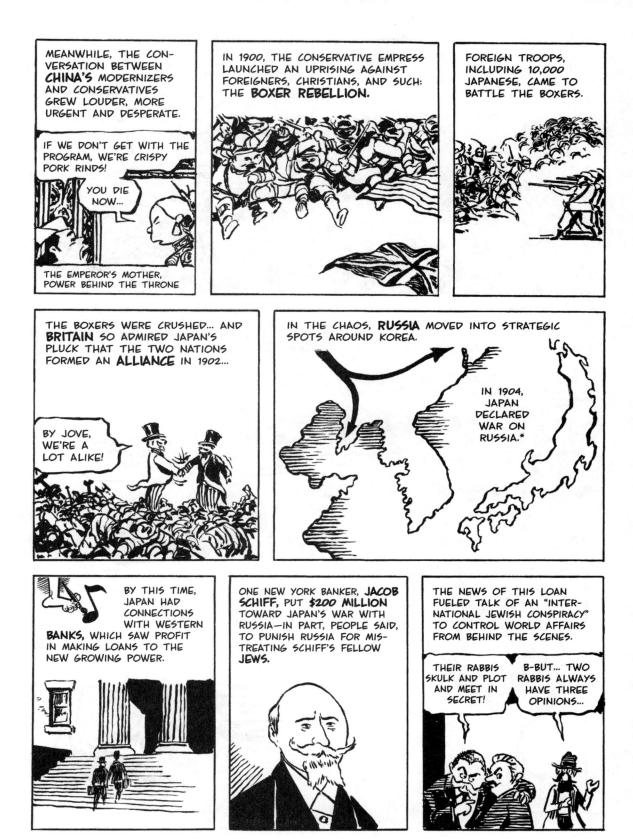

MEANWHILE, THE CONVERSATION BETWEEN **CHINA'S** MODERNIZERS AND CONSERVATIVES GREW LOUDER, MORE URGENT AND DESPERATE.

IF WE DON'T GET WITH THE PROGRAM, WE'RE CRISPY PORK RINDS!

YOU DIE NOW...

THE EMPEROR'S MOTHER, POWER BEHIND THE THRONE

IN 1900, THE CONSERVATIVE EMPRESS LAUNCHED AN UPRISING AGAINST FOREIGNERS, CHRISTIANS, AND SUCH: THE **BOXER REBELLION.**

FOREIGN TROOPS, INCLUDING 10,000 JAPANESE, CAME TO BATTLE THE BOXERS.

THE BOXERS WERE CRUSHED... AND **BRITAIN** SO ADMIRED JAPAN'S PLUCK THAT THE TWO NATIONS FORMED AN **ALLIANCE** IN 1902...

BY JOVE, WE'RE A LOT ALIKE!

IN THE CHAOS, **RUSSIA** MOVED INTO STRATEGIC SPOTS AROUND KOREA.

IN 1904, JAPAN DECLARED WAR ON RUSSIA.*

BY THIS TIME, JAPAN HAD CONNECTIONS WITH WESTERN **BANKS,** WHICH SAW PROFIT IN MAKING LOANS TO THE NEW GROWING POWER.

ONE NEW YORK BANKER, **JACOB SCHIFF,** PUT **$200 MILLION** TOWARD JAPAN'S WAR WITH RUSSIA—IN PART, PEOPLE SAID, TO PUNISH RUSSIA FOR MISTREATING SCHIFF'S FELLOW **JEWS.**

THE NEWS OF THIS LOAN FUELED TALK OF AN "INTERNATIONAL JEWISH CONSPIRACY" TO CONTROL WORLD AFFAIRS FROM BEHIND THE SCENES.

THEIR RABBIS SKULK AND PLOT AND MEET IN SECRET!

B-BUT... TWO RABBIS ALWAYS HAVE THREE OPINIONS...

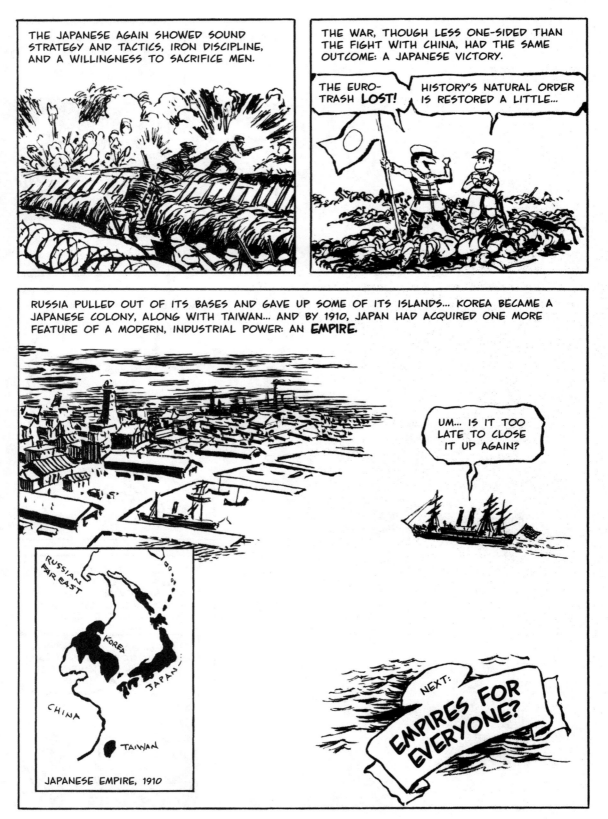

THE JAPANESE AGAIN SHOWED SOUND STRATEGY AND TACTICS, IRON DISCIPLINE, AND A WILLINGNESS TO SACRIFICE MEN.

THE WAR, THOUGH LESS ONE-SIDED THAN THE FIGHT WITH CHINA, HAD THE SAME OUTCOME: A JAPANESE VICTORY.

THE EURO-TRASH **LOST!**

HISTORY'S NATURAL ORDER IS RESTORED A LITTLE...

RUSSIA PULLED OUT OF ITS BASES AND GAVE UP SOME OF ITS ISLANDS... KOREA BECAME A JAPANESE COLONY, ALONG WITH TAIWAN... AND BY 1910, JAPAN HAD ACQUIRED ONE MORE FEATURE OF A MODERN, INDUSTRIAL POWER: AN **EMPIRE.**

UM... IS IT TOO LATE TO CLOSE IT UP AGAIN?

RUSSIAN FAR EAST

KOREA

CHINA

JAPAN

TAIWAN

JAPANESE EMPIRE, 1910

NEXT: **EMPIRES FOR EVERYONE?**

HERE'S ONE OF OUR ANCESTORS, HAPPILY SLAPPING ROCKS TOGETHER JUST TO SEE WHAT WILL HAPPEN!
(I FEEL SO TALL!)
A CHIP FLAKES OFF... A FINGER IS SLICED... AN IDEA IS BORN!
NOW PRIMATES START CHIPPING ROCKS ON PURPOSE... THEY USE THE JAGGED EDGES FOR MAKING SLICED MEAT AND ALL KINDS OF OTHER COOL STUFF!
OF COURSE, OUR TOOL USERS ALSO DISCOVER ADVANCED NEW WAYS TO BUTCHER THEIR ENEMIES...
AND THERE YOU HAVE SCIENCE IN A NUT-SHELL: SLAP ROCKS, HAVE AN IDEA, AND MAKE USEFUL NOVELTIES AND HORRIBLE WEAPONS!
IS IT WORTH IT? HMM... LET ME PUT THIS SLICED MEAT ON SOME SLICED BREAD AND CHEW ON THAT FOR A WHILE...
HI-TECH PICKLES

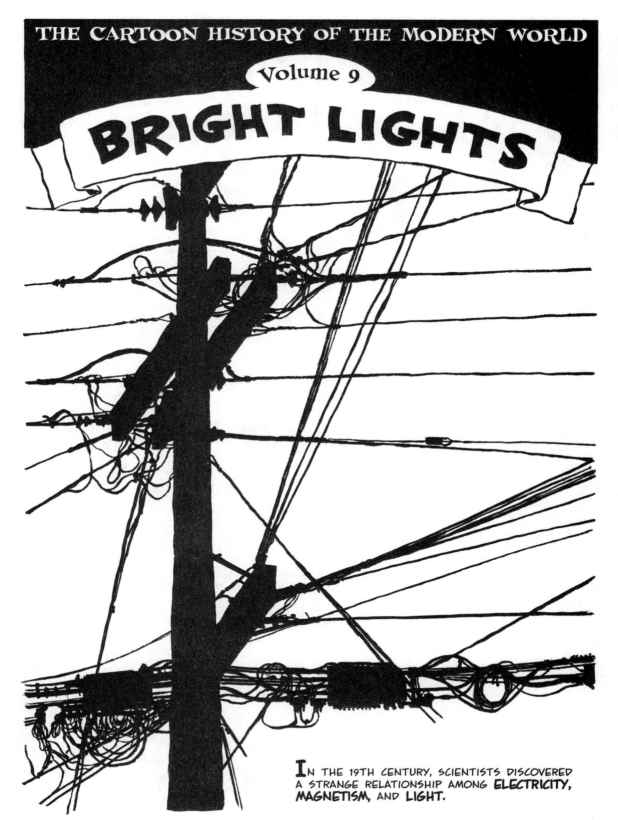

THE CARTOON HISTORY OF THE MODERN WORLD

Volume 9

BRIGHT LIGHTS

IN THE 19TH CENTURY, SCIENTISTS DISCOVERED A STRANGE RELATIONSHIP AMONG **ELECTRICITY, MAGNETISM,** AND **LIGHT.**

IN 1820, HANS CHRISTIAN **OERSTED** NOTICED THAT AN ELECTRIC CURRENT IN A WIRE WOULD DEFLECT A COMPASS NEEDLE: THE WIRE ACTED AS A **MAGNET.**

A COIL OF WIRE, IT WAS DISCOVERED, CAN BE A POWERFUL "ELECTROMAGNET" WHEN CURRENT RUNS THROUGH IT (ESPECIALLY WHEN WRAPPED AROUND AN IRON BAR).

SOMEHOW, ELECTRIC CHARGES IN MOTION GENERATE A **MAGNETIC FIELD,** A MAGNETIC INFLUENCE IN THE SPACE AROUND THEM.

A FEW YEARS LATER, MICHAEL **FARADAY** DISCOVERED A REVERSE EFFECT: A **MOVING MAGNET** WILL CAUSE AN ELECTRIC CURRENT TO RUN IN A WIRE.

IN OTHER WORDS, A MOVING MAGNET GENERATES AN **ELECTRIC FIELD,** AN ELECTRIC INFLUENCE THAT AFFECTS NEARBY CHARGES.

MORE ABSTRACTLY, A MOVING **ELECTRIC** FIELD GENERATES A **MAGNETIC** FIELD, AND A MOVING **MAGNETIC** FIELD CREATES AN **ELECTRIC** FIELD.

JAMES CLERK MAXWELL'S EQUATIONS DESCRIBED THESE STRANGE FLUXES THAT FILLED EMPTY SPACE...

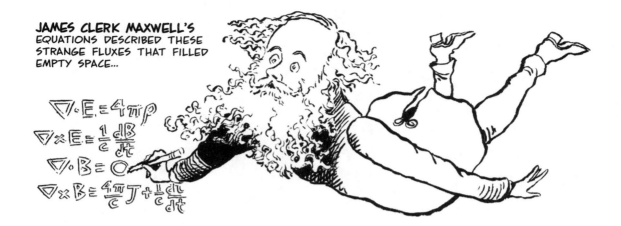

MAXWELL'S EQUATIONS PREDICT THAT A **VIBRATING** ELECTRIC CHARGE'S ELECTRIC FIELD WILL CREATE A VIBRATING MAGNETIC FIELD, WHICH CREATES AN ELECTRIC FIELD, WHICH CREATES... AND SO ON, AD INFINITUM.

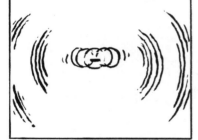

THIS DISTURBANCE IN THE FIELDS RIPPLES AWAY FROM THE CHARGE AS AN **ELEC-TROMAGNETIC WAVE.**

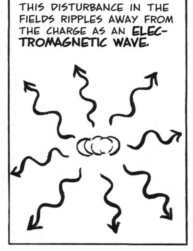

MAXWELL MEASURED THIS WAVE IN THE LAB... IT TRAVELS, HE DISCOVERED, AT THE **SPEED OF LIGHT,** 300,000 KM/SEC (KNOWN AS c TO PHYSICISTS).

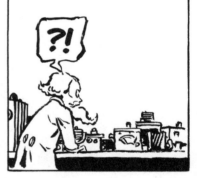

HIS CONCLUSION: IT **IS** LIGHT! WHEN THE CHARGE VIBRATES AT A RATE OF ROUGHLY 4000-7000 OS-CILLATIONS PER SECOND, ITS ELECTROMAGNETIC WAVE IS **VISIBLE LIGHT.** HIGHER OR LOWER FRE-QUENCIES CREATE OTHER, INVISIBLE WAVES... AND THESE WAVES ARE **EVERYWHERE.**

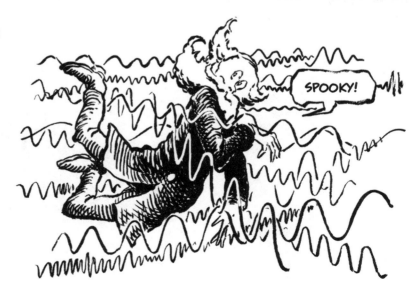

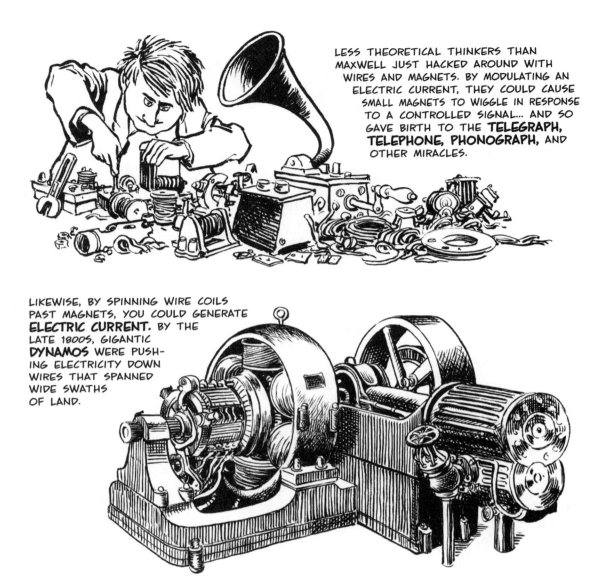

LESS THEORETICAL THINKERS THAN MAXWELL JUST HACKED AROUND WITH WIRES AND MAGNETS. BY MODULATING AN ELECTRIC CURRENT, THEY COULD CAUSE SMALL MAGNETS TO WIGGLE IN RESPONSE TO A CONTROLLED SIGNAL... AND SO GAVE BIRTH TO THE **TELEGRAPH, TELEPHONE, PHONOGRAPH,** AND OTHER MIRACLES.

LIKEWISE, BY SPINNING WIRE COILS PAST MAGNETS, YOU COULD GENERATE **ELECTRIC CURRENT.** BY THE LATE 1800S, GIGANTIC **DYNAMOS** WERE PUSHING ELECTRICITY DOWN WIRES THAT SPANNED WIDE SWATHS OF LAND.

AND SO WHOLE CITIES BECAME ELECTRIFIED!

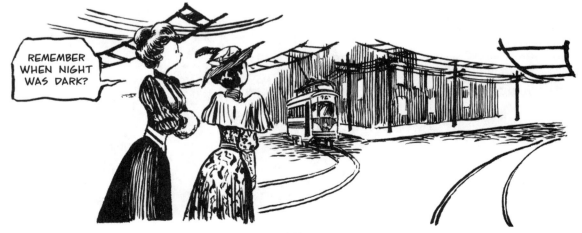

REMEMBER WHEN NIGHT WAS DARK?

IT MIGHT SEEM ALMOST CRAVEN TO QUESTION SOMETHING THAT WORKED SO WELL... BUT ELECTROMAGNETISM WAS CONFUSING... AT LEAST IT CONFUSED **ALBERT EINSTEIN.**

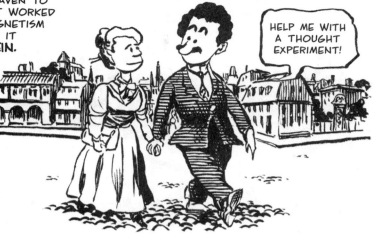

HELP ME WITH A THOUGHT EXPERIMENT!

EINSTEIN IMAGINED TWO PEOPLE (ALBERT AND MILEVA, SAY) WITH MAGNETIC COMPASSES... ELECTRIC CHARGES ARE WHIZZING BY... ALBERT **STANDS STILL,** WHILE MILEVA **FLIES ALONG** AT THE SAME SPEED AS THE CHARGES.

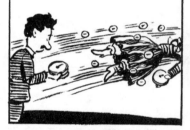

ALBERT'S COMPASS NEEDLE IS DEFLECTED, BUT NOT MILEVA'S! FROM HER POINT OF VIEW, THE ELECTRIC CHARGES ARE **NOT MOVING.**

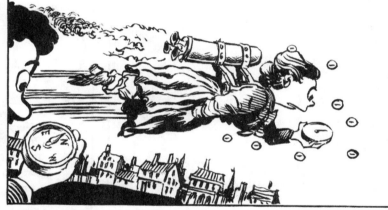

OR... MILEVA FLIES ALONG HOLDING A **PAIR** OF CHARGES... SHE SEES ONLY THEIR ELECTRIC FIELDS... BUT ALBERT SEES A **MAGNETIC** FIELD, TOO, BECAUSE OF THE MOTION. THE OBSERVERS **DISAGREE** ON WHAT FIELDS ARE PRESENT.

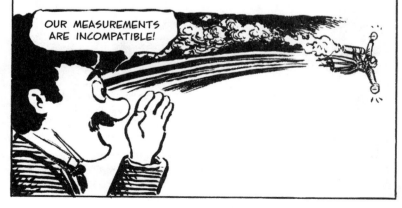

OUR MEASUREMENTS ARE INCOMPATIBLE!

IT GETS WORSE... IF MILEVA **LETS GO** OF THE TWO CHARGES, THEY FLY APART... BUT ALBERT SEES THEM SEPARATE **MORE SLOWLY** THAN MILEVA DOES, ON ACCOUNT OF THE EXTRA MAGNETIC ATTRACTION. THE OBSERVERS **MEASURE SPEED DIFFERENTLY.**

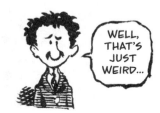

WELL, THAT'S JUST WEIRD...

155

EINSTEIN PUBLISHED HIS ODD ANALYSIS OF THIS ODDITY IN 1905: THE TWO OBSERVERS MEASURE DIFFERENT SPEEDS, HE SAID, BECAUSE FROM ALBERT'S POINT OF VIEW, MILEVA'S **TIME SLOWS DOWN.**

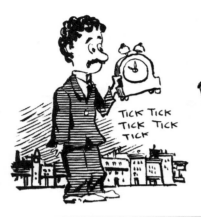

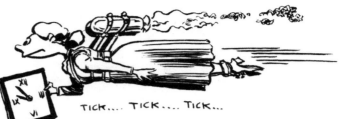

TICK TICK
TICK TICK
TICK

TICK.... TICK.... TICK...

THAT'S RIGHT... IF SHE CARRIES A CLOCK, ALBERT SEES IT RUN SLOWER THAN THE STATIONARY ONE IN HIS HAND!

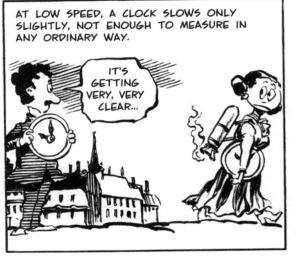

AT LOW SPEED, A CLOCK SLOWS ONLY SLIGHTLY, NOT ENOUGH TO MEASURE IN ANY ORDINARY WAY.

IT'S GETTING VERY, VERY CLEAR...

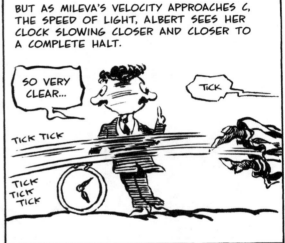

BUT AS MILEVA'S VELOCITY APPROACHES C, THE SPEED OF LIGHT, ALBERT SEES HER CLOCK SLOWING CLOSER AND CLOSER TO A COMPLETE HALT.

SO VERY CLEAR...

TICK

TICK TICK

TICK TICK TICK

AND JUST FOR A LITTLE EXTRA MIND-MELT, EINSTEIN ALSO SHOWED THAT MOVING OBJECTS GET **SHORTER** (IN THE DIRECTION OF MOTION) AND **GAIN MASS.** AS THEIR SPEED NEARS C, LENGTHS SHRINK TO ZERO, AND MASSES INCREASE WITHOUT LIMIT.

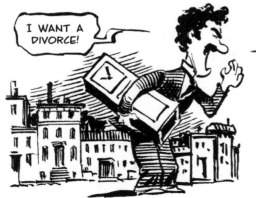

I WANT A DIVORCE!

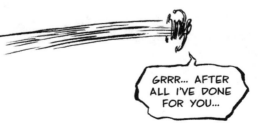

GRRR... AFTER ALL I'VE DONE FOR YOU...

THIS STRANGE TRAIN OF THOUGHT, BACKED BY UNASSAILABLE MATH, IS KNOWN AS THE **THEORY OF RELATIVITY.**

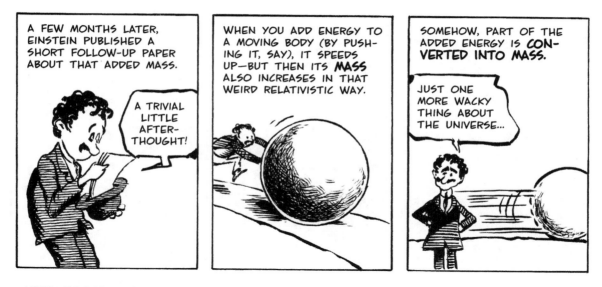

A FEW MONTHS LATER, EINSTEIN PUBLISHED A SHORT FOLLOW-UP PAPER ABOUT THAT ADDED MASS.

A TRIVIAL LITTLE AFTER-THOUGHT!

WHEN YOU ADD ENERGY TO A MOVING BODY (BY PUSHING IT, SAY), IT SPEEDS UP—BUT THEN ITS **MASS** ALSO INCREASES IN THAT WEIRD RELATIVISTIC WAY.

SOMEHOW, PART OF THE ADDED ENERGY IS **CONVERTED INTO MASS.**

JUST ONE MORE WACKY THING ABOUT THE UNIVERSE...

WHEN EINSTEIN DERIVED THE FORMULA RELATING MASS (M) TO ENERGY (E), IT WAS SURPRISINGLY SIMPLE AND DISTURBING:

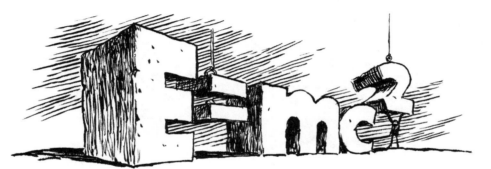

$$E = mc^2$$

DISTURBING BECAUSE C, THE SPEED OF LIGHT, IS 300,000 KM/SEC, SO C^2 IS **90,000,000,000** KM^2/SEC^2, A WHOPPING NUMBER. A VERY SMALL MASS CAN POTENTIALLY RELEASE AN IMMENSE AMOUNT OF ENERGY!

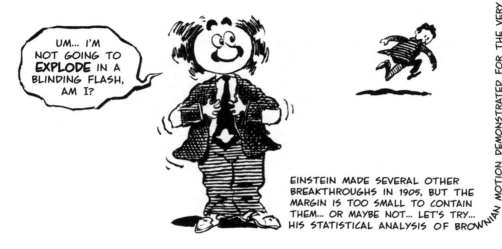

UM... I'M NOT GOING TO **EXPLODE** IN A BLINDING FLASH, AM I?

EINSTEIN MADE SEVERAL OTHER BREAKTHROUGHS IN 1905, BUT THE MARGIN IS TOO SMALL TO CONTAIN THEM... OR MAYBE NOT... LET'S TRY... HIS STATISTICAL ANALYSIS OF BROWNIAN MOTION DEMONSTRATED FOR THE VERY FIRST TIME THAT ATOMS AND MOLECULES WERE REAL PHYSICAL OBJECTS... AND HE EXPLAINED THE PHOTOELECTRIC EFFECT BY TREATING LIGHT AS A STREAM OF PARTICLES (NOT A WAVE), ANOTHER MIND-BENDING, REVOLUTIONARY IDEA THAT HELPED LAY THE FOUNDATION FOR QUANTUM MECHANICS.

WEIRD AS EINSTEIN'S IDEAS WERE, ANOTHER NEW SCIENCE, THE THEORY OF EVOLUTION, DISTURBED FOLKS MUCH MORE.
IT'S AGAINST RELIGION!
AND I CAN UNDERSTAND WHAT IT'S ABOUT...
EARLIER IN THE CENTURY, GEOLOGIST CHARLES LYELL INTERPRETED MOUNTAINS, PLATEAUS, AND THE LIKE AS THE RESULT OF SLOW PROCESSES—VERY SLOW.
IN WHICH CASE, THE EARTH MUST BE VERY OLD, MILLIONS OR BILLIONS OF YEARS.
BUT DEAR MAN, PRECISE CALCULATIONS BASED ON GENESIS PROVE THAT CREATION OCCURRED IN OCTOBER 4004 B.C.!
I KNOW... I'M IN AGONY...
WHAT COULD HAPPEN TO LIFE IN ALL THAT TIME? TWO NATURALISTS, CHARLES DARWIN AND ALFRED WALLACE, HAD THE SAME IDEA AT THE SAME TIME: LIFE EVOLVES.
LIFE EVOLVES!
LIFE EVOLVES!
AND IT EVOLVES WITHOUT ANY GUIDANCE OR DIRECTION... IT HAPPENS BECAUSE INDIVIDUALS VARY RANDOMLY IN EACH NEW GENERATION.
NATURE WEEDS OUT SOME OF THESE VARIATIONS AND FAVORS OTHERS.
OVER TIME, THESE CHANGES ADD UP... DESCENDANTS LOOK VERY DIFFERENT FROM THEIR REMOTE ANCESTORS... AND SO NEW SPECIES ARISE.

DARWIN'S MAGNUM OPUS, **THE ORIGIN OF SPECIES,** CAME OUT IN 1859, AND THE HOWLING BEGAN RIGHT AWAY.
OWWOOOOOO...
CHURCHMEN SAVAGED DARWIN FOR SAYING WE WERE KIN TO THE MONKEYS.
WE'RE NOTHING LIKE MONKEYS! NOTHING LIKE MONKEYS!
DEBATES TOOK PLACE!
IN NATURE'S PERFECTION, WE SEE THE HAND OF AN **INTELLIGENT DESIGNER...**
THEN HOW DO YOU EXPLAIN MY NOSE?
WITH ALL THIS TALK, DARWIN'S IDEA SPREAD SWIFTLY.
IT'S COOL! IT'S SIMPLE! IT EXPLAINS SO MUCH!
SOME PRO-EVOLUTION ENTHUSIASTS GOT CARRIED AWAY WITH THIS "SURVIVAL OF THE FITTEST" STUFF.
HMM... WHAT WOULD A CHIMPANZEE DO?
SOCIAL DARWINISTS SAW SOCIETY AS A COMPETITIVE STRUGGLE FOR SURVIVAL.
MUST FIND A CHIMPANZEE AND ASK ITS OPINION...
THE PEOPLE ON TOP GOT THERE BECAUSE THEY WERE "MORE FIT" THAN THOSE AT THE BOTTOM. WHEREVER YOU WERE, YOU DESERVED IT!
A MOST COMFORTING IDEA...
THIS LINE OF THOUGHT APPEALED TO THOSE WHO LIVED BY CRUSHING THEIR FELLOW HUMANS.
♪
BUT SOCIAL DARWINISM WAS NO SCIENCE... IT WAS ONLY "SCIENCE-Y"... LIKE A LOT OF THEORIES GOING AROUND AT THE TIME.
DAMMIT, DON'T YOU SEE YOU'RE STIFLING INDIVIDUAL INITIATIVE?

SCIENCEY THINKING WAS IN VOGUE... PEOPLE ADMIRED SCIENCE... TAKE **KARL MARX,** FOR EXAMPLE.
MARX LABORED IN LONDON FOR DECADES TO WORK OUT A SYSTEM OF "SCIENTIFIC SOCIALISM."
HE PENNED AN UNFINISHED PAPER MOUNTAIN CALLED *CAPITAL,* NOT REALLY SCIENCE, BUT NOT CHOPPED LIVER EITHER.
MMM... I WISH IT **WAS** CHOPPED LIVER...
QUIET! I'M WORKING!
IN HIS SCIENCEY WAY, MARX HELD THAT ALL EVENTS, IDEAS, ACTIONS, AND OPINIONS SPRING FROM **MATERIAL** CAUSES. HISTORY, LIKE PHYSICS, IS DRIVEN NOT BY IDEAS BUT BY **STUFF.**
KARL! WE'RE HUNGRY!
YOU ONLY THINK THAT BECAUSE FOOD IS INSUFFICIENT.
PEOPLE'S ATTITUDES, IDEAS, THEIR VERY CONSCIOUSNESS, COME FROM THEIR **SOCIAL CLASS** AND ITS RELATIONSHIP WITH OTHER CLASSES.
KARL! HOW COULD YOU DO THIS TO YOUR FAMILY? YOU COULD HAVE BEEN A LAWYER! A DOCTOR!
I WAS WISE TO MARRY A MIDDLE-CLASS WOMAN... A PROLETARIAN WOULD HAVE BRAINED ME WITH THE FRYING PAN BY NOW...
TAKE, FOR INSTANCE, THE IDEA OF WHITE SUPREMACY. MARX WOULD SAY THIS RESULTED FROM WHITES' NEED TO JUSTIFY WHAT THEY DID TO AFRICANS WHILE CHASING GAIN.
FIRST THE EXPLOITATION, THEN THE EXPLANATION!

HISTORY, LIKE OTHER SCIENCES, HAS LAWS, SAYS MARX. EVENTS PROCEED **DIALECTICALLY,** WHICH MEANS THAT EACH NEW DEVELOPMENT ("THESIS") PROVOKES A REACTION ("ANTITHESIS") THAT LEADS TO A NEW CREATION ("SYNTHESIS") AND SOME RESOLUTION OF "CONTRADICTIONS" WITHIN THE EXISTING ORDER.

SO, LIKE A SCIENTIST, YOU CAN PREDICT THE FUTURE?

JA! BECAUSE I UNDERSTAND THE **CONTRADICTIONS** OF CAPITALISM!

CONTRADICTION #1: CAPITAL AND LABOR ARE AT ODDS.

MARX, LIKE LOCKE, SAYS THAT **LABOR** AND LABOR ALONE CREATES **VALUE...** BUT MARX ADDS THAT THE CAPITALIST ALWAYS PAYS THE WORKER **LESS** THAN THE VALUE OF HIS LABOR AND KEEPS THE EXTRA, "SURPLUS" VALUE, I.E., THE PROFIT.

WHAT ONE GAINS, THE OTHER LOSES!

WE MADE THAT PIE CHART, AND ALL WE GET TO KEEP IS THIS CRUMMY SLICE!

CONTRADICTION #2: THE OWNER CAN EXTRACT PROFIT ONLY FROM WORKERS, THE SOLE SOURCE OF VALUE, NOT FROM MACHINERY... AND YET HE HAS TO INVEST IN MACHINERY.

AS MORE CAPITAL IS SUNK INTO FACTORIES AND EQUIP- MENT, THEN, THE RETURN ON INVESTMENT—THE **RATE OF PROFIT—MUST FALL.**

YOU CAN'T MAKE OMELETS WITHOUT USING FRYING PANS...

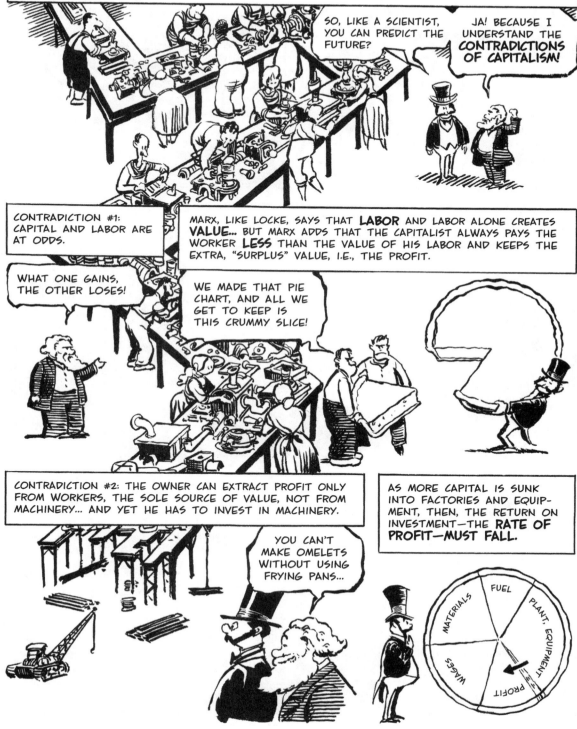

MATERIALS · FUEL · PLANT, EQUIPMENT · PROFIT · WAGES

161

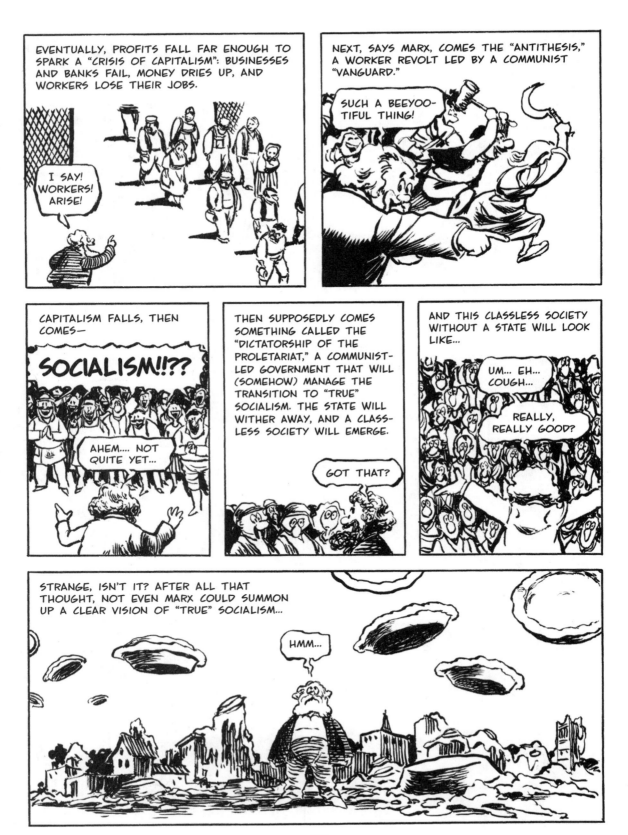

EVENTUALLY, PROFITS FALL FAR ENOUGH TO SPARK A "CRISIS OF CAPITALISM": BUSINESSES AND BANKS FAIL, MONEY DRIES UP, AND WORKERS LOSE THEIR JOBS.

I SAY! WORKERS! ARISE!

NEXT, SAYS MARX, COMES THE "ANTITHESIS," A WORKER REVOLT LED BY A COMMUNIST "VANGUARD."

SUCH A BEEYOO-TIFUL THING!

CAPITALISM FALLS, THEN COMES—

SOCIALISM!!??

AHEM.... NOT QUITE YET...

THEN SUPPOSEDLY COMES SOMETHING CALLED THE "DICTATORSHIP OF THE PROLETARIAT," A COMMUNIST-LED GOVERNMENT THAT WILL (SOMEHOW) MANAGE THE TRANSITION TO "TRUE" SOCIALISM. THE STATE WILL WITHER AWAY, AND A CLASS-LESS SOCIETY WILL EMERGE.

GOT THAT?

AND THIS CLASSLESS SOCIETY WITHOUT A STATE WILL LOOK LIKE...

UM... EH... COUGH...

REALLY, REALLY GOOD?

STRANGE, ISN'T IT? AFTER ALL THAT THOUGHT, NOT EVEN MARX COULD SUMMON UP A CLEAR VISION OF "TRUE" SOCIALISM...

HMM...

MORE SCIENCEY STUFF OF THE DAY:

PHRENOLOGY CLAIMED TO READ HUMAN CHARACTER FROM THE PATTERN OF BUMPS ON THE SKULL.

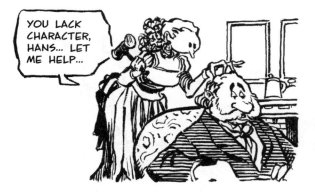

YOU LACK CHARACTER, HANS... LET ME HELP...

ANIMAL MAGNETISM EXPERIMENTED WITH HYPNOSIS (ON PEOPLE, NOT ANIMALS).

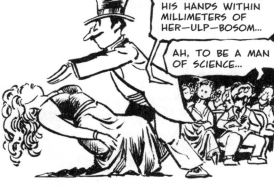

GASP! HE'S PASSING HIS HANDS WITHIN MILLIMETERS OF HER—ULP—BOSOM...

AH, TO BE A MAN OF SCIENCE...

EUGENICS AIMED TO IMPROVE HUMANITY BY ENCOURAGING "BETTER" PEOPLE TO BREED AND STOPPING "WORSE" ONES.

PAY YOU FIVE DOLLARS TO GET STERILIZED!

WHERE'D THE MONEY COME FROM? SOME KINDA PREJUDICED RICH OFAY?

HMM... WEIRDLY INTELLIGENT QUESTION...

SUPERCUTS

PSYCHOANALYSIS* CLAIMED TO CURE "HYSTERIA," A DISEASE WITH NO DEFINITION, BY UNCOVERING CHILDHOOD SEXUAL TRAUMA, REAL OR IMAGINED.

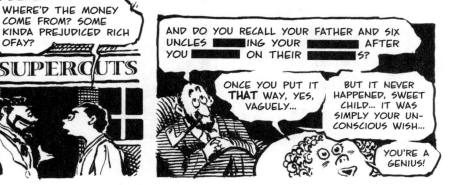

AND DO YOU RECALL YOUR FATHER AND SIX UNCLES ███████ING YOUR █████████ AFTER YOU ███████ ON THEIR ██████S?

ONCE YOU PUT IT **THAT** WAY, YES, VAGUELY...

BUT IT NEVER HAPPENED, SWEET CHILD... IT WAS SIMPLY YOUR UNCONSCIOUS WISH...

YOU'RE A GENIUS!

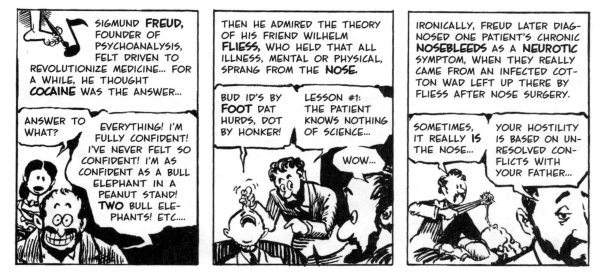

SIGMUND **FREUD**, FOUNDER OF PSYCHOANALYSIS, FELT DRIVEN TO REVOLUTIONIZE MEDICINE... FOR A WHILE, HE THOUGHT **COCAINE** WAS THE ANSWER...

ANSWER TO WHAT?

EVERYTHING! I'M FULLY CONFIDENT! I'VE NEVER FELT SO CONFIDENT! I'M AS CONFIDENT AS A BULL ELEPHANT IN A PEANUT STAND! **TWO** BULL ELEPHANTS! ETC....

THEN HE ADMIRED THE THEORY OF HIS FRIEND WILHELM **FLIESS**, WHO HELD THAT ALL ILLNESS, MENTAL OR PHYSICAL, SPRANG FROM THE **NOSE**.

BUD ID'S BY **FOOT** DAT HURDS, DOT BY HONKER!

LESSON #1: THE PATIENT KNOWS NOTHING OF SCIENCE...

WOW...

IRONICALLY, FREUD LATER DIAGNOSED ONE PATIENT'S CHRONIC **NOSEBLEEDS** AS A **NEUROTIC** SYMPTOM, WHEN THEY REALLY CAME FROM AN INFECTED COTTON WAD LEFT UP THERE BY FLIESS AFTER NOSE SURGERY.

SOMETIMES, IT REALLY **IS** THE NOSE...

YOUR HOSTILITY IS BASED ON UNRESOLVED CONFLICTS WITH YOUR FATHER...

HOW CAN YOU BLAME PEOPLE FOR SCIENCEY THINKING, WHEN THEY SAW FRESH TECHNICAL MARVELS EVERY DAY? NEW AND IMPROVED **MATERIALS**—STRUCTURAL STEEL, DURABLE "VULCANIZED" RUBBER, FUELS AND LUBRICANTS FROM REFINED PETROLEUM,* SYNTHETIC FERTILIZER, EXPLOSIVES, DYES, AND INKS—SPAWNED NEW **MACHINERY** AND **STRUCTURES**... STEEL-FRAMED SKYSCRAPERS WITH HYDRAULIC ELEVATORS TO SCALE THE HEIGHTS... CARS AND AIRPLANES POWERED BY INTERNAL COMBUSTION... GIANT PRINTING PRESSES SPEWING ILLUSTRATED NEWSPAPERS, WHICH THRILLED READERS WITH THAT DEEPLY RADICAL, IMPORTANT, AND BRILLIANT INVENTION, THE **COMIC STRIP**...

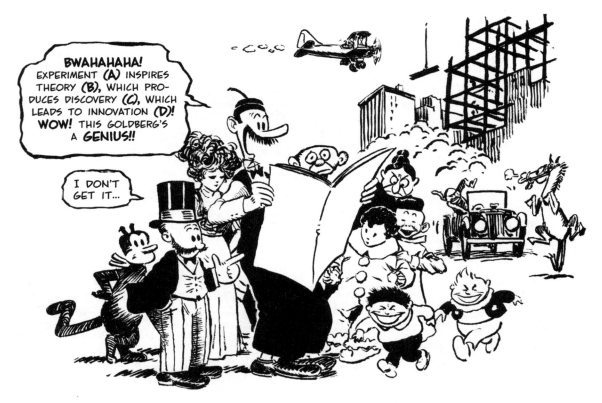

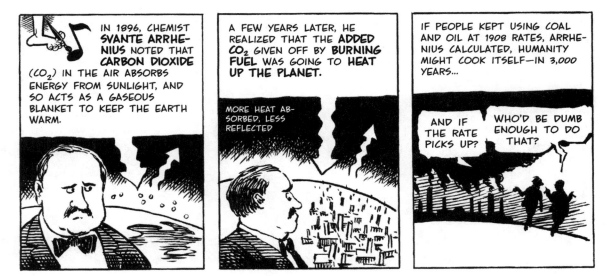

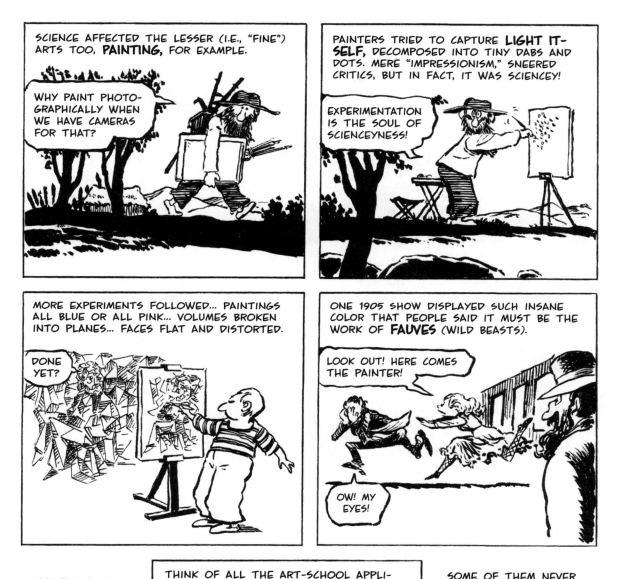

SCIENCE AFFECTED THE LESSER (I.E., "FINE") ARTS TOO, **PAINTING,** FOR EXAMPLE.

WHY PAINT PHOTOGRAPHICALLY WHEN WE HAVE CAMERAS FOR THAT?

PAINTERS TRIED TO CAPTURE **LIGHT IT-SELF,** DECOMPOSED INTO TINY DABS AND DOTS. MERE "IMPRESSIONISM," SNEERED CRITICS, BUT IN FACT, IT WAS SCIENCEY!

EXPERIMENTATION IS THE SOUL OF SCIENCEYNESS!

MORE EXPERIMENTS FOLLOWED... PAINTINGS ALL BLUE OR ALL PINK... VOLUMES BROKEN INTO PLANES... FACES FLAT AND DISTORTED.

DONE YET?

ONE 1905 SHOW DISPLAYED SUCH INSANE COLOR THAT PEOPLE SAID IT MUST BE THE WORK OF **FAUVES** (WILD BEASTS).

LOOK OUT! HERE COMES THE PAINTER!

OW! MY EYES!

MODERN ART FAVORED THE NEW, THE ODD, THE SHOCKING, AND NOT EVERYONE LIKED IT.

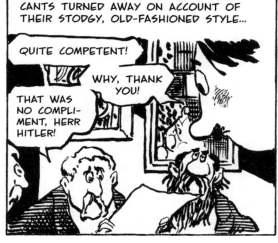

THINK OF ALL THE ART-SCHOOL APPLICANTS TURNED AWAY ON ACCOUNT OF THEIR STODGY, OLD-FASHIONED STYLE...

QUITE COMPETENT!

WHY, THANK YOU!

THAT WAS NO COMPLIMENT, HERR HITLER!

SOME OF THEM NEVER QUITE GOT OVER IT.

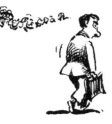

EASTERN EMPIRES

THE AUSTRO-HUNGARIAN EMPIRE EMBRACED MANY CULTURES: GERMAN, SLAVIC, HUNGARIAN, AND MORE... AND IT WORKED, SORT OF... VIENNA'S FROTHY FIZZ OF MUSIC, ART, PSYCHIATRY, PASTRY, AND WHIPPED CREAM PUT A NICE TOPPING ON THE ETHNIC TENSIONS* SEETHING BENEATH. AUSTRIA'S **GERMAN** NATIONALISTS ESPECIALLY SNEERED AT THIS "COSMOPOLITAN" MIX: THE LIBERAL PRESS, SOCIALIST IDEAS, MODERN ART, LANGUAGE-MANGLING SLAVS, AND THE JEWS.

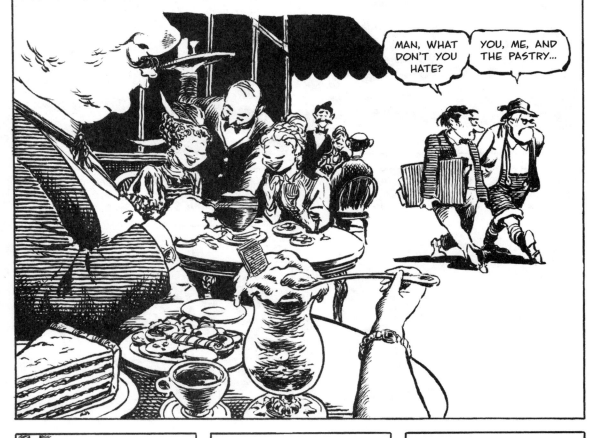

MAN, WHAT DON'T YOU HATE?

YOU, ME, AND THE PASTRY...

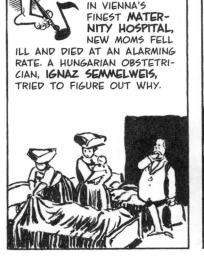

IN VIENNA'S FINEST **MATERNITY HOSPITAL**, NEW MOMS FELL ILL AND DIED AT AN ALARMING RATE. A HUNGARIAN OBSTETRICIAN, **IGNAZ SEMMELWEIS**, TRIED TO FIGURE OUT WHY.

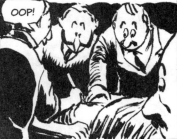

ONE DAY, A DOCTOR WAS ACCIDENTALLY NICKED DURING AN AUTOPSY... HE SOON DIED OF "CHILDBED FEVER"... AND SEMMELWEIS REALIZED THAT DOCTORS WERE CARRYING **SEPTIC GOO** STRAIGHT FROM **CORPSES** TO THE **DELIVERY ROOM.**

OOP!

WHEN HE URGED THE STAFF TO WASH THEIR HANDS, THEY JEERED THE HUNGARIAN "CRACKPOT" OUT OF VIENNA!

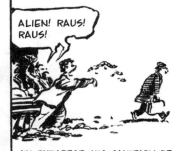

ALIEN! RAUS! RAUS!

(IN BUDAPEST, HIS SANITARY REFORMS SAVED MANY LIVES, WHILE VIENNA'S MOMS KEPT PERISHING AT A HIGH RATE FOR YEARS.)

AUSTRIA'S GERMAN NATIONALISTS ENVIED GERMANY'S GERMANS NEXT DOOR (ESPECIALLY THE WAY BISMARCK SUPPRESSED SOCIALIST PARTIES).

SO BUSINESSLIKE, SO CONSERVATIVE, SO... GERMAN...

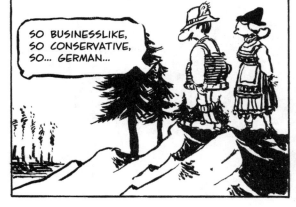

GERMANY HAD SEAPORTS, SHIPPING, AND TRADE AND INFLUENCE IN CHINA AND JAPAN.

AND THEY'RE **WAY** AHEAD OF US IN TOXIC CHEMICALS...

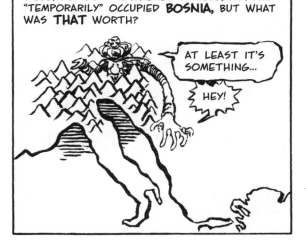

BY CONTRAST, AUSTRIA WAS LANDLOCKED, WITH NOWHERE TO GO.

WELL, ALMOST NOWHERE... IN 1878, AUSTRIA "TEMPORARILY" OCCUPIED **BOSNIA,** BUT WHAT WAS **THAT** WORTH?

AT LEAST IT'S SOMETHING...

HEY!

SO, IN VIENNA, MORE COFFEE... MORE PASTRY... MORE WALTZES, MORE PSYCHOANALYSIS... MORE **CULTURE...**

CULTURE IS GOOD!

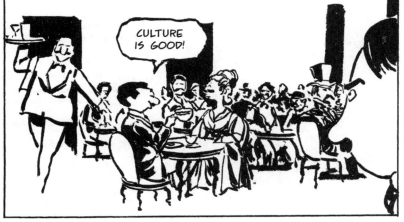

WHILE GERMANY PUSHED FOR MORE POWER, CAUTIOUSLY, AT FIRST.

IN 1885, AT THE BERLIN CONFERENCE (SEE P. 98), GERMANY LAID CLAIM TO A PIECE OF EAST AFRICA—BUT IN A NICE WAY...
JUST AN EENTSY THING, NOTHING REALLY...
YOU DESERVE IT!
IN 1888, BISMARCK'S MENTOR, THE OLD KAISER, DIED, AND THE NEW ONE, WILHELM II, TURNED OUT TO BE MUCH MORE IMPULSIVE AND FIERCE.
PLEASE! THINK OF ME AS INTUITIVE!
IMPATIENT WITH BISMARCK'S COOL CALCULATION, THE NEW KAISER PUSHED HIM ASIDE AND TOOK CHARGE OF GERMANY HIMSELF.
OBOY!
WILHELM II WANTED AN OVERSEAS EMPIRE! WARSHIPS! A BIT OF WORLD DOMINATION!
TOOT TOOT!
TOO BAD... NOT MUCH MORE OF THE WORLD WAS AVAILABLE... IRAN, MAYBE, BUT BRITAIN AND RUSSIA ALREADY HAD THEIR PAWS IN THERE...
BLOODY UNFAIR!
SO, FOR THE TIME BEING, GERMANY SOUGHT PROFIT, NOT GLORY, BY PUTTING ITS BANKS AND BUSINESSES WHERE IT COULD IN AFRICA AND ASIA.
I'M NOTHING BUT A LOAN OFFICER AND A FERTILIZER SALESMAN...
AND BUILT UP ITS MILITARY, JUST IN CASE.
IT WOULD MEAN SO MUCH TO ME TO PROJECT MY TURGID, THROBBING POWER INTO THE DELICATE FLESH OF THE WORLD...
HAVE YOU CONSULTED DR. FREUD?

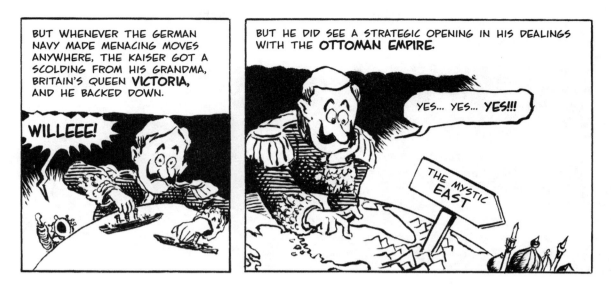

IN 1894, ON A VISIT TO THE OTTOMAN COURT, THE KAISER ANNOUNCED A GRAND PLAN TO BUILD A **RAILROAD** LINKING **CONSTANTINOPLE** TO **BAGHDAD**. AN OBVIOUS BOON TO THE TURKS, THIS TRACK WOULD ALSO GIVE GERMANY (AND AUSTRIA) A DIRECT ROUTE TO POINTS FARTHER EAST.

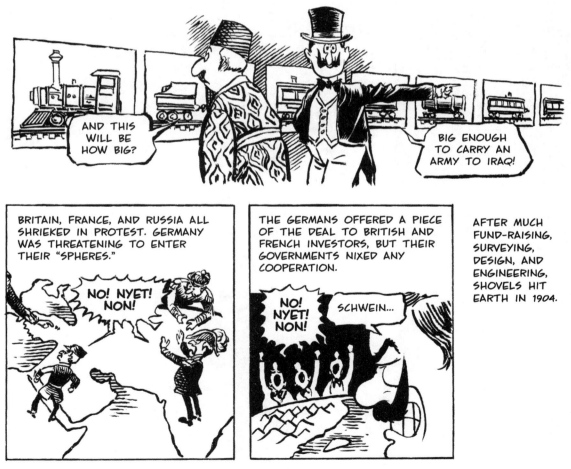

AFTER MUCH FUND-RAISING, SURVEYING, DESIGN, AND ENGINEERING, SHOVELS HIT EARTH IN 1904.

MEANWHILE, A CLASH OF EMPIRES TOOK PLACE ON THE FAR SIDE OF THE PLANET.

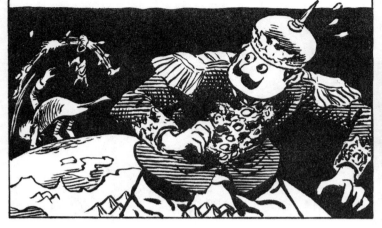

THE **UNITED STATES**, HAVING SPANNED A CONTINENT, KEPT HEADING WESTWARD.

KIND OF A HABIT, REALLY!

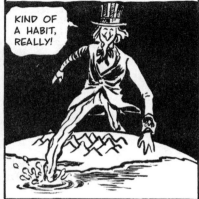

THE WESTWARD HO BOYS OF THE **McKINLEY** ADMINISTRATION CAST THEIR EYES ON THE SPANISH **PHILIPPINES,** GATEWAY TO ASIA.

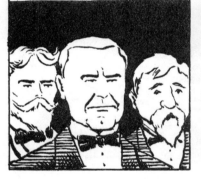

IN 1898, THE U.S. DECLARED WAR ON SPAIN AND THRASHED THE DECAYING OLD NATION.

BESIDES THE PHILIPPINES, THE U.S. PICKED UP PUERTO RICO AND CUBA TOO.

PUERTO RICO, GATEWAY TO THE CARIBBEAN!

CUBA, GATEWAY TO PUERTO RICO!

THE FILIPINOS THEN SHOCKED THE AMERICANS BY FIGHTING FOR THEIR **OWN** INDEPENDENCE, BUT AFTER MANY MASSACRES, THE AMERICANS HELD ON.

INDEPENDENCE! THE IDEA!

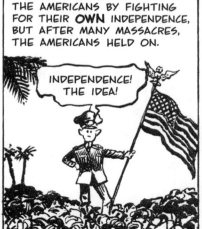

THE WAR WAS SHORT... NO ONE HELPED SPAIN... TO SOME PEOPLE, THE LESSON MUST HAVE SEEMED CLEAR—

YOU **CAN** TAKE OTHER PEOPLE'S STUFF!

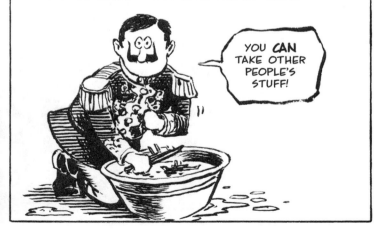

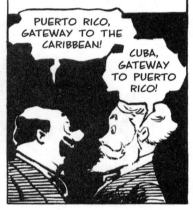

NOW BACK TO EUROPE... IN 1904, AS RAILROAD BUILDING BEGAN IN ASIA MINOR, RUSSIA WENT TO WAR WITH JAPAN—AND **LOST** (SEE P. 148).

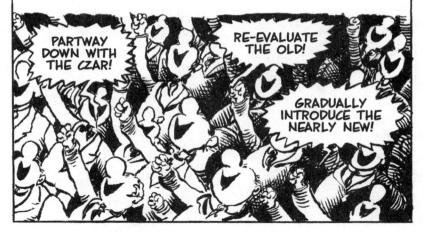

THIS DEFEAT SHOCKED RUSSIA SO BADLY THAT EVEN THE **MODERATES** TOOK TO THE STREETS.

PARTWAY DOWN WITH THE CZAR!

RE-EVALUATE THE OLD!

GRADUALLY INTRODUCE THE NEARLY NEW!

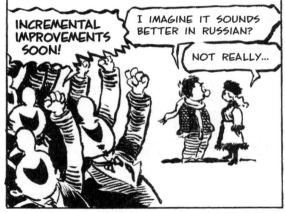

SINCE RUSSIAN RADICALS WERE ALL IN PRISON OR EXILE, THE MOB'S DEMANDS WERE MODEST.

INCREMENTAL IMPROVEMENTS SOON!

I IMAGINE IT SOUNDS BETTER IN RUSSIAN?

NOT REALLY...

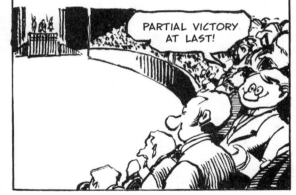

THE CZAR CAVED... AND RUSSIA FINALLY GOT A CONSTITUTIONAL GOVERNMENT WITH A PARLIAMENT, THE DUMA—WHILE KEEPING THE CZAR, TOO, FOR NOW...

PARTIAL VICTORY AT LAST!

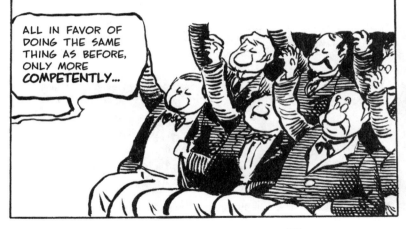

NONE OF THIS CHANGED RUSSIAN IMPERIAL AMBITIONS, NOR ITS CONCERNS ABOUT GERMANY'S PLANS IN ASIA.

ALL IN FAVOR OF DOING THE SAME THING AS BEFORE, ONLY MORE **COMPETENTLY**...

IN 1907, RUSSIA ALLIED ITSELF WITH BRITAIN AND FRANCE AGAINST GERMANY—AND SECRETLY AGREED WITH BRITAIN TO SHARE **IRAN'S** ASSETS...

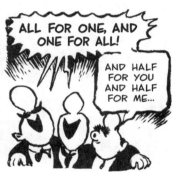

ALL FOR ONE, AND ONE FOR ALL!

AND HALF FOR YOU AND HALF FOR ME...

GERMANY, MEANWHILE, KEPT PUSHING ITS RAILWAY EASTWARD OVER TURKISH SOIL AND RUSSIAN OBJECTIONS... BUT HOW COULD THIS LINE CONNECT BACK TO AUSTRIA AND GERMANY? ONLY THROUGH THE UNSTABLE **BALKANS.**

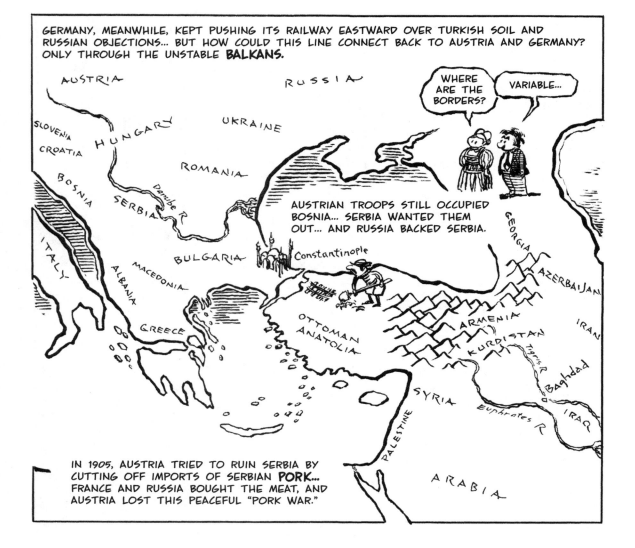

AUSTRIAN TROOPS STILL OCCUPIED BOSNIA... SERBIA WANTED THEM OUT... AND RUSSIA BACKED SERBIA.

WHERE ARE THE BORDERS?

VARIABLE...

IN 1905, AUSTRIA TRIED TO RUIN SERBIA BY CUTTING OFF IMPORTS OF SERBIAN **PORK...** FRANCE AND RUSSIA BOUGHT THE MEAT, AND AUSTRIA LOST THIS PEACEFUL "PORK WAR."

IN 1908 CAME A SHOCKER IN CONSTANTINOPLE: A GROUP OF TURKISH OFFICERS, THE "COMMITTEE FOR UNION AND PROGRESS," SEIZED POWER AND ANNOUNCED THAT THE OTTOMAN EMPIRE WOULD BECOME A MODERN, INDUSTRIAL STATE.

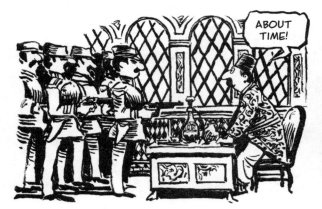

ABOUT TIME!

EUROPE CHEERED—UNTIL IT HEARD THE REST OF THE YOUNG TURKS' PROGRAM, WHICH WAS TO WIN BACK THE **BALKANS!**

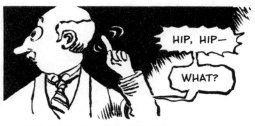

HIP, HIP—

WHAT?

NOW EVENTS ACCELERATED.

1908: AUSTRIA ABSORBS BOSNIA INTO THE EMPIRE... RUSSIA MENACES AUSTRIA... GERMANY WARNS RUSSIA... RUSSIA BACKS DOWN...

GRRRR SNARL GNASH

1908–9: BULGARIA DECLARES INDEPENDENCE FROM THE OTTOMAN EMPIRE... GREEKS, BULGARS, AND SERBS FIGHT OVER MACEDONIA.

1909: THE YOUNG TURKS TOPPLE THE SULTAN AND END THE OTTOMAN DYNASTY.

WE SIMPLY HAVE **GOT** TO GET ORGANIZED!

1909: TURKEY CARRIES OUT A "SMALL" MASSACRE OF ARMENIANS ("ONLY" 80,000) TO DISCOURAGE THEM FROM COPYING THE BULGARIANS.

1912: GREEKS, BULGARS, AND ALL STOP FIGHTING EACH OTHER AND TURN AGAINST THE TURKS.

1912: A TURKISH OFFICER, **ENVER PASHA,** MAKES HIMSELF **DICTATOR** IN CONSTANTINOPLE.

BETTER ORGANIZED, I TELL YOU!

1913: ENVER PASHA GIVES UP ALL CLAIMS TO THE BALKANS. GREEKS, BULGARS, SERBS, ALBANIANS, AND ALL START FIGHTING EACH OTHER AGAIN.

MAN! ENOUGH OF THAT!

1914: THE POWERS IMPOSE AN UNEASY PEACE... AUSTRIA STILL COVETS SERBIA... RUSSIA, BRITAIN, AND FRANCE SAY NYET, NO, NON.

GRRR GNASH
MUTTER MUTTER MUTTER

JUNE 1914: AN AUSTRIAN DUKE AND DUCHESS VISITING "AUSTRIAN BOSNIA" ARE ASSASSINATED BY A SERB.

WAR AND REVOLUTION

AUSTRIA MAKES TEN IMPOSSIBILE DEMANDS OF SERBIA—OR ELSE. SERBIA DITHERS...

"OR ELSE" WHAT? DON'T YOU WONDER?

MORE TALKING, MOST LIKELY...

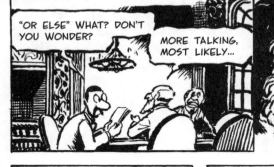

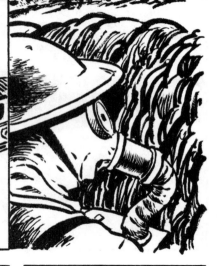

THIS TIME, RUSSIA COMMITS ITSELF TO SERBIA'S DEFENSE... A MILLION RUSSIAN SOLDIERS PACK THEIR GEAR AND START BOARDING TRAINS.

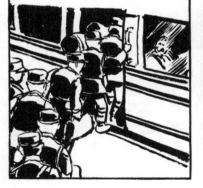

THE GERMAN ARMY TAKES THE RUSSIAN MOVES AS AN ACT OF WAR AND STARTS MOVING TOO.

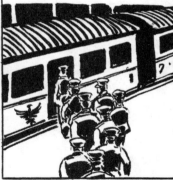

FRANCE, ALLIED WITH RUSSIA, GEARS UP FOR WAR WITH GERMANY.

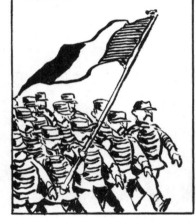

KAISER WILHELM BEGS HIS OWN ARMY TO SLOW DOWN, BUT HIS CHIEF OF STAFF, GENERAL VON MOLTKE, TELLS HIM:

ONCE THE TRAINS LEFT, THERE WAS NO GOING BACK!

THANK HEAVEN GRANDMA'S DEAD...

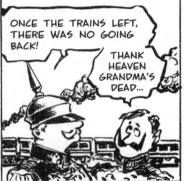

VON MOLTKE HAS A PLAN, A SCHEDULE! A QUICK SWEEP NORTH OF THE FRENCH DEFENSIVE LINE WILL REACH PARIS IN EIGHT WEEKS, **PUNKT!**

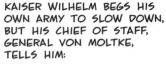

OH, ALL RIGHT THEN...

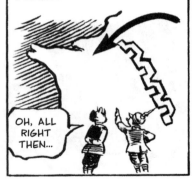

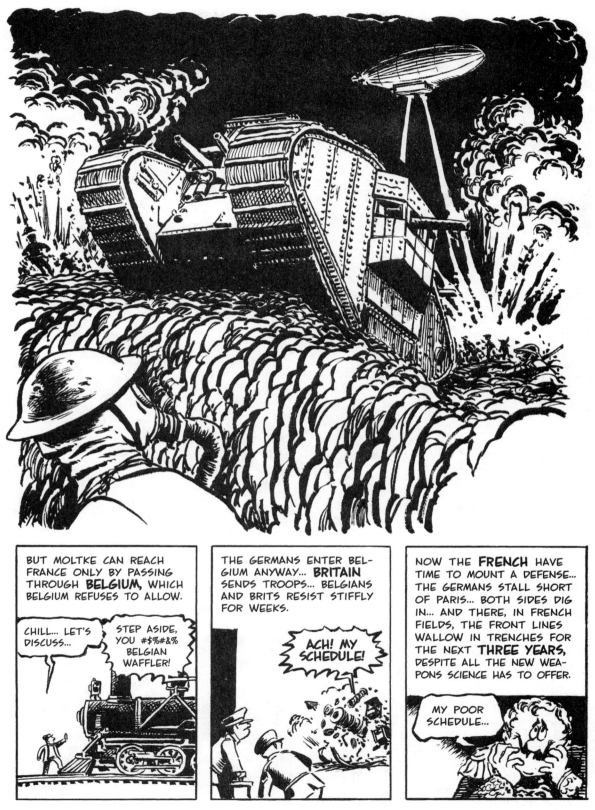

BUT MOLTKE CAN REACH FRANCE ONLY BY PASSING THROUGH **BELGIUM**, WHICH BELGIUM REFUSES TO ALLOW.

CHILL... LET'S DISCUSS...

STEP ASIDE, YOU #$%#&% BELGIAN WAFFLER!

THE GERMANS ENTER BELGIUM ANYWAY... **BRITAIN** SENDS TROOPS... BELGIANS AND BRITS RESIST STIFFLY FOR WEEKS.

ACH! MY SCHEDULE!

NOW THE **FRENCH** HAVE TIME TO MOUNT A DEFENSE... THE GERMANS STALL SHORT OF PARIS... BOTH SIDES DIG IN... AND THERE, IN FRENCH FIELDS, THE FRONT LINES WALLOW IN TRENCHES FOR THE NEXT **THREE YEARS,** DESPITE ALL THE NEW WEAPONS SCIENCE HAS TO OFFER.

MY POOR SCHEDULE...

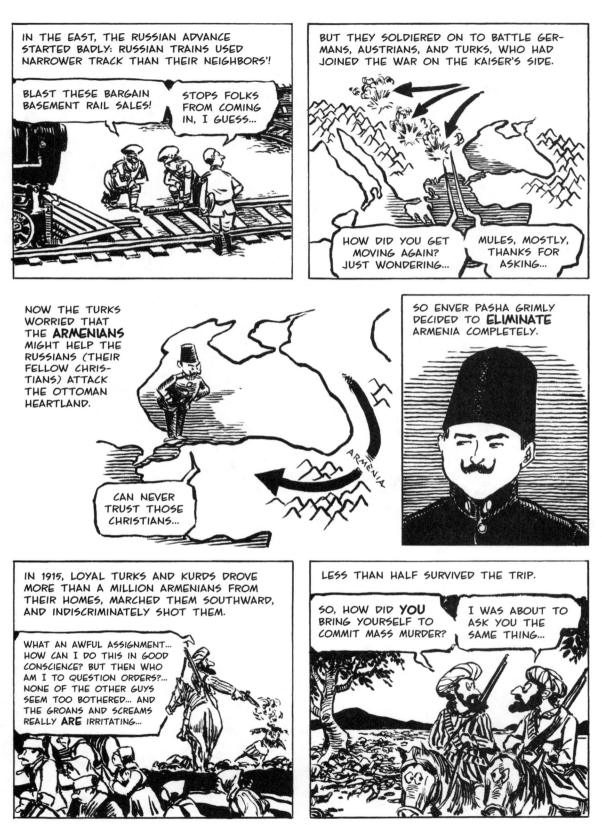

IN THE EAST, THE RUSSIAN ADVANCE STARTED BADLY: RUSSIAN TRAINS USED NARROWER TRACK THAN THEIR NEIGHBORS'!

BLAST THESE BARGAIN BASEMENT RAIL SALES!

STOPS FOLKS FROM COMING IN, I GUESS...

BUT THEY SOLDIERED ON TO BATTLE GERMANS, AUSTRIANS, AND TURKS, WHO HAD JOINED THE WAR ON THE KAISER'S SIDE.

HOW DID YOU GET MOVING AGAIN? JUST WONDERING...

MULES, MOSTLY, THANKS FOR ASKING...

NOW THE TURKS WORRIED THAT THE **ARMENIANS** MIGHT HELP THE RUSSIANS (THEIR FELLOW CHRISTIANS) ATTACK THE OTTOMAN HEARTLAND.

CAN NEVER TRUST THOSE CHRISTIANS...

ARMENIA

SO ENVER PASHA GRIMLY DECIDED TO **ELIMINATE** ARMENIA COMPLETELY.

IN 1915, LOYAL TURKS AND KURDS DROVE MORE THAN A MILLION ARMENIANS FROM THEIR HOMES, MARCHED THEM SOUTHWARD, AND INDISCRIMINATELY SHOT THEM.

WHAT AN AWFUL ASSIGNMENT... HOW CAN I DO THIS IN GOOD CONSCIENCE? BUT THEN WHO AM I TO QUESTION ORDERS?... NONE OF THE OTHER GUYS SEEM TOO BOTHERED... AND THE GROANS AND SCREAMS REALLY **ARE** IRRITATING...

LESS THAN HALF SURVIVED THE TRIP.

SO, HOW DID **YOU** BRING YOURSELF TO COMMIT MASS MURDER?

I WAS ABOUT TO ASK YOU THE SAME THING...

WHEREVER THE POWERS HAD INTERESTS, THEY FOUGHT...

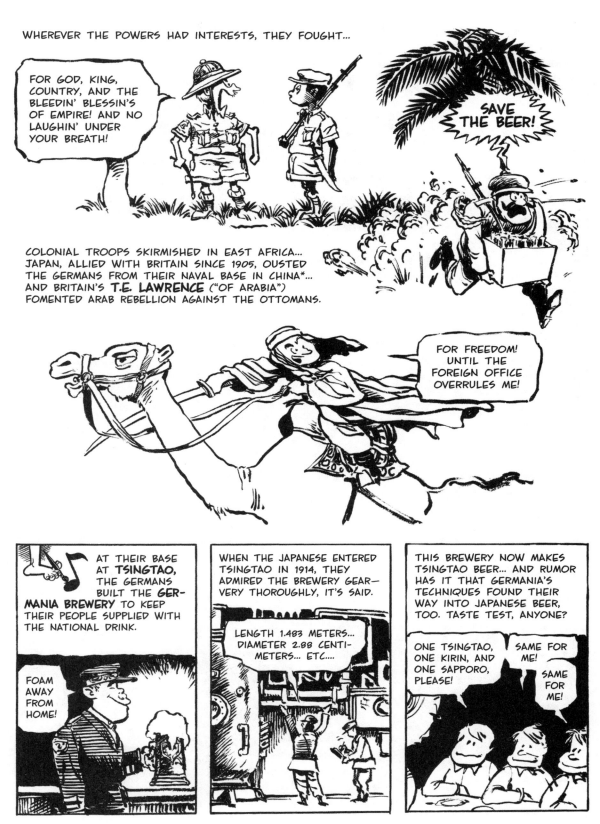

FOR GOD, KING, COUNTRY, AND THE BLEEDIN' BLESSIN'S OF EMPIRE! AND NO LAUGHIN' UNDER YOUR BREATH!

SAVE THE BEER!

COLONIAL TROOPS SKIRMISHED IN EAST AFRICA... JAPAN, ALLIED WITH BRITAIN SINCE 1905, OUSTED THE GERMANS FROM THEIR NAVAL BASE IN CHINA*... AND BRITAIN'S **T.E. LAWRENCE** ("OF ARABIA") FOMENTED ARAB REBELLION AGAINST THE OTTOMANS.

FOR FREEDOM! UNTIL THE FOREIGN OFFICE OVERRULES ME!

AT THEIR BASE AT **TSINGTAO**, THE GERMANS BUILT THE **GERMANIA BREWERY** TO KEEP THEIR PEOPLE SUPPLIED WITH THE NATIONAL DRINK.

FOAM AWAY FROM HOME!

WHEN THE JAPANESE ENTERED TSINGTAO IN 1914, THEY ADMIRED THE BREWERY GEAR—VERY THOROUGHLY, IT'S SAID.

LENGTH 1.483 METERS... DIAMETER 2.88 CENTIMETERS... ETC....

THIS BREWERY NOW MAKES TSINGTAO BEER... AND RUMOR HAS IT THAT GERMANIA'S TECHNIQUES FOUND THEIR WAY INTO JAPANESE BEER, TOO. TASTE TEST, ANYONE?

ONE TSINGTAO, ONE KIRIN, AND ONE SAPPORO, PLEASE!

SAME FOR ME!

SAME FOR ME!

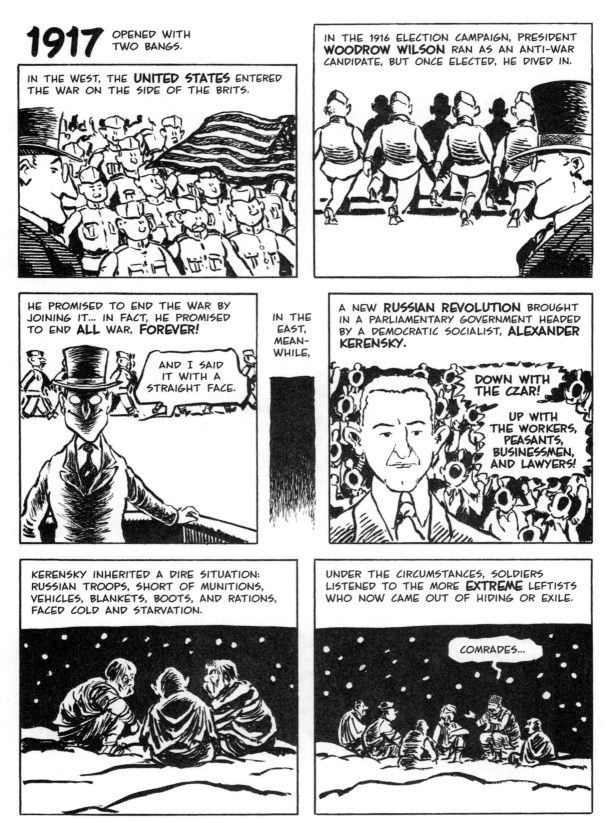

1917 OPENED WITH TWO BANGS.

IN THE WEST, THE **UNITED STATES** ENTERED THE WAR ON THE SIDE OF THE BRITS.

IN THE 1916 ELECTION CAMPAIGN, PRESIDENT **WOODROW WILSON** RAN AS AN ANTI-WAR CANDIDATE, BUT ONCE ELECTED, HE DIVED IN.

HE PROMISED TO END THE WAR BY JOINING IT... IN FACT, HE PROMISED TO END **ALL** WAR, **FOREVER!**

AND I SAID IT WITH A STRAIGHT FACE.

IN THE EAST, MEAN-WHILE,

A NEW **RUSSIAN REVOLUTION** BROUGHT IN A PARLIAMENTARY GOVERNMENT HEADED BY A DEMOCRATIC SOCIALIST, **ALEXANDER KERENSKY.**

DOWN WITH THE CZAR!

UP WITH THE WORKERS, PEASANTS, BUSINESSMEN, AND LAWYERS!

KERENSKY INHERITED A DIRE SITUATION: RUSSIAN TROOPS, SHORT OF MUNITIONS, VEHICLES, BLANKETS, BOOTS, AND RATIONS, FACED COLD AND STARVATION.

UNDER THE CIRCUMSTANCES, SOLDIERS LISTENED TO THE MORE **EXTREME** LEFTISTS WHO NOW CAME OUT OF HIDING OR EXILE.

COMRADES...

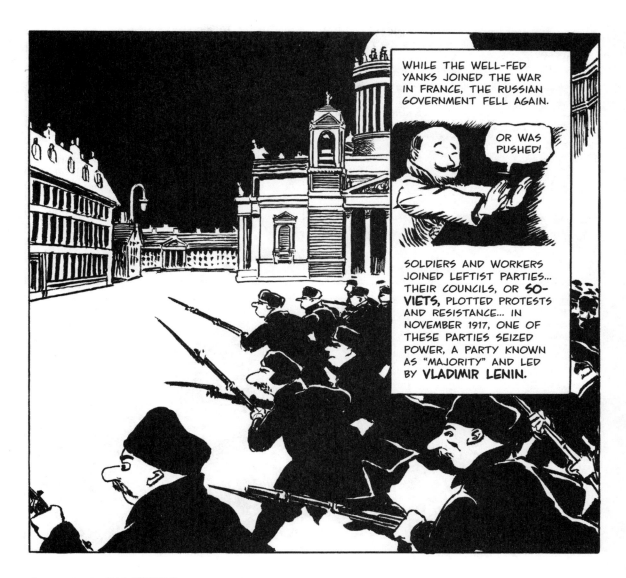

WHILE THE WELL-FED YANKS JOINED THE WAR IN FRANCE, THE RUSSIAN GOVERNMENT FELL AGAIN.

OR WAS PUSHED!

SOLDIERS AND WORKERS JOINED LEFTIST PARTIES... THEIR COUNCILS, OR **SO-VIETS,** PLOTTED PROTESTS AND RESISTANCE... IN NOVEMBER 1917, ONE OF THESE PARTIES SEIZED POWER, A PARTY KNOWN AS "MAJORITY" AND LED BY **VLADIMIR LENIN.**

"MAJORITY" (**BOLSHEVIKI** IN RUSSIAN) SAW THE WAR AS A FIGHT AMONG CAPITALISTS OVER EMPIRE, AND NOTHING TO DO WITH THE WORKERS... SO THE RED REVOLUTIONARIES IMMEDIATELY MADE PEACE WITH GERMANY AND LEFT THE OTHER POWERS TO BATTLE IT OUT.

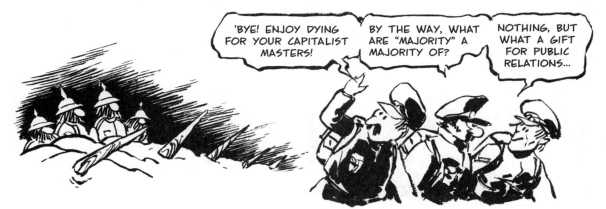

'BYE! ENJOY DYING FOR YOUR CAPITALIST MASTERS!

BY THE WAY, WHAT ARE "MAJORITY" A MAJORITY OF?

NOTHING, BUT WHAT A GIFT FOR PUBLIC RELATIONS...

GERMANY COULD NOW MOVE ITS EASTERN ARMY TO THE WEST... AND THESE SOLDIERS BROUGHT THE NEWS ABOUT RUSSIA.
IT'S AN HONEST-TO-GOD WORKERS' STATE WITHOUT BOSSES!
OR SOMETHING LIKE IT...
THEY ARGUED ABOUT SOCIALISM ALL THROUGH THE GRUELING RETREAT FROM THE WELL-ARMED, WELL-FED AMERICANS.
WHY SHOULD WE FIGHT TO FATTEN CAPITALISTS?
SILENCE, SCHWEIN! YOU DISHONOR THE GERMAN NATION! THE RACE! THE BLOOD!
OH, LIGHTEN UP, HITLER...
BY LATE 1918, TURKS AND AUSTRIANS WERE CAVING IN... GERMAN WORKERS TOOK TO THE STREETS... ON NOVEMBER 9, KAISER WILHELM FLED TO SWEDEN.
TWO DAYS LATER, THE SHOOTING STOPPED.
'BYE! NOTHING PERSONAL!
THE ALLIES—BRITAIN, FRANCE, AND THE U.S., BUT DEFINITELY NOT RUSSIA—MET IN THE MIRRORED PALACE AT VERSAILLES TO PLAN THE WORLD'S FUTURE.
BY THE WAY, DOES THIS SUIT MAKE ME LOOK FAT?
THE MIRRORS MAY EXPLAIN WHY THEIR TREATY WAS THE EXACT REVERSAL OF THE POST-NAPOLEONIC BALANCE OF POWER MADE A CENTURY EARLIER... THE VERSAILLES TREATY OF 1919 CREATED AN IMBALANCE OF POWER.
WE'VE REFLECTED LONG AND HARD!

BESIDES SHRINKING GERMANY, THE TREATY DEMANDED HUGE SUMS FROM THE LOSERS TO PAY FOR ALL THE DAMAGE.

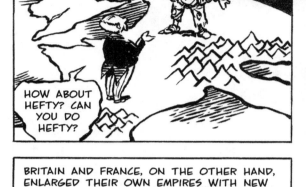

BUT WE DON'T **HAVE** HUGE SUMS!

HOW ABOUT HEFTY? CAN YOU DO HEFTY?

AUSTRIANS AND TURKS GOT WHAT THEY HAD ALWAYS DREADED: THEIR EMPIRES SPLIT INTO SMALL, ETHNIC NATIONS.

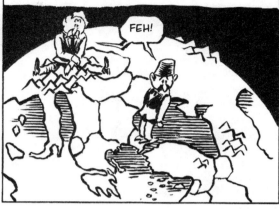

FEH!

BRITAIN AND FRANCE, ON THE OTHER HAND, ENLARGED THEIR OWN EMPIRES WITH NEW HOLDINGS IN **SYRIA, PALESTINE,** AND **IRAQ.**

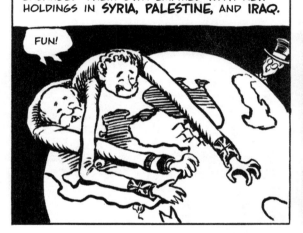

FUN!

TO BLESS THIS ARRANGEMENT, THE TREATY CREATED A NEW INTERNATIONAL ORGANIZATION, THE **LEAGUE OF NATIONS.**

LED BY US, OF COURSE!

SIGH...

(THE U.S., IRKED BY THE STANCE OF BRITAIN AND FRANCE, KEPT OUT OF THE LEAGUE.)

JUST ONE ITEM ESCAPED THE POWERS' REACH: **RUSSIA.** AFTER A CIVIL WAR AND A BRIEF ANGLO-AMERICAN INVASION, THE BOLSHEVIK ARMIES HELD ON TO RUSSIA'S VAST, MULTI-ETHNIC EMPIRE, WHICH BECAME A MARXIST "UNION OF SOVIET SOCIALIST REPUBLICS." ("SOVIET" MEANS WORKERS COUNCIL, BUT IN PRACTICE, ALL BUSINESSES WERE RUN BY THE STATE.)

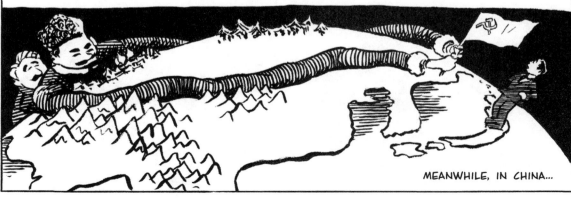

MEANWHILE, IN CHINA...

MIDDLE KINGDOM ENDS

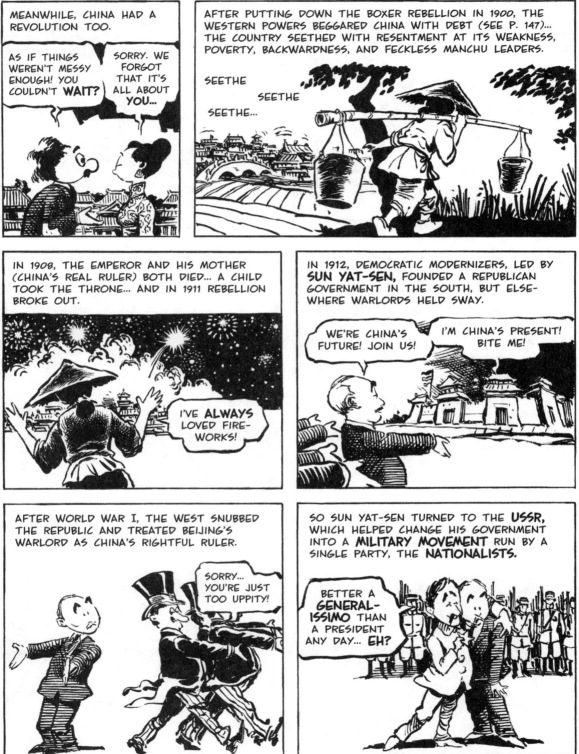

MEANWHILE, CHINA HAD A REVOLUTION TOO.

AS IF THINGS WEREN'T MESSY ENOUGH! YOU COULDN'T **WAIT**?

SORRY. WE FORGOT THAT IT'S ALL ABOUT **YOU**...

AFTER PUTTING DOWN THE BOXER REBELLION IN 1900, THE WESTERN POWERS BEGGARED CHINA WITH DEBT (SEE P. 147)... THE COUNTRY SEETHED WITH RESENTMENT AT ITS WEAKNESS, POVERTY, BACKWARDNESS, AND FECKLESS MANCHU LEADERS.

SEETHE

SEETHE

SEETHE...

IN 1908, THE EMPEROR AND HIS MOTHER (CHINA'S REAL RULER) BOTH DIED... A CHILD TOOK THE THRONE... AND IN 1911 REBELLION BROKE OUT.

I'VE **ALWAYS** LOVED FIRE-WORKS!

IN 1912, DEMOCRATIC MODERNIZERS, LED BY **SUN YAT-SEN**, FOUNDED A REPUBLICAN GOVERNMENT IN THE SOUTH, BUT ELSE-WHERE WARLORDS HELD SWAY.

WE'RE CHINA'S FUTURE! JOIN US!

I'M CHINA'S PRESENT! BITE ME!

AFTER WORLD WAR I, THE WEST SNUBBED THE REPUBLIC AND TREATED BEIJING'S WARLORD AS CHINA'S RIGHTFUL RULER.

SORRY... YOU'RE JUST TOO UPPITY!

SO SUN YAT-SEN TURNED TO THE **USSR**, WHICH HELPED CHANGE HIS GOVERNMENT INTO A **MILITARY MOVEMENT** RUN BY A SINGLE PARTY, THE **NATIONALISTS**.

BETTER A **GENERAL-ISSIMO** THAN A PRESIDENT ANY DAY... EH?

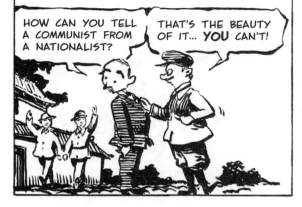

OR TWO PARTIES, REALLY... THE RUSSIANS ALSO PUT TOGETHER A SMALL CHINESE **COMMUNIST PARTY,** WHICH WORKED ALONGSIDE THE NATIONALISTS.

HOW CAN YOU TELL A COMMUNIST FROM A NATIONALIST?

THAT'S THE BEAUTY OF IT... **YOU** CAN'T!

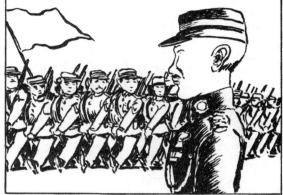

SUN YAT-SEN DIED IN 1925... THE NEW GENERALISSIMO, JAPANESE-TRAINED **CHIANG KAI-SHEK,** FELT STRONG ENOUGH TO ATTACK THE WARLORDS.

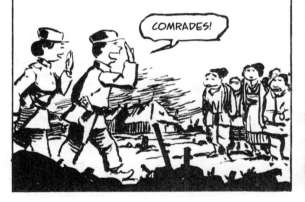

WITH EACH VICTORY, CHIANG SENT ADMINISTRATORS TO SET UP NATIONALIST RULE... AND COMMUNISTS FLOCKED TO THESE PROVINCIAL POSITIONS.

COMRADES!

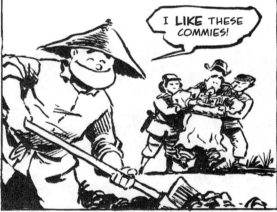

THERE THEY TOOK FROM THE RICH AND GAVE TO THE POOR!

I **LIKE** THESE COMMIES!

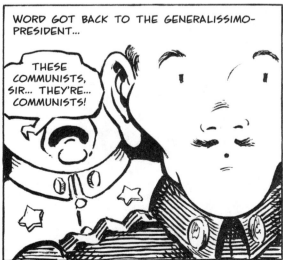

WORD GOT BACK TO THE GENERALISSIMO-PRESIDENT...

THESE COMMUNISTS, SIR... THEY'RE... COMMUNISTS!

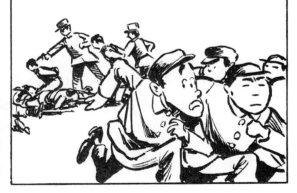

IN 1927, CHIANG TURNED HIS GUNS ON THE COMMUNISTS, KILLING HUNDREDS... BUT THOUSANDS MORE ESCAPED TO BEGIN A NEW **CIVIL WAR...**

ROARING '20s

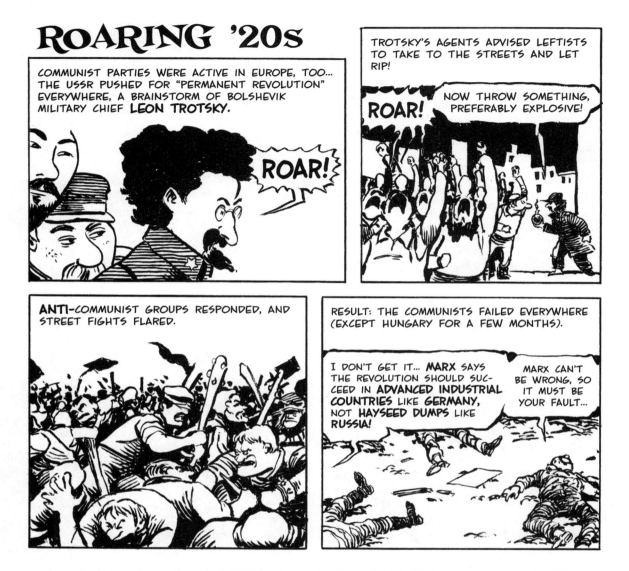

COMMUNIST PARTIES WERE ACTIVE IN EUROPE, TOO... THE USSR PUSHED FOR "PERMANENT REVOLUTION" EVERYWHERE, A BRAINSTORM OF BOLSHEVIK MILITARY CHIEF **LEON TROTSKY.**

ROAR!

TROTSKY'S AGENTS ADVISED LEFTISTS TO TAKE TO THE STREETS AND LET RIP!

ROAR!

NOW THROW SOMETHING, PREFERABLY EXPLOSIVE!

ANTI-COMMUNIST GROUPS RESPONDED, AND STREET FIGHTS FLARED.

RESULT: THE COMMUNISTS FAILED EVERYWHERE (EXCEPT HUNGARY FOR A FEW MONTHS).

I DON'T GET IT... **MARX** SAYS THE REVOLUTION SHOULD SUCCEED IN **ADVANCED INDUSTRIAL COUNTRIES** LIKE **GERMANY**, NOT **HAYSEED DUMPS** LIKE **RUSSIA!**

MARX CAN'T BE WRONG, SO IT MUST BE YOUR FAULT...

ON THE OTHER HAND, A **RIGHT-WING** LEADER, **BENITO MUSSOLINI,** ROSE TO LEAD **ITALY** IN 1922. WITHIN THREE YEARS, HIS BROWN-SHIRTED STREET FIGHTERS CRUSHED THE LEFT, THE REPUBLICAN GOVERNMENT, AND ALL DISAGREEMENT. MUSSOLINI, NOW **IL DUCE** (THE DUKE), CALLED HIS SYSTEM **FASCISM.**

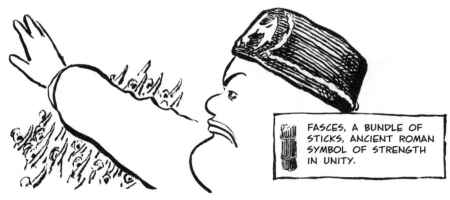

FASCES, A BUNDLE OF STICKS, ANCIENT ROMAN SYMBOL OF STRENGTH IN UNITY.

AS IN ITALY, SO IN **GERMANY:** DISGUSTED VETERANS, INCLUDING ART-SCHOOL REJECT ADOLF HITLER, FOUNDED THE "NATIONAL SOCIALISTS" OR **NAZIS,** A FASCIST-STYLE PARTY WITH AN EXTRA OBSESSION WITH RACIAL PURITY.

IN 1923, THE NAZIS DECIDED TO MAKE THEIR MOVE... GERMANY WAS IN CHAOS... PRICES WERE RISING WILDLY...

20,000 M

IN FACT, PRICES WERE RISING BY THE HOUR!

THREE MIL-LION MARKS PLEASE!

OUTRAGEOUS! SHAMEFUL! SOMEHOW JEWISH!

KEEP TALKING... NOW IT'S FOUR MILLION...

AT A RALLY IN A MUNICH BEER HALL, HITLER ANNOUNCED THAT THE TIME HAD COME FOR A **PUTSCH.**

HOW MUCH FOR THE BEER?

TWO BILLION MARKS.

THEY TROMPED OUT AND TOOK OVER A FEW GOVERN-MENT OFFICES.

HEY, THAT'S TWO BILLION **EACH!**

THE EPISODE ENDED QUICKLY, AS A FEW DOZEN POLICEMEN ROUNDED UP ALL THE PUTSCHISTS.

0,000,000 M

BUT THEIR PUNISHMENT WAS LIGHT... HITLER, THE LEADER, WAS OUT OF JAIL WITHIN MONTHS. THE NAZIS, IT SEEMED, HAD FRIENDS IN HIGH PLACES.

'BYE!

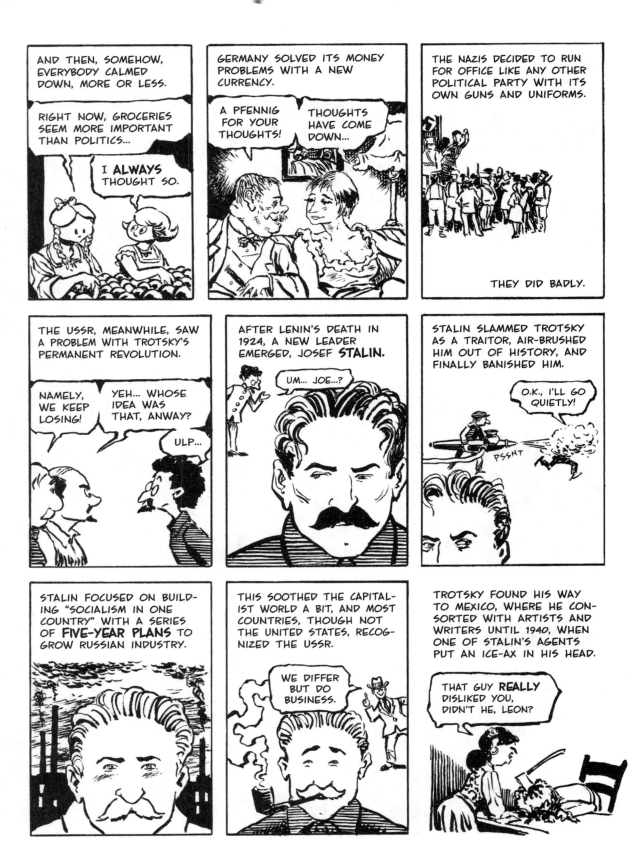

AND THEN, SOMEHOW, EVERYBODY CALMED DOWN, MORE OR LESS.

RIGHT NOW, GROCERIES SEEM MORE IMPORTANT THAN POLITICS...

I **ALWAYS** THOUGHT SO.

GERMANY SOLVED ITS MONEY PROBLEMS WITH A NEW CURRENCY.

A PFENNIG FOR YOUR THOUGHTS!

THOUGHTS HAVE COME DOWN...

THE NAZIS DECIDED TO RUN FOR OFFICE LIKE ANY OTHER POLITICAL PARTY WITH ITS OWN GUNS AND UNIFORMS.

THEY DID BADLY.

THE USSR, MEANWHILE, SAW A PROBLEM WITH TROTSKY'S PERMANENT REVOLUTION.

NAMELY, WE KEEP LOSING!

YEH... WHOSE IDEA WAS THAT, ANWAY?

ULP...

AFTER LENIN'S DEATH IN 1924, A NEW LEADER EMERGED, JOSEF **STALIN.**

UM... JOE...?

STALIN SLAMMED TROTSKY AS A TRAITOR, AIR-BRUSHED HIM OUT OF HISTORY, AND FINALLY BANISHED HIM.

O.K., I'LL GO QUIETLY!

PSSHT

STALIN FOCUSED ON BUILD-ING "SOCIALISM IN ONE COUNTRY" WITH A SERIES OF **FIVE-YEAR PLANS** TO GROW RUSSIAN INDUSTRY.

THIS SOOTHED THE CAPITAL-IST WORLD A BIT, AND MOST COUNTRIES, THOUGH NOT THE UNITED STATES, RECOG-NIZED THE USSR.

WE DIFFER BUT DO BUSINESS.

TROTSKY FOUND HIS WAY TO MEXICO, WHERE HE CON-SORTED WITH ARTISTS AND WRITERS UNTIL 1940, WHEN ONE OF STALIN'S AGENTS PUT AN ICE-AX IN HIS HEAD.

THAT GUY **REALLY** DISLIKED YOU, DIDN'T HE, LEON?

AND SO BEGAN A CAPITALIST BOOM... THE **JAZZ AGE**... MUSIC WENT UP-TEMPO, HEMLINES ROSE, NECKLINES PLUNGED... CARS, RADIOS, AND PHONOGRAPHS REVOLUTIONIZED PEOPLE'S LIVES... AND MOVIES SPREAD THESE IMAGES AND INSPIRED IMITATION ACROSS THE WORLD...

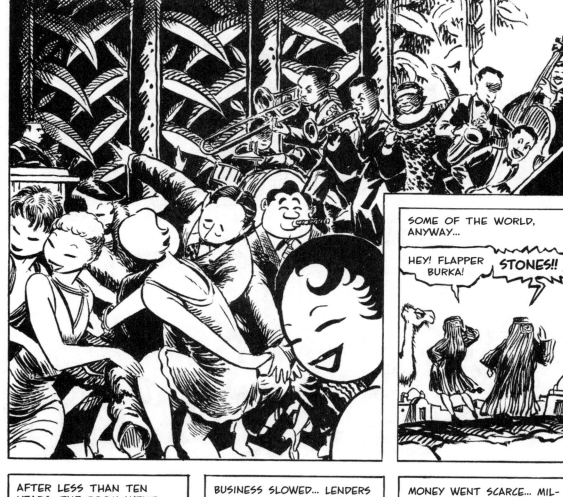

SOME OF THE WORLD, ANYWAY...

HEY! FLAPPER BURKA!

STONES!!

AFTER LESS THAN TEN YEARS, THE BOOM WENT BUST WITH A CRASH—A STOCK MARKET CRASH, THAT IS, IN OCTOBER 1929.

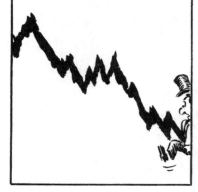

BUSINESS SLOWED... LENDERS CALLED IN LOANS... PEOPLE RAN TO THE BANKS FOR THEIR CASH—AND LEARNED THE TRUTH ABOUT BANKS.

ONLY A **FRACTION** OF YOUR DE-POSIT STAYS IN THE BUILDING... MOST OF THE MONEY IS OUT ON LOAN TO BUSINESSES... IT'S NOT HERE AND **NEVER WILL BE**...

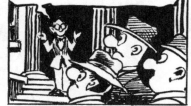

MONEY WENT SCARCE... MIL-LIONS OF PEOPLE LOST JOBS, HOMES, FARMS... PRICES AND WAGES PLUNGED...

AT LEAST WE'RE GETTING AN EDUCA-TION IN FINANCE...

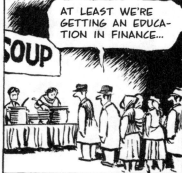

SOUP

DEPRESSED

THE DEPRESSION SPREAD WORLDWIDE, AND LIKE A DEPRESSED PLANET ANYWHERE, THE WORLD **ACTED OUT.**

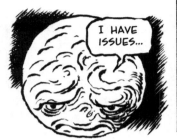

I HAVE ISSUES...

JAPAN'S NEW EMPEROR, **HIROHITO,** FORMED AN AGGRESSIVE GOVERNMENT THAT TRIED TO CHEER UP THE NATION WITH SHOCK THERAPY BY INVADING **MANCHURIA** IN 1931.

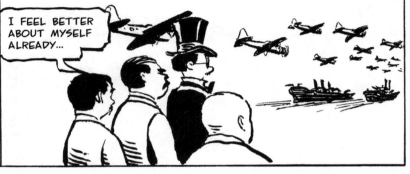

I FEEL BETTER ABOUT MYSELF ALREADY...

IN 1932, THE UNITED STATES ELECTED A DEMOCRATIC PRESIDENT, **FRANKLIN ROOSEVELT,** WHO PROMISED AMERICANS A "NEW DEAL."

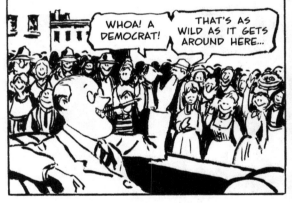

WHOA! A DEMOCRAT!

THAT'S AS WILD AS IT GETS AROUND HERE...

THIS INCLUDED A NATIONAL RETIREMENT PENSION, BANK DEPOSIT INSURANCE, NEW DAMS, BRIDGES, POST OFFICES, AND ELECTRIC GRIDS... NO WONDER ROOSEVELT WON RE-ELECTION IN 1936, 1940, AND 1944...

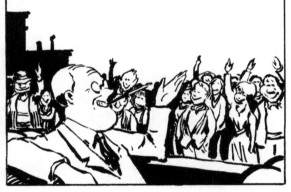

IN GERMANY, VIOLENCE BETWEEN LEFT AND RIGHT ERUPTED AGAIN... PEOPLE TURNED TO **EXTREME PARTIES** FOR ANSWERS.

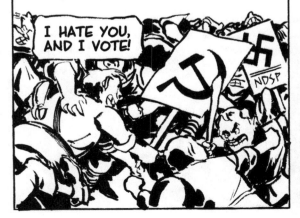

I HATE YOU, AND I VOTE!

IN 1933, THE VOTE SPLIT SEVERAL WAYS... AT **35 PERCENT,** THE NAZIS HAD MORE THAN ANYONE ELSE... SO **ADOLF HITLER** BECAME CHANCELLOR OF GERMANY.

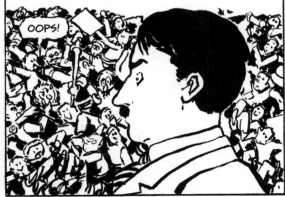

OOPS!

ONCE IN POWER, HITLER SILENCED ALL DISSENT, EVEN AMONG HIS OWN NAZIS, HUNDREDS OF WHOM WERE KILLED IN A SINGLE "NIGHT OF THE LONG KNIVES."

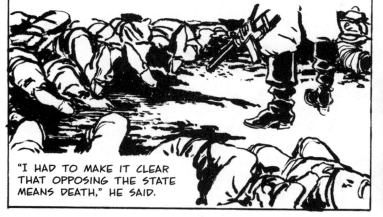

"I HAD TO MAKE IT CLEAR THAT OPPOSING THE STATE MEANS DEATH," HE SAID.

AS PROMISED, THE NAZIS PUT DOWN THE JEWS... NEW LAWS BARRED JEWS FROM GOVERNMENT, THE PROFESSIONS, AND MARRYING "ARYANS." EVERYONE WAS CLASSIFIED BY RACE, BASED ON BIRTH RECORDS GOING BACK FOR GENERATIONS.

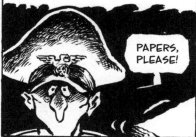

PAPERS, PLEASE!

GERMAN INSTITUTIONS PURGED THEIR JEWS... OUT WENT DOCTORS, LAWYERS, STUDENTS, AND PROFESSORS, LIKE **ALBERT EINSTEIN,** WHO FLED IN 1933.

UM... YOU DON'T THINK GETTING RID OF OUR TOP SCIENTISTS MIGHT BE... UM... STUPID?

A JEWISH IDEA!

THE NAZIS CELEBRATED THEMSELVES AND COWED EVERYONE ELSE WITH MASSIVE, REGIMENTED RALLIES.

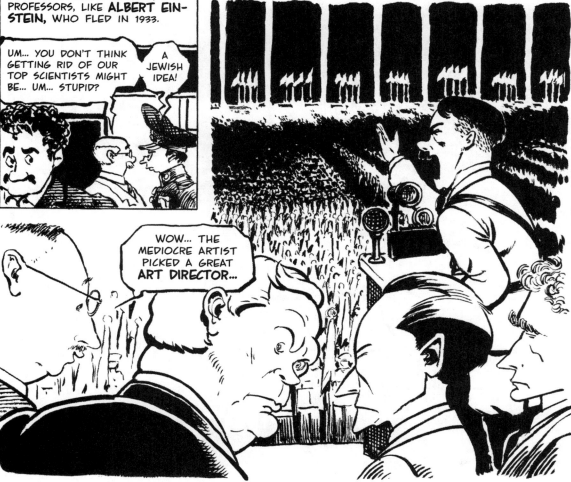

WOW... THE MEDIOCRE ARTIST PICKED A GREAT **ART DIRECTOR...**

ELSEWHERE, MEANWHILE...

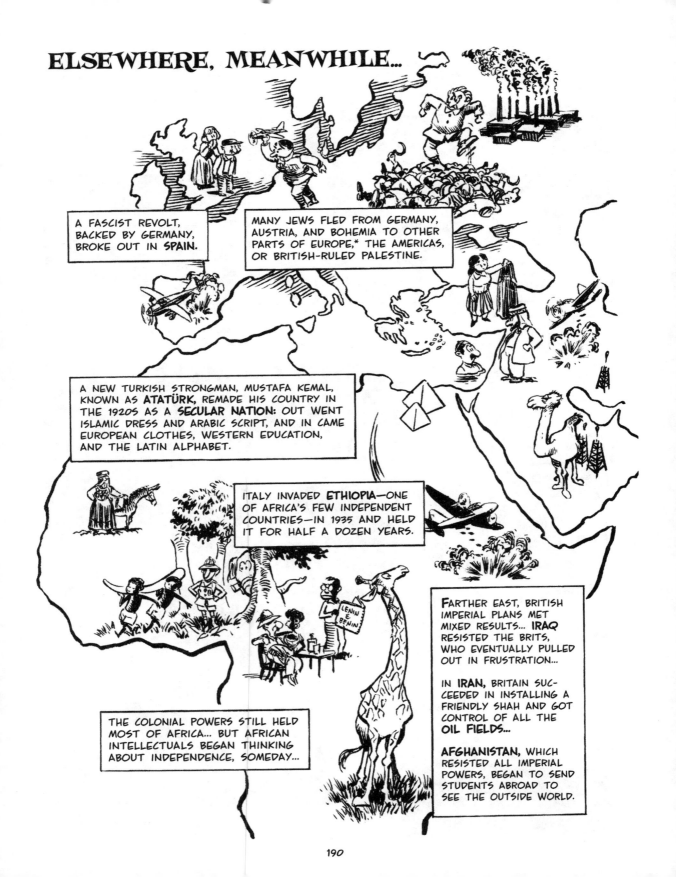

A FASCIST REVOLT, BACKED BY GERMANY, BROKE OUT IN **SPAIN**.

MANY JEWS FLED FROM GERMANY, AUSTRIA, AND BOHEMIA TO OTHER PARTS OF EUROPE,* THE AMERICAS, OR BRITISH-RULED PALESTINE.

A NEW TURKISH STRONGMAN, MUSTAFA KEMAL, KNOWN AS **ATATÜRK**, REMADE HIS COUNTRY IN THE 1920S AS A **SECULAR NATION**: OUT WENT ISLAMIC DRESS AND ARABIC SCRIPT, AND IN CAME EUROPEAN CLOTHES, WESTERN EDUCATION, AND THE LATIN ALPHABET.

ITALY INVADED **ETHIOPIA**—ONE OF AFRICA'S FEW INDEPENDENT COUNTRIES—IN 1935 AND HELD IT FOR HALF A DOZEN YEARS.

FARTHER EAST, BRITISH IMPERIAL PLANS MET MIXED RESULTS... **IRAQ** RESISTED THE BRITS, WHO EVENTUALLY PULLED OUT IN FRUSTRATION...

IN **IRAN**, BRITAIN SUC-CEEDED IN INSTALLING A FRIENDLY SHAH AND GOT CONTROL OF ALL THE **OIL FIELDS**...

AFGHANISTAN, WHICH RESISTED ALL IMPERIAL POWERS, BEGAN TO SEND STUDENTS ABROAD TO SEE THE OUTSIDE WORLD.

THE COLONIAL POWERS STILL HELD MOST OF AFRICA... BUT AFRICAN INTELLECTUALS BEGAN THINKING ABOUT INDEPENDENCE, SOMEDAY...

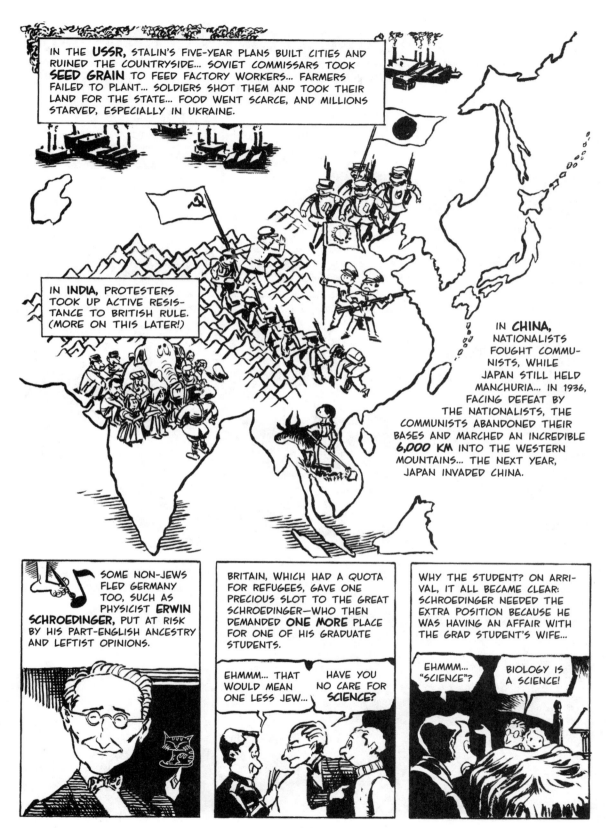

IN THE **USSR,** STALIN'S FIVE-YEAR PLANS BUILT CITIES AND RUINED THE COUNTRYSIDE... SOVIET COMMISSARS TOOK **SEED GRAIN** TO FEED FACTORY WORKERS... FARMERS FAILED TO PLANT... SOLDIERS SHOT THEM AND TOOK THEIR LAND FOR THE STATE... FOOD WENT SCARCE, AND MILLIONS STARVED, ESPECIALLY IN UKRAINE.

IN **INDIA,** PROTESTERS TOOK UP ACTIVE RESISTANCE TO BRITISH RULE. (MORE ON THIS LATER!)

IN **CHINA,** NATIONALISTS FOUGHT COMMUNISTS, WHILE JAPAN STILL HELD MANCHURIA... IN 1936, FACING DEFEAT BY THE NATIONALISTS, THE COMMUNISTS ABANDONED THEIR BASES AND MARCHED AN INCREDIBLE **6,000 KM** INTO THE WESTERN MOUNTAINS... THE NEXT YEAR, JAPAN INVADED CHINA.

SOME NON-JEWS FLED GERMANY TOO, SUCH AS PHYSICIST **ERWIN SCHROEDINGER,** PUT AT RISK BY HIS PART-ENGLISH ANCESTRY AND LEFTIST OPINIONS.

BRITAIN, WHICH HAD A QUOTA FOR REFUGEES, GAVE ONE PRECIOUS SLOT TO THE GREAT SCHROEDINGER—WHO THEN DEMANDED **ONE MORE** PLACE FOR ONE OF HIS GRADUATE STUDENTS.

EHMMM... THAT WOULD MEAN ONE LESS JEW...

HAVE YOU NO CARE FOR **SCIENCE?**

WHY THE STUDENT? ON ARRIVAL, IT ALL BECAME CLEAR: SCHROEDINGER NEEDED THE EXTRA POSITION BECAUSE HE WAS HAVING AN AFFAIR WITH THE GRAD STUDENT'S WIFE...

EHMMM... "SCIENCE"?

BIOLOGY IS A SCIENCE!

WAR AND REVOLUTION (CONTINUED)

UNDER HITLER, GERMANY BUILT UP ITS ARMY AGAIN, WHILE BRITAIN AND FRANCE DID NOT...

NAZI MARCHERS FAVORED AN ELEVATED GAIT KNOWN, FOR SOME REASON, AS THE GOOSE STEP.

> I FEEL LIKE A CHORUS GIRL...

> OW! WHO GOOSED ME?

BY '38, HITLER HAD ENOUGH KICK TO DEMAND CONTROL OF AUSTRIA AND PART OF CZECHOSLOVAKIA... BRITAIN AND FRANCE, TOO WEAK TO RESIST, STOOD ASIDE.

> DON'T WORRY! IT'S THE LAST THING I'LL EVER WANT!

KICK ME   KICK ME

THE NAZIS ROLLED INTO THEIR NEW TERRITORY TO WILD CHEERS AND BEASTLY TREATMENT OF POLITICAL OPPONENTS AND JEWS.

AS BRITAIN AND FRANCE FRANTICALLY REARMED, GERMANY MADE A SURPRISE PACT WITH THE **USSR**.

> PSST!

> WHAT?

HITLER AND STALIN—UNTIL THEN BITTER ENEMIES—QUIETLY AGREED TO DIVIDE **POLAND**.

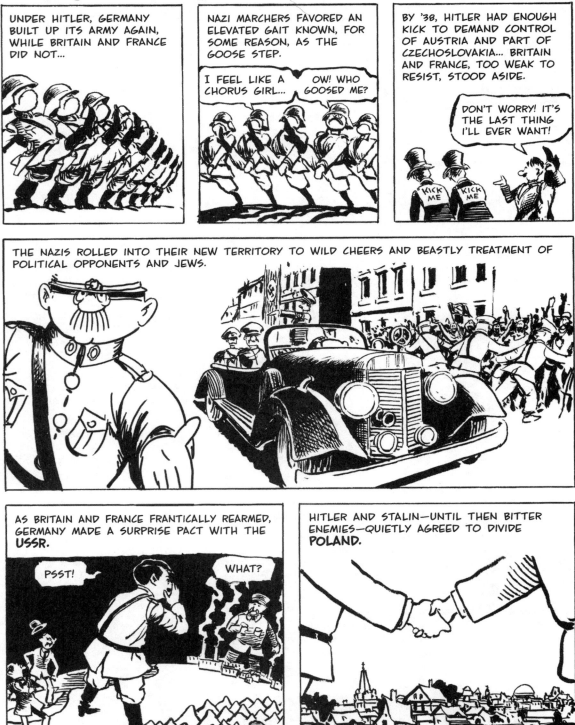

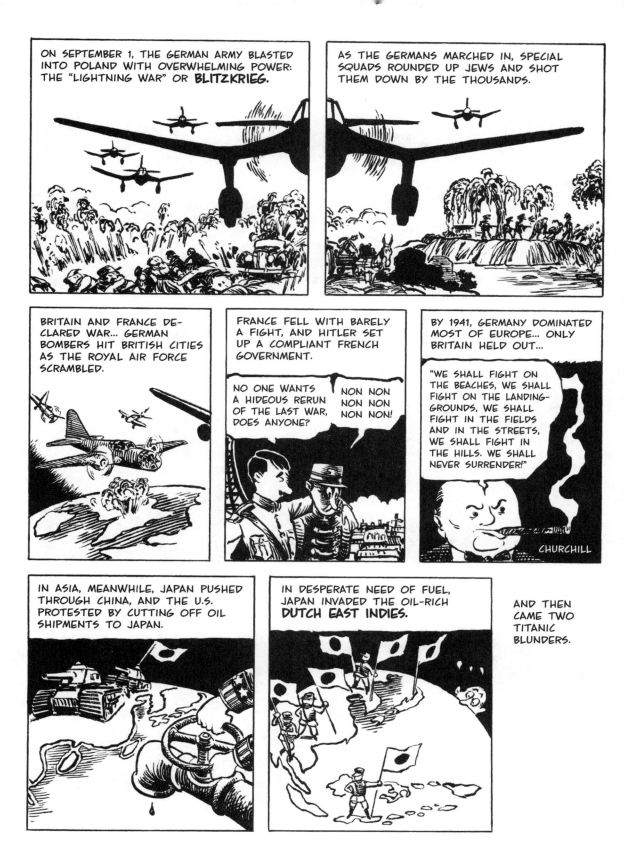

ON SEPTEMBER 1, THE GERMAN ARMY BLASTED INTO POLAND WITH OVERWHELMING POWER: THE "LIGHTNING WAR" OR **BLITZKRIEG.**

AS THE GERMANS MARCHED IN, SPECIAL SQUADS ROUNDED UP JEWS AND SHOT THEM DOWN BY THE THOUSANDS.

BRITAIN AND FRANCE DECLARED WAR... GERMAN BOMBERS HIT BRITISH CITIES AS THE ROYAL AIR FORCE SCRAMBLED.

FRANCE FELL WITH BARELY A FIGHT, AND HITLER SET UP A COMPLIANT FRENCH GOVERNMENT.

NO ONE WANTS A HIDEOUS RERUN OF THE LAST WAR, DOES ANYONE?

NON NON NON NON NON NON!

BY 1941, GERMANY DOMINATED MOST OF EUROPE... ONLY BRITAIN HELD OUT...

"WE SHALL FIGHT ON THE BEACHES, WE SHALL FIGHT ON THE LANDING-GROUNDS, WE SHALL FIGHT IN THE FIELDS AND IN THE STREETS, WE SHALL FIGHT IN THE HILLS. WE SHALL NEVER SURRENDER!"

CHURCHILL

IN ASIA, MEANWHILE, JAPAN PUSHED THROUGH CHINA, AND THE U.S. PROTESTED BY CUTTING OFF OIL SHIPMENTS TO JAPAN.

IN DESPERATE NEED OF FUEL, JAPAN INVADED THE OIL-RICH **DUTCH EAST INDIES.**

AND THEN CAME TWO TITANIC BLUNDERS.

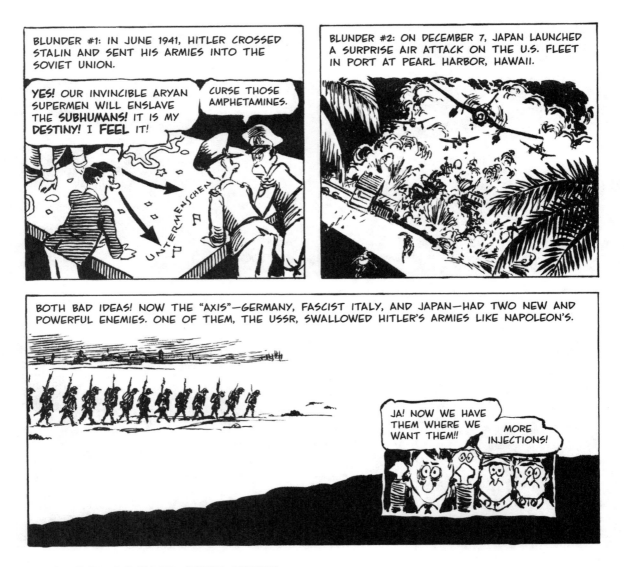

BLUNDER #1: IN JUNE 1941, HITLER CROSSED STALIN AND SENT HIS ARMIES INTO THE SOVIET UNION.

BLUNDER #2: ON DECEMBER 7, JAPAN LAUNCHED A SURPRISE AIR ATTACK ON THE U.S. FLEET IN PORT AT PEARL HARBOR, HAWAII.

BOTH BAD IDEAS! NOW THE "AXIS"—GERMANY, FASCIST ITALY, AND JAPAN—HAD TWO NEW AND POWERFUL ENEMIES. ONE OF THEM, THE USSR, SWALLOWED HITLER'S ARMIES LIKE NAPOLEON'S.

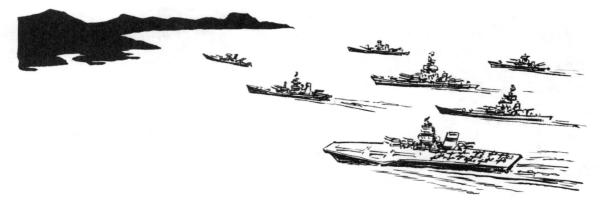

THE OTHER, THE UNITED STATES, REBUILT ITS NAVY AT TOP SPEED AND STEAMED INTO BATTLE AGAINST JAPAN.

AFTER TWO RUSSIAN (I.E., COLD) WINTERS, THE SOVIET ARMY PUSHED THE GERMANS BACK WITH TERRIBLE LOSSES ON BOTH SIDES...
WHILE BRITISH AND AMERICAN BOMBERS FLATTENED OR INCINERATED ONE GERMAN CITY AFTER ANOTHER.
(DESPITE THE ALLIED BOMBING OF CIVILIANS, AN ESTIMATED 85 PERCENT OF ALL WAR DEATHS WERE ON THE ALLIED SIDE—MAINLY RUSSIANS, CHINESE, AND JEWS.)
LOSSES OR NO, THE NAZIS STILL FOUND RESOURCES TO SPEND ON "SOLVING" THE "JEWISH PROBLEM."
WE'RE RUNNING OUT OF TIME!
SOLDIERS CORRALED JEWS... TRAINS MOVED THEM... CAMPS HOUSED THEM... POISON GAS KILLED THEM... OVENS BURNED THEIR BODIES...
HURRY HURRY HURRY!
AS THE RUSSIANS POUNDED INTO POLAND, THEY FOUND CAMPFULS OF THE STARVING AND THE DEAD.
#%$!!
IF YOU'RE GON' BE LIKE THAT, YOU'LL NEVER FEEL MY PAIN...
IN JUNE 1944, AMERICAN, BRITISH, AND ANTI-GERMAN FRENCH ARMIES ENTERED FRANCE... PUSHED INTO GERMANY... AND FOUND MORE DEATH CAMPS.
BERLIN
PARIS
IN APRIL 1945, THE ALLIES REACHED BERLIN, HITLER COMMITTED SUICIDE, AND GERMANY QUICKLY SURRENDERED.
WE HOPE YOU'VE LEARNED YOUR LESSON!
THERE'S A LESSON?
WHAT IS THE LESSON?
CAPITALISM! DEMOCRACY!
COMMUNISM!
UH-OH...

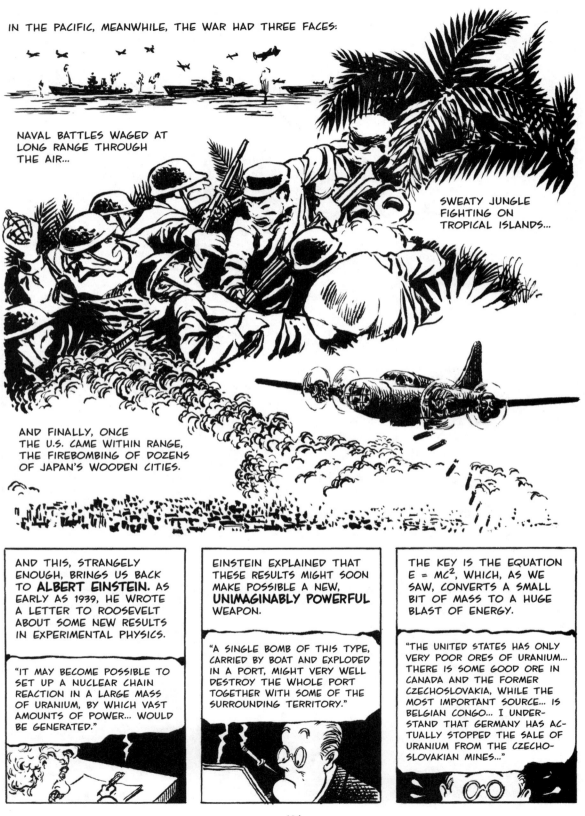

IN THE PACIFIC, MEANWHILE, THE WAR HAD THREE FACES:

NAVAL BATTLES WAGED AT LONG RANGE THROUGH THE AIR...

SWEATY JUNGLE FIGHTING ON TROPICAL ISLANDS...

AND FINALLY, ONCE THE U.S. CAME WITHIN RANGE, THE FIREBOMBING OF DOZENS OF JAPAN'S WOODEN CITIES.

AND THIS, STRANGELY ENOUGH, BRINGS US BACK TO **ALBERT EINSTEIN.** AS EARLY AS 1939, HE WROTE A LETTER TO ROOSEVELT ABOUT SOME NEW RESULTS IN EXPERIMENTAL PHYSICS.

"IT MAY BECOME POSSIBLE TO SET UP A NUCLEAR CHAIN REACTION IN A LARGE MASS OF URANIUM, BY WHICH VAST AMOUNTS OF POWER... WOULD BE GENERATED."

EINSTEIN EXPLAINED THAT THESE RESULTS MIGHT SOON MAKE POSSIBLE A NEW, **UNIMAGINABLY POWERFUL** WEAPON.

"A SINGLE BOMB OF THIS TYPE, CARRIED BY BOAT AND EXPLODED IN A PORT, MIGHT VERY WELL DESTROY THE WHOLE PORT TOGETHER WITH SOME OF THE SURROUNDING TERRITORY."

THE KEY IS THE EQUATION $E = MC^2$, WHICH, AS WE SAW, CONVERTS A SMALL BIT OF MASS TO A HUGE BLAST OF ENERGY.

"THE UNITED STATES HAS ONLY VERY POOR ORES OF URANIUM... THERE IS SOME GOOD ORE IN CANADA AND THE FORMER CZECHOSLOVAKIA, WHILE THE MOST IMPORTANT SOURCE... IS BELGIAN CONGO... I UNDERSTAND THAT GERMANY HAS ACTUALLY STOPPED THE SALE OF URANIUM FROM THE CZECHO-SLOVAKIAN MINES..."

196

THE WAR DEPARTMENT
BUILT A CITY IN THE NEW
MEXICO DESERT WHERE
AMERICA'S TOP PHYSICISTS
WORKED ON THE NEW
EXPLOSIVE FOR FOUR YEARS.

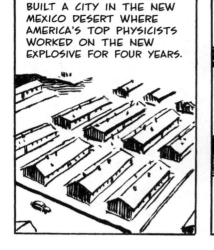

BY THE TIME THE BOMB WAS
FINISHED, IN JULY 1945,
GERMANY HAD ALREADY
SURRENDERED.

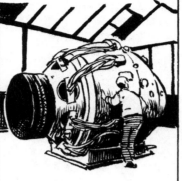

BUT JAPAN FOUGHT ON...
AN INVASION OF JAPAN
WOULD FACE RELENTLESS
RESISTANCE... SO PRESIDENT
TRUMAN (ROOSEVELT
HAVING DIED FOUR MONTHS
EARLIER) GAVE THE NOD,
AND A B-29 HEADED FOR
JAPAN WITH A SINGLE BOMB
IN ITS BAY.

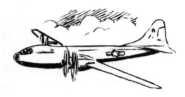

HIROSHIMA, AUGUST 6, 1945: THE
EXPLOSION BEGAN WITH A BLINDING
FLASH OF WHITE LIGHT, AS BRIGHT AS
DAY EVEN THROUGH CLOSED EYELIDS.

THEN THE BLAST, THE HEAT, THE TOWERING CLOUD... AND HIROSHIMA WAS GONE.

STILL JAPAN HELD OUT... ON AUGUST 9, A SECOND NUCLEAR BOMB OBLITERATED NAGASAKI, AND JAPAN SURRENDERED.

A THEORY ABOUT LIGHT HAD PRODUCED SOMETHING VERY DARK... THE DARKEST INVENTION OF AN ENLIGHTENED AGE...

EINSTEIN'S THEORY DEFIED COMMON SENSE, AND SO DID ITS APPLICATION: IF **ONE** ATOMIC BOMB WAS A WEAPON, A FEW **THOUSAND** MIGHT BE THE END OF US ALL... BUT PEOPLE BUILT MORE OF THEM ANYWAY.

IT'S MILITARY LOGIC!

NEXT:
BEYOND REASON?

IN JUST 50 MORE PAGES THIS CARTOON HISTORY IS COMING TO AN—ULP—END...
I'LL TAKE MY LEAVE AND BE NO MORE... CROSS THAT MYSTERIOUS BOUNDARY BETWEEN NOW AND AFTERWARD... PASS ON TO... WHERE?
WHERE INDEED? IN THE COURSE OF THIS HISTORY, WE'VE SEEN MANY PEOPLE WHO CLAIMED TO KNOW THE FUTURE, BOTH IN THIS WORLD AND THE NEXT...
SEERS AND SEEKERS, PUNDITS AND PROPHETS... SO FAR-SIGHTED... SO PERSUASIVE... SO FULL OF FAITH IN THEIR OWN VISIONS!
PROPHECY
HISTORY
TOO BAD NONE OF 'EM AGREE ABOUT ANYTHING...
FLIP
FLIP
FLIP
BUT HEY, I LOVE A SURPRISE! DON'T YOU?

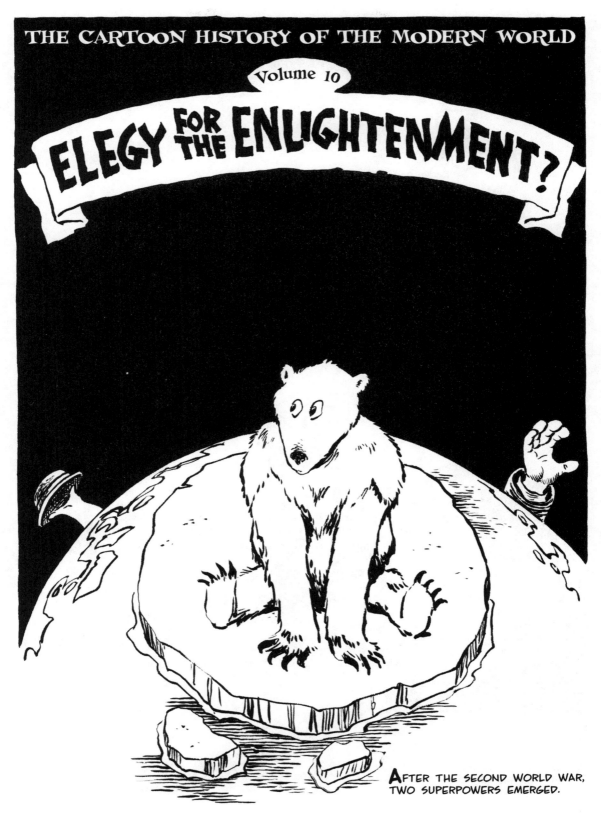

THE CARTOON HISTORY OF THE MODERN WORLD

Volume 10

ELEGY FOR THE ENLIGHTENMENT?

AFTER THE SECOND WORLD WAR, TWO SUPERPOWERS EMERGED.

OF ALL COUNTRIES IN THE WAR EXCEPT POSSIBLY CHINA, THE **SOVIET UNION** HAD SUFFERED THE MOST. TWENTY MILLION OF ITS PEOPLE—ONE IN TEN—HAD DIED... MAJOR CITIES LAY RUINED... BUT BECAUSE OF ITS SIZE, MUCH WAS SPARED... AND NOW, WITH ARMIES OCCUPYING MOST OF EASTERN EUROPE, DICTATOR **JOSEF STALIN** SAW A NEW OPPORTUNITY TO SPREAD THE SOVIET SYSTEM.

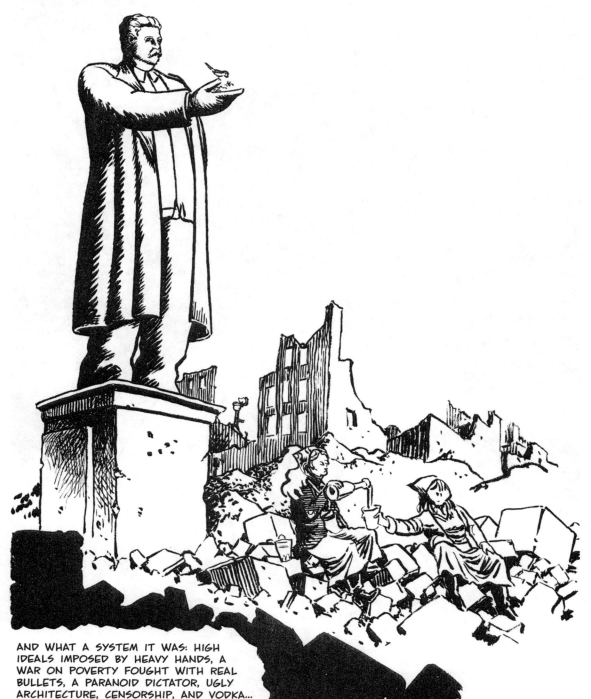

AND WHAT A SYSTEM IT WAS: HIGH IDEALS IMPOSED BY HEAVY HANDS, A WAR ON POVERTY FOUGHT WITH REAL BULLETS, A PARANOID DICTATOR, UGLY ARCHITECTURE, CENSORSHIP, AND VODKA...

THE **UNITED STATES** HAD LOST 600,000 SONS OVERSEAS, BUT AT HOME ITS MINES, OIL WELLS, FACTORIES, BRIDGES, CITIES, HIGHWAYS, POWER PLANTS, AND DAMS STILL STOOD INTACT, AND NOW ITS ARMIES AND NAVIES WERE STATIONED AROUND THE WORLD.

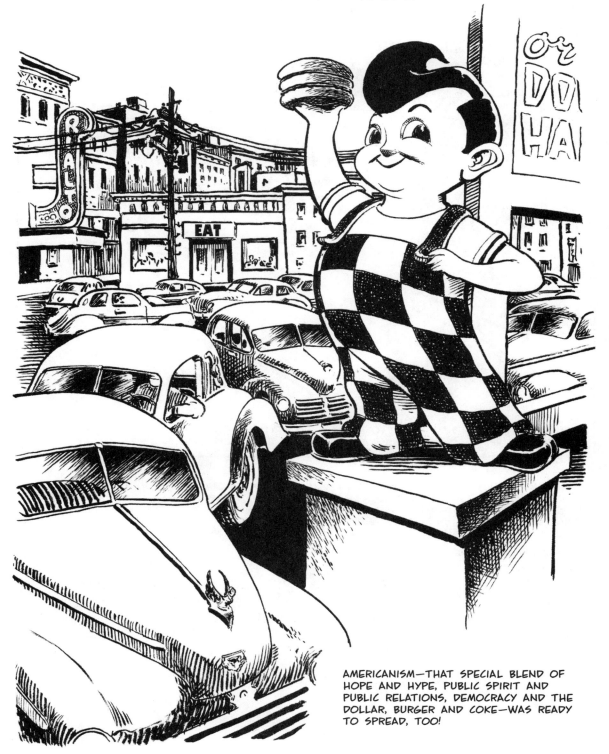

AMERICANISM—THAT SPECIAL BLEND OF HOPE AND HYPE, PUBLIC SPIRIT AND PUBLIC RELATIONS, DEMOCRACY AND THE DOLLAR, BURGER AND COKE—WAS READY TO SPREAD, TOO!

DESPITE THEIR DIFFERENCES, THE TWO GIANTS FOUND WAYS TO GET ALONG, AT FIRST... WITH FOUR DOZEN OTHER COUNTRIES, THEY CREATED THE **UNITED NATIONS,** AN INTERNATIONAL ORGANIZATION NICELY DEMOCRATIC, EXCEPT THAT ANY ONE OF THE FIVE POWERS—THE U.S., USSR, BRITAIN, FRANCE, OR CHINA—COULD VETO THE PROCEEDINGS.

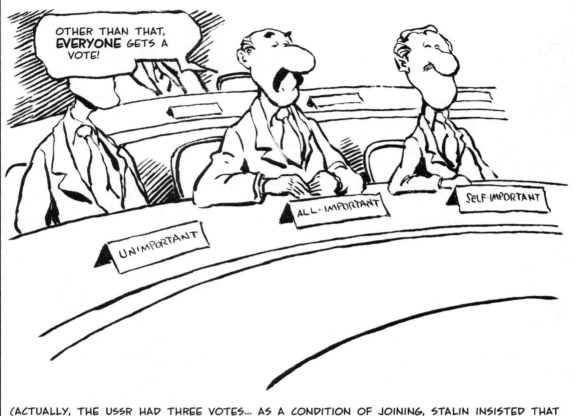

(ACTUALLY, THE USSR HAD THREE VOTES... AS A CONDITION OF JOINING, STALIN INSISTED THAT TWO OF HIS "REPUBLICS," BYELORUSSIA AND UKRAINE, GET THEIR OWN SEATS.)

THEY CHATTED LIKE CHUMS... AGREED THAT SOVIET TROOPS WOULD PULL OUT OF **EASTERN EUROPE...** AGREED THAT **KOREA** SHOULD BE INDEPENDENT... AGREED THAT MAYBE, JUST MAYBE, **NUCLEAR WEAPONS** MIGHT BE PUT UNDER SOME KIND OF INTERNATIONAL CONTROL... BUT ALL THIS TURNED OUT TO BE NOTHING BUT TALK...

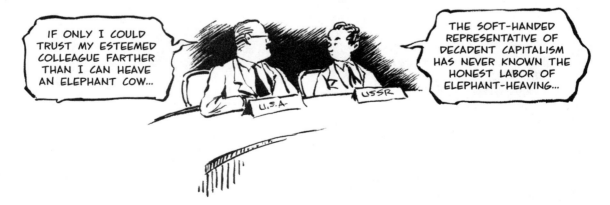

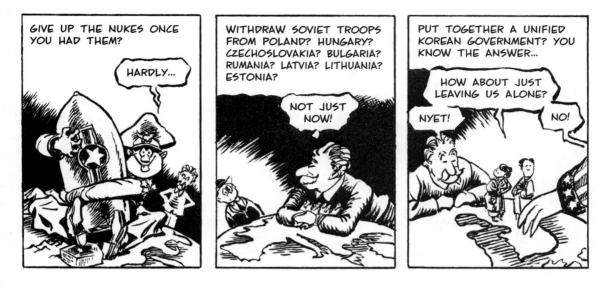

AND MORE: THE TWO TOOK OPPOSITE SIDES IN A GREEK CIVIL WAR... THE USSR BLOCKADED BERLIN TO FORCE OUT THE AMERICANS, BUT THE AMERICANS REFUSED TO BE OUSTED... AND SOON ONE HEARD THE CALLS TO WAR.

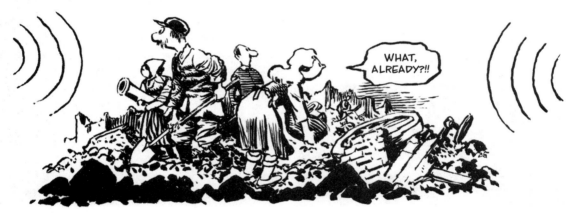

BY 1948, THE USSR HAD ABSORBED THE BALTIC STATES AND INSTALLED LOYAL GOVERNMENTS IN EASTERN GERMANY AND ALL THE OTHER COUNTRIES IT OCCUPIED. THE WESTERN POWERS FORMED **NATO**, A MILITARY ALLIANCE AGAINST THE SOVIETS, AND THE SOVIET BLOC FORMED THE **WARSAW PACT**, A MILITARY ALLIANCE AGAINST NATO.

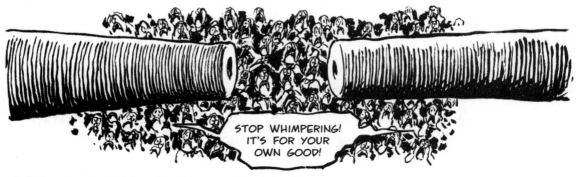

(NATO = NORTH ATLANTIC TREATY ORGANIZATION)

205

BOTH SIDES TALKED UP THEIR VISION OF THE WORLD. THE U.S. PUT DEMOCRACY INTO GERMAN AND JAPANESE SCHOOLBOOKS AND PROMOTED ELECTIONS.*

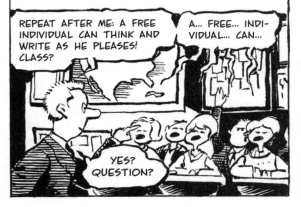

REPEAT AFTER ME: A FREE INDIVIDUAL CAN THINK AND WRITE AS HE PLEASES! CLASS?

A... FREE... INDIVIDUAL... CAN...

YES? QUESTION?

IT ALSO SECRETLY PAID THE POLITICAL PARTIES IT FAVORED AND SABOTAGED THE OPPOSITION.

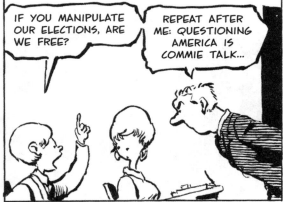

IF YOU MANIPULATE OUR ELECTIONS, ARE WE FREE?

REPEAT AFTER ME: QUESTIONING AMERICA IS COMMIE TALK...

IN THE EAST, THE COMMUNISTS PUT MARX AT THE CENTER OF EVERYTHING AND SUPPRESSED "INCORRECT" THINKING, WRITING, AND ART.

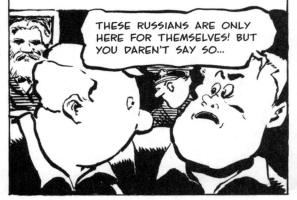

THESE RUSSIANS ARE ONLY HERE FOR THEMSELVES! BUT YOU DAREN'T SAY SO...

THIS INVOLVED NETWORKS OF INFORMERS AND SECRET POLICE.

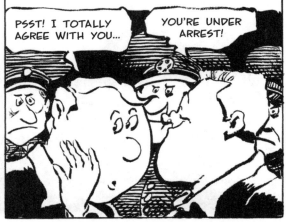

PSST! I TOTALLY AGREE WITH YOU...

YOU'RE UNDER ARREST!

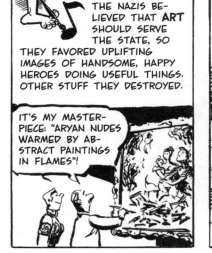

THE NAZIS BELIEVED THAT **ART** SHOULD SERVE THE STATE, SO THEY FAVORED UPLIFTING IMAGES OF HANDSOME, HAPPY HEROES DOING USEFUL THINGS. OTHER STUFF THEY DESTROYED.

IT'S MY MASTERPIECE: "ARYAN NUDES WARMED BY ABSTRACT PAINTINGS IN FLAMES"!

BUT THEY DID LOVE THE CLASSICS! THROUGHOUT THE WAR, EUROPEAN MUSEUMS TRIED TO KEEP THEIR COLLECTIONS OUT OF NAZI HANDS.

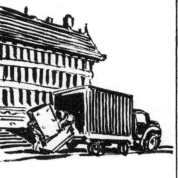

AFTER IT WAS OVER, THE U.S. SENT SCHOLARS AND SHOWS TO REVIVE GERMANY'S APPRECIATION OF MODERNISM AND ART FOR ART'S SAKE.

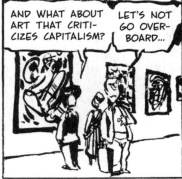

AND WHAT ABOUT ART THAT CRITICIZES CAPITALISM?

LET'S NOT GO OVERBOARD...

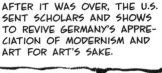

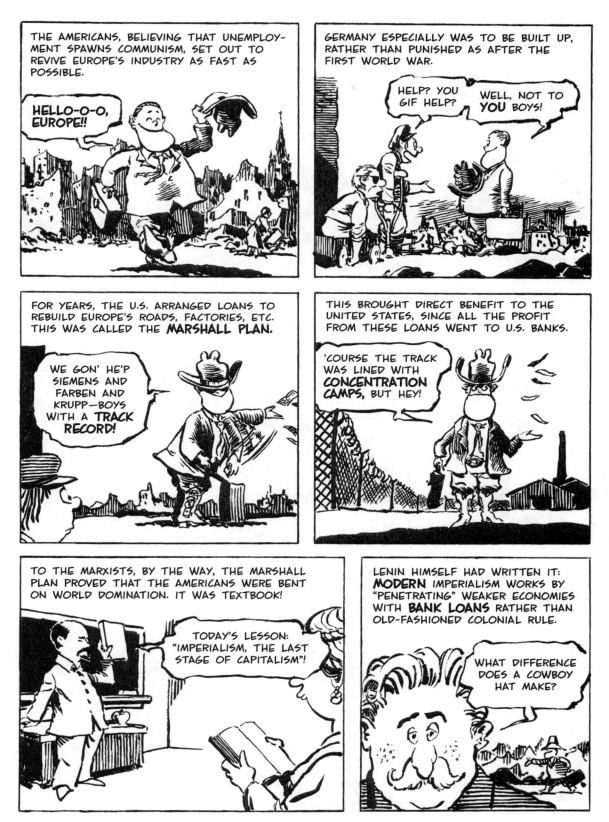

THE AMERICANS, BELIEVING THAT UNEMPLOYMENT SPAWNS COMMUNISM, SET OUT TO REVIVE EUROPE'S INDUSTRY AS FAST AS POSSIBLE.

HELLO-O-O, EUROPE!!

GERMANY ESPECIALLY WAS TO BE BUILT UP, RATHER THAN PUNISHED AS AFTER THE FIRST WORLD WAR.

HELP? YOU GIF HELP?

WELL, NOT TO **YOU** BOYS!

FOR YEARS, THE U.S. ARRANGED LOANS TO REBUILD EUROPE'S ROADS, FACTORIES, ETC. THIS WAS CALLED THE **MARSHALL PLAN.**

WE GON' HE'P SIEMENS AND FARBEN AND KRUPP—BOYS WITH A **TRACK RECORD!**

THIS BROUGHT DIRECT BENEFIT TO THE UNITED STATES, SINCE ALL THE PROFIT FROM THESE LOANS WENT TO U.S. BANKS.

'COURSE THE TRACK WAS LINED WITH **CONCENTRATION CAMPS,** BUT HEY!

TO THE MARXISTS, BY THE WAY, THE MARSHALL PLAN PROVED THAT THE AMERICANS WERE BENT ON WORLD DOMINATION. IT WAS TEXTBOOK!

TODAY'S LESSON: "IMPERIALISM, THE LAST STAGE OF CAPITALISM"!

LENIN HIMSELF HAD WRITTEN IT: **MODERN** IMPERIALISM WORKS BY "PENETRATING" WEAKER ECONOMIES WITH **BANK LOANS** RATHER THAN OLD-FASHIONED COLONIAL RULE.

WHAT DIFFERENCE DOES A COWBOY HAT MAKE?

HOW NOW, MAO?

THE HEAT BETWEEN MOSCOW AND WASHINGTON MIGHT HAVE COOLED, EXCEPT FOR A NEW UPHEAVAL IN **CHINA.**

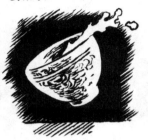

CHINESE NATIONALISTS AND COMMUNISTS HAD BEEN FIGHTING BITTERLY SINCE 1927 (SEE P. 183)... BUT NOW, IN 1945, ALL THE WESTERN POWERS URGED THEM TO RECONCILE.

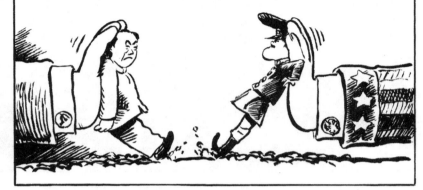

THE U.S. HAD REASONS FOR CALLING FOR PEACE.

WAR'S OVER, CHINA'S A MESS, THE REDS ARE OUTNUMBERED!

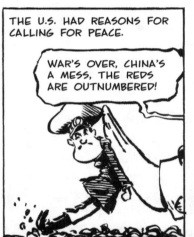

STALIN HAD HIS REASONS TOO.

YEAH! WHAT?

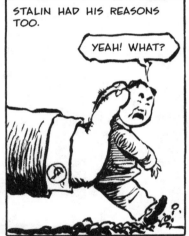

STALIN'S MARXISM DENIED THAT A PLACE LIKE CHINA—A PEASANT COUNTRY WITH FEW INDUSTRIAL WORKERS—COULD BE READY FOR SOCIALISM.

SEE?

I'M NOT LOOKING!

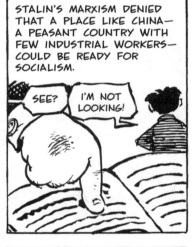

EVEN WORSE, THE CHINESE COMMUNIST LEADER, **MAO ZEDONG,** THOUGHT THE PEASANTS COULD **MAKE** THE REVOLUTION—EVEN THOUGH "EVERYONE KNEW" THAT PEASANTS WERE NARROW-MINDED, SELFISH, AND CONSERVATIVE.

THAT'S WHY I SHOT SO MANY OF 'EM!

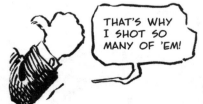

STALIN HATED TO THINK THAT THIS WACKY PSEUDO-MARXIST MIGHT END UP IN CHARGE OF A COUNTRY AS IMPORTANT AS CHINA.

I ADMIT IT... HE MAKES ME FEEL A LITTLE **INSECURE**...

UH-OH!

LOOK OUT!

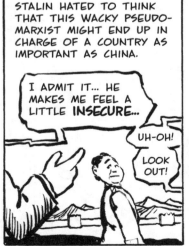

SO... TALK IT WOULD BE.

UNDERSTAND?

YES... "DAD"!

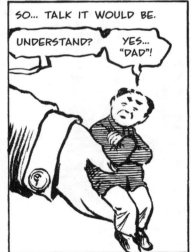

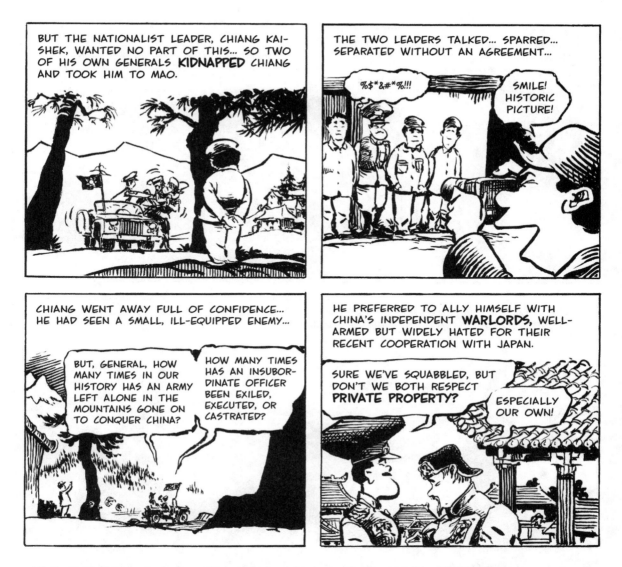

BUT THE NATIONALIST LEADER, CHIANG KAI-SHEK, WANTED NO PART OF THIS... SO TWO OF HIS OWN GENERALS **KIDNAPPED** CHIANG AND TOOK HIM TO MAO.

THE TWO LEADERS TALKED... SPARRED... SEPARATED WITHOUT AN AGREEMENT...

%$*&#*%!!!

SMILE! HISTORIC PICTURE!

CHIANG WENT AWAY FULL OF CONFIDENCE... HE HAD SEEN A SMALL, ILL-EQUIPPED ENEMY...

BUT, GENERAL, HOW MANY TIMES IN OUR HISTORY HAS AN ARMY LEFT ALONE IN THE MOUNTAINS GONE ON TO CONQUER CHINA?

HOW MANY TIMES HAS AN INSUBORDINATE OFFICER BEEN EXILED, EXECUTED, OR CASTRATED?

HE PREFERRED TO ALLY HIMSELF WITH CHINA'S INDEPENDENT **WARLORDS,** WELL-ARMED BUT WIDELY HATED FOR THEIR RECENT COOPERATION WITH JAPAN.

SURE WE'VE SQUABBLED, BUT DON'T WE BOTH RESPECT **PRIVATE PROPERTY?**

ESPECIALLY OUR OWN!

WITH THIS SUPPORT, CHIANG FELT SECURE... HE DISCHARGED **500,000 SOLDIERS,** MEN WITH MILITARY TRAINING, NO JOBS, NO MONEY, AND EARS FOR THE COMMUNIST RECRUITERS!

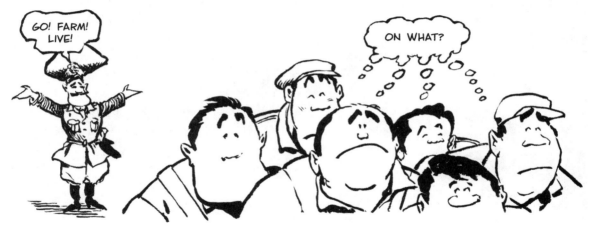

GO! FARM! LIVE!

ON WHAT?

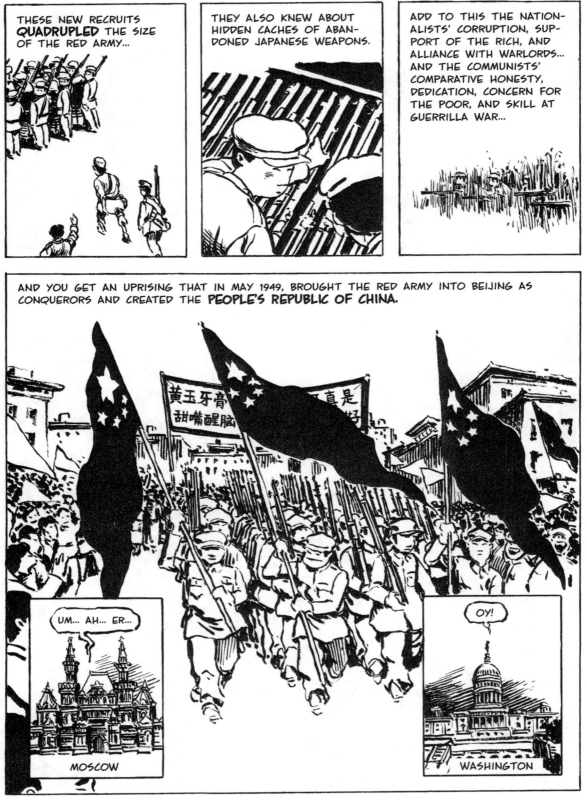

THESE NEW RECRUITS **QUADRUPLED** THE SIZE OF THE RED ARMY...

THEY ALSO KNEW ABOUT HIDDEN CACHES OF ABANDONED JAPANESE WEAPONS.

ADD TO THIS THE NATIONALISTS' CORRUPTION, SUPPORT OF THE RICH, AND ALLIANCE WITH WARLORDS... AND THE COMMUNISTS' COMPARATIVE HONESTY, DEDICATION, CONCERN FOR THE POOR, AND SKILL AT GUERRILLA WAR...

AND YOU GET AN UPRISING THAT IN MAY 1949, BROUGHT THE RED ARMY INTO BEIJING AS CONQUERORS AND CREATED THE **PEOPLE'S REPUBLIC OF CHINA.**

UM... AH... ER...

MOSCOW

OY!

WASHINGTON

MEANWHILE, CHIANG KAI-SHEK AND HIS FOLLOWERS FLED TO THE SIZABLE ISLAND OF TAIWAN.

AND THERE THE **REPUBLIC OF CHINA** REMAINS TO THIS DAY.

BACK IN NEW YORK, THE USSR ASKED THE U.N. TO RECOGNIZE THE NEW CHINESE GOVERNMENT... THE U.S. OBJECTED... SO TAIWAN KEPT THE "CHINA SEAT"... AND THE RUSSIANS WALKED OUT OF THE U.N. IN PROTEST.

%$#$ AMERICAN PUPPET THEATER!

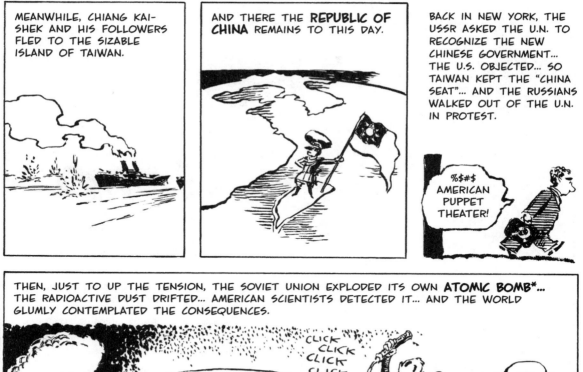

THEN, JUST TO UP THE TENSION, THE SOVIET UNION EXPLODED ITS OWN **ATOMIC BOMB***... THE RADIOACTIVE DUST DRIFTED... AMERICAN SCIENTISTS DETECTED IT... AND THE WORLD GLUMLY CONTEMPLATED THE CONSEQUENCES.

CLICK CLICK CLICK CLICK CLICK CLICK

AW, MANNNN...

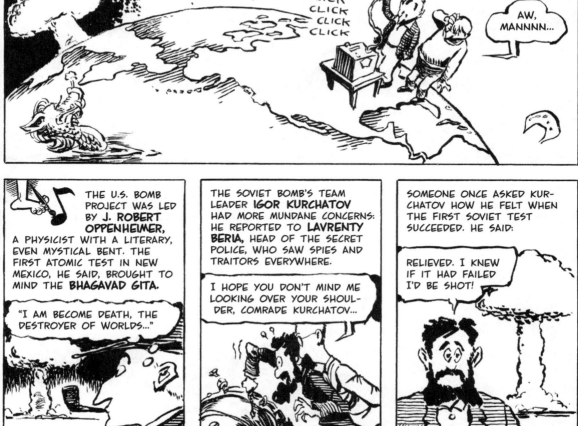

THE U.S. BOMB PROJECT WAS LED BY **J. ROBERT OPPENHEIMER,** A PHYSICIST WITH A LITERARY, EVEN MYSTICAL BENT. THE FIRST ATOMIC TEST IN NEW MEXICO, HE SAID, BROUGHT TO MIND THE **BHAGAVAD GITA.**

"I AM BECOME DEATH, THE DESTROYER OF WORLDS..."

THE SOVIET BOMB'S TEAM LEADER **IGOR KURCHATOV** HAD MORE MUNDANE CONCERNS: HE REPORTED TO **LAVRENTY BERIA,** HEAD OF THE SECRET POLICE, WHO SAW SPIES AND TRAITORS EVERYWHERE.

I HOPE YOU DON'T MIND ME LOOKING OVER YOUR SHOULDER, COMRADE KURCHATOV...

SOMEONE ONCE ASKED KURCHATOV HOW HE FELT WHEN THE FIRST SOVIET TEST SUCCEEDED. HE SAID:

RELIEVED. I KNEW IF IT HAD FAILED I'D BE SHOT!

WAR AGAIN, ALREADY?

THE COMMUNIST WORLD, SURPRISED AT ITS OWN SUCCESS, LOOKED TO EXPAND EVEN FURTHER.

LET'S TRY KOREA!

U.S.-SOVIET FRICTION HAD SPLIT KOREA: A STALINIST DICTATOR RULED THE NORTH... A U.S.-BACKED "STRONGMAN" SAT IN THE SOUTH... AND BOTH OF THEM CLAIMED THE WHOLE COUNTRY.

WHAT'S THE DIFFERENCE BETWEEN A DICTATOR AND A STRONGMAN?

YOU EVER SEE A DICTATOR IN A LEOTARD?

HUH!

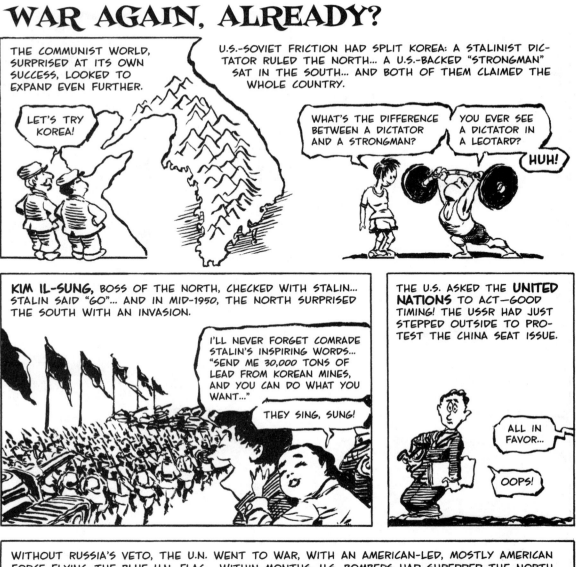

KIM IL-SUNG, BOSS OF THE NORTH, CHECKED WITH STALIN... STALIN SAID "GO"... AND IN MID-1950, THE NORTH SURPRISED THE SOUTH WITH AN INVASION.

I'LL NEVER FORGET COMRADE STALIN'S INSPIRING WORDS... "SEND ME 30,000 TONS OF LEAD FROM KOREAN MINES, AND YOU CAN DO WHAT YOU WANT..."

THEY SING, SUNG!

THE U.S. ASKED THE **UNITED NATIONS** TO ACT—GOOD TIMING! THE USSR HAD JUST STEPPED OUTSIDE TO PROTEST THE CHINA SEAT ISSUE.

ALL IN FAVOR...

OOPS!

WITHOUT RUSSIA'S VETO, THE U.N. WENT TO WAR, WITH AN AMERICAN-LED, MOSTLY AMERICAN FORCE FLYING THE BLUE U.N. FLAG... WITHIN MONTHS, U.S. BOMBERS HAD SHREDDED THE NORTH KOREAN ARMY AND ITS SUPPLY LINES, WHILE GROUND TROOPS PUSHED NORTH ALL THE WAY TO THE CHINESE BORDER.

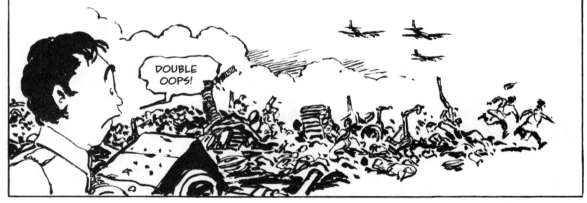

DOUBLE OOPS!

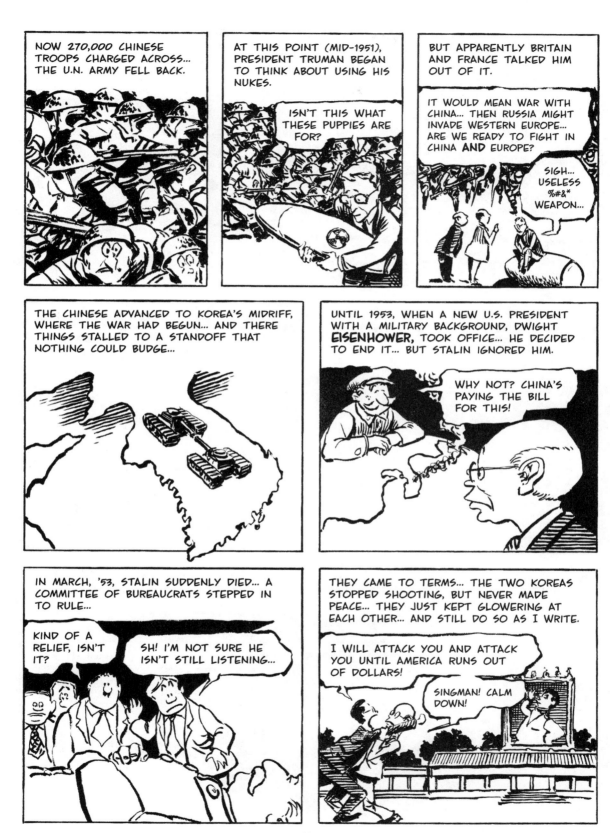

NOW 270,000 CHINESE TROOPS CHARGED ACROSS... THE U.N. ARMY FELL BACK.

AT THIS POINT (MID-1951), PRESIDENT TRUMAN BEGAN TO THINK ABOUT USING HIS NUKES.

ISN'T THIS WHAT THESE PUPPIES ARE FOR?

BUT APPARENTLY BRITAIN AND FRANCE TALKED HIM OUT OF IT.

IT WOULD MEAN WAR WITH CHINA... THEN RUSSIA MIGHT INVADE WESTERN EUROPE... ARE WE READY TO FIGHT IN CHINA **AND** EUROPE?

SIGH... USELESS %#&* WEAPON...

THE CHINESE ADVANCED TO KOREA'S MIDRIFF, WHERE THE WAR HAD BEGUN... AND THERE THINGS STALLED TO A STANDOFF THAT NOTHING COULD BUDGE...

UNTIL 1953, WHEN A NEW U.S. PRESIDENT WITH A MILITARY BACKGROUND, DWIGHT **EISENHOWER,** TOOK OFFICE... HE DECIDED TO END IT... BUT STALIN IGNORED HIM.

WHY NOT? CHINA'S PAYING THE BILL FOR THIS!

IN MARCH, '53, STALIN SUDDENLY DIED... A COMMITTEE OF BUREAUCRATS STEPPED IN TO RULE...

KIND OF A RELIEF, ISN'T IT?

SH! I'M NOT SURE HE ISN'T STILL LISTENING...

THEY CAME TO TERMS... THE TWO KOREAS STOPPED SHOOTING, BUT NEVER MADE PEACE... THEY JUST KEPT GLOWERING AT EACH OTHER... AND STILL DO SO AS I WRITE.

I WILL ATTACK YOU AND ATTACK YOU UNTIL AMERICA RUNS OUT OF DOLLARS!

SINGMAN! CALM DOWN!

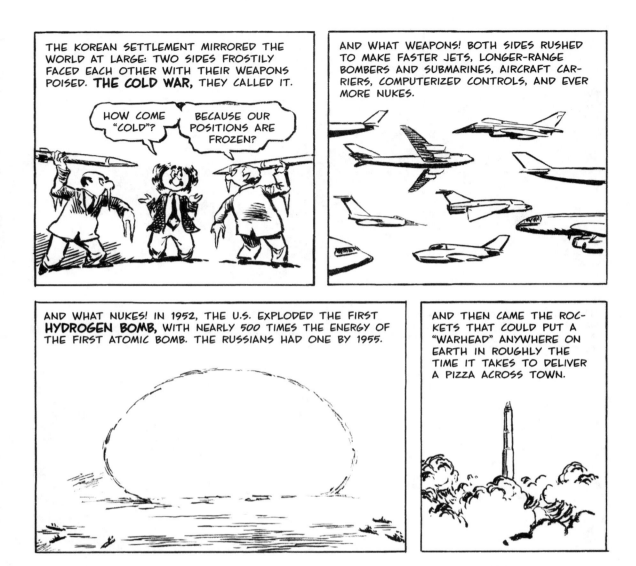

THE KOREAN SETTLEMENT MIRRORED THE WORLD AT LARGE: TWO SIDES FROSTILY FACED EACH OTHER WITH THEIR WEAPONS POISED. **THE COLD WAR,** THEY CALLED IT.

HOW COME "COLD"?

BECAUSE OUR POSITIONS ARE FROZEN?

AND WHAT WEAPONS! BOTH SIDES RUSHED TO MAKE FASTER JETS, LONGER-RANGE BOMBERS AND SUBMARINES, AIRCRAFT CARRIERS, COMPUTERIZED CONTROLS, AND EVER MORE NUKES.

AND WHAT NUKES! IN 1952, THE U.S. EXPLODED THE FIRST **HYDROGEN BOMB,** WITH NEARLY 500 TIMES THE ENERGY OF THE FIRST ATOMIC BOMB. THE RUSSIANS HAD ONE BY 1955.

AND THEN CAME THE ROCKETS THAT COULD PUT A "WARHEAD" ANYWHERE ON EARTH IN ROUGHLY THE TIME IT TAKES TO DELIVER A PIZZA ACROSS TOWN.

RELAXING TIME, THE 1950S... I STILL REMEMBER THE SCHOOL "DUCK AND COVER" AIR RAID DRILLS... DUCK UNDER YOUR DESK AND COVER THE NAPE OF YOUR NECK WITH YOUR HAND...

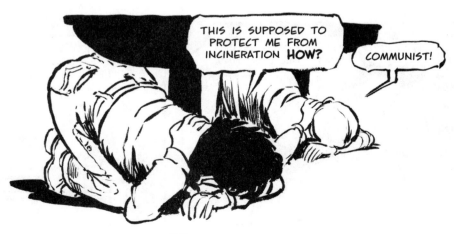

THIS IS SUPPOSED TO PROTECT ME FROM INCINERATION **HOW?**

COMMUNIST!

NEW COLONIES FOR OLD

WHILE THE SUPERPOWERS WERE BREATHING FIRE, THE WORLD HAD OTHER THINGS ON ITS MIND. IN ASIA, AFRICA, AND LATIN AMERICA, THE GREAT EUROPEAN EMPIRES WERE **BREAKING UP**—OR DOWN, DEPENDING ON WHERE YOU STOOD.

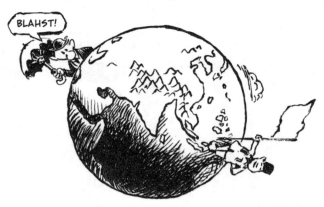

BLAHST!

FIRST TO GO WAS THE **NETHERLANDS EAST INDIES,** THE FABLED INDIES WHERE NUTMEG GROWS AND PETROLEUM FLOWS.

DURING THE WAR, WHILE GERMANY OCCUPIED THE NETHERLANDS, JAPAN MOVED INTO THE INDIES, ARRESTED THE DUTCH, AND SET UP A LOCAL DICTATOR, **SUKARNO.**

ASIA FOR THE ASIANS!

UNNATURAL! UNCHRISTIAN! UNPROFITABLE!

WITH THE JAPANESE DEFEAT, SUKARNO DECLARED INDEPENDENCE FOR THE COUNTRY NOW CALLED **INDONESIA...** THE DUTCH, WEAKENED BY WAR, HAD TO YIELD.

UNCHRISTIAN!

UNNATURAL!

BUT NOT NECESSARILY UNPROFITABLE...

EVERYWHERE THE CREAKY OLD POWERS FACED INDEPENDENCE MOVEMENTS IN THE COLONIES... AND EVERYWHERE THE NEW POWERS JOCKEYED FOR INFLUENCE.

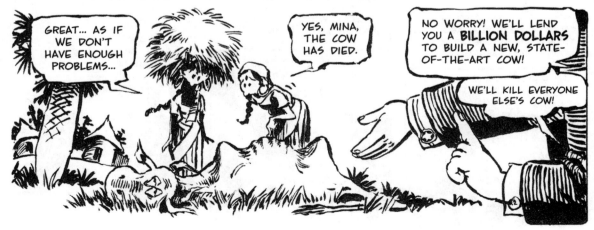

GREAT... AS IF WE DON'T HAVE ENOUGH PROBLEMS...

YES, MINA, THE COW HAS DIED.

NO WORRY! WE'LL LEND YOU A **BILLION DOLLARS** TO BUILD A NEW, STATE-OF-THE-ART COW!

WE'LL KILL EVERYONE ELSE'S COW!

CONSIDER INDIA... FOR DECADES, ACTIVISTS HAD BEEN PUSHING THE BRITISH TO "QUIT INDIA."
PUSHING HOW, SAHIB? WITH BOMBINGS? ASSASSINATIONS? SABOTAGE?
MUCH, MUCH WORSE...
INDIA HAD MANY POLITICAL PARTIES, BUT ONLY ONE, THE INDIAN NATIONAL CONGRESS, HAD THE GENIUS OF BRITISH-TRAINED LAWYER MOHANDAS GANDHI.
TO HIT BRITISH COMMERCE, GANDHI URGED INDIANS TO HAND-SPIN THEIR OWN COTTON, NOT WEAR WESTERN THREADS.
NOW IF WE EACH DO AN HOUR A DAY...
MERCHANTS, LAWYERS, ETC.
HE SHED HIS WESTERN SUIT FOR A DHOTI... LEARNED TO SPIN... AND APPLIED INDIAN SPIRITUAL TRADITIONS TO PRACTICAL POLITICS.
IS HE SPINNING OR MEDITATING?
BOTH.
HIS PHILOSOPHY HAD NO ROOM FOR ANGER OR HATRED... PROTESTERS DELIBERATELY DISOBEYED UNJUST LAWS AND CALMLY TOOK BEATINGS AND ARREST.
"I CAN THINK OF MANY THINGS WORTH DYING FOR, BUT NONE WORTH KILLING FOR."
BY COMPARISON, THE BRITS LOOKED MEAN, PETTY, AND GREEDY.
I SEE WHAT YOU MEAN, SAHIB...
IT'S BLOODY UNFAIR!!
IN THE 1930S, SOME AFRICAN-AMERICANS CAME TO INDIA TO TALK TO GANDHI ABOUT THEIR OWN STRUGGLES AGAINST DISCRIMINATION.
HAVE YOU CONSIDERED SPINNING?
WE'VE ALREADY DONE ENOUGH WITH COTTON, THANKS!
ONE OF THE VISITORS, BENJAMIN MAYS, LATER BECAME PRESIDENT OF MOREHOUSE COLLEGE, WHERE HE TAUGHT MARTIN LUTHER KING, JR.
BOY, IF YOU DON'T STUDY HARDER, I'M GOING TO WHUP YOUR—I MEAN, AS GANDHI USED TO SAY...
AND SO GANDHIAN NONVIOLENCE CAME TO THE AMERICAN CIVIL RIGHTS MOVEMENT OF THE '50S AND '60S.
WHAT WOULD THE MAHATMA DO?

GANDHI'S MESSAGE AND TACTICS MADE THE CONGRESS INDIA'S BIGGEST PARTY BY FAR, WITH MILLIONS JOINING ITS PROTESTS AND ATTENDING ITS RALLIES. PEOPLE CALLED HIM THE **MAHATMA,** OR GREAT SOUL.

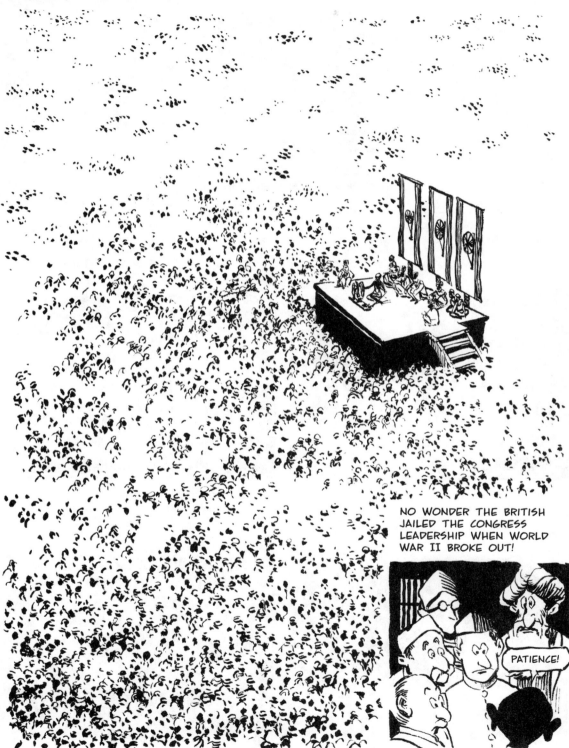

NO WONDER THE BRITISH JAILED THE CONGRESS LEADERSHIP WHEN WORLD WAR II BROKE OUT!

PATIENCE!

AFTER THE WAR, THE EXHAUSTED BRITS COULD NO LONGER RESIST INDIA'S CALLS FOR INDEPENDENCE.
BLAHST! WHERE ARE THE POLICE?
EHMMM.... THOSE ARE THE POLICE...
IN 1947, THE TWO SIDES BEGAN DISCUSSING THE TRANSFER OF POWER...
BUT THERE TURNED OUT TO BE MORE THAN TWO SIDES!
COW-HATER!
IDOLATOR!
MANY INDIAN MUSLIMS SAW BRITAIN AS PROTECTION AGAINST THE COUNTRY'S 400 MILLION HINDUS.
RATHER THAN SHARING INDEPENDENCE WITH A HINDU MAJORITY, INDIA'S MUSLIM LEAGUE AGITATED FOR THEIR OWN SEPARATE STATE: PAKISTAN.
SOMEPLACE PURE AND RIGHTEOUS AND JUST!
JUST WHAT?
MUHAMMAD ALI JINNAH
NEVER MIND THAT THE NON-SECTARIAN CONGRESS, WITH LEADERS OF ALL SORTS, FAVORED EQUAL RIGHTS FOR EVERYONE.
IT'S STILL TOO HINDU!
HINDUS SAW PAKISTAN AS A BETRAYAL OF THE INDEPENDENCE MOVEMENT.
LONG LIVE PAKISTAN!
DEATH TO PAKISTAN!

CONGRESS LOYALISTS WATCHED IN SHOCK AS FURIOUS HINDUS TURNED THESE MARCHES INTO RIOTS THAT KILLED HUNDREDS.

BRITAIN AND CONGRESS AGREED: TO MAKE PEACE, THEY MUST YIELD... SO LINES WERE DRAWN, AND PAKISTAN PLANNED.

WITH THE BLEEPIN' WISDOM OF SOLOMON!

BUT NO PEACE CAME... RIOTS BECAME MASSACRES... WHOLE COMMUNITIES FLED THEIR HOMES TO CROSS THE BORDER ONE WAY OR THE OTHER... BY MOST ESTIMATES, A MILLION DIED...

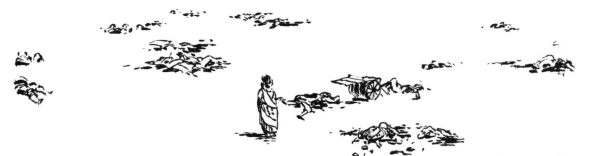

ON JANUARY 1, 1948, BOTH INDIA AND PAKISTAN CELEBRATED THEIR INDEPENDENCE.

A MONTH LATER, A MILITANT HINDU GUNMAN ASSASSINATED GANDHI FOR LETTING PAKISTAN GET AWAY.

AFTER 60 YEARS, THE TWO COUNTRIES REMAIN ENEMIES.

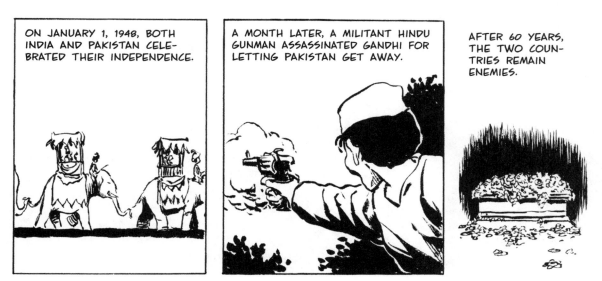

YOU DON'T HAVE TO BE JEWISH TO SAY "OY!"

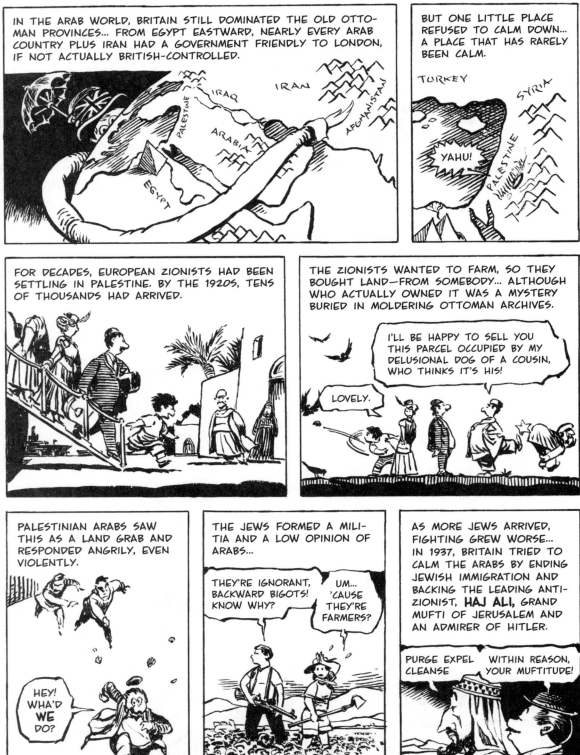

IN THE ARAB WORLD, BRITAIN STILL DOMINATED THE OLD OTTO-MAN PROVINCES... FROM EGYPT EASTWARD, NEARLY EVERY ARAB COUNTRY PLUS IRAN HAD A GOVERNMENT FRIENDLY TO LONDON, IF NOT ACTUALLY BRITISH-CONTROLLED.

BUT ONE LITTLE PLACE REFUSED TO CALM DOWN... A PLACE THAT HAS RARELY BEEN CALM.

YAHU!

FOR DECADES, EUROPEAN ZIONISTS HAD BEEN SETTLING IN PALESTINE. BY THE 1920S, TENS OF THOUSANDS HAD ARRIVED.

THE ZIONISTS WANTED TO FARM, SO THEY BOUGHT LAND—FROM SOMEBODY... ALTHOUGH WHO ACTUALLY OWNED IT WAS A MYSTERY BURIED IN MOLDERING OTTOMAN ARCHIVES.

I'LL BE HAPPY TO SELL YOU THIS PARCEL OCCUPIED BY MY DELUSIONAL DOG OF A COUSIN, WHO THINKS IT'S HIS!

LOVELY.

PALESTINIAN ARABS SAW THIS AS A LAND GRAB AND RESPONDED ANGRILY, EVEN VIOLENTLY.

HEY! WHA'D WE DO?

THE JEWS FORMED A MILITIA AND A LOW OPINION OF ARABS...

THEY'RE IGNORANT, BACKWARD BIGOTS! KNOW WHY?

UM... 'CAUSE THEY'RE FARMERS?

AS MORE JEWS ARRIVED, FIGHTING GREW WORSE... IN 1937, BRITAIN TRIED TO CALM THE ARABS BY ENDING JEWISH IMMIGRATION AND BACKING THE LEADING ANTI-ZIONIST, **HAJ ALI,** GRAND MUFTI OF JERUSALEM AND AN ADMIRER OF HITLER.

PURGE EXPEL CLEANSE

WITHIN REASON, YOUR MUFTITUDE!

AS EUROPE CAME TO THE BOIL, ZIONISTS GOT FEISTIER... SOME JEWS, TOO VIOLENT FOR THE DEFENSIVE MILITIA, FORMED A SECRET ORGANIZATION, THE **IRGUN,** THAT TERRORIZED ARABS... AND OF COURSE ARABS TERRORIZED JEWS RIGHT BACK.

TRULY BIBLICAL!

WHEN THE WORLD WAR BEGAN, BRITAIN FOUND ITSELF IN A (KOSHER?) PICKLE.

HMMM... WE HATE HITLER... WE LIKE THE ARABS, WHO HATE THE JEWS... THE JEWS HATE HITLER... THE GRAND MUFTI LIKES HITLER...

BOTHER!

FOLLOWING THIS LINE OF THOUGHT, BRITISH OFFICERS BEGAN TRAINING JEWISH VOLUNTEERS FOR WAR.

HEAD TRAINER COL. ORDE WINGATE, EVANGELICAL CHRISTIAN

AFTER THE WAR, HORDES OF DISPLACED EUROPEAN JEWS LOOKED FOR SHELTER IN PALESTINE, AND THE BRITS WAFFLED.

WHAT ARE WE, A BLEEDIN' CHARITY?

HELP!

IN MID-1945, JEWISH TERRORISTS BLEW UP THE KING DAVID HOTEL, WHERE BRITISH GENERALS LODGED... 85 DIED.

STICKY BLOODY WICKET!

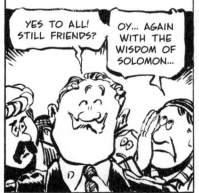

SO... AS IN INDIA, THE BRITISH OFFERED TO SPLIT THE COUNTRY INTO TWO SLIVERS, JEWISH AND ARAB.

YES TO ALL! STILL FRIENDS?

OY... AGAIN WITH THE WISDOM OF SOLOMON...

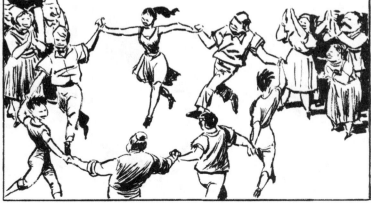

THE JEWS LOVED IT... THE ARABS HATED IT... THE U.N. OKAYED IT... SO IN 1948 AN INDEPENDENT ISRAEL APPEARED FOR THE FIRST TIME IN ROUGHLY 2,003 YEARS.

NOW EUROPE'S DISPLACED JEWS FLOODED ISRAEL AND IMPATIENTLY DROVE OUT MORE ARABS.
PALESTINIAN REFUGEES POURED INTO NEIGHBORING LANDS: LEBANON, JORDAN, SYRIA, EGYPT.
BROTHERS! SISTERS! WELCOME! WHO'S PAYING?!
MANY FOUND HOUSING AND JOBS, BUT THE POOREST WENT TO "TEMPORARY" CAMPS THAT STILL TEEM WITH PEOPLE 60 YEARS LATER.
JERUSALEM'S MUFTI HAJ ALI LOBBIED ARAB NATIONS TO WIPE OUT THE NEW STATE, WHOSE NAME NO ONE EVEN DEIGNED TO UTTER... AND ARABS SAID YES.
BY GOD, HONOR DEMANDS ARAB UNITY AGAINST, ER, THE ZIONIST ENTITY! BY THE WAY, WILL THOSE DOGS THE SYRIANS BE INVOLVED?
BUT EACH ARAB NATION SUSPECTED THE OTHERS OF GOING IN FOR GAIN, NOT FOR HONOR, SO THEIR EFFORTS LACKED COORDINATION AND OOMPH.
ATTACK! ATTACK!
YOU ATTACK!
THE ISRAELIS, MEANWHILE, BOUGHT HEAVY WEAPONS FROM CZECHOSLOVAKIA (WITH STALIN'S APPROVAL).
ULP! HIS EYES SEEM TO FOLLOW YOU EVERYWHERE!
TELL ME ABOUT IT...
RESULT: ISRAEL DEFEATED THE ARABS.
JEWS FLYING PLANES?
ISRAEL SURVIVED... MORE PALESTINIANS FLED... THE ARAB COUNTRIES SMOLDERED... AND BRITAIN'S HOPES SLOWLY FADED.
AH, WELL, WE'LL ALWAYS HAVE HONG KONG...

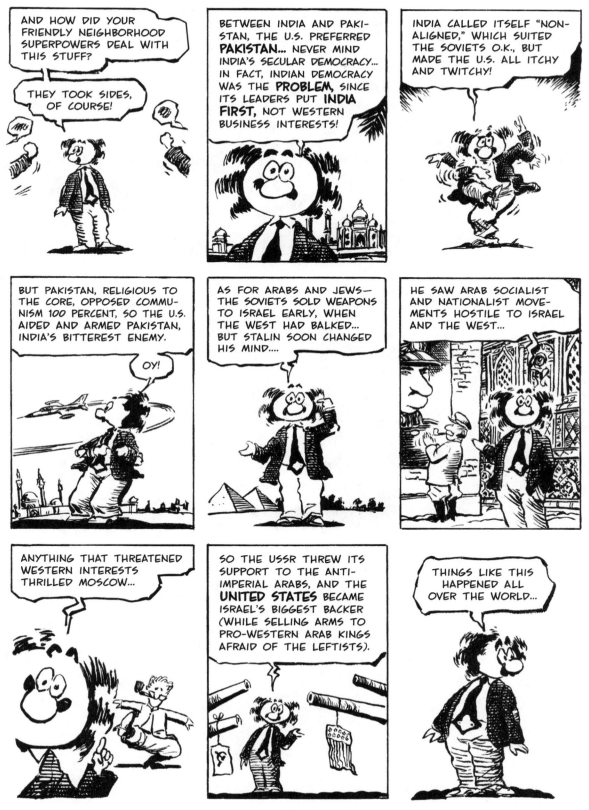

AND HOW DID YOUR FRIENDLY NEIGHBORHOOD SUPERPOWERS DEAL WITH THIS STUFF?

THEY TOOK SIDES, OF COURSE!

BETWEEN INDIA AND PAKISTAN, THE U.S. PREFERRED **PAKISTAN**... NEVER MIND INDIA'S SECULAR DEMOCRACY... IN FACT, INDIAN DEMOCRACY WAS THE **PROBLEM,** SINCE ITS LEADERS PUT **INDIA FIRST,** NOT WESTERN BUSINESS INTERESTS!

INDIA CALLED ITSELF "NON-ALIGNED," WHICH SUITED THE SOVIETS O.K., BUT MADE THE U.S. ALL ITCHY AND TWITCHY!

BUT PAKISTAN, RELIGIOUS TO THE CORE, OPPOSED COMMUNISM 100 PERCENT, SO THE U.S. AIDED AND ARMED PAKISTAN, INDIA'S BITTEREST ENEMY.

OY!

AS FOR ARABS AND JEWS— THE SOVIETS SOLD WEAPONS TO ISRAEL EARLY, WHEN THE WEST HAD BALKED... BUT STALIN SOON CHANGED HIS MIND....

HE SAW ARAB SOCIALIST AND NATIONALIST MOVEMENTS HOSTILE TO ISRAEL AND THE WEST...

ANYTHING THAT THREATENED WESTERN INTERESTS THRILLED MOSCOW...

SO THE USSR THREW ITS SUPPORT TO THE ANTI-IMPERIAL ARABS, AND THE **UNITED STATES** BECAME ISRAEL'S BIGGEST BACKER (WHILE SELLING ARMS TO PRO-WESTERN ARAB KINGS AFRAID OF THE LEFTISTS).

THINGS LIKE THIS HAPPENED ALL OVER THE WORLD...

SPY VS. SPY

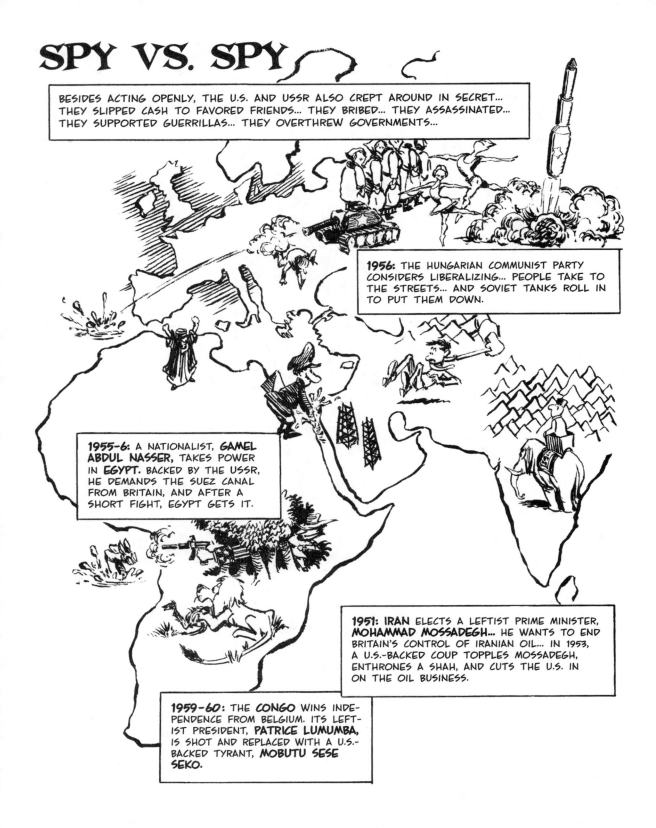

BESIDES ACTING OPENLY, THE U.S. AND USSR ALSO CREPT AROUND IN SECRET...
THEY SLIPPED CASH TO FAVORED FRIENDS... THEY BRIBED... THEY ASSASSINATED...
THEY SUPPORTED GUERRILLAS... THEY OVERTHREW GOVERNMENTS...

1956: THE HUNGARIAN COMMUNIST PARTY CONSIDERS LIBERALIZING... PEOPLE TAKE TO THE STREETS... AND SOVIET TANKS ROLL IN TO PUT THEM DOWN.

1955-6: A NATIONALIST, **GAMEL ABDUL NASSER**, TAKES POWER IN **EGYPT**. BACKED BY THE USSR, HE DEMANDS THE SUEZ CANAL FROM BRITAIN, AND AFTER A SHORT FIGHT, EGYPT GETS IT.

1951: IRAN ELECTS A LEFTIST PRIME MINISTER, **MOHAMMAD MOSSADEGH...** HE WANTS TO END BRITAIN'S CONTROL OF IRANIAN OIL... IN 1953, A U.S.-BACKED COUP TOPPLES MOSSADEGH, ENTHRONES A SHAH, AND CUTS THE U.S. IN ON THE OIL BUSINESS.

1959-60: THE **CONGO** WINS INDEPENDENCE FROM BELGIUM. ITS LEFTIST PRESIDENT, **PATRICE LUMUMBA**, IS SHOT AND REPLACED WITH A U.S.-BACKED TYRANT, **MOBUTU SESE SEKO**.

MEANWHILE, THE TWO POWERS TRIED TO SHOWCASE THEIR SYSTEMS TO THE WORLD... THE U.S. LIGHTENED UP ON ITS DARKER-SKINNED CITIZENS... ITS FACTORIES SPEWED TELEVISIONS, CARS, APPLIANCES... WHILE THE USSR POINTED TO ITS NARROW GAP BETWEEN RICH AND POOR, ITS CLASSICAL MUSIC AND DANCE, AND ITS ROCKET SCIENCE. IN 1957, MOSCOW SHOCKED WASHINGTON BY LAUNCHING THE FIRST **ARTIFICIAL SATELLITE**, SPUTNIK, INTO EARTH ORBIT.

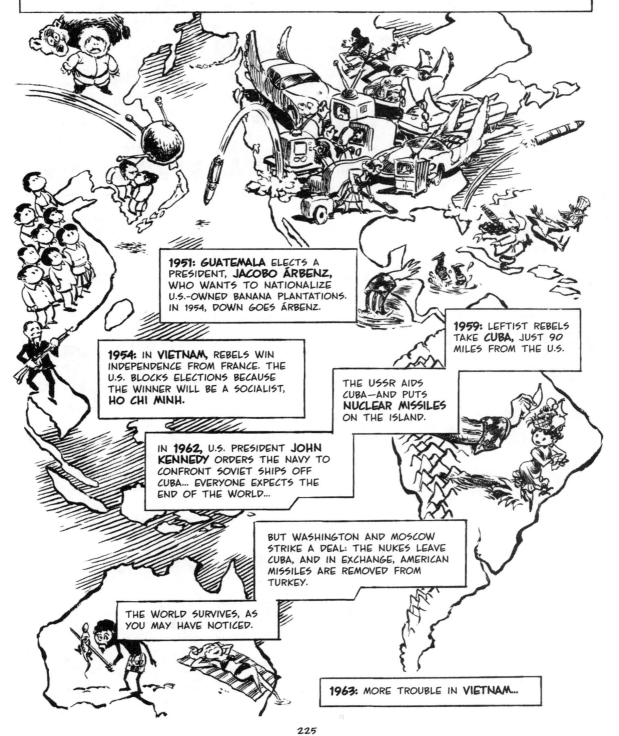

1951: GUATEMALA ELECTS A PRESIDENT, **JACOBO ÁRBENZ**, WHO WANTS TO NATIONALIZE U.S.-OWNED BANANA PLANTATIONS. IN 1954, DOWN GOES ÁRBENZ.

1954: IN **VIETNAM**, REBELS WIN INDEPENDENCE FROM FRANCE. THE U.S. BLOCKS ELECTIONS BECAUSE THE WINNER WILL BE A SOCIALIST, **HO CHI MINH.**

1959: LEFTIST REBELS TAKE **CUBA**, JUST 90 MILES FROM THE U.S.

THE USSR AIDS CUBA—AND PUTS **NUCLEAR MISSILES** ON THE ISLAND.

IN **1962**, U.S. PRESIDENT **JOHN KENNEDY** ORDERS THE NAVY TO CONFRONT SOVIET SHIPS OFF CUBA... EVERYONE EXPECTS THE END OF THE WORLD...

BUT WASHINGTON AND MOSCOW STRIKE A DEAL: THE NUKES LEAVE CUBA, AND IN EXCHANGE, AMERICAN MISSILES ARE REMOVED FROM TURKEY.

THE WORLD SURVIVES, AS YOU MAY HAVE NOTICED.

1963: MORE TROUBLE IN **VIETNAM**...

THE "SIXTIES"

LIKE KOREA, VIETNAM WAS LONG AND DIVIDED, WITH A STALINIST NORTH AND A SOUTH RULED BY A PRO-WESTERN, DICTATORIAL "PRESIDENT."

BUT UNLIKE KOREA, SOUTH VIETNAM HAD **JUNGLES**, WHERE ITS RESISTANCE FIGHTERS, THE **VIET CONG**, COULD HIDE.

IN THE EARLY 1960S, THE U.S. SENT ARMS AND ADVISERS TO HELP THE SOUTH VIETNAMESE GOVERNMENT FIGHT THE REBELS.

THIS DID NOTHING TO SLOW VIET CONG ATTACKS... IN FACT, THEY GREW WORSE.

DANG!

THE U.S. BLAMED CORRUPT VIETNAMESE LEADERS... SO, WITH KENNEDY'S BLESSING, SOUTH VIETNAM'S BOSS DIEM WAS SHOT AND RE-PLACED WITH A COLONEL, **NGUYEN CAO KY.**

KENNEDY NEVER FOUND OUT HOW LITTLE DIFFERENCE THIS MADE: HE WAS SHOT TOO, JUST THREE WEEKS LATER (NOVEMBER 22, 1963).*

KENNEDY'S KILLER, **LEE HARVEY OSWALD**, TEXAN, FORMER MARINE, COMMUNIST, AND GLORY HOG, BORE SEVERAL GRUDGES, AMONG THEM HIS HATRED OF AMERICAN TREATMENT OF CUBA.

A FEW MONTHS BEFORE THE ASSASSINATION, HE WENT TO THE SOVIET EMBASSY IN MEX-ICO CITY—A VISIT THE FBI HAS ALWAYS CALLED INNOCENT.

THE EVIDENCE SHOWS THAT OSWALD WAS THE ONLY GUNMAN... BUT DID HE **PLAN** THE ASSASSINATION ALONE? WE MAY NEVER KNOW...

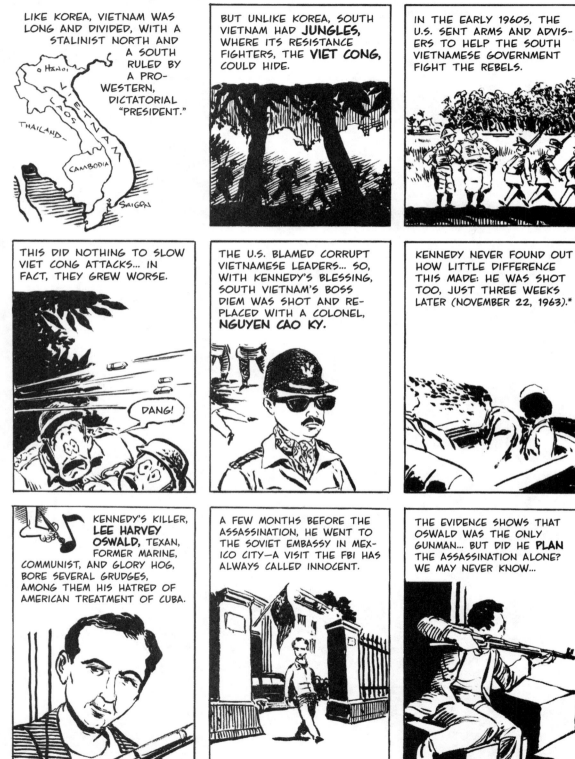

FIGHTING IN VIETNAM GOT HOTTER... KENNEDY'S SUCCESSOR **LYNDON JOHNSON** SENT MORE AMERICAN "MILITARY ADVISERS," AND THEN COMBAT TROOPS.

THEY MADE NO PROGRESS... SO JOHNSON SENT MORE TROOPS... AND MORE... UNTIL **550,000** AMERICANS WERE THERE BY 1968.

THE U.S. DROPPED MORE EXPLOSIVES ON LITTLE VIETNAM THAN IN ALL OF WORLD WAR II... WITHERED THE JUNGLE WITH TOXIC CHEMICALS... FIREBOMBED VILLAGES... HERDED THE PEOPLE INTO FORTIFIED CAMPS... USED ELECTRONIC SENSORS, COMPUTERS, NIGHT VISION, AND OTHER HIGH TECHNOLOGY... BUT STILL THE U.S. COULD NOT WIN...

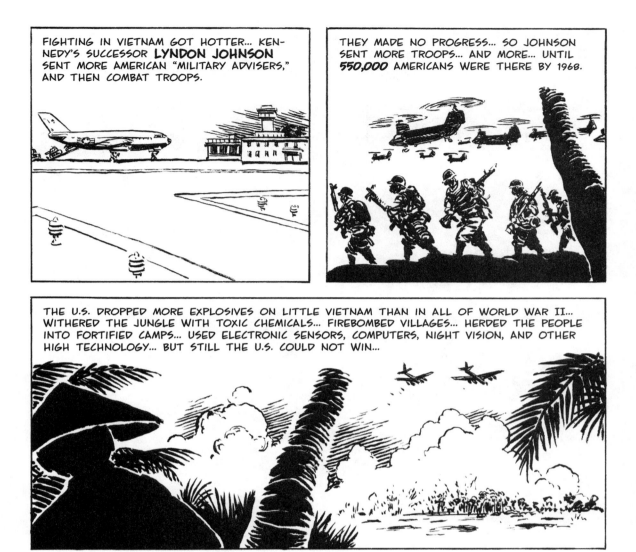

AND ALL THIS APPEARED ON TELEVISION!

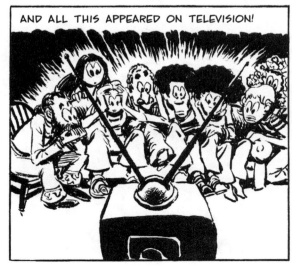

THE ENDLESS IMAGES OF FIRE AND DEATH TURNED MILLIONS OF AMERICANS AGAINST **THEIR OWN GOVERNMENT**—AND NOT QUIETLY, EITHER.

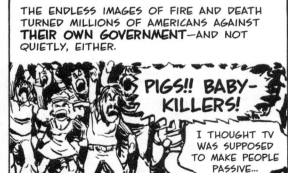

PIGS!! BABY-KILLERS!

I THOUGHT TV WAS SUPPOSED TO MAKE PEOPLE PASSIVE...

THIS MOVEMENT OPPOSED MORE THAN THE WAR... IT PUT DOWN EVERYTHING OLD... THE YOUNGER GENERATION SAW WORLD POLITICS AS A **"POWER TRIP,"** A MINDLESS, ABSURD GAME... AND PROPOSED TO REPLACE OLD, MISGUIDED HABITS WITH NEW ONES: PEACE, LOVE, DRUG-INDUCED ECSTASY, PAISLEY, PATCHED BELL-BOTTOMS, AND SEX WITHOUT HANG-UPS.* LIFE WAS A DAY IN THE PARK!

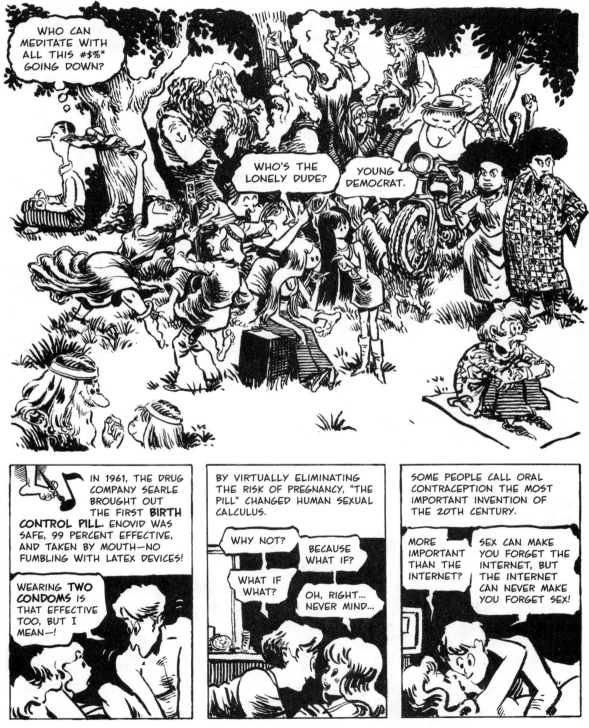

THIS MATURING
GENERATION,
THE "BABY
BOOM" BORN
AFTER WORLD
WAR II, LOOKED
DIFFERENT IN
DIFFERENT
COUNTRIES.

FRANCE, 1968: LEFTIST STUDENTS RIOTED, CLOSED THE UNIVERSITIES, THEN TOOK THEM OVER.

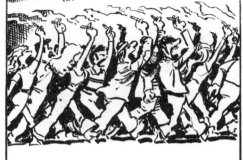

CZECHOSLOVAKIA: ANTI-SOVIET PROTESTERS WAVED FLOWERS AT RUSSIAN TANKS.

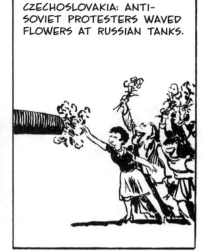

CHINA: THE BIGGEST, STRANGEST STUDENT DEMONSTRATIONS OF ALL—AND GOVERNMENT-SPONSORED!

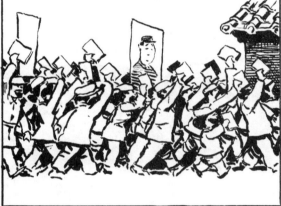

PARTY CHAIRMAN MAO ZEDONG, HIS WIFE JIANG JING, AND A FEW PALS HAD THE BRIGHT IDEA TO USE THAT YOUTHFUL ZEAL TO **SUPPRESS** ALL **DISSENT**!

BRILLIANT, REALLY!

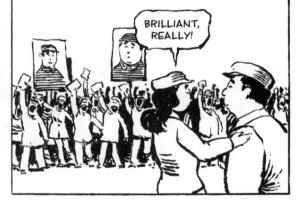

MILLIONS OF STUDENT "RED GUARDS," RAISED TO WORSHIP MAO AS AN ORACLE, CALLED OUT THEIR PROFESSORS AND BROWBEAT THEM WITH QUOTES FROM MAO'S WORKS—AND SOMETIMES HEAVIER THINGS—UNTIL THE OLD GEEZERS DIED OR CONFESSED... GIVEN A CHANCE TO YELL AT THEIR TEACHERS, KIDS WILL DO THE DARNEDEST THINGS...

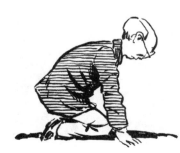

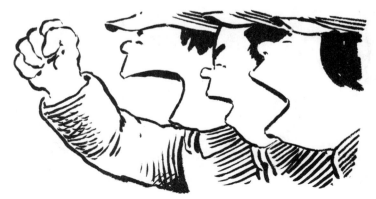

ALL THIS TIME, THE U.S. WAS BOMBING VIETNAM, NORTH AND SOUTH, AND STILL GETTING NOWHERE...

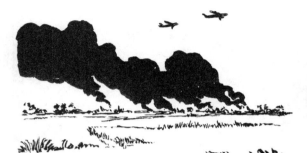

... WHILE THE AMERICAN ANTI-WAR MOVEMENT SPAWNED REVOLUTIONARY GROUPS THAT FOUND MAINSTREAM SUPPORT.

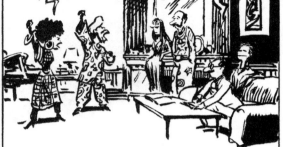

OFF THE PIG!

TO WHOM DO I MAKE OUT THE CHECK?

THE GOVERNMENT LOOKED FOR SOME WAY OUT OF THE MESS.

OFF THE PIG! OFF THE PIG!*

THIS WILL TAKE NOTHING SHORT OF GENIUS...

LUCKILY, I AM HERE!

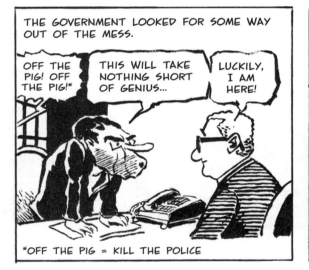

*OFF THE PIG = KILL THE POLICE

PRESIDENT **RICHARD NIXON**, FAMOUSLY DEVIOUS, AND HIS PROFESSORIAL ADVISER **HENRY KISSINGER** HATCHED A NEW GAMBIT: MAKE FRIENDS WITH **CHINA**.

ZIS VILL MAKE THE ZOVIETZ ZO **PAHRANOID**...

LOVE IT, HENRY! LOVE IT LOVE IT LOVE IT!

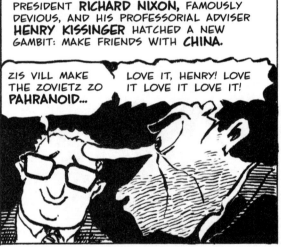

CHINA, THEY FINALLY REALIZED, HAD ITS DIFFERENCES WITH RUSSIA... FOR INSTANCE, CHINA MISTRUSTED NORTH VIETNAM. NOT ALL COMMUNISTS WERE ALIKE!

EHMMM... "DEAR CHAIRMAN MAO," AHEM... "I ADMIRE YOUR WAY WITH THE YOUNG PEOPLE..." YES... GOOD... OKAY... "CAN YOU GIVE ME SOME POINTERS?" HMM, TOO ABJECT? ETC.

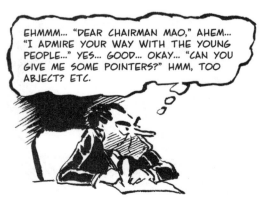

SO... NIXON WENT TO CHINA AND MET MAO, AND BEIJING FINALLY GOT THE CHINA SEAT AT THE UNITED NATIONS.

SIC THEM ON THEIR PROFESSORS, AND THEY'LL EAT OUT OF YOUR HAND.

HOW COULD I EVER HAVE HATED YOU?

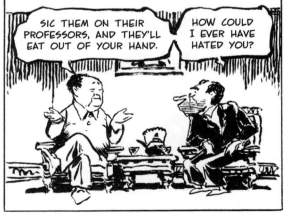

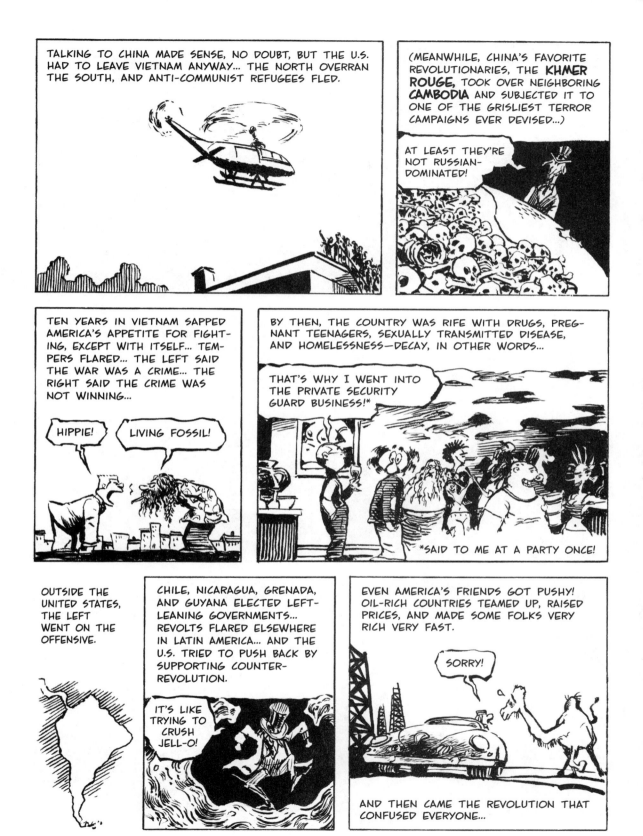

TALKING TO CHINA MADE SENSE, NO DOUBT, BUT THE U.S. HAD TO LEAVE VIETNAM ANYWAY... THE NORTH OVERRAN THE SOUTH, AND ANTI-COMMUNIST REFUGEES FLED.

(MEANWHILE, CHINA'S FAVORITE REVOLUTIONARIES, THE **KHMER ROUGE,** TOOK OVER NEIGHBORING **CAMBODIA** AND SUBJECTED IT TO ONE OF THE GRISLIEST TERROR CAMPAIGNS EVER DEVISED...)

AT LEAST THEY'RE NOT RUSSIAN-DOMINATED!

TEN YEARS IN VIETNAM SAPPED AMERICA'S APPETITE FOR FIGHTING, EXCEPT WITH ITSELF... TEMPERS FLARED... THE LEFT SAID THE WAR WAS A CRIME... THE RIGHT SAID THE CRIME WAS NOT WINNING...

HIPPIE!

LIVING FOSSIL!

BY THEN, THE COUNTRY WAS RIFE WITH DRUGS, PREGNANT TEENAGERS, SEXUALLY TRANSMITTED DISEASE, AND HOMELESSNESS—DECAY, IN OTHER WORDS...

THAT'S WHY I WENT INTO THE PRIVATE SECURITY GUARD BUSINESS!*

*SAID TO ME AT A PARTY ONCE!

OUTSIDE THE UNITED STATES, THE LEFT WENT ON THE OFFENSIVE.

CHILE, NICARAGUA, GRENADA, AND GUYANA ELECTED LEFT-LEANING GOVERNMENTS... REVOLTS FLARED ELSEWHERE IN LATIN AMERICA... AND THE U.S. TRIED TO PUSH BACK BY SUPPORTING COUNTER-REVOLUTION.

IT'S LIKE TRYING TO CRUSH JELL-O!

EVEN AMERICA'S FRIENDS GOT PUSHY! OIL-RICH COUNTRIES TEAMED UP, RAISED PRICES, AND MADE SOME FOLKS VERY RICH VERY FAST.

SORRY!

AND THEN CAME THE REVOLUTION THAT CONFUSED EVERYONE...

HIDDEN FACES

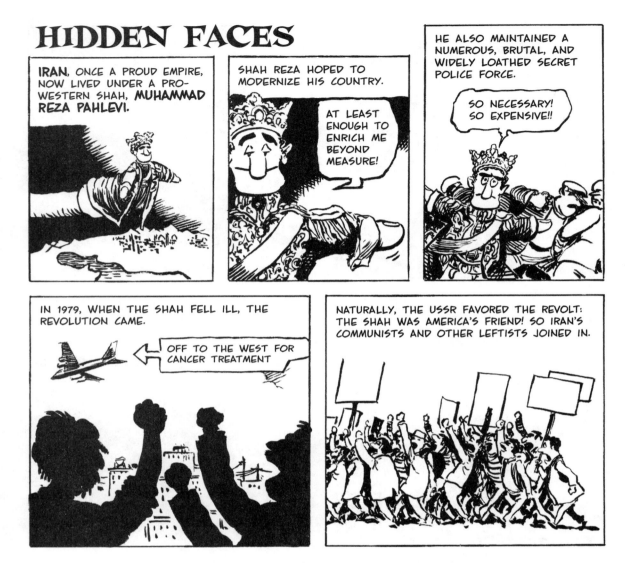

IRAN, ONCE A PROUD EMPIRE, NOW LIVED UNDER A PRO-WESTERN SHAH, MUHAMMAD REZA PAHLEVI.

SHAH REZA HOPED TO MODERNIZE HIS COUNTRY.

AT LEAST ENOUGH TO ENRICH ME BEYOND MEASURE!

HE ALSO MAINTAINED A NUMEROUS, BRUTAL, AND WIDELY LOATHED SECRET POLICE FORCE.

SO NECESSARY! SO EXPENSIVE!!

IN 1979, WHEN THE SHAH FELL ILL, THE REVOLUTION CAME.

OFF TO THE WEST FOR CANCER TREATMENT

NATURALLY, THE USSR FAVORED THE REVOLT: THE SHAH WAS AMERICA'S FRIEND! SO IRAN'S COMMUNISTS AND OTHER LEFTISTS JOINED IN.

BUT SURPRISE! THE MASSES IN THE STREET CHOSE ANOTHER DIRECTION COMPLETELY: THAT OF AYATOLLAH RUHOLLAH KHOMEINI, A SHI'ITE IMAM WHO CALLED FOR AN ISLAMIC "REPUBLIC" UNDER AN ALL-POWERFUL AYATOLLAH (GUESS WHICH ONE).

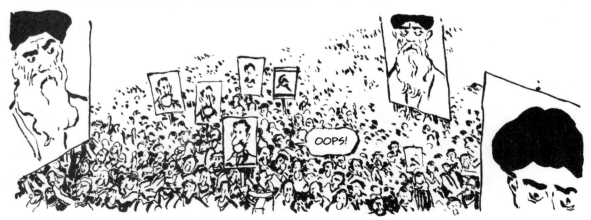

OOPS!

A STUNNED WORLD WATCHED KHOMEINI'S ZEALOTS BAN MUSIC, ALCOHOL, FILM, BOY-GIRL MINGLING, BARE-HEADED WOMEN, ETC.... AND OFF TO THE SHAH'S OLD PRISON WENT LEFTISTS AND OTHER "UN-ISLAMIC" ELEMENTS.

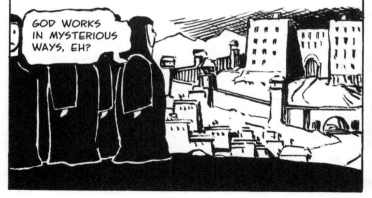

GOD WORKS IN MYSTERIOUS WAYS, EH?

SHI'ITE MULLAHS CROSSED THE BORDER TO PREACH THE REVOLUTION IN IRAQ, AFGHANISTAN, AND SOVIET CENTRAL ASIA.

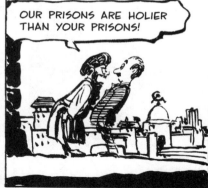

OUR PRISONS ARE HOLIER THAN YOUR PRISONS!

IN EARLY 1979, SHI'ITES REVOLTED IN HERAT, AFGHANISTAN.

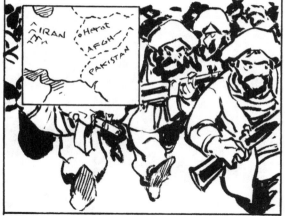

IRAN · Herat
AFGH.
PAKISTAN

THEIR TARGET: AFGHANISTAN'S COMMUNIST-LED GOVERNMENT, WHICH HAD SEIZED POWER IN A COUP JUST A YEAR EARLIER.

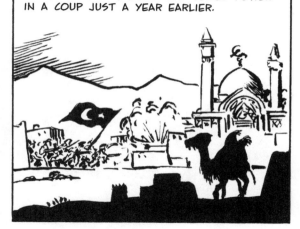

THIS RELIGIOUS REVOLT CONFOUNDED THE RUSSIANS' MARXIST IDEAS.

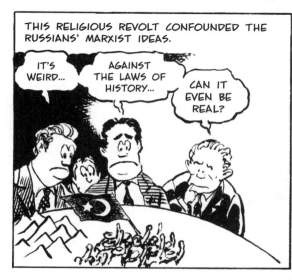

IT'S WEIRD...

AGAINST THE LAWS OF HISTORY...

CAN IT EVEN BE REAL?

THEY VOWED TO HOLD AFGHANISTAN AT ALL COSTS... IN DECEMBER 1979, SOVIET TROOPS ENTERED AFGHANISTAN TO DEFEND THE PRO-SOVIET GOVERNMENT.

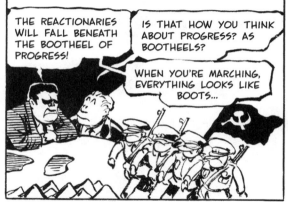

THE REACTIONARIES WILL FALL BENEATH THE BOOTHEEL OF PROGRESS!

IS THAT HOW YOU THINK ABOUT PROGRESS? AS BOOTHEELS?

WHEN YOU'RE MARCHING, EVERYTHING LOOKS LIKE BOOTS...

LUCKILY FOR RUSSIA, IRAN WAS TOO BUSY PICKING A FIGHT WITH IRAQ TO BOTHER WITH AFGHANISTAN.
SADDAM HUSSEIN IS THE ENEMY OF ISLAM!
YOU ARE!
SO THE AFGHANS FOUGHT ALONE—AND SHOWED WHY THEY HAD NEVER BEEN CONQUERED.
ОЙ!!
SIX YEARS LATER, THE WAR STILL DRAGGED ON, AND PEOPLE BEGAN CALLING IT "RUSSIA'S VIETNAM."
MILLIONS OF AFGHANS FLED THE FIGHTING, MOSTLY EASTWARD TO REFUGEE CAMPS IN PAKISTAN, WHERE PAKISTANI AND AMERICAN AGENTS OFFERED SUPPLIES AND TRAINING.
HI THERE! WE'RE HERE TO HELP AS LONG AS WE NEED YOU! CHOCOLATE?
IN 1986, THE U.S. STARTED SHIPPING THE AFGHANS SHOULDER-FIRED STINGER MISSILES, WITH COMPUTERIZED GUIDANCE.
AM'RIKA GO TO MOON... AFGHANISTAN NO GO TO THE MOUNTAIN!*
*SAID TO ME BY A SHOPKEEPER IN HERAT IN 1970.
A COUPLE OF MEN WITH A FEW STINGERS COULD TAKE RUSSIAN HELICOPTERS OUT OF THE SKY—AND WITHOUT AIR POWER, THE SOVIETS COULD NOT WIN.
AM'RIKA IS A GREAT FRIEND OF ISLAM!

MEANWHILE, BACK AT HOME, THE RUSSIAN PEOPLE STILL LIVED IN CROWDED, BADLY BUILT APARTMENTS, WAITED FOR HOURS TO BUY GROCERIES, AND RISKED ARREST FOR COMPLAINING.

THE USSR ALSO FACED A NEW CHALLENGE FROM THE U.S.: THE AMERICAN PRESIDENT, **RONALD REAGAN,*** HAD STARTED A RAPID NEW BUILDUP OF ARMS.

I COULD USE SOME NEW ARMS!

FACED WITH ALL THIS, THE COMMUNISTS WENT FOR **REFORM**, OR "RESTRUCTURING," THE SLOGAN OF THE NEW PARTY CHAIRMAN, **MIKHAIL GORBACHEV.**

GOOD LUCK, GORBY!

GORBACHEV MET REAGAN, AND FOR THE FIRST TIME EVER, THE SUPERPOWERS AGREED TO SCRAP SOME OF THEIR NUKES.

WE'RE JUST A COUPLE OF HIPPIES!

UM...

IN '88, THE RUSSIAN VOWED TO LEAVE AFGHANISTAN... BY EARLY 1989, ALL SOVIET TROOPS WERE OUT.

EVERYONE WILL LOVE ME!

APPALLED BY SOCIAL DECAY IN POST-SIXTIES AMERICA, PRESIDENT REAGAN'S WIFE, NANCY, MOUNTED A **PUBLIC RELATIONS** CAMPAIGN AGAINST **DRUG USE.** ITS CATCHPHRASE:

JUST SAY NO!

NO!

YOUR CARTOONIST ONCE HEARD MRS. REAGAN EXPLAIN ON A TV TALK SHOW WHY SHE HAD MADE THIS HER CAUSE.

BECAUSE, DICK [OR WAS IT MERV? OR JOHNNY?], DRUGS ARE **SUCH** A DOWNER!

THE FIRST LADY CLEARLY HAD **NO IDEA** THAT "DOWNER" MEANT "SEDATIVE"—A WORD FROM THE DRUG CULTURE!

THE WHOLE EXPERIENCE HAS BEEN A RUSH..., LIKE, WOW... COSMIC...

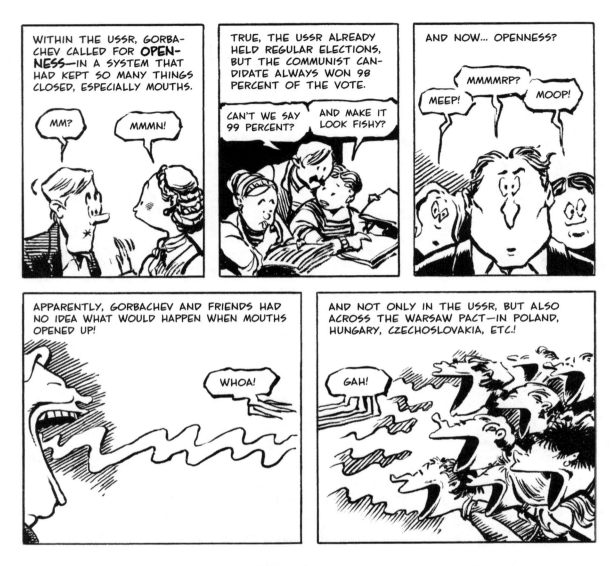

DEMONSTRATIONS ERUPTED ACROSS EASTERN EUROPE... AND, TO THE AMAZEMENT OF ALL, NEARLY EVERY COMMUNIST GOVERNMENT HELD ELECTIONS, **LOST** THEM, AND QUIETLY **DISSOLVED.** BY 1990(!), THE WARSAW PACT WAS FINISHED, AND WITH IT THE COLD WAR.

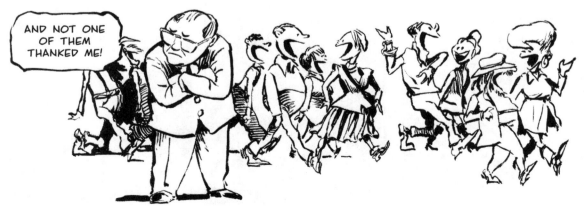

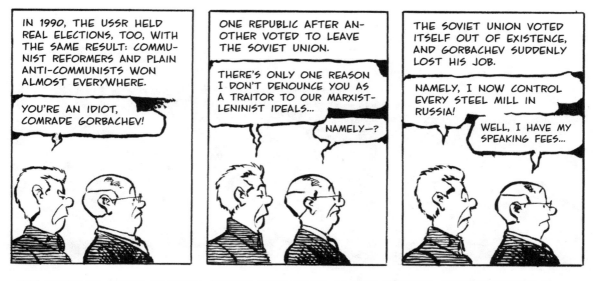

IN 1990, THE USSR HELD REAL ELECTIONS, TOO, WITH THE SAME RESULT: COMMUNIST REFORMERS AND PLAIN ANTI-COMMUNISTS WON ALMOST EVERYWHERE.

YOU'RE AN IDIOT, COMRADE GORBACHEV!

ONE REPUBLIC AFTER ANOTHER VOTED TO LEAVE THE SOVIET UNION.

THERE'S ONLY ONE REASON I DON'T DENOUNCE YOU AS A TRAITOR TO OUR MARXIST-LENINIST IDEALS...

NAMELY—?

THE SOVIET UNION VOTED ITSELF OUT OF EXISTENCE, AND GORBACHEV SUDDENLY LOST HIS JOB.

NAMELY, I NOW CONTROL EVERY STEEL MILL IN RUSSIA!

WELL, I HAVE MY SPEAKING FEES...

THE REPUBLICS, MOST OF THEM, REMADE THEMSELVES AS THE **COUNCIL OF INDEPENDENT STATES,** WITH A MORE OR LESS DEMOCRATIC RUSSIA MORE OR LESS AT THE HEAD.

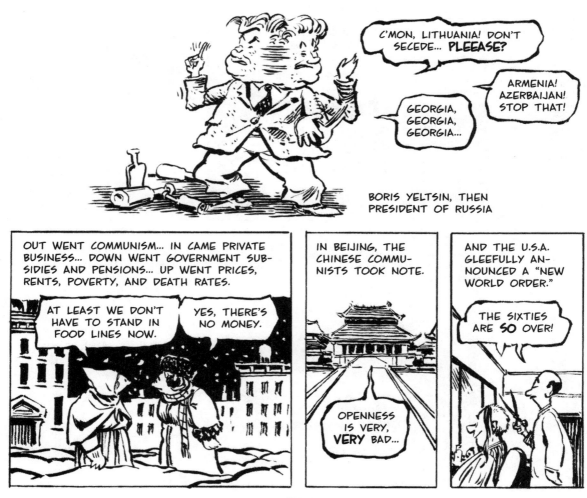

C'MON, LITHUANIA! DON'T SECEDE... **PLEEASE?**

ARMENIA! AZERBAIJAN! STOP THAT!

GEORGIA, GEORGIA, GEORGIA...

BORIS YELTSIN, THEN PRESIDENT OF RUSSIA

OUT WENT COMMUNISM... IN CAME PRIVATE BUSINESS... DOWN WENT GOVERNMENT SUBSIDIES AND PENSIONS... UP WENT PRICES, RENTS, POVERTY, AND DEATH RATES.

AT LEAST WE DON'T HAVE TO STAND IN FOOD LINES NOW.

YES, THERE'S NO MONEY.

IN BEIJING, THE CHINESE COMMUNISTS TOOK NOTE.

OPENNESS IS VERY, **VERY** BAD...

AND THE U.S.A. GLEEFULLY ANNOUNCED A "NEW WORLD ORDER."

THE SIXTIES ARE **SO** OVER!

ORDER! ORDER!

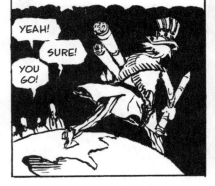

AS THE SOLE SURVIVING SUPER-POWER, THE U.S. THOUGHT IT COULD POLICE THE WORLD. COULD IT?

YEAH!

SURE!

YOU GO!

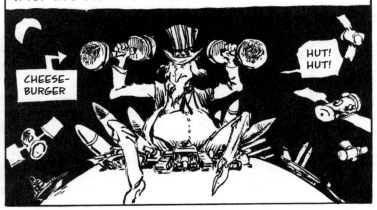

MAYBE... THE COUNTRY WAS RICH... POWERFUL... HAD MILITARY BASES WHEREVER YOU LOOKED...

CHEESE-BURGER

HUT! HUT!

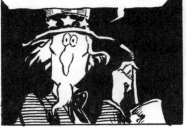

THE U.S. CONSUMED MORE FUEL THAN ANYONE... SO NATURALLY IT WANTED **OIL** IN STEADY SUPPLY FROM FRIENDLY SUPPLIERS.

OTHERWISE, HOW WILL I GET TO THE DRIVE-IN?

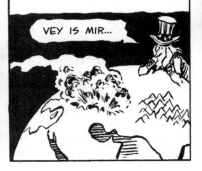

MOST OIL WAS AROUND THE **PERSIAN GULF,** WHERE IRAQ LEANED TOWARD RUSSIA, AND IRAN HATED AMERICA WHILE BATTLING IRAQ...

VEY IS MIR...

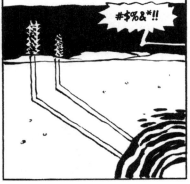

IRAN AND IRAQ FINALLY MADE PEACE IN 1988... BUT IRAQ QUICKLY STARTED A NEW WAR.

#$%&*!!

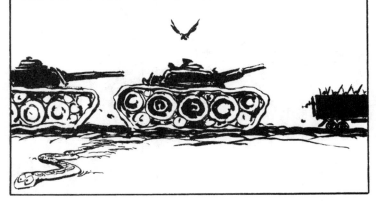

IRAQ ACCUSED ITS SOUTHERN NEIGHBOR **KUWAIT** OF TAP-PING SLANTWISE INTO IRAQI OIL FIELDS... KUWAIT MERELY SHRUGGED... SO IRAQ **INVADED** KUWAIT, A COUNTRY FRIENDLY TO THE UNITED STATES.

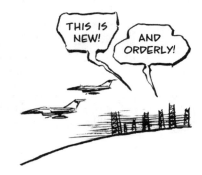

BACKED BY THE U.N., DOZENS OF COUNTRIES JOINED A U.S.-LED DEFENSE OF KUWAIT... THE SAUDIS EVEN ALLOWED AN AMERICAN AIR BASE ON THEIR SACRED SOIL...

THIS IS NEW!

AND ORDERLY!

IN LATE 1990, AN OVERWHELMING AIR AND GROUND ASSAULT MADE SHORT WORK OF THE IRAQI ARMY.

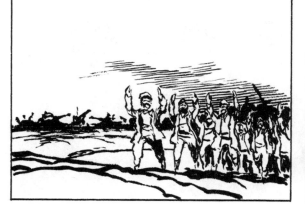

BUT THE U.S. DECIDED TO LEAVE IRAQI BOSS **SADDAM HUSSEIN** IN POWER AS A CHECK ON IRAN.

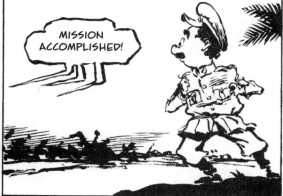

MISSION ACCOMPLISHED!

ALLIED GROUND TROOPS LEFT IRAQ... BUT THE U.S. HEMMED IN SADDAM NORTH AND SOUTH WITH "NO-FLY" ZONES... AND STARVED HIS COUNTRY WITH A BAN ON TRADE...

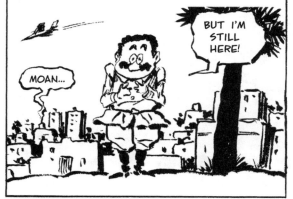

MOAN...

BUT I'M STILL HERE!

TO POLICE THE REGION, THE U.S. KEPT ITS AIR BASE IN SAUDI ARABIA.

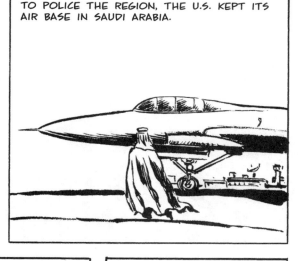

THE PRESENCE OF ARMED INFIDELS ON ISLAM'S HOLIEST SOIL OFFENDED SOME MUSLIMS, INCLUDING A RICH ZEALOT NAMED **USAMA BIN LADIN.**

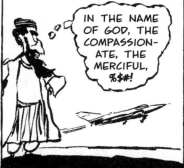

IN THE NAME OF GOD, THE COMPASSIONATE, THE MERCIFUL, %$#!

BIN LADIN HAD ALREADY RAISED A PRIVATE ARMY TO FIGHT SADDAM HUSSEIN... BUT THE SAUDIS REBUFFED HIS VOLUNTEERS... SO HE TURNED HIS IRE AGAINST THEM AND THEIR AMERICAN SPONSORS.

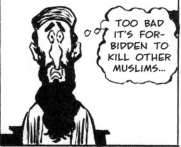

TOO BAD IT'S FORBIDDEN TO KILL OTHER MUSLIMS...

THE SAUDIS BANISHED HIM FROM THE KINGDOM...

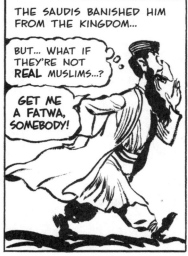

BUT... WHAT IF THEY'RE NOT **REAL** MUSLIMS...?

GET ME A FATWA, SOMEBODY!

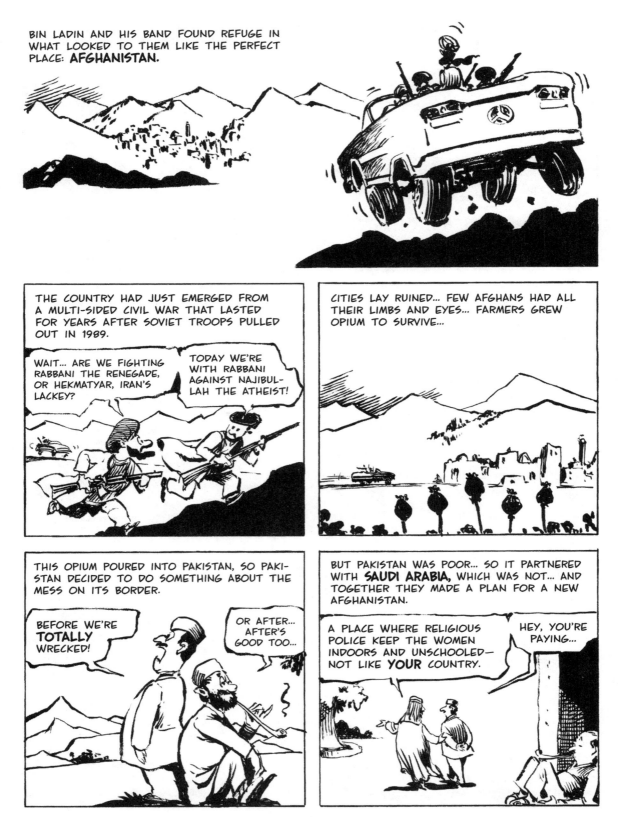

BIN LADIN AND HIS BAND FOUND REFUGE IN WHAT LOOKED TO THEM LIKE THE PERFECT PLACE: **AFGHANISTAN.**

THE COUNTRY HAD JUST EMERGED FROM A MULTI-SIDED CIVIL WAR THAT LASTED FOR YEARS AFTER SOVIET TROOPS PULLED OUT IN 1989.

WAIT... ARE WE FIGHTING RABBANI THE RENEGADE, OR HEKMATYAR, IRAN'S LACKEY?

TODAY WE'RE WITH RABBANI AGAINST NAJIBUL-LAH THE ATHEIST!

CITIES LAY RUINED... FEW AFGHANS HAD ALL THEIR LIMBS AND EYES... FARMERS GREW OPIUM TO SURVIVE...

THIS OPIUM POURED INTO PAKISTAN, SO PAKISTAN DECIDED TO DO SOMETHING ABOUT THE MESS ON ITS BORDER.

BEFORE WE'RE **TOTALLY** WRECKED!

OR AFTER... AFTER'S GOOD TOO...

BUT PAKISTAN WAS POOR... SO IT PARTNERED WITH **SAUDI ARABIA,** WHICH WAS NOT... AND TOGETHER THEY MADE A PLAN FOR A NEW AFGHANISTAN.

A PLACE WHERE RELIGIOUS POLICE KEEP THE WOMEN INDOORS AND UNSCHOOLED— NOT LIKE **YOUR** COUNTRY.

HEY, YOU'RE PAYING...

PAKISTANI AGENTS SEARCHED AFGHANISTAN FOR A RIGHTEOUS LEADER TO BANKROLL.
THEY FOUND THEIR MAN IN KANDAHAR: MULLAH OMAR, A ONE-EYED VETERAN WITH A SOLID 7TH-CENTURY VIEW OF THE WORLD.
IT USED TO BE 14TH-CENTURY, BUT THEN I LOST ONE EYE...
MY MAN!
ARMED WITH WEAPONS, SUVS, AND A SENSE OF ROUGH JUSTICE, OMAR'S FOLLOWERS, THE TALIBAN (= STUDENTS) CONQUERED MOST OF AFGHANISTAN IN NO TIME.
LOVE THE SUVS! I'M YOURS!
IN CAME PUBLIC STONINGS AND AMPUTATIONS... OUT WENT WOMEN FROM SCHOOLS AND THE WORKFORCE... IN CAME BEARDS... OUT WENT MUSIC, MOVIES, KITE FLYING...
THESE GUYS MAKE IRANIAN AYATOLLAHS LOOK LIKE WOMEN!
WHAT DO WOMEN LOOK LIKE? I FORGET...
AT THIS POINT USAMA BIN LADIN, THE FUGITIVE ARAB, SHOWED UP. HE AND THE TALIBAN FELL IN LOVE... BIN LADIN RECRUITED HUNDREDS OF FOREIGN ZEALOTS HAPPY TO BASE THEIR JIHAD IN AFGHANISTAN.
UMM... YOU'RE SURE YOU'RE HAPPY?
YOU SHOULD SEE US WHEN WE'RE GRIM!
(A SAUDI INTELLIGENCE OFFICIAL REPORTEDLY ASKED THE TALIBAN TO EXPEL BIN LADIN... MULLAH OMAR RESPONDED BY POURING COLD WATER OVER HIS OWN HEAD TO SHOW HOW BADLY HE NEEDED TO COOL OFF AFTER HEARING SUCH AN INFLAMMATORY SUGGESTION...)
YOU'RE LIKE A FATHER TO US, BUT PLEASE! DON'T ASK AGAIN!

MULLAH OMAR OVERLOOKED ONE PROBLEM: USAMA HAD HIS OWN **FOREIGN POLICY**... BUT THEN, THE MULLAH HAD BARELY LEFT KANDAHAR.

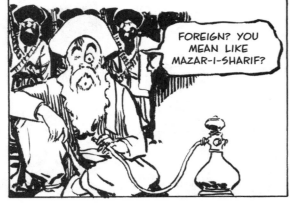

FOREIGN? YOU MEAN LIKE MAZAR-I-SHARIF?

WHILE THE TALIBAN, AS PAKISTAN'S FRIEND, TALKED BUSINESS WITH THE U.S.A., USAMA PLOTTED TO ATTACK IT.

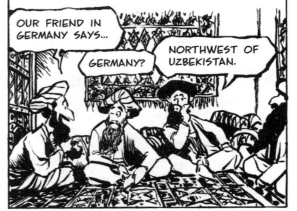

OUR FRIEND IN GERMANY SAYS...

GERMANY?

NORTHWEST OF UZBEKISTAN.

USAMA'S JIHADIS SPECIALIZED IN SUICIDE BOMBINGS... THEIR AGENTS CIRCLED THE WORLD IN SEARCH OF WOULD-BE MARTYRS.

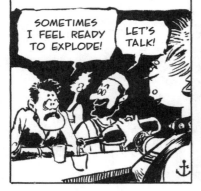

SOMETIMES I FEEL READY TO EXPLODE!

LET'S TALK!

THE PROMISE: ENTRY INTO HEAVEN... THE DISCIPLINE: CONSTANT PRAYER, UP TO THE END... THE TECHNIQUE: WHATEVER MODERN TECHNOLOGY HAD TO OFFER!

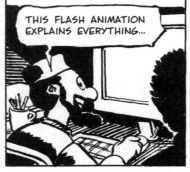

THIS FLASH ANIMATION EXPLAINS EVERYTHING...

THE TERRORISTS STRUCK SEVERAL TIMES IN THE 1990S: THE WORLD TRADE CENTER PARKING GARAGE IN NEW YORK, A U.S. WARSHIP IN YEMEN, U.S. AND ISRAELI EMBASSIES IN KENYA...

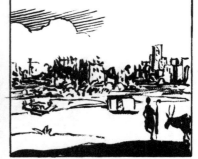

IN LATE 2000, A GROUP OF 19 JIHADIS ENTERED THE UNITED STATES.

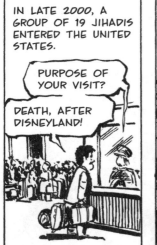

PURPOSE OF YOUR VISIT?

DEATH, AFTER DISNEYLAND!

SOME OF THEM TOOK CLASSES IN FLYING JUMBO JETS.

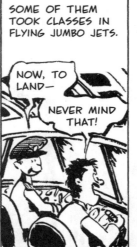

NOW, TO LAND—

NEVER MIND THAT!

ON SEPTEMBER 11, 2001, THEY SPLIT UP AND BOARDED FOUR COMMERCIAL FLIGHTS FROM THE EAST COAST.

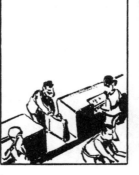

ARMED ONLY WITH KNIVES AND BOX-CUTTERS, THEY HIJACKED THE PLANES.

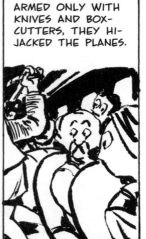

PRAYING ALL THE WAY, THE HIJACKERS STEERED THE GREAT PLANES... ONE CRASHED IN THE PENNSYLVANIA WOODS... ONE DROVE INTO THE PENTAGON, HEADQUARTERS OF THE U.S. MILITARY.

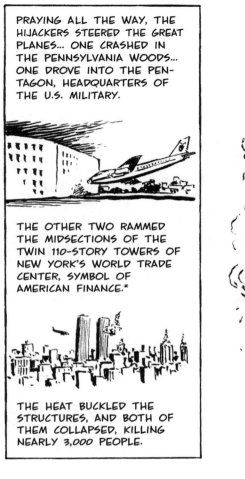

THE OTHER TWO RAMMED THE MIDSECTIONS OF THE TWIN 110-STORY TOWERS OF NEW YORK'S WORLD TRADE CENTER, SYMBOL OF AMERICAN FINANCE.*

THE HEAT BUCKLED THE STRUCTURES, AND BOTH OF THEM COLLAPSED, KILLING NEARLY 3,000 PEOPLE.

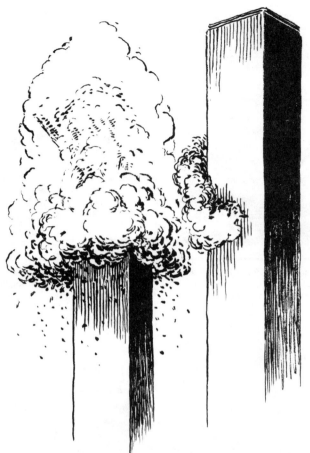

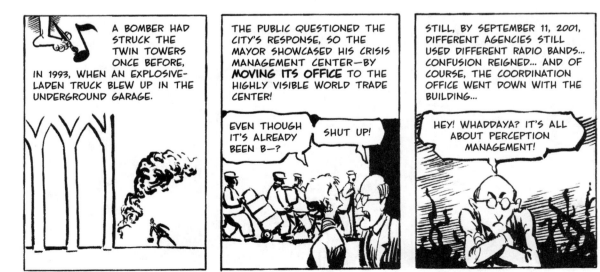

A BOMBER HAD STRUCK THE TWIN TOWERS ONCE BEFORE, IN 1993, WHEN AN EXPLOSIVE-LADEN TRUCK BLEW UP IN THE UNDERGROUND GARAGE.

THE PUBLIC QUESTIONED THE CITY'S RESPONSE, SO THE MAYOR SHOWCASED HIS CRISIS MANAGEMENT CENTER—BY **MOVING ITS OFFICE** TO THE HIGHLY VISIBLE WORLD TRADE CENTER!

EVEN THOUGH IT'S ALREADY BEEN B—?

SHUT UP!

STILL, BY SEPTEMBER 11, 2001, DIFFERENT AGENCIES STILL USED DIFFERENT RADIO BANDS... CONFUSION REIGNED... AND OF COURSE, THE COORDINATION OFFICE WENT DOWN WITH THE BUILDING...

HEY! WHADDAYA? IT'S ALL ABOUT PERCEPTION MANAGEMENT!

THE AMERICAN PRESIDENT, **GEORGE W. BUSH,** ANNOUNCED THE DAWN OF A NEW ERA, THE AGE OF PURE GOOD AND EVIL, WITH NOTHING IN BETWEEN.
AND WE'RE THE GOOD GUYS, BY THE WAY!
HE DEMANDED THAT AFGHANISTAN TURN OVER USAMA BIN LADIN.
MULLAH OMAR REFUSED.
TELL THE INFIDELS THAT USAMA IS OUR GUEST... AS CIVILIZED PEOPLE, THEY'LL UNDERSTAND HOSPITALITY!
SO THE U.S. "GOT INVOLVED" IN AFGHANISTAN AGAIN, THIS TIME MORE DIRECTLY.
FACED WITH U.S. BOMBS FROM THE SKY AND ANTI-TALIBAN AFGHANS ON THE GROUND, THE TALIBAN QUICKLY RETREATED.
WELL, BY GOD, THEY'RE NOT SO CIVILIZED AFTER ALL!
THEY TOOK TO THE MOUNTAINS ALONG THE PAKISTANI BORDER AND WAITED FOR ANOTHER DAY.
WE'LL BE BACK WITHIN TEN YEARS...
U.S. SPECIAL FORCES TRACKED BIN LADIN TO SOME FORTIFIED CAVES...
THEN SENT IN LOCAL AFGHAN MILITIAS TO CAPTURE THE PRIZE.
ALL RIGHT! **YOU** MEN WILL HAVE THE **HONOR** OF DOING THE **RISKY** STUFF!
SOMEHOW, THE TERRORIST MASTERMIND ESCAPED.
UM... SORRY!

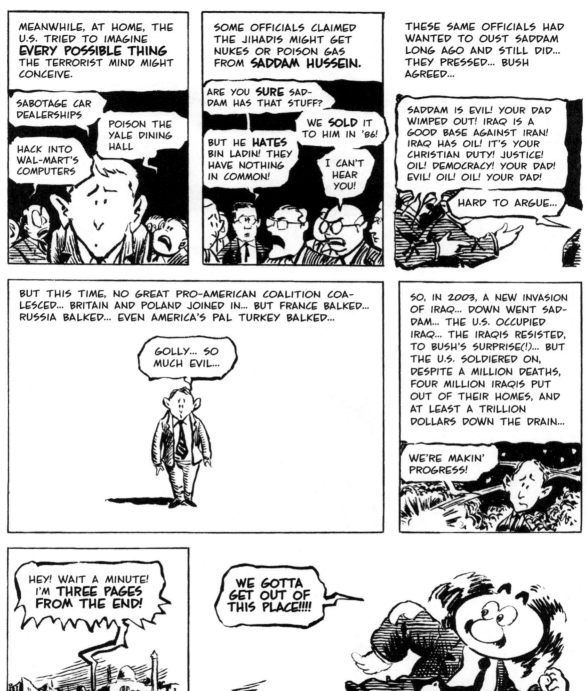

MEANWHILE, AT HOME, THE U.S. TRIED TO IMAGINE **EVERY POSSIBLE THING** THE TERRORIST MIND MIGHT CONCEIVE.

SABOTAGE CAR DEALERSHIPS

HACK INTO WAL-MART'S COMPUTERS

POISON THE YALE DINING HALL

SOME OFFICIALS CLAIMED THE JIHADIS MIGHT GET NUKES OR POISON GAS FROM **SADDAM HUSSEIN.**

ARE YOU **SURE** SADDAM HAS THAT STUFF?

WE **SOLD** IT TO HIM IN '86!

BUT HE **HATES** BIN LADIN! THEY HAVE NOTHING IN COMMON!

I CAN'T HEAR YOU!

THESE SAME OFFICIALS HAD WANTED TO OUST SADDAM LONG AGO AND STILL DID... THEY PRESSED... BUSH AGREED...

SADDAM IS EVIL! YOUR DAD WIMPED OUT! IRAQ IS A GOOD BASE AGAINST IRAN! IRAQ HAS OIL! IT'S YOUR CHRISTIAN DUTY! JUSTICE! OIL! DEMOCRACY! YOUR DAD! EVIL! OIL! OIL! YOUR DAD!

HARD TO ARGUE...

BUT THIS TIME, NO GREAT PRO-AMERICAN COALITION COALESCED... BRITAIN AND POLAND JOINED IN... BUT FRANCE BALKED... RUSSIA BALKED... EVEN AMERICA'S PAL TURKEY BALKED...

GOLLY... SO MUCH EVIL...

SO, IN 2003, A NEW INVASION OF IRAQ... DOWN WENT SADDAM... THE U.S. OCCUPIED IRAQ... THE IRAQIS RESISTED, TO BUSH'S SURPRISE(!)... BUT THE U.S. SOLDIERED ON, DESPITE A MILLION DEATHS, FOUR MILLION IRAQIS PUT OUT OF THEIR HOMES, AND AT LEAST A TRILLION DOLLARS DOWN THE DRAIN...

WE'RE MAKIN' PROGRESS!

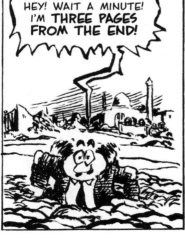

HEY! WAIT A MINUTE! I'M **THREE PAGES** FROM THE END!

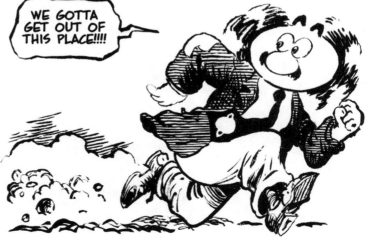

WE GOTTA GET OUT OF THIS PLACE!!!!

SHEESH! WHILE I WAS GAPING AT AMERICA'S WASTE OF FORTUNE, LIFE, AND REPUTATION, THE REST OF THE WORLD WAS MOVING ON...
INDIA, DESPITE ITS DOZENS OF LANGUAGES, HALF A BILLION PAUPERS, AND RELIGIOUS AND ETHNIC TENSIONS, HAS BOOMING SOFTWARE AND MANUFACTURING INDUSTRIES...
CHINA, STILL RUN BY THE COMMUNIST PARTY, OR SOMETHING CALLING ITSELF THAT, NOW FOLLOWS THE SLOGAN, "TO GET RICH IS GLORIOUS"...
EUROPE, AT PEACE FOR 60 YEARS (EXCEPT IN THE BALKANS, BUT WHAT CAN YOU EXPECT?), HAS FORMED AN ECONOMIC UNION THAT NOW INCLUDES MORE THAN 25 COUNTRIES, ALL DEMOCRATIC.
THE MIDDLE EAST STILL HAS MOSTLY AUTOCRATIC GOVERNMENTS, EXPLOSIVE ISLAMISTS, AND CONFLICT: ISRAELIS VERSUS PALESTINIANS, ARABS VERSUS IRANIANS, SUNNIS VERSUS SHI'ITES...
AFRICA? A MIXED BAG... NEARLY ALL THE OLD COLONIES ARE FREE, BUT NOT ONE AFRICAN COUNTRY HAS DELIVERED PROSPERITY TO ITS PEOPLE... THE SAHARA STILL GROWS... AIDS AFFLICTS MILLIONS...
SOUTH AMERICA—I CAN ONLY APOLOGIZE FOR GIVING IT SHORT SHRIFT IN THESE PAGES. SORRY, SOUTH AMERICA!

AND I HAVEN'T EVEN MENTIONED THE SUDDEN **ECONOMIC COLLAPSE** THAT BEGAN IN THE MONTHS I'VE BEEN DRAWING THESE PAGES...
I MISS YOU, TANTA!
SLAM
OR DESCRIBED HOW WE'RE DEPLETING OIL, FISH, AND FORESTS... POURING SLUDGE FROM MINES, POWER PLANTS, AND FEEDLOTS... SPEWING GASES FROM OUR CHIMNEYS AND TAILPIPES... POLLUTING AND HEATING OUR **ONE AND ONLY PLANET...**
OR TALKED ABOUT THE TEAMS OF SCIENTISTS, PLANNERS, AND ACTIVISTS WHO SEEK CONSTRUCTIVE, HUMANE SOLUTIONS TO OUR PROBLEMS!
WHRRR
POP
WHRRR
HOW WILL IT ALL TURN OUT? **I HAVE NO IDEA!!!** THIS TIME MACHINE **STINKS** AT **PREDICTION!**
ZHWZH
SNAP
CLICK
BUT THIS MUCH I KNOW FOR SURE: **THE END IS NEAR...**
RUMBLE
RUMBLE
RUMBLE
OF THIS BOOK, I MEAN!

OH! OH! OH! IT'S HERE! ONE MORE TURN OF THE PAGE, AND I'LL BE ON THE "OTHER SIDE"!!!
IS IT OBLIVION, OR A PORTAL TO—

THE END

BIBLIOGRAPHY

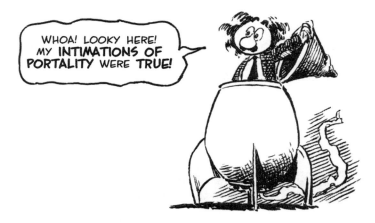

BELAUNDE, V., ***BOLÍVAR AND THE POLITICAL THOUGHT OF THE SPANISH AMERICAN REVOLUTION,*** NEW YORK: OCTAGON BOOKS, 1967. A WIDE-RANGING LATIN-AMERICAN PERSPECTIVE.

BOSHER, J., ***THE FRENCH REVOLUTION,*** NEW YORK: W.W. NORTON, 1988. UNUSUALLY COOL, MEASURED, ANALYTICAL TREATMENT, ESPECIALLY GOOD ON THE YEARS BEFORE 1789.

CARROLL, J., ***CONSTANTINE'S SWORD, THE CHURCH AND THE JEWS,*** NEW YORK: HOUGHTON MIFFLIN, 2001. THE WHOLE LONG, SORRY STORY.

CHANG, H-P., ***COMMISSIONER LIN AND THE OPIUM WAR,*** NEW YORK: W.W. NORTON, 1964. SLENDER, INCISIVE ACCOUNT OF THE DRUG TRADE, THE PEOPLE WHO PUSHED IT, AND THOSE WHO RESISTED.

CLEVELAND, W., ***A HISTORY OF THE MODERN MIDDLE EAST,*** SECOND EDITION, BOULDER, CO: WESTVIEW PRESS, 2000.

CLOETE, W., ***AFRICAN PORTRAITS, A BIOGRAPHY OF PAUL KRUGER, CECIL RHODES, AND LOBENGULA,*** LONDON: COLLINS, 1946. DATED AND REPETITIVE, THOROUGHLY CONDESCENDING TO THE MATABELE AND OTHER "KAFFIRS," DEEPLY SYMPATHETIC TO THE BOERS. GOOD READ, THOUGH!

COLE, H., ***CHRISTOPHE, KING OF HAITI,*** NEW YORK: VIKING PRESS, 1967. THE LIFE OF A PRINCIPLED, HARD-WORKING, FARSIGHTED, INSUFFERABLE TYRANT.

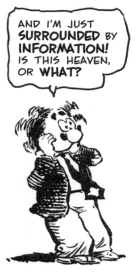

COLL, S., ***GHOST WARS: THE SECRET HISTORY OF THE CIA, AFGHANISTAN, AND BIN LADIN FROM THE SOVIET INVASION TO SEPTEMBER 10, 2001,*** NEW YORK: PENGUIN PRESS, 2004. WHAT IT SAYS. REQUIRED READING!!!!!

DAVIS, M., ***LATE VICTORIAN HOLOCAUSTS, EL NIÑO FAMINES AND THE MAKING OF THE THIRD WORLD,*** LONDON: VERSO, 2001. A NEW-LEFT HISTORIAN DESCRIBES THE FORGOTTEN RELATIONSHIP BETWEEN BRITISH IMPERIAL POLICIES AND FAMINE IN THE COLONIES.

DE TOCQUEVILLE, A., TRANS. S. GILBERT, ***THE OLD RÉGIME AND THE FRENCH REVOLUTION,*** NEW YORK: ANCHOR BOOKS, 1955. ONE BRILLIANT BOOK.

EQUIANO, O., ***THE INTERESTING NARRATIVE OF THE LIFE OF OLAUDAH EQUIANO, OR GUSTAVAS VASSA,*** DOWNLOADABLE EITHER AS TEXT OR HTML AT HTTP://WWW.GUTENBERG.ORG/ETEXT/15399. IN HIS OWN WORDS, FIRST PUBLISHED IN 1789.

FORREST, A., ***THE FRENCH REVOLUTION AND THE POOR,*** NEW YORK: ST. MARTIN'S, 1981. DESCRIBES THE GOVERNMENT'S TAKEOVER OF POOR RELIEF AND HOSPITALS FROM THE CHURCH.

GALBRAITH, J. K. *MONEY, WHENCE IT CAME, WHERE IT WENT,* BOSTON: HOUGHTON MIFFLIN, 1975. WITTY, SOMETIMES SELF-CONSCIOUSLY SO, BUT WISE TOO. GOOD ACCOUNT OF ACCOUNTS.

GANDHI, M., *AN AUTOBIOGRAPHY,* BOSTON: BEACON PRESS, 1957. A MOST EXTRAORDINARY FELLOW.

GOLDHAGEN, D. J., *HITLER'S WILLING EXECUTIONERS, ORDINARY GERMANS AND THE HOLOCAUST,* NEW YORK: ALFRED A. KNOPF, 1996. HYPEREMOTIONAL DESCRIPTION, WHETHER ACCURATE OR NOT, OF A GERMANY THOROUGHLY STEEPED IN HATE.

GUÉRIN, D., *CLASS STRUGGLE IN THE FIRST FRENCH REPUBLIC,* LONDON: PLUTO PRESS, 1977. SOME GOOD OBSERVATIONS AND SCHOLARSHIP BECLOUDED BY FORMULAIC MARXIST PHRASES.

GULAM H. S., TRANS. ABDUS SALAM, *RIYAZ-US-SALITIN, THE HISTORY OF BENGAL,* AVAILABLE ONLINE AT HTTP://PERSIAN.PACKHUM.ORG/PERSIAN. AN AMAZING COMPENDIUM OF PERSIAN MATERIAL IN TRANSLATION.

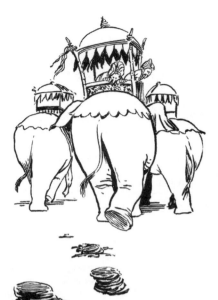

HERZL, T., *THE JEWISH STATE,* ONLINE IN FULL AT HTTP://WWW.JEWISHVIRTUALLIBRARY.ORG/JSOURCE/ZIONISM/HERZL2.HTML.

HITLER, A., *MEIN KAMPF,* AVAILABLE ONLINE AT HTTP://WWW.HITLER.ORG/WRITINGS/MEIN_KAMPF/. A GOOD PICTURE OF OLD VIENNA AS SEEN BY ITS RABID GERMANO-PHILES; BUT SOME OF HIS REMINISCENCES MAY BE FAULTY, A COMMON PROBLEM IN MEMOIRS, I'M TOLD!

HITTI, P. K., *THE NEAR EAST IN HISTORY,* PRINCETON, NJ: D. VAN NOSTRAND CO., 1961.

HOCHSCHILD, A., *KING LEOPOLD'S GHOST,* BOSTON: HOUGHTON MIFFLIN, 1998. DESCRIBES THE MASSACRE OF HALF THE CONGO BY THE AGENTS OF A WORLD-CLASS ROYAL WEASEL AND THE INTERNATIONAL PROTEST CAMPAIGN THAT BARELY SLOWED HIM DOWN.

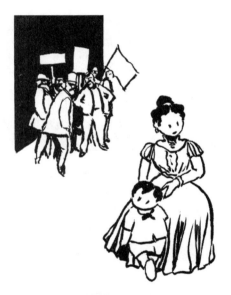

HUME, D., *A TREATISE OF HUMAN NATURE,* ONLINE AT HTTP://WWW.CLASS.UIDAHO.EDU/MICKELSEN/TOC/HUME%20TREATISE%20TOC.HTM.

JANSEN, M. B., *THE MAKING OF MODERN JAPAN,* CAMBRIDGE, MA: HARVARD U. PRESS, 2000.

JOSEPHINE, EMPRESS, *MEMOIRS OF THE EMPRESS JOSEPHINE,* IN TWO VOLUMES, READABLE (IN A COOL "FLIP-BOOK" FORMAT) AND DOWNLOADABLE AT HTTP://WWW.ARCHIVE.ORG/DETAILS/MEMOIRSOFEMPRESS01JOSEIALA AND HTTP://WWW.ARCHIVE.ORG/DETAILS/MEMOIRSOFEMPRESS02JOSEIALA. OVERWROUGHT AT TIMES, BUT IT DOES PAINT A PICTURE OF LIFE IN THE SUGAR ISLANDS, AT THE FRENCH COURT DURING THE REVOLUTION, AND LATER AT NAPOLEON'S SIDE.

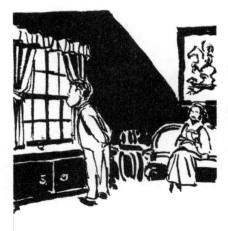

KANT, I., **CRITIQUE OF PURE REASON,** ONLINE AT HTTP://WWW.HKBU.EDU.HK/~PPP/CPR/TOC.HTML. TAKES ON THE HUME-INSPIRED PROBLEM OF HOW WE CAN REASON USING CONCEPTS DERIVED PURELY FROM OUR MINDS. GOOD TREATMENT FOR INSOMNIA OR JET LAG, TOO.

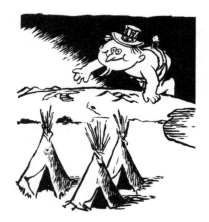

LAW, R., ED., **FROM SLAVE TRADE TO 'LEGITIMATE' COMMERCE,** CAMBRIDGE, ENGLAND: CAMBRIDGE U. PRESS, 2002. A VALIANT ATTEMPT TO ASSESS THE EFFFECT OF THE END OF THE SLAVE TRADE ON WEST AFRICA, THOUGH CONTRIBUTORS ALL CAUTION THAT EVIDENCE IS RELATIVELY MEAGER.

LIMERICK, P. N., **THE LEGACY OF CONQUEST,** NEW YORK: W.W. NORTON, 1987. ESSAYS REINTERPRETING THE HISTORY OF THE AMERICAN WEST.

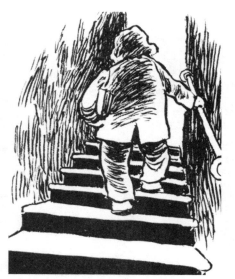

MADELIN, L., **THE REVOLUTIONARIES (1789–1799),** BRISTOL, ENGLAND: ARROWSMITH, 1930. OFTEN UNFLATTERING CHARACTER SKETCHES OF FRENCH REVOLUTIONARY FIGURES, THOUGH THE AUTHOR ADMIRES DANTON *MALGRÉ LUI.*

MARX, K., AND F. ENGELS, **THE COMMUNIST MANIFESTO,** AVAILABLE ONLINE AT HTTP://WWW.ANU.EDU.AU/POLSCI/MARX/CLASSICS/MANIFESTO.HTML, AMONG OTHER PLACES.

MELSON, R. F., **REVOLUTION AND GENOCIDE,** CHICAGO: U. OF CHICAGO PRESS, 1992. ON ARMENIAN GENOCIDE AND THE HOLOCAUST. A WELCOME CONTRAST TO GOLDHAGEN.

MILL, J., **THE HISTORY OF BRITISH INDIA,** AT HTTP://OLL.LIBERTYFUND.ORG/TOC/0381.PHP.

MILLER, J. C., **WAY OF DEATH, MERCHANT CAPITALISM AND THE ANGOLAN SLAVE TRADE 1730–1830,** MADISON, WI: U. OF WISCONSIN PRESS, 1988. MANY NUGGETS OF INFORMATION EMBEDDED IN A MATRIX OF PROSE ALTERNATELY POETIC AND ACADEMIC. COULD BE SHORTER.

MORRIS, A. C., ED., **THE DIARY AND LETTERS OF GOUVERNEUR MORRIS,** IN TWO VOLUMES, NEW YORK: SCRIBNER'S, 1888. THE ONE-LEGGED, WITTY U.S. FOUNDING-FATHER FINANCIER'S ACCOUNT OF PARIS DURING THE FRENCH REVOLUTION.

NAKASH, Y., **THE SHI'IS OF IRAQ,** PRINCETON, NJ: PRINCETON U. PRESS, 1995.

PARK, M., **TRAVELS IN THE INTERIOR OF AFRICA** (IN TWO VOLUMES), AVAILABLE BY MAIL ORDER FROM HTTP://WWW.KESSINGER.NET. A RIVETING ACCOUNT OF THE SLAVE TRADE BY A JUDICIOUS OBSERVER WHO SPOKE THE LANGUAGE AND PENETRATED DEEP UP THE NIGER RIVER IN 1795.

PETRIE, F. L., **SIMON BOLÍVAR,** NEW YORK: JOHN LANE, 1910. CONFUSING, DETAILED, BUT CONVINCING PORTRAIT OF BOLÍVAR'S CHARACTER.

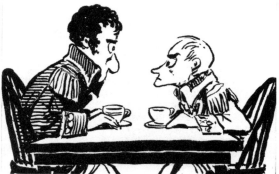

ROBERTS, B., **CECIL RHODES, FLAWED COLOSSUS,** NEW YORK: W.W. NORTON, 1988. FLAWED BIOGRAPHY.

ROCK, D., **ARGENTINA,** 1516–1987, BERKELEY, CA: U. OF CALIFORNIA PRESS, 1987.

SALE, K., *REBELS AGAINST THE FUTURE*, READING, MA: ADDISON-WESLEY, 1995. ABOUT THE LUDDITES.

SARMIENTO, D., TRANS. K. ROSS, *FACUNDO*, BERKELEY, CA: U. OF CALIFORNIA PRESS, 2003. A BITTER ARGENTINIAN MASTERPIECE ABOUT THE RISE OF DICTATORS FROM GAUCHO ROOTS.

SCHAMA, S., *CITIZENS*, NEW YORK: ALFRED A. KNOPF, 1989. NARRATES THE FRENCH REVOLUTION FROM MANY PERSPECTIVES, WITH GREATER SYMPATHY FOR ITS ARISTOCRATIC VICTIMS THAN ITS POLITICAL LEADERS OR FRANCE'S STARVING FARMERS.

SCHEVILL, F., *HISTORY OF THE BALKAN PENINSULA*, NEW YORK: FREDERICK UNGAR, 1966. FIRST PUBLISHED IN 1922, WHEN THE BALKAN WARS AND WWI WERE FRESH MEMORIES.

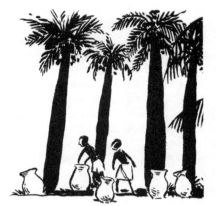

THOMAS, H., *THE SLAVE TRADE*, NEW YORK: SIMON & SCHUSTER, 1997. MUCH GREAT INFORMATION, BUT NOT ALWAYS EASY TO FOLLOW, AND SOME STRANGE ERRORS, SUCH AS THAT COTTON MATHER WAS A UNITARIAN(!).

WALEY, A., *THE OPIUM WAR THROUGH CHINESE EYES*, PALO ALTO, CA: STANFORD U. PRESS, 1972. JUDICIOUS, SENSITIVE DISCUSSION AND TRANSLATION OF ASSORTED CHINESE DIARIES AND DOCUMENTS.

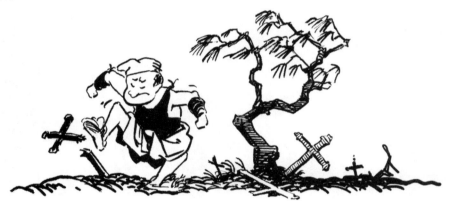

WALKER, B. L., *THE CONQUEST OF AINU LANDS, ECOLOGY AND CULTURE IN JAPANESE EXPANSION, 1590–1800*, BERKELEY, CA: U. OF CALIFORNIA PRESS, 2006.

WHITE, R., *"IT'S YOUR MISFORTUNE AND NONE OF MY OWN," A NEW HISTORY OF THE AMERICAN WEST*, NORMAN, OK: U. OF OKLAHOMA PRESS, 1991. NICE LITTLE PARAGRAPHS ABOUT ABALONE, KELP, CHINESE FISHERMEN, AND PACIFIC FISH STOCKS.

WILBER, D. N., *CLANDESTINE SERVICE HISTORY, OVERTHROW OF PREMIER MOSSADEQ OF IRAN, NOVEMBER 1952–AUGUST 1953*, PUBLISHED ONLINE AT HTTP://WEB.PAYK.NET/POLITICS/CIA-DOCS/PUBLISHED/ONE-MAIN/MAIN.HTML, 2006. CONTEMPORARY ACCOUNT BY THE "EXECUTIVE PRODUCER" OF THE CIA'S REGIME-CHANGE PROGRAM.

WROBEL, P., *THE JEWS OF GALICIA UNDER AUSTRIAN-POLISH RULE, 1876–1918*, ONLINE AT HTTP://WWW.JEWISHGEN.ORG/GALICIA/HTML/JEWS_OF_GALICIA.PDF.

INDEX

ABOUT THE AUTHOR

ORIGINALLY TRAINED AS A MATHEMATICIAN, LARRY GONICK DROPPED OUT OF GRADUATE SCHOOL AT HARVARD TO PURSUE A CAREER WRITING AND DRAWING COMICS ABOUT HISTORY, SCIENCE, AND OTHER BIG SUBJECTS. HIS FIRST CARTOON HISTORY, *YANKEE ALMANACK*, AN ACCOUNT OF COLONIAL MASSACHUSETTS AND THE AMERICAN REVOLUTION, WAS SERIALIZED IN THE *BOSTON GLOBE* SUNDAY COMICS SECTION DURING THE U.S. BICENTENNIAL, 1975-76. AFTER ITS INEVITABLE CONCLUSION, HE TURNED TO WORLD HISTORY AS A SUBJECT THAT PROMISED TO TAKE MORE TIME TO EXHAUST. THIS BOOK IS THE FIFTH AND FINAL INSTALLMENT OF A THIRTY-YEAR SERIES THAT ALSO INCLUDES *THE CARTOON HISTORY OF THE UNIVERSE I, II, AND III*, AND *THE CARTOON HISTORY OF THE MODERN WORLD, PART 1*. *THE CARTOON HISTORY OF THE UNIVERSE III* WON THE HARVEY AWARD, THE OSCAR OF COMICS, AS BEST ALBUM OF ORIGINAL MATERIAL IN 2003.

See What You Can Learn with Cartoons!

THE CARTOON HISTORY OF THE MODERN WORLD PART I
From Columbus to the U.S. Constitution

ISBN 978-0-06-076004-5 (paperback)

Follow humanity from Christopher Columbus to the United States' emergence as a world superpower, the technological revolution, and the resurgence of militant religion.

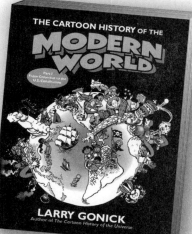

THE CARTOON HISTORY OF THE MODERN WORLD PART II
From the Bastille to Baghdad

ISBN 978-0-06-076008-3 (paperback)

From the beginning of the Enlightenment to the environmental crisis of today's world, Gonick concludes (for the moment) his engagingly epic history of human kind.

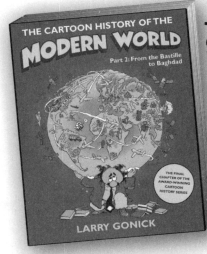

THE CARTOON HISTORY OF THE UNITED STATES

ISBN 978-0-06-273098-5 (paperback)

From the first English colonies to the Gulf War, fill in the gaps of your United States history knowledge with this entertaining and helpful guide.

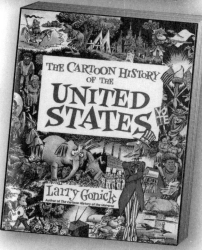

THE CARTOON GUIDE TO CHEMISTRY

ISBN 978-0-06-093677-8 (paperback)

A complete course in college level chemistry that covers both the history and the basics of multiple divisions of chemistry.

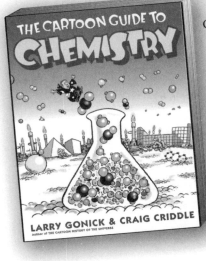

THE CARTOON GUIDE TO GENETICS

ISBN 978-0-06-273099-2 (paperback)

Having trouble deciphering your genetic code? Do dominant genes make you feel recessive? Let this cartoon guide ease you through molecular biology and the basics of genetic engineering.

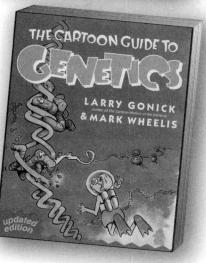

THE CARTOON GUIDE TO STATISTICS

ISBN 978-0-06-273102-9 (paperback)

Learn all the central ideas of modern statistics: the summary and display of data, probability in gambling and medicine, random variables, and much more.

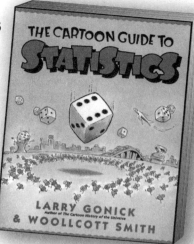

THE CARTOON GUIDE TO PHYSICS

ISBN 978-0-06-273100-5 (paperback)

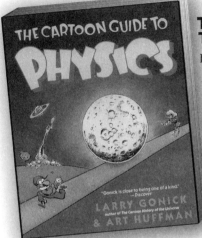

A crash course in physics if you think a negative charge is something that shows up on your credit card bill or that Ohm's law dictates how long to meditate.

THE CARTOON GUIDE TO THE ENVIRONMENT

ISBN 978-0-06-273274-3 (paperback)

Use this handy guide to pave your way to environmental literacy regarding crucial issues such as food webs, human population growth, sources of energy and raw materials, and deforestation.

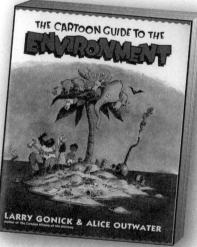

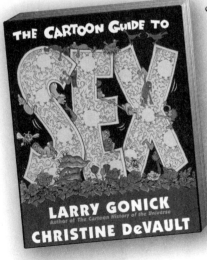

THE CARTOON GUIDE TO SEX

ISBN 978-0-06-273431-0 (paperback)

From first eye contact to the therapist's couch, from the world's sexiest animal to the dating jungle, this cartoon guide covers everything you've always wanted to know about sex.

OVERDUES
5¢ A DAY

10/09

ISLAND PARK PUBLIC LIBRARY
176 Long Beach Road
Island Park, NY 11558
Phone: 432-0122